CHINA
SCAPEGOAT

The Diplomatic Ordeal of John Carter Vincent

CHINA SCAPEGOAT

The Diplomatic Ordeal
of John Carter Vincent

GARY MAY
University of Delaware

Introduction by
John K. Fairbank

Waveland Press, Inc.
Prospect Heights, Illinois

For information about this book, write or call:

Waveland Press, Inc.
P.O. Box 400
Prospect Heights, Illinois 60070
(312) 634-0081

For Joanna and Jeffrey

CONTENTS

Preface

It has never been easy being an American diplomat. From the beginning of our history the American people and their representatives in government have viewed the activities of their diplomats with suspicion and mistrust, and often with outright hostility. American diplomatic history is replete with examples of ambassadors, ministers, or special presidential emissaries languishing in foreign posts, their recommendations ignored, their efforts unappreciated.

The "diplomat as scapegoat" is also an established tradition. The Anglo-American treaty negotiated by John Jay in 1794 helped to avoid war with England but it also precipitated a national political crisis which nearly ruined Jay's career. Jay was hung in effigy, and specialists in early American graffiti scrawled this message across fences: "Damn John Jay! Damn everyone that won't damn John Jay! Damn everyone that won't put lights in his windows and sit up all night damning John Jay!" A half-century later Nicholas Trist received similar treatment for negotiating the end of the war between the United States and Mexico. While securing the Treaty of Guadalupe Hidalgo, Trist was called an "impudent and unqualified scoundrel" by James K. Polk, and although the treaty was later ratified by the Senate and confirmed by the president, it took the government twenty-two years to pay Trist for his services.

But nothing in the past quite equaled the abuse sustained by John Carter

9

Vincent, a career Foreign Service officer blamed for the "loss of China" in the 1940s and 1950s. Vincent's diplomatic career spanned twenty-eight years and coincided with critical moments in Chinese history: In the 1920s he was in Ch'ang-sha during the most serious antiforeign uprising since the Boxer Rebellion. Ten years later, he was in Mukden and Dairen, an eyewitness to the Japanese takeover of Manchuria. On December 7, 1941, he was in Chungking, and spent the next two years observing the disintegration of Chiang Kai-shek's Nationalist government and the growth of Mao Tse-tung's Communist movement. As counselor of the American embassy in Chungking, and later, director of the State Department's Office of Far Eastern Affairs, he urged the United States to force Chiang to reform his regime before China fell to the Japanese, or more likely, the Communists.

Vincent's China service made him, as he once said, "the obvious target" for those political extremists and opportunists unable or unwilling to understand what his long years in China had taught him: that China was never owned by the United States and was not hers to lose. "It was the sheer and protracted stupidity of the National Government that lost China," Vincent argued. ". . . Nothing short of an American military protectorate, in fact if not in name, could have saved China." When some in the Pentagon recommended this course in the late 1940s, Vincent fought and helped defeat them, at great personal cost. With the Communist victory in 1949, Vincent became a "China scapegoat," and like Jay and Trist before him, was blamed for developments he had feared and predicted.

Ironically, the man who was the "obvious target" of partisan attack has not been the obvious subject of historical study. Vincent's career has not received the attention it deserves: While the memoirs and dispatches of other China hands like John Paton Davies, Jr., O. Edmund Clubb, and John S. Service have been published and discussed, Vincent's work has been overlooked and his importance forgotten. He was the only diplomat of his generation to observe the Chinese revolution of the 1920s, the Japanese take-over of the 1930s, the Chinese civil war of the 1940s, both on the scene and as a prominent member of the State Department. More importantly, Vincent's personality and his view of Chinese politics and American policy, reveal the strengths and weaknesses of American liberalism, as personal philosophy and diplomatic guide; therefore, his life story may help us as we grope toward new approaches in politics and foreign policy in the years after Vietnam and Watergate.

Vincent's experience also sheds light on how America's diplomacy affects its domestic life. The cold war, and the fall of China, led to the development, under President Harry S. Truman, of a "loyalty bureaucracy," the forerunner of that "invisible government" of federal agencies which have corrupted civil liberties in the years since 1945. The Freedom of Information Act gave this historian access to FBI, State Department, and Civil Service Commission records which allowed him to describe the heretofore secret operations of the machinery which destroyed not only John Carter Vincent's career but those of other valuable public servants. What the record reveals gives us little reason to feel nostalgic about either Harry Truman or the 1950s.

Writing history is a collective enterprise and there are a great many persons whose assistance made this study possible. My greatest debt is to the late John Carter Vincent and Mrs. Elizabeth Vincent, who generously permitted me access to their personal papers and always answered my inquiries fully and fairly. Other members of the Vincent family were also helpful: Mr. and Mrs. John C. Vincent, Jr., Mrs. Sheila Vincent Cox, and Mrs. Margaret Vincent Smith.

I also extend my appreciation to the skillful archivists at the Hoover Institution on War, Revolution, and Peace, the Franklin D. Roosevelt, Harry S. Truman, and Dwight D. Eisenhower libraries, the Library of Congress and the National Archives, and the Universities of Iowa, Michigan, and Oklahoma.

A number of friends and associates of John Carter Vincent granted me personal interviews which were of great value. They are Claude A. Buss, Everett F. Drumright, John K. Fairbank, Adrian S. Fisher, Monroe Karasik, Abbott Moffat, John S. Service, Walter S. Surrey, Ross Terrill, and James C. Thomson, Jr.

I am also happy to acknowledge the financial aid given me by the John R. and Dora Haynes Foundation, the Hattie M. Strong Foundation, the Harry S. Truman Institute of National and International Affairs, the American Foreign Service Association, the Carnegie Endowment for International Peace, and the University of Delaware General Research Fund.

This study had its origins as a doctoral dissertation under the direction of Professor Robert Dallek; I thank him for his patience and consideration. Professors Dorothy Borg, Warren Cohen, John K. Fairbank, and Mrs. Annalee Jacoby Fadiman also read the dissertation and offered helpful advice. Professors Waldo H. Heinrichs, Jr. and Ross Terrill read the entire 910-page manuscript and provided superb guides which helped me to produce this book. I owe a special debt of gratitude to my colleague and friend, Professor Raymond Wolters. He too read the long manuscript, suggested revisions, and just as essential, gave the encouragement so important to the apprentice historian.

11   Preface

Mrs. Antonia Turman typed the manuscript beautifully, Mrs. Sharon Smith listened patiently to my many complaints and reminded me of my goals, and Ira Conrad and Larry Agran, good friends and able attorneys, provided me with helpful legal advice. Joan Tapper of New Republic Books, gave excellent editorial advice, and Carolyn McKee did a thorough job of copy-editing.

Those closest to me have shared the pain and pleasure inherent in any work of scholarship—and they are the most difficult to thank. Without the support (both spiritual and financial) of my parents and grandparents, none of what follows would have been completed. And two very special people have been constant sources of imagination and joy: my wife, Gail, and daughter, Joanna. This book belongs to them.

Newark, Delaware   GM
August 2, 1978

Introduction

We now know that nations, like people, can go crazy. They may act on assumptions quite contrary to reality and plunge into unnecessary disasters. For example, Japan with 80 million people in the 1930s felt compelled to expand by force, whereas Japan today with over 100 million prospers by expanding on a different basis. America plunged blindly into Vietnam to stop an assumed Russo-Chinese-Vietnamese monolith. That monolith, if it ever existed, has now splintered from within while we continue to pay high prices for our folly. Today again fear and hatred, misplaced sentiment, reckless ambition, try constantly to warp our public judgment. The humane intelligence that keeps us in balance by generalizing about every day's reality is asked to accept strident oversimplifications.

The Chinese revolution has tested most severely our capacity to make sense of the world. Would we have fallen into the folly of Vietnam in the 1960s if we had not suffered the shock of China going Communist in the 1940s? Our wasted expenditures in Vietnam have helped us into the inflationary quagmire of the 1970s. Whether or not the gods are out to destroy us, we have surely been afflicted with a degree of public madness. The "loss of China" issue was in fact only a small aspect of the Great Fear of the cold war and Joe McCarthy era. In the stress of new and strange

13

problems, unreason took power among us, with all its mistaken beliefs and fervent righteousness.

The story of John Carter Vincent, told in this book by Gary May, is a case study of unreason triumphant. It illustrates the process. But it also shows how one man survived intact.

John Carter Vincent looked distinguished, as a diplomat should, yet his slight build and soft Georgia accent, still rare in the days before the Carter presidency, made him seem easily approachable. He had a disarming knack of conversing with strangers so naturally on everyday topics that they at once became friendly acquaintances, possible friends. He liked people in their diversity and quickly sensed their views and motives.

Vincent rose to the top of the China Service partly by seniority but mainly because he was a man of broad grasp and cool judgment. He was not a careerist of obsessive ego nor an axe-grinder or true believer in one cause. He was not combative but understanding and patient, concerned not for himself but for the working out of diplomatic problems. While acutely intelligent, he was not primarily an intellectual. His faith was not in any creed but in the values of liberalism. He was a man of good will with an open mind, and his belief in humane and rational conduct gave him a self-confidence and imperturbability that stood him in good stead. In brief, he was the polar opposite of what his attackers alleged him to be.

Gary May's fast-moving account uses new evidence and brings out new facets of this sordid and yet edifying story. Vincent, because of his position as the top professional on China policy in the State Department, was attacked the earliest, in 1947. The campaign by which he was then pursued for the following six years until his retirement in 1953 can best be understood in anthropological terms. The public madness of the time was expressed in a ritual of vicarious vengeance in which the determination to victimize and destroy a supposed symbol of evil overrode all considerations of credibility and legal procedure. The result was injustice on a truly incredible scale. So-called evidence was adduced which no novelist would dare put in a work of fiction lest it immediately lose all verisimilitude. Hearsay from ex-Communists was believed simply because they had once been Communists. The self-selected agents of righteous vengeance mouthed slogans of freedom while imitating the evils of unfreedom. They were motivated by a gamut of desires for notoriety or political advantage, out of feelings of inferiority and anti-intellectualism, personal frustration or sheer opportunism. Some were high-minded but stupid and credulous. They had their day because novel dangers had stymied the public's critical faculty.

Far from being the achievement of Joe McCarthy, the witch hunt of the early 1950s was a widespread effort by some of the best people, scions of first families, rock-ribbed descendants of the Puritans of impeccable lineage. Men of good repute in positions of high responsibility were moved by base passions of fear and aggrandizement. These men somehow felt most threatened and became most intent upon destroying their prey. Their superpatriotism colored the scene with pious statements. It now appears, as John Carter Vincent did not know at the time, that several major organs of the American government conspired to railroad him. These included duly constituted committees of the legislative branch, that sacrosanct despot, J. Edgar Hoover of the FBI, and in the end the cynically righteous secretary of state, John Foster Dulles.

The real message of Gary May's book lies in the steady and rational conduct of Vincent himself. He first had the experience of constructing an American policy vis-a-vis the Chinese revolution. With historical hindsight it is easy to see that there has seldom been a more completely lost cause than the effort to preserve the American position in China as the revolution came to a climax. Nationalism alone was enough to eject the Americans from their privileges. As the Communist movement in China gained leadership of nationalist sentiment and received the tacit mandate to save the country and its people, there was nowhere for the Americans to go but out. Recent speculation that we could somehow have been friends with Mao when he came to power overlook the larger forces at work. How could a movement bent on expunging the century-long humiliations of the unequal treaties effect a compromise with the vested interests that the unequal treaties had produced?

In this hopeless situation, Vincent and his colleagues kept on trying to do two things—first, to report the fact that the Communists were winning the acquiescence of the populace and thereby organizing superior military power, and second, to urge a policy of abstention that would not try to command the tides of change and take arms against the Chinese revolution that the Communists now led. The Vincent formula for meeting our China problem did not work out as more than a non-success, but it was the best that anyone could suggest at the time, namely, to support liberalism in Chinese politics and stand against solutions by military violence. As we can see now, the Foreign Service officers in China were in a no-win position, for neither side in the Chinese revolution subscribed to liberal principles. Historians run the risk of supinely accepting what happened when it might have been better, but it is hard to see how Stilwell's taking nominal command of the Chinese armies in 1944 or Mao Tse-tung's coming to Washington in 1945, or in fact any other move, could have basically altered the outcome of American defeat. Our defeat in China in fact was inherited from the British and was long overdue, but we could not understand this.

Once back in Washington in charge of the Far Eastern division, Vincent, working with Dean Acheson, devised our most sincere effort to unscrew the inscrutable—the Marshall mission of 1946 to mediate in the Chinese civil war. Gary May brings out the fact that General Marshall at first differed with Vincent and believed that arms to Chiang Kai-shek would help his cause of mediation. Only through experience did he come around to Vincent's view that military support of Chiang would make him less likely to seek a nonviolent solution. Students of diplomacy will conclude, I think, that Vincent made the best of a bad job. Because General Marshall had learned the Chinese realities on the spot, when he became secretary of state in 1947 he saved us from intervening in what could only have been a super-super-Vietnam.

Mr. May's lively account shows how resiliently and patiently Vincent stood up to the ordeal of attempted slow destruction that was visited upon him between 1947 and 1953. Having been myself a marginal figure in the who-lost-China furor, I can only admire the accuracy and artistry with which Gary May has depicted the procedures. Although my job as a Harvard professor was never at stake, I was privileged to have a day before the McCarran committee and a couple of other days before an army review board, set up especially to determine whether I should be allowed to go to Japan. Thus I can understand the feelings of others who were questioned by the well-named Sourwine or the righteous Robert Morris who later became a judge. In the review board procedure I had the experience of sympathizing with three good men and true, innocent of any China experience, who were sworn to judge my attitudes in a far-off Chinese situation where the good guys in public esteem were Communists and the bad guys were our allies. The most striking thing about such situations is the dissonance between Chinese fact and American morality, when one tries to apply the values of one culture to the situation in another.

In this book the record of how the State Department and its Foreign Service officers were scapegoated is now given its capstone. O. Edmund Clubb, one of the most experienced and competent of these officers, our last consul general in Hanoi and also in Peking, has given his account in *The Witness and I* (Columbia University Press, 1975). John S. Service, the brilliant reporter who had the most contact with Mao, has written *The Amerasia Papers: Some Problems in the History of U.S.-China Relations* (University of California, Center for Chinese Studies, 1971). John Paton Davies, Jr., who was General Stilwell's principal advisor on loan from the State Department, has written *Dragon by the Tail: American, British, Japanese, and Russian Encounters with China and One Another* (Norton,

1972). John K. Emmerson, in *The Japanese Thread: A Life in the U.S. Foreign Service* (Holt, Rinehart and Winston, 1978) has recounted the wild suspicions engendered by his skilled service with Japanese prisoners of war in Yen-an. These men most directly involved were only the most prominent of those many, many public servants subjected to loyalty-security investigations.

Of them all, John Carter Vincent was the foremost in policy-making and in responsibility. It was typical of him that he undertook no writing in his own defense because he retained confidence not only in himself but in the common sense of historical judgment. He was in fact not a martyr at all, because he was not destroyed. They tried but they failed. He stands forth in these pages simply as a hero.

Cambridge, Mass.   JOHN K. FAIRBANK
November 1978

scapegoat: 1: a goat upon whose head are symbolically placed the sins of the people after which he is sent into the wilderness in the biblical ceremony for Yom Kippur   2: a person or thing bearing the blame for others.

1

The Making of a China Hand

The confidential telegram from the secretary of state arrived at the American consulate general in Tangier, Morocco, on the evening of December 15, 1952, and it was delivered immediately to the American minister, John Carter Vincent. The message did not concern relations between the United States and Morocco, however. It was completely personal in nature and tragic in circumstance. The Department of State was notifying him that the Civil Service Commission's Loyalty Review Board had just completed its examination of Vincent's record and concluded that there was "reasonable doubt" of his loyalty to the United States.[1] The Board was recommending, therefore, that his services be "terminated," and for the present, he was suspended from duty. The news was shocking, but it did not surprise him: For the last five years his career had been a subject of major controversy.

As a member of the Foreign Service and Department of State for over twenty years, Vincent had been responsible for the development and execution of American foreign policy in China. Between 1941 and 1947 he served as counselor of the American embassy in Chungking, chief of the State Department's Division of Chinese Affairs and then director of the Office of Far Eastern Affairs, a position that is today the assistant secretary of state for East Asia and the Pacific.

21

As the chief public spokesman for the China policy of presidents Roosevelt and Truman, Vincent had long been attacked by congressional critics and special interest groups, who hoped to win political capital from America's troubled relationship with China. In 1947, his promotion to career minister had been delayed for six months because of accusations that he had "notoriously and harmfully distorted the American position" in Asia. In 1950 Senator Joseph McCarthy had called him a Communist spy and then sent an agent to Europe to destroy Vincent's career. In 1951 an ex-Communist had told Senate investigators that Vincent had been a member of the Communist Party, an action that led the State Department to issue its own charges against him. Private citizens had written letters calling him "a liar, perjurer and traitor," and one had urged that he "blow [his] brains out."[2] Now the Civil Service Commission wanted him dismissed from the Foreign Service.

"Spy," "Communist," "perjurer," "traitor"—these were frightening and bizarre words to describe a man who had been born in the American heartland, a descendant of a family with roots deep in American history.

John Carter Vincent was born in Seneca, Kansas, on August 19, 1900, the third son of Frank and Beulah Carter Vincent. His arrival (although certainly not unexpected) was somewhat sudden. When Beulah's labor pains began early that morning, Frank rushed off to get the doctor and his mother-in-law. When they returned, he discovered that he had another son: "big enough to go to meeting barefoot," noted an uncle who had come along for the show. "Somehow or other the rogue got in, and claimed to be of our kith and kin."[3]

Vincent inherited not only his uncle's dry wit but his family's love of travel and adventure, all qualities essential for success in foreign service.

Vincents had arrived on the American continent from England at the end of the seventeenth century, settling first in Rhode Island then moving on to Ohio early in the nineteenth century. Professionally, they were farmers, preachers, and doctors, but they were also spirited and romantic—sometimes too much so. One relative, Susannah North, was burned as a witch in Salem, Massachusetts, in 1692; another was among the first to open the Ohio Valley to settlement, while a third was a "pronounced abolitionist" who ran an underground railroad in Oberlin, Ohio, on the eve of the Civil War. It was in New Oberlin that his father, Frank, was born in 1862.[4]

The Carters, his mother's family, came to the United States early in the nineteenth century. They too were eager for adventure and found it along the eastern frontier. Young John Carter was always fascinated by the tales he heard about his mother's great-great-grandfather, Augestine Hunt, who seemed to possess the gift of prophecy. Scouting along the Susquehanna River one day in the early 1800s, Hunt sensed trouble and told his party of twenty-one men that they should return to camp. His colleagues laughed at him, but being independent (another family trait) he left anyway. That night a band of Indians attacked those Hunt left behind and all perished.[5]

Just as interesting was Vincent's maternal grandfather who had prospected for gold in Australia and California. Although he never struck it rich in either place, the small amount of gold he did find was sufficient to excite John Carter, who always enjoyed hearing of his exploits. Eventually, Ohio became the Carters' home and it was there that his mother Beulah was born in 1864.[6]

It was in Ohio that Beulah Carter and Frank Vincent grew up, met, and married. Not long after their marriage in 1888, they moved to Seneca, Kansas, where Frank opened the Vincent and Drees General Store. The business prospered and so did the family. Within ten years, the Vincents had three sons and a daughter: Edward Martin (called "Ned"), Frank Brooks, John Carter, and Margaret Elizabeth. But with each pregnancy, Beulah grew progressively weaker: She had contracted tuberculosis, a disease that had already killed two brothers. In 1906, the family moved to Macon, Georgia, where it was hoped that the warmer climate might restore her health. Frank opened a real estate and insurance office, and both Vincents became active in the city's Baptist Church. Unfortunately, Beulah's condition did not improve; she had to be isolated from the rest of the family and lived in a special tent behind the Vincent house on Pierce Street. A year after moving to Macon, she died.[7]

Beulah's sister Louise tried to fill the void left by her passing, and cousin Carrie Carter, a fifty-five-year-old spinster, came to live with the Vincents for three years, until Frank remarried in 1910.[8]

John Carter's new step-mother was Lula Velma Fulghum, a thirty-six-year-old teacher and superintendent in the Macon public school system. It was she who probably had the greatest impact on the future diplomat's personality. "She was a deeply devout person," her granddaughter would later recall, "who not only paid lip service to her faith, but who was actively involved in many church activities. Her Christian belief permeated itself into the home. The Bible was read aloud daily, and all the Vincent children gained a knowledge and understanding of many biblical stories. Prayers before meals and before going to bed were an important part of their life style." She was intellectual as well as religious: Together she and John

Carter (as he was always called, in southern style) would select books and read aloud, and the boy and later man would always remember how he was encouraged "to keep an open mind and read. . . ." Later in life, Vincent became something of an authority on nineteenth-century English poetry and could quote long passages he and his stepmother had memorized.[9]

Prompted by Lula, Vincent became a devoted attendant of the Vineville Baptist Church, where both his parents taught Sunday school classes, and he was often tempted to become a Baptist minister. But he eventually found organized religion too doctrinaire to suit him: "At an early age while still going through the religious routine of the family and the church I developed doubts about religion as thought and practised; disliked St. Peter and St. Paul heartily but clung to the Sermon on the Mount." Despite these reservations, the early religious training left its mark. All his life Vincent tried to follow the Baptist injunction to "do good, seek justice, [and] correct oppression."[10]

Though he would spend his boyhood in typical pursuits (including hunting, soccer, and baseball—for a time he dreamed of being a professional pitcher), he was a serious, responsible young man. "Nobody ever had to tell me to go out and cut kindling or get firewood for the stove," he later remembered. "And if I had chickens around the place, I usually looked after them." (His first birthday present from Lula was a "pair of little bantams, the tiny rooster gaily colored as autumn leaves, the little hen demurely brown." Nearly forty years later, when he was minister to Switzerland, he was still raising hens in the legation basement.) Determined to rely on his own resources, he earned extra money by helping his father collect rents and "during vacations . . . packed peaches from Georgia to Virginia." From these jobs he would earn fifteen to twenty-five dollars a week, enough to pay his extracurricular expenses during the school year.[11]

After graduating from Vineville Grade School in 1914, Vincent majored in foreign languages, English, and history at Sidney Lanier High School. His best grades were in the humanities, his worst in what was then called "domestic science": manual training, drawing, and shop. His attention was not limited to the classroom: National and world events also captured his imagination. His boyhood hero and fellow southerner, Woodrow Wilson, was president, and Wilson's religious idealism appealed to the young man. When the president led the nation into World War I, to "make the world safe for democracy," sixteen-year-old Vincent was impatient to go abroad and do his part. In 1918 he tried to join the armed forces but without success.

Vincent volunteered before he was drafted, but his slight, ninety-nine-pound frame failed to meet the minimum weight requirement. With characteristic determination, he put himself on a diet of chocolate malts and quickly gained sixteen pounds, enough to get him by his army physical. In October he entered the Student Army Training Corps at Mercer University, but his military career ended abruptly a month later with the armistice. He found himself marching down Cherry Street in Macon commemorating the coming of peace, "the most unhappy looking soldier in the whole crowd because it looked like my last chance to get abroad."[12]

In early 1919, Vincent began his college studies at Clemson, a small school in rural South Carolina. He soon found the curriculum as parochial as the environment. Breakfast often consisted of bread and syrup and the school was run like the military academy it had once been. Not long after his entrance, a rebellion erupted among a group of student busboys who were dissatisfied with their wages and quickly spread throughout the college, ending in a "walkout" of the freshman and sophomore classes. Caught up in the drama, Vincent packed his bags and joined his classmates (who had facetiously dubbed themselves "the Bolsheviks") in walking ten miles to catch the nearest train for home. Though the college administration later promised to improve conditions at Clemson and invited the students to return without penalty, Vincent decided that he would not complete the four-year term. He returned to finish his first year and transferred to Mercer University in Macon, an institution he felt could better prepare him for a career of public service.[13]

At Mercer, he pursued more deeply those subjects that had long fascinated him: history, journalism, and foreign languages. He joined the Quill Club, where Mercer's budding writers read and criticized each other's short stories and essays; twice he edited the student yearbook, and in 1921 was elected vice-president of the School of Journalism. Yet he found the writer's world limited and lonely, and friends urged him in other directions. J. Clay Walker, his professor of modern languages, encouraged him "to go into the foreign service, to get out, go abroad, and do things." But Vincent could not make a final decision. He knew the life of a farmer or small town businessman was not for him. He was much too interested in people and ideas to spend the rest of his life in remote and secluded Macon. As graduation approached, he vacillated between religious and secular careers: becoming a Baptist missionary (his stepmother's choice) or joining the Consular Service. In the end, he decided to give the Consular Service a try; if accepted he would have an opportunity to travel and perform public service. But should he find the life of a consul unrewarding, he could always resign and pursue another career. Whatever the eventual outcome, his life would be spent following Wilson's call to "lift your eyes to the horizons . . . , let your thoughts and imagination run abroad throughout the world . . . . [Go] out and make the world more comfortable and happy."[14]

In June 1923, Vincent received his bachelor's degree in English (with a minor in journalism) from Mercer University. That summer he worked in his father's real estate office and studied for the oral and written examinations for the Consular Service. "You answered a few simple questions," he was encouraged to believe, "and you got through with it." Arriving in Washington the following January to take the examinations, he had a rude awakening: It "was much more difficult than I thought it was going to be."

First, he was examined orally by a panel consisting of Assistant Secretary of State Leland Harrison, and other high-ranking diplomatic and consular officials. Groups of five candidates were questioned about international law, contemporary history, and diplomatic usage. One question dealt with the Austrian seizure of Herzegovina during World War I. The examiners went down the row of nervous young men, looking for someone who knew of the incident. By chance, Vincent "happened to have been reading up on it and knew it backward and forward." His familiarity with this complex event impressed the board.

Besides intellectual ability, the oral examination was designed to test the judgment and propriety of the applicants. One candidate made the mistake of wearing knickers to the examination. "Those were the days prospective diplomats weren't supposed to wear 'knickers'—at least before the board," Vincent recalled. "Doing so was a large mark against him. He couldn't answer the questions anyway, but even if he had been able to, I think the Plus Fours would have killed him." Vincent was neatly dressed, knew the answers, and passed the examination with a score of eighty.[15]

The written examination was more rigorous. Here, he scored seventy-six, four points below the acceptable minimum. Suddenly, it seemed that his consular career was over before it had even begun.

Fortunately, the board of examiners weighed the written and oral examinations equally, and it was Vincent's performance on the latter that gave him another opportunity to join the Consular Service. With the helpful intervention of his state's senior senator, Walter George, the State Department offered Vincent the position of clerk, provided that he repeat the written examination within the next year. On April 16, 1924, he accepted and became (provisionally) a member of the Consular Service of the United States.[16]

Vincent requested Copenhagen as his first assignment, but, with characteristic efficiency, the State Department ordered him to a post a world away: to Ch'ang-sha, capital of China's Hunan Province. He accepted the assignment unhappily, believing that he would be "bored to death in that isolated spot." He prepared himself by purchasing two pair of glasses ("in case my eyes gave out from reading") and a flute to play "when reading became a bore." But he was also experiencing other emotions.

"One night before my departure," he later remembered, "I had one of those hair-raising dreams that makes you wake up in a cold sweat. I dreamed that I was right in the middle of the Boxer Rebellion and getting the worst of it." From his childhood, he recalled the stories he had read in the *Baptist Youth Companion*, describing American missionaries being attacked, tortured, and killed by mobs of angry Chinese. Undaunted, he departed Macon with his books, glasses, and flute.[17]

Had Vincent been aware of the history of Ch'ang-sha and the surrounding province, he would not have anticipated boredom. Ch'ang-sha, called by the Chinese "the city that cannot be conquered," had been for centuries a battleground of social, political, and intellectual revolution—"the abode of romantic poets, of speculative philosophers, and of great lovers and soldiers."[18] In the first decades of the twentieth century, Hunan was "a bitterly anti-foreign province."[19] American diplomats stationed there and in nearby Hankow noted the presence of placards attacking foreigners—placards "of the most outrageous character, pictorial ones so degrading and filthy as to be unfit for any persons to see." Chinese agitators in Ch'ang-sha urged their followers to "begin the killing. . . , kill foreigners and their officials! Put to death the foreign students and foreign children."[20] Vincent's dream would prove to be prophetic; the books he brought along to fill his idle hours would go unread, the glasses would break, and the ebony flute "split open from disuse." Only twenty-three and a stranger to China, fate and the Department of State were soon to place him inside the "moving tornado" that was the modern Chinese revolution.[21]

Vincent saw his first home in China from the deck of a river steamer as it plowed its way through the muddy waters of the River Hsiang. It was May 1924, and spring had come to Hunan Province. In the distance, he could see blue clad farmers planting new green rice in treeless fields. Then the wooded islands of Pien Shan and Chun Shan came into view, the latter fabled in Chinese history as the visiting place of the concubines of the Emperor Shun. Passing a covey of brightly colored junks, his ship turned into Tungting Lake, the final approach to Ch'ang-sha, "the city of the long sands."[22]

Leaving the ship, he found himself surrounded by a Chinese crowd:

beggars, with their hands outstretched, children pulling at his pants legs, rickshaw drivers fighting for the chance to take him to his destination. Finally, the victor picked up his bags and motioned Vincent to climb aboard. He was too exhausted from his long voyage and too excited by the scene around him to realize how uncomfortable and dangerous was his ride through the city's narrow and slimy streets. Running fast, the coolie barely avoided collision with other rickshaws and with the people and pigs that filled the avenue. Vincent held on tight, fearing that at any moment he might be thrown overboard, an inglorious way to announce his arrival in Ch'ang-sha.

Somehow he managed to arrive safely at the American Consulate, a two-story white brick building topped with an American flag. A Chinese ushered him into the office of his new boss, Consul Carl D. Meinhardt, who examined carefully the new clerk which the State Department had sent him. Meinhardt found a man of medium height and slight build, dressed in a blue pin-striped suit and matching bow tie. The body may have looked frail, but the face was strong: a wide mouth, over which jutted a firm straight nose, penetrating blue eyes and bushy brows. His sandy hair was worn long, unparted, and piled on top of the head. Seventeen years residence in Georgia had also left its mark: The young man spoke with a distinct southern drawl. Meinhardt was happy to see him. For months he had operated the office alone, with the help of three Chinese who spoke only "pidgin English." Despite Vincent's youth and unfamiliarity with China, he would be a valuable addition to his staff.[23]

During the next few days, Vincent learned more about his new post and duties. The consular district in Hunan Province which Meinhardt and Vincent (and their Chinese assistants) serviced was like many American outposts in China in the 1920s. Representatives of Standard Oil, Dupont Chemical, and the Singer Sewing Machine Company lived and worked in Ch'ang-sha, vying with their British, French, and Japanese competitors for the profits to be reaped from the rich soil. Over three hundred American missionaries were also working to convert the Chinese to Christianity at twenty-three separate stations throughout the province.[24] The American Navy was represented by the presence of the gunboat, U.S.S. *Villalobos*. It was Vincent's responsibility to protect American lives and promote American interests in the area.

His daily activities were more mundane. His first duty was to help run the tiny legation office and to report on political developments in the district to the State Department once every month. Most of his time was spent answering inquiries from American firms interested in selling their products or establishing branch offices in Ch'ang-sha. On one occasion, for example, it was his sad duty to inform the Merchants' Association of New York that he did not think it profitable to open "an agency . . . for collapsable corsets," since to his knowledge Chinese women did not wear them.[25]

Although Vincent missed his family and friends at home, he had little trouble adjusting to life in China. In fact, the secluded foreign enclave where he lived and worked was not very different from Macon. "Nearly everyone is constantly going or coming from teas and dinner parties," he wrote his sister not long after arriving, "everyone is dependent on everyone else for amusement and . . . everyone seems to be enjoying themselves immensely." He was quick to make friends and soon he was well known to the American community in the city. "Never was anyone treated more cordially than your brother has been here," he told Margaret, "the old men call him 'son,' the Yale [-in-China] boys take him in as one of them, young ladies . . . sew the buttons on his clothes, patch his trousers, mend his gloves and have him to dinner." He even won first prize at a New Year's Eve costume ball, thanks to his popularity with the ladies. He went as St. Peter; his costume "consisted chiefly of a sheet draped Romanesquely over a pair of poor shoulders, a bare arm, feet encased in white socks and gross sandles, a half powdered head surmounted by a large halo and a white beard . . . revealing a Piedmont cigarette." At midnight he "passed out with the old year." "The interpretation I gave of St. Peter that night is still occupying first place at dinner conversations," he noted a few days later, with one missionary friend remarking that "it wasn't how much you looked like Saint Peter as how much you didn't look like him that won the prize."[26]

Despite the social activities and the leisurely pace of work, he was uncertain whether to remain in the Consular Service or accept an invitation to join his friends in missionary work at the headquarters of nearby Yale-in-China. In February 1925, he took again that "damned" Foreign Service examination which he had failed the year before. For fourteen hours during a two day period, he was tested on international, maritime, and commercial law; political and commercial geography; arithmetic; modern languages (French, German, or Spanish); natural, industrial, and commercial resources of the United States; political economy; American history, government, and institutions; and modern history since 1850 (including Europe, Latin America, and the Far East).[27]

This time, Vincent achieved a passing score of at least 80 in seven of the eight sections and in American history, government, and institutions he earned a perfect one hundred.[28] A short time later he received official confirmation that he had been appointed a foreign service officer, unclassified, and vice-consul of career. "No congratulations appreciated," a disgruntled Vincent wrote his sister. "Until I received the news I planned to take a vacation. Now I cannot. Before, Mr. Meinhardt could give me permission, now I have to write to the State Department to get more than two days leave. Oh well."[29]

April found him just as undecided about his future. "'What are your plans? More clear I hope than when I last approached you on the theme,'" he asked himself in a bit of free verse written to his sister late that month.

> "As clear," I sighed, "as mud; behold the little bird, he plans not nor premeditates and yet I find that his unchartered state does not impair his song."
>
> "Quite so," replied my sage companion," but does the little bird . . . get very far; progress, I mean to say."
>
> "And who, in Jesus' name, has asked my little bird for progress? is't not enough that he lives, flies and sings without demanding that he go to hell or heaven?"[30]

Less than a month after John Carter wrote these lines, events in Shanghai changed Chinese history and the course of his own life.

On May 30, a brigade of British police in Shanghai fired on a group of Chinese students and workers who had been protesting working conditions in a foreign textile mill. Twelve Chinese were killed and seventeen were wounded, but it was only the beginning of a new period of revolutionary violence against the western imperialists who were dominating China. In June, the trouble spread to Hankow and Canton, and in a repetition of the "May 30th Incident," more Chinese were killed and wounded. Suddenly all of China seemed to be united in its determination to drive out the foreigners.

The turmoil unleashed by the events of May and June 1925, were symptomatic of the political cataclysm that the country had been experiencing since 1911. The Revolution of 1911 had brought an end to the reign of the Ch'ing Dynasty, but it had failed to create a unified national government to take its place. Instead, China dissolved into geographical fragments, each controlled by a different political or military strongman. The leader of the Chinese revolution, Sun Yat-sen, had established his own Kuomintang regime in Canton and looked forward to the day when he could defeat the northern warlords and reunify the country.[31]

Unable to win financial support from the western powers (who preferred a fragmented China under their control), Sun had turned to Soviet Russia for assistance, and the Russians, hoping to manipulate the Chinese revolution for their own purposes, responded by giving valuable military and financial aid to the Canton regime, while at the same time recognizing the established government of warlord Wu Pei-fu in Peking.[32]

Before the full effect of Russian assistance could be felt, however, Sun Yat-sen died, and the Kuomintang was left leaderless. Of those aspiring to succeed Sun the most important was Chiang Kai-shek. Chiang had been born in Chekiang in 1886 and educated at military academies in Pao-ting and Tokyo, where he had joined the Kuomintang. Despite his membership, he was never a revolutionary, and the years after 1911 found him living and working among financial gangster elements in Shanghai. In 1924 he visited Soviet Russia to learn the tactics of political revolution and he then returned to China to direct the Whampoa Military Academy, a position that catapulted him to the front rank of the party. Sun's death in March 1925 opened the fissures between the left and right in the Kuomintang and Chiang emerged as the leader of the conservative faction, which feared that the influence of the Soviets (and the violence that followed the Shanghai incident) would lead to the communist conquest of China.[33]

Despite their political differences, Kuomintang leaders could now depend on an army that was growing in strength and expertise. Deciding that the moment had come to fulfill Sun's dream of national unity, in the summer of 1926 they launched a campaign aimed at destroying the warlords and capturing Peking.[34]

As Chiang's army marched north, Ch'ang-sha was torn by violence. In both the city and the countryside, peasants, workers, and students organized themselves into revolutionary unions and created havoc at Yale-in-China and other mission stations. "There is madness in the air that moves as fast as the wind," noted Ruth Kauke, who was visiting her missionary relatives at Fu Siang Mission in late summer 1926. "From day to day more laborers and students are deciding that they must have their own way . . . and a strike or parade is immediately under way. They demand the most ridiculous things: no religion in school; the power to dismiss teachers; the power to tell teachers what they must do; and they want a Chinese principal."[35]

Revolutionary soldiers occupied church property, where to the horror of American missionaries, they slept, drank, and washed themselves from the communal well, and cooked dinners of fish, rice, and red peppers. Some missionaries tried to forcibly eject the soldiers (one septuagenarian beat at them with his cane) but the soldiers laughed and threatened to kill them. "A few years ago they would have respected the foreigners' wishes," Mrs. Kauke wrote a friend, "but now the soldiers say 'this isn't yours, this is China. . . .' They've seen enough of foreigners in their own land to realize that the white man is not a God."[36]

Meinhardt and Vincent sought redress from the local Chinese government, and also urged worried Americans to remain cool. Vincent thought stronger measures were necessary and recommended that armed naval guards be dispatched to protect mission buildings but he received no immediate reply from the State Department. Their failure to turn back the Chinese revolution frequently angered their missionary constituents. "It is very plain that America does not guard her interests out here so efficiently and thoroughly as do the British and the Japanese," Mrs. Kauke commented. "They have a dozen men on the job where we have only one and a very poor one at that. The Vice Consul here in charge at present is only a youngster with no experience. And our gun-boats are a joke."[37] (Mrs. Kauke, a young, attractive widow later changed her mind about Vincent when he asked her for a date).[38]

In mid-December, conditions improved slightly, and Meinhardt decided to return to the United States on home leave, leaving Vincent in charge of the consulate. He was not gone long before the situation took a new turn for the worse.

As Christmas approached, representatives of American business in the interior found their activities restricted once again by what Vincent described as "unsettled conditions, agitation of antiforeign labor unions, and military demands."[39] Of the three, he believed that the radical labor movement was the most dangerous. "The farmers', students', and laborers' unions are a growing menace," he reported to Minister John V.A. MacMurray in Peking. "Through either ignorance or indifference they frequently cause trouble for the agents of American firms. The Tobacco Product Corporation has suffered at their hands in several towns and their propaganda and troublemaking is reacting unfavorably on the business of the Standard Oil Company. The continual threat of strikes and the impossible demands which accompany these threats is having an unfavorable effect on foreign and Chinese business alike."[40]

Because of the crisis in the countryside, Vincent spent Christmas Day at the office. The Christian holiday gave antiforeign Chinese another opportunity to strike out at those they accused of importing an alien faith into China. Vincent visited the local commissioner of foreign affairs and demanded that he give protection to American and Chinese Christians, but the commissioner's proclamation only protected those who resided in the city and did not extend into the interior. There, "Chinese Christians were intimidated, churches were entered and congregations scattered, and some missions reported broken windows [and] benches."[41]

Exhausted after a long day at the consulate, Vincent stopped off at one of the foreigner's clubs before returning home for the night. As he sipped a drink and chatted with his friend Lieutenant Commander Allen E. Smith of the U.S.S. *Villalobos*, a messenger arrived to report that the French postal commissioner "was being held by a mob" and needed his assistance. (Since there was no French consul in the city and the British consul had recently died, Vincent had agreed to watch over French interests in the province. He therefore felt responsible for Commissioner de Jauriaus's safety.)[42] Smith agreed to join Vincent on his mission and armed with only a flashlight the two set out into the "dark misty night" to search for the helpless Frenchman. After "groping" their way about the streets of Ch'ang-sha for almost an hour, they finally entered a compound where a crowd of seventy-five "dark clad Chinese" surrounded the building in which they believed de Jauriaus was being held prisoner.

Pushing his way through the crowd, Vincent announced in "loud, controlled words . . . : American Gunboat, where is Monsieur de Jauriaus?" For twenty minutes the crowd stared blankly at the two Americans. While Vincent remained calm, Smith began to sense trouble and looked for a place where they could put their backs against the wall. Finally, three men came out of the adjoining building. One of them was the French commissioner, whom Vincent and Smith marched from the compound. De Jauriaus was unhurt, having capitulated to the Chinese demands before "they began to string him up by the thumbs." But French interests were still secure, he informed Vincent, for when he signed the agreement he also indicated that he did so under duress, thus making the document null and void. Vincent and Smith saw him safely home and returned to their own quarters. Surely, it had been the strangest Christmas Day the young diplomat had ever spent.[43]

The new year, 1927, did not bring stability to Hunan Province: Agitation by radical students, peasants, and workers continued, and it was not long before every mission school had ceased to function. "They will stop at nothing," E.D. Chapin reported from the American Presbyterian Mission at Ch'ang-te:

> When the school closed they took away the balance of the money in the treasury of the Y.M.C.A. and have been using the money to finance their campaign of villification against Christianity. . . . They came to the school . . . and seized . . . books, magazines and other things of the Y.M.C.A. to which they had no right. . . . they would not dare to act in so high-handed [a] way were it not that they have the support of the Bolshevistic Students' Union and of the Kuomintang which has been helping them openly. . . . The school is closed because the students urged on by the Reds . . . made such demands that it was impossible to carry on any longer.[44]

When the Kuomintang threatened to seize empty school buildings to transform them into a military academy, Vincent advised Chapin and the other missionaries at Ch'ang-te to do all that they could to prevent confiscation. "We received your wire instructing us to take a firm stand against their taking them for military purposes," Chapin wrote Vincent "and will do so if they come again, though if they really intend to take them there is little that we can do."[45]

Vincent urged Americans to resist Chinese seizure of their property. "Close the schools, keep them closed, and keep the Chinese out of them," he wrote the Reverend Charles H. Derr of the American Presbyterian Mission in Hengchow. "Close your hospitals and schools rather than make concessions to the Chinese which would limit your control," he also told Dr. Stephen C. Lewis at Cheng-chou. "You should await more settled conditions before making agreements with the Chinese. . . . Unless the situation becomes more serious than it is at the present a few missionaries should remain at the various stations to protect property and endeavor to counteract the anti-Christian propaganda."[46] With the American position under attack everywhere in China, Vincent was determined to protect his country's interests at almost any cost.

But not if it meant the loss of American lives. When revolutionary violence erupted anew at Hankow on January 3 and the British government decided to evacuate women and children from Ch'ang-sha, Vincent sent letters to all American missions in the province recommending that nonessential personnel make plans for a speedy withdrawal. The first group of seventy Americans left Ch'ang-sha on January 25, and one hundred more followed a few days later (including John Carter's sister Margaret, who had been visiting him during the past few months).[47]

Nearly every mission station accepted Vincent's advice without question, and the withdrawal proceeded smoothly with only a few exceptions, some comic, others pathetic. The missionaries at Hengchow informed Vincent that it was impossible to leave because they were having a "ladies meeting at the mission" and those at Han-shou simply could not make up their minds what to do. On the afternoon of January 31, he wired both groups "in English" and ordered them to "withdraw to Hankow immediately." Despite these problems, he seemed to be enjoying himself: "Keep your feet dry, have a good time, and don't worry about me," he wrote his sister, "I'm right in the middle of China where I wanted to be."[48]

Vincent expressed more serious concern to Consul General Francis Lockhart in Hankow: "Each day brings its developments and incidents . . . which serve to convince me of the impossibility of Americans continuing their missionary work . . . as long as . . . the present [Chinese] Government exists."[49] "The Nationalist Government has done nothing to prevent agitation and strikes," he wrote Minister MacMurray in Peking, a few days later. "Effective educational and medical work is not possible."[50]

Above all, he was distressed by the obstruction of missionary efforts in Hunan. "Although I am not a missionary," he wrote Dr. E. D. Vanderburgh of the Presbyterian Mission at Hsiang-t'an, "I have been intimately associated with American missionaries for the past two years . . . and I believe that I have a sympathetic understanding of your difficulties and desires." While he found much that was distasteful in missionary activities, he believed that it was his responsibility as vice-consul to guarantee Americans the "right" to bring western religion and culture to China.[51]

The problem was to develop a system that would protect American interests without threatening American lives or relations with revolutionary China. Vincent recognized the difficulty inherent in such a task: "If, out of the welter of conflicting treaty rights and national aspirations, of idealism, Communism, imperialism and demagogy," he wrote to a friend, "one is able to forecast events and decide on a plan of action one is fortunate."[52] As the American economic and religious position in China deteriorated in January and February 1927, he tried to devise that "plan of action." Initially, his program of partial evacuation and resistance to radical demands was suffcent to preserve American rights, but it was only a palliative and could not remedy the American-China problem. To grant the demands of the students, laborers, or government was no solution: To him it meant "absolute loss of control by the foreigners."[53]

Since the provincial government refused to respect American rights under the old system of extraterritoriality, Vincent believed that a new "form of legal or treaty status" should be established which could "be used as a basis of negotiating with the local authorities."[54] When the American people were critical of "gunboat diplomacy," and Secretary of State Frank Kellogg was urging President Coolidge to negotiate a revision of extraterritoriality that would eliminate foreign privileges in China,[55] Vincent was recommending that the system be amended to preserve American prerogatives, not abolish them. Like Minister MacMurray and other members of the treaty port community in China, Vincent had little sympathy for Chinese radicalism and opposed a plan that would end extra-territoriality completely. "I . . . should be very loathe to reside in Chungking or Ch'ang-sha," he wrote his sister, "without [some] semblance of extraterritorial rights . . . and without—and this is much more important—a gunboat."[56] After all, Vincent had to deal with the explosive situation in Ch'ang-sha on a daily basis, while those at home had time and distance to help them judge developments more objectively.

Events, one quite personal, the other national, distracted Vincent from his reflections on the treaty system. On February 13, 1927, he received a telegram from his twenty-five-year-old sister Margaret announcing her marriage to his friend Allen "Hoke" Smith, the captain of the U.S.S. *Villalobos*. He was "surprised, shocked, and saddened," so disturbed in fact that he failed to file his monthly report to the State Department. That night sleep eluded him and in the early morning hours he wrote to his sister and her new husband. ". . . I didn't send you to Shanghai to get married," he told Margaret, but faced with a fait accompli, the twenty-six-year-old bachelor offered her advice.

> [Be] more than a husband and wife to each other . . . [R]emember that your continued happiness is going to depend on more than love. Patience and understanding and respect are some very essential ingredients of married happiness. Take care of yourself physically (remember your mother always). . . . [M]ake him covet your respect and admiration. Admiration is a wonderful thing in married life; and it's admiration of personality and mentality that really counts. Be ambitious: for yourself and for Hoke . . . I expect Hoke to be an Admiral some day. I want you to be ready for his every promotion and be *promoted with him.*

To Hoke he wrote: "She is my only sister. She has been my companion for twenty-five years. I love her better than I ever will anyone else and am very deeply interested in her welfare and happiness. Her marriage is of far more concern to me than my own will be . . . . Be companions; be advisors to each other; be partners in accomplishment; be promoters of each other's welfare, happiness and success." Finally he fell asleep and awoke happier in the morning: "Best of luck and joy to you both," he appended to his note to Margaret, then ran off to write his report to Washington.[57]

A month later he had reason to be thankful that Margaret was safe in Shanghai. On March 24, Nationalist troops entered Nanking, burning and looting foreign homes, and attacking American and European citizens. Although only six foreigners died during the "Nanking Incident," thousands fled China in the weeks that followed; most never returned.[58]

Among them were the last remaining Americans in Vincent's district. Three days after the tragedy in Nanking, Minister MacMurray ordered Vincent to evacuate all American citzens from Hunan; those who refused to go were to be warned that they remained "entirely at their own risk."[59] The vice-consul followed these instructions immediately, and when it was announced that the American consulate would soon be closed, disorder intensified in the city. On Monday, April 4, a strike against all American firms was ordered by the radical labor and student's union, and all Chinese who worked for foreigners were told to walk off their jobs. "Feeling ran high," Vincent later wrote Margaret. "Pete [Dorrance, the Manager of Standard Oil] was besieged in his office by a group of coolies and forced to agree to unreasonable demands. All employees of American firms and missions walked out, including those at the consulate."[60] Three days later, after making certain that almost every American had been evacuated (over three hundred had already left), Vincent closed and sealed the consulate. With the help of American sailors, he carried the office archives aboard the U.S.S. *Palos*, which then sailed from Ch'ang-sha.[61]

Vincent arrived in Hankow on April 9 to find the foreign community frightened and dismayed by the effects of the Chinese revolution. He did not share their anxieties or their attitudes. "After the rather tense last week in Ch'ang-sha," he told his sister,

> I could not keep from laughing at the . . . Hankow people who were unable to attend their clubs [and] offices unmolested, [despite] the two dozen or more men of war to protect them. The American and British men [are] living aboard the ships and the little German children [are] running about the street. I haven't seen a coolie try to eat one of them since I have been here. The principal grievance, I have found, is that coolies are permitted to walk on the sidewalk. . . . In Hankow, I, who never suspected myself of being pro-Chinese am 'branded' as such by these rabid haters of anything that savors of China. It disgusts me.[62]

His dislike for Hankow made him miss Ch'ang-sha all the more, and he longed for some word of conditions in the province from clerk J. S. Pan who had remained behind to watch over American interests. A few weeks after his arrival, he received his first bit of news from Ch'ang-sha, but it did little to brighten his spirits. "Ch'ang-sha has been under the control of the Communist Party since April 8th," Pan wrote Vincent. "From April 8th to April 30th there existed a reign of terror. Many innocent rich men met death; their property was either stolen or confiscated. The Unions are controlling the city; the provincial government exercises no authority. Every day four to six people are executed in front of the Educational Hall. There is a parade against foreigners . . . every day." Vacant mission property was now occupied by the labor and students' unions. The Yale College in Ch'ang-sha was still an educational institution, but it was run by the Chinese and for purposes that few Yale alumni would have sponsored. In the interior, conditions were even worse than usual: American missions had been looted and occupied, and movable articles were sold at public auction.[63]

Troubled by these developments, Vincent conferred with the foreign minister of the Nationalist government, Eugene Chen. He found him "interesting, intelligent and capable" but was disappointed that Chen could not assure him that order would soon be restored. The best way to protect American interests until a responsible government came to power, Chen asserted, was to support the Nationalist regime by reopening the American consulate in Ch'ang-sha. ("Such a move was desired because it would do much to restore confidence in the government which he represents," Vincent noted.) Skillfully avoiding the trap that Chen seemed to be setting, Vincent replied that the consulate would remain closed until there was "a stable government . . . in control of the province and convincing assurance . . . given that American life and property would be given adequate protection and compensation paid for losses."[64] Vincent left the meeting "convinced that there was nothing [Chen] or the government he represents could do to rectify matters in Hunan."[65]

Vincent remained pessimistic even while Chiang Kai-shek moved to take control of the revolutionary movement and channel it in more moderate directions. That same April, Chiang ordered his troops to attack the Communist and non-Communist radicals in Shanghai, and during a three-day bloodbath the Kuomintang was purged of its liberal and Communist membership. During the next nine months, Chiang's fortunes rose and fell, but in January 1928, he finally defeated the radicals and took control of the party and the Nationalist government now based in Nanking. He resumed the Northern Expedition to unify China under the banner of a conservative Kuomintang, and on July 3, the Nationalists formally occupied Peking. China was "united" for the first time since the fall of the Manchus in 1911.

The unity was more nominal than real. Outer Mongolia, Tibet, Sinkiang Uighur, and especially Manchuria were still virtually autonomous and powerful Chinese warlords like Li Tsung-jen of Kwangsi Chuang, Yen Hsi-shan of Shansi, and Feng Yu-hsiang and Chang Hsueh-liang of northern China remained cool to Chiang's invitation to give up their independent status and join the Nationalists. The authority of China's new government "extended to only five provinces in the lower Yangtze region" and its armies were still outnumbered by those of Chiang's provincial rivals. Beset by a variety of military, economic, and political problems, it seemed likely that the Chinese regime would follow its predecessors and vanish before the year was out.

Vincent had had an opportunity to observe these problems first hand, during a brief visit to Ch'ang-sha a few months earlier. He found conditions in the city in mid-May as unstable as when he had left the year before. "Yale was dismal," he later informed Margaret, "the island was dismal, and it rained all the time I was there." From J. S. Pan he learned that "Hunan is in almost as bad shape as it was a year ago . . . the Communists are active, the government is broke, and . . . business is at a standstill. . . . Chinese soldiers still occupy almost every mission station in the interior." To see his beloved city in ruins was particularly saddening and he was happy to leave as soon as his business was completed. "I am sorry I went back," he later noted. "I [would] rather remember it as it was, than see it as it is—a poorly kept graveyard of so many pleasant times and happy associations, a cabaret at ten o'clock of the succeeding morning."[66]

Vincent's trip to Ch'ang-sha, and his observations of war-torn Hankow, convinced him that "law and order" would not soon return to China, an assessment that he hoped was shared by his superiors in Washington, despite their eagerness to recognize the existence of Chiang's regime. He was concerned that "enthusiasts" in the State Department would see the creation of the Nationalist government as a sign that "permanent stability" had been restored, and would therefore "give up all those 'unequal treaty rights' under which we foreigners are allowed to exist in China." Despite exposure to the "rabid" China-haters of Hankow, his attitude toward the average Chinese was indifferent, and he was especially skeptical of those "working for their betterment," a "task" that he judged "difficult" and "disappointing."[67]

Although he shared many of the sentiments of the anti-Chinese "treaty port foreigners," his view of the Chinese revolution was remarkably objective and sound. Unlike the missionaries and businessmen he served, he did not see the revolution as Bolshevik-inspired but the result of an outburst of nationalism which was colliding with the interests of the western powers. And while many Americans responded hysterically when their prerogatives were being challenged, Vincent remained cool and detached. Edwin Deeks Harvey of Yale-in-China told Consul General Nelson T. Johnson "that under the very great strains [sic] that came upon Mr. Vincent he never lost his poise, either with Chinese officials or sometimes obstreperous American citizens; and that by calm persistence on an unostentatious evacuation, he got everybody under his care to leave the province." Consul General F. P. Lockhart, in an efficiency report written in August 1927, noted that Vincent "possesses an unusual amount of patience and maintains a serenity of mind which is of great value." And Minister MacMurray himself informed the State Department that Vincent "combined an alertness in seeing and meeting situations with a conspicuously sound judgment when, as was frequently the case, he had to act on his own discretion in matters of the most vital import to American lives and interests."[68] These qualities of poise, calm, patience, and serenity would receive even stronger testing in the years ahead, but for now Vincent was pleased and flattered to receive accolades from his government and missionary constituents.

Although at the age of twenty-seven he was now a famous figure in the Yangtze Valley, Vincent really knew little about China and its ancient language, culture, and history. To give its officers in the Far East a knowledge of China, the State Department required that they receive formal training in Chinese affairs at the American legation, so in May 1928, Vincent was ordered to proceed to Peking to begin his service as a "language officer." Disappointed that Ch'ang-sha was no longer a "livable place" and disgusted with life in Hankow, he received his new instructions with pleasure: "I am to report for language study no later than October first," he informed his sister, " . . . I shall gladly obey."[69]

After the "limited" life of Macon, and the remoteness of Ch'ang-sha and Hankow, Peking was "utopia." For the next two years Vincent's home was the intellectual and cultural center of China. "Here the old Mandarin class mingled with venal adventurers, the new China throbbed with plans and hopes for reform, foreigners lived a charmed, hedonistic existence and the silent Altar of Heaven lay in eternal marble perfection open to the sky."[70]

But it was a paradise to be studied as well as enjoyed. As a language officer attached to the American legation, Vincent's primary responsibility was to learn to speak and read the Chinese language competently and to absorb Chinese history, politics, geography, and commerce from his teachers and his texts. For twenty-seven years, the State Department had been training its young diplomats in Chinese affairs and Vincent's life in Peking followed the historic pattern of his predecessors in the China Service.[71]

Like the men who came before him, Vincent was given quarters in the San Kuan Miao (or "students' mess") "an enchanting old Chinese temple of historic fame," where it was rumored that one of the Manchu emperors had committed suicide. "The approach was through a circular moon gate," one of Vincent's colleagues later noted. "The buildings were laid out in a series of outer and inner courtyards . . . in such a way that one did not lead straight into the next, so there would be no easy entry for obnoxious spirits."[72] After Vincent had found his way through this exotic maze, he was introduced to Clarence J. Spiker, the "Chinese secretary," the man responsible for giving Vincent and the other students their reading lists and Chinese teachers.

Because Vincent was no stranger to China, his course of study differed slightly from the others who had just arrived. His first assignment was to enroll in the North China Union Language School for a one-quarter course in Chinese. The "Peking Language School" (as it was known to its students) employed one hundred teachers and "taught the direct method for fast results." Chinese, because of its complicated tonal system (there are four tones in Mandarin, eight in Cantonese) is best taught where students can hear and speak the language in daily drill. "The Teacher would say something in Chinese," Vincent later remembered, "and then all the students were supposed to repeat it, to fix your ear." After his morning lesson Vincent would return to his quarters for additional practice with the Chinese scholars who had been selected to assist him. Though a student of foreign languages since his days at Vineville Grade School, he was never able to master Chinese. Despite his years in Ch'ang-sha, Hankow, and Peking, his Chinese was only good enough "to do polite conversation at a dinner table, or josh along with a rickshaw coolie."[73]

The newer students worked individually with their Chinese teachers in their quarters in the students' mess. The teacher spoke little, if any, English so the student had to make his way unaided through the forest of Chinese vocabulary. If he felt baffled and confused, he was not alone. "The Chinese Teacher had not the slightest knowledge of how he proposed to teach me, or how I was supposed to learn," one of Vincent's colleagues later complained. After several hours of this arduous routine, the student was left by himself to study his Chinese character cards, begin his readings in Chinese history, politics, and geography, and perhaps to wonder why he had ever wished to join the China Service.[74]

At mid-morning, the students would gather in the communal eating hall for a cup of hot Chinese tea and conversation. The older, more cynical students would warn the newcomers "that studying Chinese too much [would] certainly affect one's intellect very adversely." To avoid becoming a useless Sinologue, they were urged to choose a hobby, lest they "became so immersed in the study of Chinese that [they] should lose all touch with the practical side of life and thus be of little use to [their] country." Polo, horseback riding, and ice skating were all available in Peking and every day could be a holiday, if the students so desired. On the other hand, the more scholarly could ignore these recommendations and return to their studies.[75]

Vincent was more likely to seek diversion. "I should have realized that when my college career was completed, my days as a student were over," he told his sister in 1929. Like his fellow students, he tried polo, but as "a simple Georgah [sic] peach packer" felt out of place; he also "found the damned horse uncomfortable and hated getting covered with mud from the track." Most of his free time was spent swimming in the legation pool with his friend James McHugh, a naval officer who was also studying in Peking. It was McHugh who told Vincent of the arrival in Peking of two American women who had been traveling through Europe and the Orient: Lucille Swann, a sculptor, and Elizabeth Spencer, a writer. "If they're good looking invite them over for a swim," Vincent instructed McHugh. They were very attractive indeed, McHugh assured Vincent, and a meeting was arranged.[76]

Vincent found them both "charming and good looking," he wrote his sister. "They are a delight to me because of their keen interest in the artistic side of the Chinese and their knowledge of Western art. They are like an invigorating sea breeze after the smug diplomatic atmosphere and small talk air-pockets of Peking."[77] The three became close friends and Vincent was admitted into their social circle, where he observed the royal life of the foreigner in Peking.

For thirty-five dollars a month Mex. (approximately seventeen dollars in American currency) the two women rented a house that had three wings—one for servants, one for guests, and one for residents. Outside there were two courtyards, and surrounding the grounds and house were "high, thick walls and a great locked portal for seclusion."[78]

They had five servants. Wong, the Number One Boy, "hires all the servants, fires them, manages them, prepares our bath, serves our meals, polishes our shoes, keeps track of the household accounts, feeds our kitten . . . and protects and serves us in every imaginable way;" he earned nine dollars a month. The cook, "a funny pixie like creature who is never seen outside her dungeon kitchen and who bows often and low at a chance encounter with his two Missies," cost them seven dollars a month. They also had two personal rickshaw coolies, Ting and Tong, who for four dollars a month each, built the morning fire in the grate, cleaned out the courtways, and stood ready to carry them wherever they wished to go. And finally, there was their own "Amah," "with the gentlest face, who sits all day long on her tiny feet sewing and mending"—cost: twenty cents gold per day. "We are being thoroughly and magnificently spoiled," Elizabeth told her mother. " . . . This is the kind of utopian existence one dreams of but never expects to achieve."[79]

Vincent's own life was less luxurious, but lavish nonetheless. He had his own number one boy to care for his daily needs and his apartment in the San Kuan Miao consisted of five rooms, two bathrooms, and a pantry—all decorated in Chinese fashion: "ceilings and walls a heavy cream with the beams in the living room done in . . . Chinese red, green, yellow and black design and those in the bedroom blue and gold. The conglomeration of colours," he believed, gave one "a mental picture of a perfect crazy quilt."[80] There was certainly nothing like it in Macon.

Unfortunately, his life was not as leisurely as that of his companions. Come October 1929 he would have to take his first annual examination in Chinese studies, and as the summer ended, he returned to his studies.

Not having taken his subjects very seriously during the previous year, he was not optimistic. His written Chinese, he admitted later, "was lamentably weak, [his] spoken none too good, and as for Chinese history, geography, trade and law—[he] knew as much as the average person who had lived in China for five years, but that wasn't enough."[81] For weeks, he studied day and night, his bedroom a mess of papers, books, letters, and magazines scattered everywhere. By the end of September he felt better prepared and his spirits brightened. "With the aid of twenty-five percent luck," he believed that he might be able to pass. "But fate and Mrs. MacMurray had other plans," Vincent later observed.[82]

On the morning of September 29, the wife of Minister John V. A. MacMurray telephoned John Carter to invite him to join Mrs. MacMurray and her party on a two week trip to Shensi Province west of Peking. They planned to leave three days hence, the first of October. Vincent explained that his examination was scheduled for that day, but he would consult the assistant Chinese secretary and return the lady's call. After securing permission, Vincent informed Mrs. MacMurray that it would be his pleasure to accompany them on their journey. His exam could wait until he returned in mid-October.

Vincent was pleased to be going and honored that he had been invited. "More congenial and interesting company could not be found in Peking." Along with Mrs. MacMurray, the group included Mrs. John Magruder, Mrs. Dorthey McHugh, and Andrew Hangoa of the United States Army. "Lois MacMurray gave the party rank," he later wrote his sister, "Helen [Magruder] gave it brains and Doty interest. Andy was manager and I was super-cargo and my own sweet self." For the next two weeks they traveled through Shensi by train, bus, mule, litter, and foot, "seeing what there was to be seen but mostly enjoying each other, the relaxation of being away from Peking, and the freedom of the open country."[83]

Back in Peking, he had only ten days in which to prepare for the examination. There could be no more delays. He attacked his studies as never before, and spent over twelve hours a day (including Saturdays and Sundays) poring over his books. But by the eve of the examination he was still unprepared. Of the thousand characters he was expected to know, he had mastered only seven hundred. Now he felt that he needed more than "twenty-five percent luck" to pass.

The examination, which ran from Monday through Friday, was organized into two sections consisting of questions on the language (written and spoken), and Chinese politics, commerce, geography, and history. Despite his anxiety, luck was still with him. He enjoyed the brief and simple conversation in Chinese with his examiner and on the written portion was delighted to discover that he was able to identify at least ninety-three of the one hundred characters selected for translation. The section on politics and history covered the areas that he had anticipated: the Opium Wars and the Taiping Rebellion, nationalism and sectionalism in modern Chinese history, and Sino-American relations since the day of the China traders. These topics did not prove to be a problem. The part devoted to Chinese commerce was a bit more difficult, however. Here he was asked to name the principal products of Szechwan Province. "How the hell can I answer this," he thought, "when the Chinese themselves don't know." He listed the few that came to mind and completed the examination. He left the room confident of success, and a bit surprised that he had done as well as he had, a fact confirmed a short time later when he was informed that he had received a passing score.[84]

That ordeal behind him, he was free again to renew his acquaintances at a celebration party. Among the guests were his friends from the legation swimming pool, who continued to be the most interesting of companions.

The object of Vincent's attention was Elizabeth (Betty) Spencer, who, he had learned, was thirty-two years old and a divorcee from Chicago. She had a lovely face and figure, golden brown hair, and eyes that sparkled with wit and warmth. In many ways she was John Carter's total opposite: worldly where he was somewhat provincial, volatile and quick to anger where he was calm. But they also shared a number of common interests: a taste for classical music and great literature, and a love of travel and adventure. Together, they made an unusual and fascinating couple. In Betty, John Carter had found an ideal companion with whom to explore China.

Their first major excursion together (which included her friend Lucille) was to the western hills, fifteen miles from Peking. They set out one chilly morning in November, Betty and Lucille clad in their "flashy leopard coats," and John Carter "wearing a huge sweater and wool mittens," looking, Betty later admitted, like a cross between "an aristocrat and a bum."[85]

They went by rickshaw to the railroad station, "caught the train by a squeak," and settled into the open coal car where the majestic Peking countryside was spread out before them. After admiring the sights for a while they went into the "coolie coach" for "warmth, conversation . . . [and] a bit of brandy and Chinese food." They returned to the open car just in time to catch their first glimpse of one of the greatest wonders of the world, the Great Wall of China. "It creeps over mountains, down passes, miles and miles of it," Betty wrote her mother in astonishment. "Over one point we could see the Mongolian Plains sweeping out and out as far as our eyes could reach." Later, they went sightseeing on foot, encountering "a small farm with a Chinese family running it as their forefathers did about a thousand years ago." John Carter thought it an ideal opportunity to practice his Chinese, and the party was invited to stay for a lunch of "garlic rice and meatballs." The Chinese asked "the most outrageous questions of Betty and Lucille: How old we are—if we are both his wives—how much John Carter makes—what he does with his money." Vincent translated hurriedly for his friends who urged him to say that they were both "twenty-five" and "his two favorite concubines." Before returning to the city, they spread out a blanket "under the shade of that great, old Wall . . . and talked and laughed until train time."[86]

Betty and John Carter's affection for one another made even the stuffy diplomatic life of Peking somehow bearable. In early 1930, Nelson T. Johnson arrived to replace John V.A. MacMurray as minister, producing a series of social gatherings that Vincent, as senior language officer, was expected to attend. He did not enjoy them very much but at least they gave him another chance to be with Betty.

"Going to a dinner party in Peking is an experience in itself," Betty reported to her mother. "You feel so elegant and secure seated in your rickshaw, wrapped up in fur coats, . . . [with] your legs and feet in blankets—just like sleigh riding. I always . . . feel like a Russian princess, especially when the little silver bells of the rickshaw sound clear in these cold, moonlit nights." As Betty and Lucille glided along slowly toward the legation compound, they could see the faces of the Chinese who lined the city streets: "the beggars and women with babies at their breasts, old men dragging on crutches and little girls in pigtails braided with bright red string." The rickshaw came to a halt amidst the sea of Chinese street merchants who called to the foreigners and offered them their wares: "velvet slippers and pieces of jade, empty patent medicine bottles and taffey [sic] apples on long red sticks." When they were able to move faster again the sounds of the street grew faint and they were encased by the night, the silence interrupted only by the "soft pat pat of the coolie's feet, so well coordinated and swift . . . that one is not conscious of a human being between the shafts."[87]

Finally, after a series of "unending . . . walls and temples," they rolled through the huge archway that guarded the American legation and arrived at the home of Mahlon F. Perkins, the counselor of legation and host of the evening's celebration. At the door they were greeted by four Chinese servants who took their wraps and directed them to the seating list that defined their place at the dinner table. Mrs. Perkins was a close friend of Betty's and knowing of her fondness for John Carter arranged to have them seated together.

The house was furnished "exactly" to Betty's taste: The walls of the drawing room were a "pale green," and the chairs were covered in "rose and white chintz." There she met the new American minister and the other guests. Nelson T. Johnson was "fat, with red hair, . . . so completely the traveling salesman it is indescribable." Johnson was a warm and gregarious bachelor, and Betty did not believe that he was the right type of man to represent the United States in a foreign land. "He squeezed Mrs. Howe and me . . . to indicate his friendly and enthusiastic feelings towards us," she noted in her diary, "exactly as a certain cheap type of man does. Socially he is not much to be proud of." Also in attendance were some of the community's more interesting diplomatic characters, including "the funny little Belgian Minister who wears a monocle and insists on talking French all the time" and the French minister whose affair with an American was "creating the biggest scandal in Peking at the moment." ("He is the smartest European diplomat dealing with the Chinese," Betty was told, "so all of his personal vagaries are borne with by the French Government otherwise he would probably be recalled.")

During dinner, Betty was seated next to John Carter and, much to her displeasure, Nelson T. Johnson. She found him "boring," "vulgar," and "pompous," but for his sake (and John Carter's) she "oohed and aahed at his stupid stories," while making sure that she followed her hostess's lead in finishing courses in unison. For one "awful moment," Betty feared that she was lagging behind when she noticed that the "Minister ha[d] finished his fish" before she had even begun to eat hers.[88]

There were other nights like this, and afternoon walks with John Carter in Sun Yat-sen Park and visits to the Ming tombs.[89] As spring turned to summer, Betty and John Carter discovered that they were falling in love. But like all love affairs, there were complications and doubts, expectations and disappointments, good moments and bad. To her mother, her closest friends, and most of all to herself, she listed the "credits and debits" of John Carter Vincent.

"He is good for me," she explained to her friend Florence Reynolds, "because he is one of those fortunate human beings who seem to have been born adjusted to life, and [he] doesn't have to tear me down in the frantic process of building himself up. [But] he is in his too early thirties, has most of his career to make, hasn't a cent, and cannot help but be immature in some ways." Could she adjust to being the wife of a diplomat in the China Service? "Will I fit in," she wondered, "will the life seem petty and restricted; will I irk at being cut off from the civilized world?" But all the doubts could vanish in an instant when she remembered that he had "impeccable taste and a love for music, intense eyes, and an indulgent attitude toward all my foibles, [all of which] will probably be my undoing."[90]

Despite the intensity of her feelings ("I am not distinguished for my clear and unemotional . . . way of conducting my life," she once wrote in self-analysis), the "undoing" was not quickly or easily achieved. As the fall approached and John Carter prepared to take his second and final examination, she found it difficult to make a decision. "I am not in a very settled state," she wrote her mother in mid-September 1930. "Marrying again seems almost impossible to me in thought. I must confess that I wish you were here to give me your candid opinion on this burning question. . . . I can't face the fact of being without him and a good part of the time I can't face marriage with him. I'm in a hell of a fix."[91]

While Betty turned the "burning question" over and over again in her mind, John Carter forced himself to concentrate on the impending examination. During the previous year he had studied a number of works on various subjects, including commercial geography and consular and diplomatic practice. In the final days, he reviewed his notes on Hawks Potts' *Outline of Chinese History*, Arnold's *China: A Commercial and Industrial Handbook*, and Richards's *Comprehensive Geography of the Chinese Empire* as well as his list of collateral readings which numbered over twenty books. Once again, the language presented a special difficulty. ("How many times I have regretted my decision to study this damned language!" he had once written to his sister.) In the second year's course he had been required to finish reading his principal text, *Shih Yung Hsin Chung Hua Yu*, master *Bullock's Progressive Exercises in the Chinese Written Language* and Soothill's *Phonetics*, and memorize five hundred new selections from *Peck's Character Cards*. In addition, he might be called on to translate any of the "Fifty Selected Chinese Communications" and "Fifteen Selected Newspaper Clippings" that had also been assigned for study. It had been a difficult program compared to that experienced by the early language officers, and Vincent felt no better prepared than he had the year before when his "luck" had been so good. But ironically, "fate" intervened again to make his task an easier one.

On the day before he was scheduled to take his examination, he received word from the State Department that he had been appointed to the rank of full consul and that he should proceed as soon as possible to a new post at Tsinan. Theoretically, such appointments depended on the student's performance on the final examination (as well as his general record), but for some reason the department had already made the decision in his case. Knowledge of his guaranteed promotion gave him the psychological boost that he needed to complete the exam, and he passed satisfactorily.[92]

Looking "thin" and feeling "exhausted" after two hectic years spent in study, travel, and romance, he looked forward to the "quiet of a smaller place" where there would be time "to read, think and lead a very leisurely regular life." And there would be the woman of his choice to share it, for at last, Betty had "decided quite definitely to marry John Carter." Before the wedding, however, she would return to Chicago to visit her mother, whom she had not seen in over two years.

On October 29, the day before John Carter was scheduled to leave for Tsinan, they gave themselves a farewell party. Predictably, Betty felt sad and "looked rather weepy and emotional, partly by the thought that [they] might be seeing each other for the last time, and partly because of several potent cocktails." All afternoon the apartment was crowded with old friends and well-wishers and John Carter and Betty found it difficult to have a quiet moment alone. Finally, they slipped into the bathroom where they could talk undisturbed. He reassured her "that there were no more decisions to make." There was no reason why Betty should "get dramatic over a few months separation," and if she were as certain as he was, then the marriage had already taken place.

"Now I feel sure that it is only a matter of time," she wrote her mother the following day. "You want me to come home to help you which I want to do, but . . . it is [in] no way a test of my desire to marry John Carter. He doesn't feel it as a test either, but only a duty to be performed towards you which I want to do because I love you and because you have never failed me. All of this he understands and that is why I am coming home. . . . John Carter . . . does not ignore things like 'consideration,' 'duty,' 'obligation' and all those words we were both raised on."[93]

And so they parted, Betty for America, and John Carter for Tsinan. Vincent's years in Peking had been important in his intellectual and emotional development. He had expanded his knowledge of China, and through Betty, was now aware of new developments in music, art, and literature. Like the other young Americans who had come to the legation before him, he had struggled to learn Chinese, partied in the students' mess, and explored the streets of Peking. Only a few months past his thirtieth birthday and already a full consul, he was now a full-fledged member of the China Service.

Vincent's assignment to Tsinan was brief and uneventful. The capital and commercial center of the northeastern, coastal, Shantung Province, Tsinan was just beginning to recover from the ravages of war and revolution which had disrupted Chinese life since the 1920s. Only three months before his arrival in October 1930, Shantung had been a battleground between the armies of Chiang Kai-shek and the forces of two of China's most powerful warlords, Yen Hsi-shan and Feng Yu-hsiang. But by the end of the year an uneasy peace had been established, giving Vincent the quiet life he desired after the hectic years in Peking. There were, of course, the usual consular chores to perform: writing reports on political developments in the area once every month and watching out for the interests of 328 Americans who lived and worked in the province. But he had ample time "to read, think and lead a very leisurely regular life."[94]

Such a life made him miss Betty all the more. "It frightens me when I realize how much I have grown to count on your life and our eternal companionship," he wrote her shortly after arriving in Tsinan. "I can think of anyone else's death and my own without much interest. The thought of yours makes my heart stand still and my breath come short. . . . That part of me which is worth living would be lost if I lost you. It was almost extinct when I met you a year and a half ago. I was at the smallest, meanest period of my life then. . . . [But] I came back with you and I am eternally grateful."[95]

His relationship with Betty and exposure to art, music, and literature in Peking left him dissatisfied with life in the American community in Tsinan. "I have people in for dinner," he informed Betty on one occasion, "become enthusiastic over Brahms and am met with polite smiles. I mention subjects which interest me now, beauty as a substitute for religion, the aridness of modern writing, the fallacy of economic America, the want of culture in American education. . . . People look at me as if they thought I were queer or a college freshman. . . . I get no response because I do not care to talk of the rate of exchange, Mrs. B's operation, last night's bridge game, or the servant problem. For a year you . . . trained me; now I am made to feel like a fool if I admire the color of Shantung's clay terraces under the glow of a fading sunset."[96]

He was most unhappy with the missionaries, whose activities he had so vigorously defended as vice-consul in Ch'ang-sha. He found the pastor of Tsinan's Church of God Mission, for example, "a funny looking little chap who should be selling fake jewelry at a county fair. He is the buddy of one of the officials of the Tsingtao Race Club which holds the crookedest meetings in China. I don't think I am being unfair to the man," he wrote

Betty, "when I say that he manifested a more lively and sincere interest in ponies than he did in Chinese souls." Despite his earlier affection for missionaries, he now believed that "a Christian interest . . . in a Chinese soul is probably one of the world's most misdirected ventures."[97]

In contrast to his dislike of certain missionaries and businessmen was his growing admiration for the Chinese. His favorite was General Han Fu-chu, the chairman of the Shantung government and the province's ruling tuchun. "General Han seems to be motivated by no schemes of individual aggrandizement or ambitions for the unification of the province by military means," Vincent reported to the State Department in December. "It appears that he has accepted the status-quo and is determined to maintain peaceful relations both with the generals within the province and with those on its borders."[98] Privately, Vincent called Han "the most friendly, unassuming Chinese officer I have ever met,"[99] and the general returned his affection by inviting Vincent to breakfast with him and his associates and review provincial troops. The admiration he felt for Han was also beginning to extend to the Chinese people themselves: "I become more and more convinced that it is not government that the Chinese want and need," he told a missionary on December 20, "it is strict non-interference in their affairs. Allowed freedom from warfare and governmental interference they can govern themselves and . . . cope with such disturbances as banditry and communism."[100]

Because his relationships with the Chinese were pleasing and his workload light, it was with real regret that he learned in January 1931 that he was being transferred to an important post in the office of the American consulate at Mukden, Manchuria. "The thought of going to Mukden frightens me," he wrote Betty on February 1. "I do not want responsibility; I do not want to have to maintain a position; in short, I do not want to feel that I am getting older. I loved the total absence of all this in Peking; the carefreeness of being myself. In Mukden I shall have to be the colleague of men twenty years my senior. I shall have to be circumspect in my swearing, drinking, dress and actions for fear of offending my community. Here it is bad enough; there it will be worse. Give a long thought to this my dear, before you marry me," he counseled, "and then marry me anyway."[101]

Marry him she did, on March 28, the very day of her arrival in Tsinan. "My wedding was to my taste exactly," she later wrote her mother. "When I arrived John said, 'we'll be married at five o'clock this afternoon by Dr. Stanly, a red-headed Congregational Minister who heads the Shantung Christian College here, and who is one of the most liberal, intelligent and lovable men I have ever met.' . . . Stanly and his wife, bringing an angel food cake for the wedding cake, came over at five and with John's young

Vice-Consul as witness we were wed. Just like that." Later in the evening members of the foreign community joined them at Vincent's residence "to drink champagne and look the bride over." Since Vincent had kept the news of his impending marriage a secret, his guests were surprised to discover the reason for the celebration. When invited earlier that day to meet "Mrs. Vincent, most of them thought John's mother had arrived, or maybe he was playing a joke," but despite some initial bewilderment "we had a gay time."

The following morning they set out on their honeymoon which was to be spent in an ancient Buddhist temple located on the outskirts of Tsinan. "The day was sunny," the bride later recalled, "and I was carried most of the way in a chair while John walked. It was the loveliest trip I have ever taken. Up and down low mountains, all the hillsides terraced with winter wheat . . . making patches of brilliant green against the rugged grey of the rocks. . . . The scenery would sink into the homelike intimacy of the valley towns or farmlands stretching out in squares of green and brown. . . . Our boy had gone ahead with plenty of food, cots and bedding, so by the time we arrived the nicest guest room in the temple was all in order even to flowers and our best tea cloth on the table." Two days later they returned to the consulate and "took up the job of being married seriously."[102] In early April they left Tsinan for Manchuria.

"Mukden is politically the most important place in China today," explorer and journalist Roy Chapman Andrews told Betty when he learned that she and her husband would soon be living there. "All the fireworks will be in Mukden . . . this summer."[103] Andrew's judgment was accurate and his prediction correct. For years Manchuria, on China's northern frontier, had attracted foreign penetration for its riches in land, minerals, and water power. Japan, particularly, had over one billion yen invested in Manchurian railroads and other businesses by 1931. As Japan's population multiplied and her economy collapsed in the wake of the Great Depression, she grew increasingly dependent on Manchuria as a source of food and raw materials and a haven for starving and homeless Japanese. But China now had a new national government which had come to power on the wave of antiforeign sentiment. Andrews and other observers believed that war between the two countries was imminent, and the Vincents would not be far from its center.

The tension produced by Japanese and Chinese rivalry made its presence felt principally in Mukden, Manchuria's capital and the headquarters of Japan's Kwantung Army and South Manchuria Railway Company. "Mukden is not a bad place," Vincent wrote his sister shortly after arriving, " but it is the least likable that I have struck in China. It is an ungracious city. The continuing interests of Russians, Japanese and Chinese during the past thirty years . . . have not fostered kindly feeling nor charm. The territory has developed but the development has been forced by Russian and Japanese aspirations and Chinese defense. The contention has imposed itself upon the Chinese people (they lack the natural easy going charm of their brethran within the wall). It has also impressed itself upon the very appearance of the city. . . . It is a heterogeneous place of . . . Chinese who have lost their traditions; of poor White Russians and scheming Reds; of aggressive Japanese. It is a bastard town." He too predicted war: "Manchuria has been a battleground twice," he told Margaret in July, "it will be one again. Many years will pass before it happens I hope (I hope it doesn't happen at all) but the signs are not wanting that it will happen. The ground is good and the seeds have been planted. Let us wish that they are killed by a virtuous blight before they reach maturity and bear fruit."[104]

Tragically, the "virtuous blight" never appeared, and the seeds of war grew and bore fruit. On the night of September 18, 1931, an explosion destroyed a small section of track on the South Manchuria Railway's main line a few miles north of Mukden. The Kwantung Army held the Chinese responsible and occupied the province.[105]

Word of the Japanese invasion reached Vincent while he was inspecting a newly built Chinese harbor at Hu-lu-tao. His first reaction was shock and surprise (despite his earlier predictions), because before leaving Mukden he had been assured by Consul-General Hayashi that he could leave the city "without concern over immediate developments." Angered and also somewhat embarrassed at being away from his post during the crisis, Vincent made immediate arrangements to return.

His train arrived on the outskirts of the capital at two o'clock on the morning of September 21. Japanese soldiers came aboard and upon identifying himself as the American consul, Vincent was ordered at bayonet point to detrain and climb into a nearby rickshaw. After many delays, he was finally "delivered" to his consulate. "The Japanese military had completely taken over the city and were everywhere," he later recalled.[106]

During the next several days, Vincent tried to learn all that he could about the incident on the South Manchuria railway line. On September 25 he was invited by Japanese officials to visit the site of the hostilities and to hear Lieutenant-Colonel Shimato of the Kwantung Army describe the events that had occurred almost a week earlier. Vincent was told that at approximately 10:30 p.m. on September 18 a Japanese patrol was passing a point on the South Manchuria railway line five miles north of Mukden when they were startled by the sound of an explosion. "Running back," they claimed to have seen "several Chinese in uniform fleeing down the embankment." The officer in command ordered his men to open fire and a number of the "saboteurs" were killed. (To support his story Shimato showed Vincent "the badly decomposed bodies of two Chinese in uniform" and the signs of blood on the railway track.) After the last few Chinese soldiers had fled and Japanese reinforcements arrived, the patrol was ordered to attack a Chinese military depot at Pei Ta Ying; other forces were sent on to the Mukden Commercial Settlement and the Chinese Walled City.[107]

Vincent was not persuaded that Shimato's story was accurate. "It is not a convincing account," he noted in a memorandum on September 26, "and the carefulness with which evidence is displayed tends more to arouse than allay suspicion." What actually occurred on the night of September 18 would probably never be known, he concluded, but it was certain that the incident "was decidedly desirable from the Japanese Army standpoint and quite as undesirable from the Chinese viewpoint. The Japanese Army wanted, openly and anxiously, action in Manchuria," and the explosion provided the "desired provocation for action."[108]

In the weeks following the Japanese invasion of Manchuria, the city of Mukden existed in a state of diplomatic limbo. The traditional system of provincial government disappeared overnight, and the Japanese refused to define the authority that now controlled most of southern Manchuria. "Military occupation (although denied by the Japanese)," Vincent reported to Washington, was the term which best "seemed to describe the situation." Japanese soldiers "with fixed bayonets" patrolled the streets in front of the consulate general; certificates of identity were required of all consular servants "in order that they might pass through the streets unmolested by troops"; American and British diplomats were frequently stopped and forced to identify themselves; and it was now necessary for Vincent and his colleagues to contact the Japanese to transact business which prior to September 18 had been conducted with the Chinese.[109]

"We talk, eat and sleep the Manchurian situation," Betty wrote her mother in October. "I follow reports, dispatches, newspaper stories, sit around the bar at the Yamato hotel after office hours with John Carter gleaning the latest reports on Japanese atrocities, stupidities and lies. We drive home and are accosted by a Jap police who almost sticks a bayonet in us; . . . John goes to the Japanese Consulate, we return with one of their officers and the policeman is told the proper place of a foreign official in Mukden still enjoying, Thank God, the rights of extraterritoriality." She and her husband agreed with journalist Chester Rowell who told them that "the center of the world today is in Mukden and probably not many people at home realize it . . . That is, the whole question of disarmament, League of Nations, the moral progression of the world since the World War will totter if Japan gets away with this aggressively military move in Manchuria. . . . [T]he moral issues involved in this struggle will set the pace for the rest of the world for the next hundred years and it is swell to be as active a part of it as the wife of the consul in Mukden can be. . . . So you can envy me and not worry ever about my being here." Her greatest regret was that she might miss some important development when she went to Peking in December to give birth to their first child. "At least my child will be born at a thrilling time in China and if pre-natal influences on its mind have any effect, it should be an internationally minded diplomat or a permanent member of the League of Nations of 1961. John and I often envy him or her the ability to see what will happen within the next fifty years—the world seems so tipsy at the moment it would be fun to see the outcome."[110]

A year later, in the fall of 1932, Vincent and his wife and new daughter, Sheila Elizabeth, left Mukden to take charge of the American consulate in Dairen, the chief trading center of the southern Manchuria. From that vantage point, he observed the final Japanese takeover of Manchuria and concluded that their new puppet state of "Manchukuo" would not provide the economic security they desired. As soon as the Kwantung Army reached this realization, Vincent predicted, they would move on to richer territories.[111]

Although Japan was casting a covetous eye on northern China and inner Mongolia, Vincent believed that the true Japanese goal would eventually be south, toward the Dutch East Indies and Australia. "If allowed to continue merrily along the present path," Vincent wrote his sister in August 1934, "the Japanese will make a bid for the control of the Dutch East Indies (from whence they get oil), the Malay Straits (which will enable them to keep open their connection with India from whence they get much of their cotton and iron) and Australia (from whence their wool comes). Those four articles make up seventy-five per cent of Japan's imports. They are vital to her." Once Japan secured her position in Manchuria and northern China, she would move toward these vital areas, Vincent argued, unless the United States and Great Britain actively tried to prevent it.

It was important that the western powers try to prevent the Japanese domination of East Asia. Japan's attempt to win "control over the destinies of the Far East from Canton to Singapore" was in Vincent's mind a direct violation of "the rights and privileges which foreigners have accumulated here over a period of one hundred years" as well as a threat to American security in the Pacific. He earnestly hoped that something could be done to improve relations between Japan and the western powers, but nothing was to be gained by "making further concessions to Japan." "A united front by England and America which might bring the Japanese to their senses would be the best solution," Vincent told his sister.[112]

Vincent received an opportunity to influence American policy toward Japan and China in February 1936 when he was transferred to the State Department. During the next three years he served on the China desk in the department's Far Eastern Division and it was from that position that he urged his government repeatedly to block Japanese expansion in East Asia.

The America to which the Vincents returned in 1936 was still suffering the effects of the worst economic collapse in its history. Between eight and ten million Americans remained unemployed, and national income, payrolls, and profits continued to slide downward. Public and congressional opinion was intensely isolationist, reflecting the American people's view that national problems came first. There was little chance that the United States would launch an internationalist foreign policy, despite the growth of fascism in Europe and the Far East.

Betty and John Carter quickly learned these sad facts for themselves and they grieved for their stricken nation. They were both committed New Dealers who admired Franklin Roosevelt greatly, but they were often impatient because progress came slowly and painfully. Betty was especially upset about the disparities in wealth and power she observed in the nation's capital. On one occasion she attended a garden party at the estate of Under Secretary of State Sumner Welles, where she saw "thousands and thousands of dollars worth of exotic plants, terraced gardens, miles of woodland all carefully manicured. They must have a dozen gardeners," she wrote her mother, "and the most beautiful house I have ever seen." The next day she helped take an indigent child to the hospital "to see if it is his heart or T.B. that makes him so tired—or maybe it is just lack of food." The child's belly was distended and his posture swayback; her own diagnosis, soon confirmed by the doctors, was malnutrition. "He can't get a quart of milk to drink," she wrote in anger and anguish, "and the Sumner Welles have elaborate terraced gardens and swimming pools. . . . " Perhaps remembering her own rich existence in Peking, she added: "I wish I could live the only life I believe to be wholly moral—complete self denial and giving your coat to the other one who may be colder than you."[113]

Her husband shared these concerns, but he was even more pessimistic about the Far Eastern situation. There, Japan continued her invasion of northern China, and in July 1937 full-scale war erupted between the two powers. Vincent hoped the crisis might end Roosevelt's apparent disinterest in world affairs.

For a moment it looked like Vincent's hopes would be realized. In response to the troubled situation in the Orient (and Europe), the president delivered an address in October in which he called for a "quarantine" against "international outlaws." Isolationists believed that such measures (however vague) would lead the United States into another disastrous foreign war and they attacked the president with unrestrained savageness. The backlash caused Roosevelt to drop his notion of a quarantine: The country, he was now more convinced than ever, was too burdened with economic problems to assume any foreign responsibilities. Supporters of collective security (like the Vincents) saw little chance now that the government would reverse its policy. Their predictions came true a month later when the United States failed to play an active role at the Brussels Conference convened to discuss the Far Eastern crisis. While some European diplomats were willing to consider sanctions against Japan, Roosevelt would go no further than a declaration of moral condemnation. After a few weeks of futile deliberations, the assembly adjourned, a testament to the failure of western statesmanship.[114]

These developments convinced Vincent that the White House and the State Department did not fully appreciate the threat of Japanese militarism, so in 1938 he launched a personal campaign which he hoped would change American policy toward Japan. In a series of memorandums written to Stanley K. Hornbeck, advisor on political relations to the secretary of state, and Maxwell Hamilton, chief of the Far Eastern Division, Vincent presented his views on Japanese imperialism and recommended policies designed to prevent its further spread.

Japanese militarism, Vincent argued, was "psychologically an aggressive force" which could "not be expected to become satiated on successful aggression or deterred from aggression by normal economic and political considerations." The president's hope that Japan would become exhausted by her involvement in China had not been realized. "The same predictions were made when Japan took Manchuria," Vincent emphasized. "I was in Manchuria in 1931-32 and I do not recall that anyone in a position to know, including Japanese civilian officials, actually thought that Japanese military aggression would stop in Manchuria, and it is not believed that Japanese aggression . . . in China will stop there."[115]

Once again, Vincent predicted that Japan would eventually move south toward the Dutch East Indies and the Malay peninsula. This development would "take on a character and assume proportions menacing" to the United States. Japan was an "expanding state" whose ambitions were not limited to the Asiatic continent. To the south lay the Philippines, America's last defensive stronghold in the Pacific.[116]

To prevent a Japanese advance, Vincent recommended that the United

States give economic aid to China and apply diplomatic and economic sanctions against Japan, measures designed to "embarrass the Japanese in their attempts to conquer China." Such steps would not "get Japan out of China," he admitted, but they might help prevent Japan "from consolidating her position in China" and therefore discourage her from other aggressive adventures. The United States had a "very great and urgent obligation nationally and internationally," he told his State Department superiors, "to do what we can . . . toward influencing the course of the present conflict along lines favorable to the Chinese."[117]

Hornbeck shared Vincent's views and frequently sent copies of his memorandums to Secretary of State Cordell Hull, who called them "excellent." But other officials offered different opinions and advice. From Tokyo, Ambassador Joseph Grew argued that cutting off loans and credits (as Vincent suggested) would only enable Japanese militarists to assume complete control of the government (Vincent believed they were already in control). Japanese experts in the Far Eastern Division, more sympathetic to Japan than the China hands, agreed with Grew that economic warfare would discredit the civilians, encourage the army, and "accelerate Japanese-American relations straight down the hill."[118]

Despite the vigor with which Hornbeck and Vincent argued their views, those of Grew dominated policy-making in 1938-39. The president was still unwilling to challenge Japan. America was too weak militarily, and isolationism too strong for any major initiatives. Economic and diplomatic sanctions were therefore rejected. American policy remained (in the words of one career diplomat) "the eternal question mark."[119]

For such "wholehearted supporters of the New Deal" as Vincent and his wife, it was painful indeed to see Franklin Roosevelt retreat from the defense of those liberal principles that he seemed to symbolize so superbly. "I don't mention the world situation and what the Japs are doing to the Chinese because if I did I might not be able to sleep tonight. . . ," Betty wrote her mother in November 1938. "What a spineless foreign policy I think we have that has not raised a finger to stop such barbarities. J.C. and I are a bit cynic[al] concerning Mr. R—there is a large Jewish vote in America but a very small Chinese one[;] today he is stern over Germany but you couldn't get even a stern note to the Japanese out of him or Mr. Hull— no matter what excesses they may go against us or the Chinese. Wait and see—however, they will regret such shortsightedness . . . and bring disaster down on our heads as well as the Chinese. Damn them all I say. I'm glad that J.C. constantly raises his small voice for what he and I consider to be right. I have told him I would rather he would lose his job a thousand times over than temporize over such important matters as the spiritual

[and] practical future of these United States. In this, I feel as right as Jesus Christ did."[120]

Although Vincent found his work in the State Department "fascinating," the failure of Roosevelt's leadership left him depressed and eager to leave Washington—a city, he and Betty had come to conclude, "where people are prone to become ingrown, selfishly calloused and cheaply ambitious." It was with great pleasure therefore that he received the news in February 1939 that he had been selected to join the American delegation to the International Labor Organization in Geneva. "I look forward to the leisure of Geneva," Betty told her mother as soon as she heard the news. "I know life will be so much slower there and I know how much good it will do John Carter. . . . I think a foreign post with two hours for lunch and not too much rush work will be excellent for his health and soul."[121]

Unfortunately, the day of the leisurely foreign service post had passed; three months after the Vincents arrived in Geneva, Germany invaded Poland, and Britain and France declared war. Word of Chamberlain and Daladier's decision reached Vincent as he arrived at the office of the ILO on the morning of September 3. Betty had gone for a swim at a nearby lake and heard the report as it was broadcast over a loudspeaker set up on the shore. It had been "so beautiful a day," she later recalled,

> the plage was full of people, the lake blue and dotted with little white sailing craft. . . . About fifteen minutes after we arrived the loudspeaker . . . suddenly announced that Great Britain was at war with Germany. It was most dramatic—no one had heard the news before and slowly we all gathered around . . . and listened. Absolute silence except for the cries and laughter of the little children playing around. The announcement lasted about five minutes and it was a very sober crowd that returned to the water and the diving stand. Somehow the contrast was too cruelly ironic—the plage is always a gay place on a summer holiday . . . with mountains in the distance and great white clouds and the lake festooned everywhere with bright flowers. It was a charming picture and until the loudspeaker began its sinister message everyone seemed so happy and gay.

Across the lake, she saw the League of Nations, its white pillars gleaming brightly in the sun: "I doubt that anyone but me remembered it was there within eyesight . . . , the last ironic monument to the European tragedy."[122]

What did the conflict in Europe mean to the United States? To Vincent, there were two wars being fought simultaneously. One was the war of nations fighting to preserve wealth and empire. The other was the war of peoples fighting to win social justice and equality. The former, in Vincent's view, meant "nothing" to America, while the latter meant everything. "The

British and the French are fighting primarily for the British and the French," he wrote family and friends at home in March 1940. "They can make a fairly good case that they are fighting for democracy and liberty and justice. But not a good enough case for me. . . . England and France are [not] the seats of freedom and democracy . . . [and] it was their shortsightedness . . . that brought on this war. It is not our war."[123]

Behind the "smokescreen of battles," "great social forces were at work," and their future development was of more importance to the United States than the victory or defeat of European empires. "During recent decades there has been a growing dissatisfaction on the part of the subordinate majority with the static dominant minority," Vincent argued. "And that dissatisfaction is gradually translating itself into a dynamic revolt against anti-social national sovereignties and anti-social free capitalism. . . . The dynamic social revolt is a stronger force than Nazism and will engulf it when [it] has spent its destructive force." In short, nineteenth-century political democracy was being "liquidated" by the war and it was his hope that "social and economic democracy" would follow. For the present, he recommended that the United States avoid involvement in the European war, put its "own house in order and develop a more cooperative frame of mind." Then when the war ended (preferably through a negotiated peace) the United States should "lend all the support we can for a fair economic and social reconstruction irrespective of political considerations."[124]

Vincent's hope that the war might end through compromise was never realized. By the spring of 1940, the period of *Sitzkrieg* was over and soon Norway, Denmark, and France were under Nazi domination. The "deep, deep churnings of Europe" were being felt in the Far East as well. There, Japan was expressing increased interest in the Dutch East Indies and French Indo-China and in late September signed a Tripartite Pact with Germany and Italy providing "recognition of a Japanese Greater East Asia sphere which included the colonies of Holland, France, Britain and Portugal." In response, the United States halted shipments of iron and steel scrap to Japan and increased aid to China. War between the two countries now seemed closer than ever.

By some strange quirk of fate, Vincent had been an eyewitness to war three times during his career: in Ch'ang-sha, when the armies of Chiang Kai-shek fought the warlords, in Mukden, when the Japanese attacked, and in Geneva when the British and French mobilized. In late summer 1940, he received a telegram that was to make him again an observer of war: By order of the secretary of state he was to return to Washington as soon as possible and then proceed alone to a new post in the American consulate general at Shanghai. After an absence of five years he was to return to

China. Both the nation and the man had changed during the sixteen critical years since his career began there in 1924. China was now fighting for her life, not just for political identity but for the preservation of her national sovereignty. Vincent was different too: From a provincial Wilsonian, he had grown into a staunch New Dealer with a well-developed political philosophy that was to have a profound effect on his view of Chinese affairs in the 1940s. But whatever the differences—he was 40 years old now, his hair greying, his body even more thin and frail—his personality was fundamentally unchanged. Throughout the 1930s, men who observed him at work and later wrote evaluations of his character and performance noted continually his "poise," "good judgment," and "sound common sense"; he was a man "not easily swayed by excitement." He was, above all, a "steady," even-tempered man. "There are no great variations in him or his nature," wrote one Foreign Service inspector in 1932. " . . . In fact there is a highly satisfactory evenness when all of his qualities are analysed which in itself begets confidence. . . ," and indicates a "sound stratum of underlying worth."[125] That stratum consisted of numerous layers: his early religious training, the self-reliance and independence developed during youth and reawakened during the crises in Ch'ang-sha and Mukden, and the sensitivity and compassion nurtured by his wife. These qualities of character would prove to be invaluable in helping him survive the exciting and eventually tragic years that lay ahead.

2

Assistant Ambassador

In February 1941, Vincent boarded the S.S. *Pierce* bound for Shanghai.[1] Everything seemed to conspire to make his journey exceedingly gloomy and depressing. The weather was terrible: There was "ice all over the ship, . . . flurries of snow," and only "glimpses of sun" to warm him as he stood at the shipboard railing staring out to sea. Twenty-eight feet of water poured into the ship's holds, slowing her down to barely eleven knots instead of the customary seventeen. "The Captain thinks there is a jinx aboard," the steward informed Vincent confidentially.[2]

Dinners at the captain's table did little to dispel the gloom. Vincent found the captain "pleasant enough, although his stories run a little too much to the sex complexes and difficulties of female passengers on his ships." He tried telling his own favorite stories, including a description of the student strike at Clemson in which he had styled himself "a Bolshevik." But his conservative companions failed to see the humor in the students' pranks, and conversation turned to the more important topic of international politics. Alfred Kohlberg, a Jewish businessman, told the group that in a struggle between fascism and socialism, fascism would be the victor. "We would rather have fascism than socialism," he remarked, "the entrepreneur and property would be safer." Vincent was "irritated" by such talk. Once men were given simple economic security, he countered, freedom had little to fear from either fascism or communism. Drawing on the ideas of his political heroes, Jefferson, Lincoln, and Wilson, he argued that the world needed a "government organized and administered by and on behalf of the people, responsive to the present day popular upsurge rather than [to] the interests of privilege and property. With that slogan," he proclaimed "you'll not find it difficult to get people to fight—and win." But Kohlberg remained unconvinced. Vincent gave little thought to his debate with the small, rotund exporter, but, as it turned out, it was one of the most important incidents in his life. His defense of Jeffersonian democracy and account of his days as a "Clemson Bolshevik" convinced Kohlberg that Vincent was a Communist, and he would spend the next ten years trying to destroy Vincent's career. But that was hardly conceivable now, and Vincent spent the rest of the evening in his cabin reading Kenneth Robert's *Oliver Wiswell,* a novel of America's revolutionary past, and writing Betty his thoughts on America's equally revolutionary future.[3]

"I reckon we are going into this war blindly trying to preserve something that is already spoiled in half the world. . . ," he told his wife. "The issue is drawn in the Far East and it seems to me that only a miracle can prevent a conflict, a conflict springing fundamentally from the same causes as that in Europe. . . . Japan . . . no less than Germany, is operating as a destructive force and the United States as the conservative force. . . . We find ourselves, without consciously having pursued that path, the heir and defender of the British system in the Far East. . . . Japan has thrown off the [democratic] facade to challenge the century old western position in Asia. Japan has nothing constructive to offer. . . , neither has Germany."

What worried Vincent most was that the United States would have "nothing constructive" to offer its own citizens or the people of the world. Like progressives of an earlier generation, Vincent feared that American involvement in a conflict in Europe or the Far East would mean an end to domestic reform.

To avoid that calamity, he urged that "social reform and social objectives . . . be made a prerequisite to entrance into the war." Nazism had to be destroyed, he insisted, but "we must recognize that [Hitler]. . . represents a challenge; not simply a wild and bloody threat. A challenge calls for something positive to meet it if we are to come out of this war . . . prepared to construct something worthwhile. If we are entering it simply to preserve a social system erroneously described as 'democracy' which has glaringly proven itself a failure during the past twenty years . . . then I have grave doubts about our entering the war and graver doubts about the outcome. . . . I see us fighting to preserve and conserve rather than to create a new society of dynamic possibility." Unless Americans "enlisted on the side of [progressive] forces rather than on the side of the status quo" at home and around the world, the United States was in danger of losing—not the war, but, more importantly, the peace that was to follow. The only answer, he told Betty, was "the inevitability of change. . . . It's a sad world, my dear."[4]

His tenure in Shanghai was brief. In the spring, changes in American representation in the Far East brought him at last into a position of real influence in the development of American China policy. Nelson T. Johnson, ambassador to China for eleven years, was transferred to Australia[5] and replaced by veteran China expert, Clarence E. Gauss. Gauss had known Vincent for many years and invited him to become first secretary of the American embassy located now at China's war-torn capital in Szechwan Province. Vincent accepted, and in early June left Shanghai by way of Hong Kong for Chungking.[6]

"Chungking," he wrote his sister upon arrival, "is indescribable." He saw it first from the air at sunrise, having left Shanghai after dark, "a necessity imposed by the Japanese [who] considered Chinese commercial planes legitimate military prey." As the plane descended to the airport ("a runway and a few bamboo huts on a little flat island in the Yangste [sic]") he caught a glimpse of the majestic rocky cliffs on which Chungking was built.[7]

Once a minor trade port on the upper Yangtze, isolated from the outside world and under the domination of various warlords, Chungking was now the capital of China. But unlike the beleaguered cities of London or Paris, it was a city unloved, especially by its own inhabitants. "What is the matter with Chungking?" one Chinese official wondered in the summer of 1941. "Everything!"[8]

The weather was insufferable. Summers were hot and sticky, winters cold and rainy. On an average day the temperature might fluctuate between one hundred degrees at noon and forty degrees at midnight, causing one Chinese to describe the weather as "four seasons in one day but one season throughout the whole year."[9]

While the weather sapped the strength of its citizens, it gave vitality to the flies, mosquitos, and rats that populated the streets and alley-ways. The "rats run around everywhere in broad daylight with full impunity," one writer remarked, "and at night they take complete possession of darkened rooms. Local yarns have it that in Chungking cats are oftener afraid of rats than vice versa. It must be the good grace of providence, that has kept the bubonic plague from breaking out here."[10] But the grace of providence was not complete, because malaria and dysentery were frequent disabilities and it was only the very strong who did not suffer a daily attack of "Chungking tummy" caused by putrid water and food that spoiled quickly in the summer sun.

Such were the defects of nature; those produced by man were worse. A wartime inflation ran rampant, wiping out salaries and life savings overnight. A loaf of bread cost a dollar and twenty cents; milk, two dollars a pint; eggs, three dollars per dozen; meat, two dollars a pound. A simple uniform for an office boy cost fifty-two dollars, the same amount a Chinese official paid for tailor-cut serge and worsted suits at Shanghai in the years before the war. By mid-1941, the cost of living in Chungking was up one thousand percent.[11]

Japan's invasion of China also brought her bombers into the skies over Chungking, especially during the months that stretched from April to November. To Vincent, the bombing of the city was "disgusting." They "fly over usually about noon," he noted, "or on moonlit nights, late in the evening, so arrogantly and so safely; [they] bomb this ugly city of grey brick, plaster, and bamboo, trying to break the people's morale but only destroying little shops and huts with collected possessions of a lifetime. . . . Afterward, the poor people stolidly, unemotionally, go . . . about trying to find things in the debris. Gangs very efficiently clean . . . up and repair . . . telephone and light wires. What a LIFE."[12]

Despite these hardships, he was not unhappy. "There is a job of work to do," he wrote Margaret, "and we are trying to do it."[13] That job kept him extremely busy during the next few months while he began to acquaint himself with his new surroundings, his new colleagues, and his new responsibilities as first secretary.

His home for the next two years was the American embassy, a dilapidated building that reminded him of a Japanese brothel. Unlike its European counterparts, the American embassy was not located in the city proper but on the south bank of the Yangtze. To reach the center of the city, Vincent and other officials had to walk down a "steep staircase alley," cross the river "on the ramshackle passenger ferry," and then climb laboriously up another "long flight of steps," a journey that usually took an hour.[14]

If Vincent was in luck, a car would be waiting at the top of the stairs to transport him to his destination, but he was rarely so fortunate. The embassy had no personal vehicle and the ambassador often complained to State Department officials that he had to "beg a ride from the naval . . . or the military attaché," to whom the Chinese had given "five or six Fords."[15] Without a car, one traveled on foot or by rickshaw, a necessity that inflation had made a luxury. Traveling about Chungking, Vincent learned before long, was "something like the movements in Dante's *Inferno*."[16]

Vincent's choice of analogies was more accurate than he first supposed. Relations between American officials in Chungking, he discovered, were strained to the breaking point: "You cannot imagine . . . the situation here now," he wrote Betty in late July. "I expect an explosion any time."[17]

The cause of the crisis was the ambassador's inability to coordinate American efforts to assist the Chinese. New agencies sprang up daily, complicating procedures and enlarging the responsibilities of the embassy. There were officials in charge of commercial relations, cultural relations, industrial relations, and most importantly, military relations. Here there existed no clear chain of command but a variety of competing organizations all under the nominal direction of Brigadier General John Magruder's American Military Mission to China (AMMISCA).[18] Americans also worked for the Nationalist government, bringing to bear on the problems of Chinese economics and politics their own special knowledge and experience.[19] And, to exacerbate tensions further, there were the frequent visits of American dignitaries sent to Chungking on investigative missions for President Franklin Roosevelt.[20]

The resulting bureaucratic confusion was deeply disturbing to Ambassador Clarence E. Gauss, a thirty-four-year veteran of the China Service. The fifty-five-year-old diplomat was "an intense man," noted one who served under him, with a "thin mouth turned down at the corners in [a] near sneer, eyes a prismed blue as they peered out through thick lenses. When one first met him the smile that grimaced his pallid face . . . was as disconcerting as his customary chill gaze."[21] He took his work as seriously as he did himself. When it came to operating the American embassy, Gauss was a "strict constructionist."[22] He was sharply critical of the way American economic and military planners bypassed his office in their dealings with the Chinese. He believed that "matters of high policy . . . should be channeled through the Ambassador, the Department of State can inform War and Navy." Consequently, Gauss found it especially troublesome working with General Magruder and Colonel James McHugh, the naval attaché who "had come to be regarded as the assistant Ambassador" when he served under Nelson Johnson. Both men were highly respected by the Chinese who often turned to them for assistance instead of to Ambassador Gauss. "It requires some tact to maintain harmony and close collaboration." Gauss explained to Hornbeck.[23]

The arrival of Presidential Assistant Lauchlin B. Currie in early June also annoyed the sensitive ambassador. Currie was director of lend lease for China, and his visits were regarded as a national holiday by the Chinese who believed that this one man controlled the flow of tanks, trucks, and economic loans from Washington to Chungking. "The Chinese are . . . buzzing no end wondering what he will bring," Nelson Johnson had commented on Currie's last visit. "Will it be a lower cost of living for them and their families, [or] more guns to help them in their attack on the Japanese[?]"[24] As on his last sojourn, the Chinese worked to insure Currie's favor by showering him with attention, while Ambassador Gauss remained ignored and isolated in his residence on the South Bank. Surrounded by "advisors and pipe-lines to the states." Guass felt, according to Vincent, "boxed, bottled, and bitched."[25] The result of all this confusion was an embassy in near administrative chaos.

As Gauss's "First Secretary and right hand man," Vincent hoped "to bring about some kind of coordination" among the various American agencies in Chungking. He respected and admired his chief, but found him a "difficult man" to live with and to work for. "I'd bet on him any time as prosecuting attorney and would entrust a million dollar case to him as my corporation lawyer," he wrote Lauchlin Currie in August. "Gauss is . . . a straight shooter but a limited one. . . . I should not want to be stranded with him on a desert island. Chungking comes close enough to it."[26] As for his own position in the embassy, Vincent saw himself working somewhere "between the Devil [i.e., Gauss] and the deep blue sea [i.e., Currie's lend lease division]. . . . I have a decided preference for the deep blue sea. But I have an allegiance to the Devil which comes first—must come first if I am to be of any use here at all, if I am to stay here in fact. My effectiveness is dependent upon the confidence which G[auss] places in me."[27]

He saw his role as that of a bridge between Chungking and Washington over which information and advice might travel unobstructed by personal or bureaucratic roadblocks. He would definitely not act as an agent of Currie's office: "Any suggestion that I too was a pipeline," he informed him, ". . . would completely destroy my usefulness. . . . If I am to be a bridge (which I am trying to be) it must be on the understanding that I have my feet planted firmly on [Gauss]. So—if there is anything you want me to do, count on me but don't be surprised if I do it . . . in a First Secretary-ish . . . way."[28] He was determined, above all, to "get this place running for the American government—not for individuals—or get out."[29] Given all of the complexities of personal and diplomatic life in Chungking, it would prove to be a formidable task.

Bureaucratic politics did not consume all of his time, however. Once again, there was much to be learned about China. Except for his three-month stay in Shanghai, Vincent had not been directly exposed to Chinese life for over six years. There were many unanswered questions on his mind: Had China gained economic and political stability since 1935? What were the latest developments in the perpetual conflict between the Communists and the Nationalists? What effect was the war with Japan having on Chinese politics and economics? And, most important, what kind of policy would best promote American interests in the Orient? As he had done in Ch'ang-sha, Hankow, Mukden, and Dairen, he began to explore his new terrain and make contacts with those Americans and Chinese from whom he could acquire accurate information about Chinese personalities and policies.

In August, Vincent prepared an informal report for Lauchlin Currie which reflected his views after three months in Chungking. The Nationalist government, he had discovered with increasing concern, was economically disorganized and politically unstable. Spending from six hundred million to one billion dollars a month, the government was operating at a deficit of over four hundred million dollars monthly. Shortages of food and commodities plus a rising currency inflation were "driving prices up, way up." There were simply "not enough resources in the country to support the government on its present scale . . . [and] loose economic and political organization . . . will not permit effective price control." Without economic stabilization he did not believe China could begin to solve her problems or maintain an adequate defense against further Japanese invasion.[30]

Developments in politics were equally discouraging. Despite the existence of the "united front" between the Communists and the Nationalists, neither faction was sincerely working toward the public goal of permanent cooperation. "There is . . . a fundamental difference in outlook," Vincent emphasized, "and there is besides deep-seated personal animosity. The Kuomintang leaders . . . interpret united front as unification under the Kuomintang. . . . The Kuomintang aspires to a 'democracy' in which everybody votes the Kuomintang 'ticket.' It is shot through with one party . . . ideas . . . [;] they smack . . . pretty much of fascism. They want the Communist group to lose its identity; the Communists insist on retaining it. . . . Chow [sic] En-lai, whom I have seen many times,[31] assures me that there will be no break in relations—not now—but also no real cooperation."[32]

The situation in the Far East, he concluded his report to Currie, was only part of a complex global puzzle. It would be disastrous for Americans to focus all their energies on one part but to lose sight of the more important whole. Events in Eastern Europe, where the Russians were fighting for their lives, would probably affect developments in Asia more than anything that the Americans could presently devise or deliver. "I hope we are sending the Russians everything we can," he wrote. "If they lose, there won't be much sense or need in sending things to England and China; if they win it won't be necessary."[33] To keep China in the war without endangering America's global interests was Vincent's prescription for policy after three months in Chungking; it would remain one of his most basic political principles in the months and years ahead.

The Russians held their bloody ground at Stalingrad, but the collision of interests in the Far East that Vincent had predicted seven years before occurred finally on December 7, 1941. America was in the war, and China was no longer the object of disinterested concern. Now she was America's only ally against the onslaught of the Japanese in the Orient. The partnership between China and the United States that was sealed at Pearl Harbor was not an alliance of equals but one of "client" and "patron," the most difficult kind of relationship to sustain without animosity and resentment felt by one side or the other.

But for now there was only jubilation in Chungking. After a decade of war, China was now allied with the great western powers. "Kuomintang officials went about congratulating each other as if a great victory had been won," writer Han Suyin later recalled.[34] With the economic and military arsenals of the United States and Great Britain at his disposal, Chiang could direct his efforts toward achieving that most cherished of goals: the preservation of his own power against his military and political rivals. For him, the war against the Japanese was over. "Pearl Harbor Day in America," a perceptive American noted in Chungking, "was Armistice Day out here."[35]

Chiang moved quickly to assure the democracies that they had his support—and more. On December 8, he called a conference of British and American representatives to propose the creation of a united global front against the Axis powers. An alliance consisting of China, Britain, America, Russia, and the Netherlands, he argued, could defeat the Japanese within months, if the allies united to defeat Japan first and deal with Germany afterward. But his Pacific first strategy won him few friends among the British and Americans in Chungking, or Washington, who were committed to a strategy of Europe first.

Vincent and Gauss also found Chiang's strategy preposterous and made their position known in a telegram to the secretary of state on December 14.[36] "Chiang may be unintentionally misleading in his statement on the part that China may be counted on to play in the struggle," Vincent wrote Hull on Gauss's behalf. "His plans seem . . . to have a touch of unreality derived from a somewhat grandiose . . . conception of his and China's role . . . His proposal for a general headquarters in Chungking to plan and direct Far Eastern strategy is manifestly impracticable. . . . The Chinese army does not possess the aggressive spirit, training, equipment or supplies for any major offensive or expedition." Vincent's goals in December were the same as when he had written Currie in August: "Keeping Chinese forces active against the Japanese, bolstering Chinese morale and helping to arrest the trend toward economic chaos." To achieve these purposes the ambassador and his first secretary recommended the creation of a "joint military council" and "information service" to give the Chinese the feeling that they were participating in military planning and operations, and most importantly, some kind of financial aid "to support the Government credit and to encourage small-scale production of consumer goods."[37]

Vincent and Gauss correctly expected that the Chinese would soon request expanded economic assistance. On December 30, Chiang's formal request for an Anglo-American credit of $1 billion was unveiled during a meeting between the generalissimo and the ambassador. Chiang was in an expansive mood: Every major power had responded cordially to his message of December 8 and joint British, Chinese, and American military discussions were proceeding favorably. China, he announced, would offer the allies "a vast manpower . . . to help in the fight against Japan." In return, Chiang asked formally for "a substantial political loan" of about $1 billion—both to meet financial difficulties and as a sign that Britain and America believed in the ultimate victory of the democracies.

Gauss agreed to inform his government of Chiang's request and went on to give the generalissimo some good advice about the realities of American politics. Only the Congress could grant the president such funds, Gauss noted, and before doing so, would want to know precisely how the money would be spent. As Vincent watched and took notes, the two men sparred with one another over just how exact the Chinese request should be. Chiang insisted on the funds immediately; a detailed description of "requirements and expenditures" could come later. Gauss appealed for more information about specific Chinese needs, but "General Chiang's replies," Vincent noted, "were evasive." There the matter stood, and the conference ended.[38]

It was a disturbing meeting and the confrontation between the ambassador and the generalissimo left Vincent and Gauss angry and depressed. The ambassador was in no mood to attend the New Year's Eve party to be given the following evening by Finance Minister H. H. Kung (to which the Chiangs had also been invited), so he declined the invitation. Though invited separately, Vincent also declined. He was "disappointed" but would do nothing to offend his sensitive chief.[39]

New Year's Eve was spent instead at a club party and dance. He went "because . . . years of training in small outposts had taught [him] that the inmates must be self-reliantly cooperative and the facts are never as bad as the prospects." His mood did not improve during the next few days, however, and he busied himself by writing letters to his family[40] and taking long walks alone in the woods. Try as he might, he could not escape the gloom produced by the events of the last few weeks. Here both the "facts" and the "prospects" seemed equally bad.

"We must get out of the old frame of mind that 'one Marine can lick ten Japanese,'" he wrote Betty on January 4, "and substitute for it a determination to translate our potential superiority in productive capacity and manpower into a real superiority." He insisted that the United States rely on its own resources, despite Chiang's invitation to use China as a base to mount an offensive against Japan. "We must win this war in the Pacific; win by closing in . . . as a superior naval power not through trick aid from this quarter or that. We must forget all the glorious speeches made last summer about 'polishing off' the Japanese as a minor menace and recognize that we have a first class war on our hands which cannot be won by talk of bombing the hell out of Tokyo from this or that untenable quarter or by encouraging the Chinese . . . to start an offensive for which they have neither the spirit nor the material."[41]

The time spent alone thinking, and especially his moments with Betty (even if they were only through letters) helped to fortify him for the difficult work ahead.

Chiang's request for a loan called for a position paper from the ambassador, and Vincent spent the second week of the new year preparing one. It was to be the most important dispatch that Gauss had sent to the State Department since Pearl Harbor, and his first secretary devoted all of his time and effort to it.

In Vincent's view, an Anglo-American loan of $1 billion was extravagant and impractical. "A credit of no more than half that amount," he wrote Betty, "would produce the psychological and political effects desired and take care of all conceivable (and perhaps some inconceivable) financial and economic demands. The billion dollar credit desired would be misleading and invite attempts at misuse."[42] Vincent's concern about the loan and the uses to which it might be put reflected his growing hostility toward the government that the United States was supporting in China. En route to Shanghai the year before, he had expressed the fear that the United States might one day be fighting to "preserve and conserve rather than to create a new society of dynamic possibility." What he had feared then, now seemed to be coming true in Asia. Chiang's government, he had concluded after six months in Chungking, had more in common with America's fascist enemies than she did with her democratic friends.

"We have here," he noted privately, "an 'oliplutarchy' . . . which, bent on its own preservation, bodes [no] good for China; nor for the world for that matter. . . . The Kuomintang is a congerie of conservative personalities and cliques primarily concerned with the perpetuation of party control and of their positions in the party."[43] Briefly, he described for his wife the leading personalities in Chinese politics with whom he had become all too familiar during his months in Chungking. First, there were the militarists: General Ho Ying-chin, minister of war, "who, consciously or sub-consciously adhere[s] to a type of military fascism through party-domination"; Chen Li-fu, Kuomintang party boss who believed "to a point of fanaticism in regeneration of the Chinese people through a centralized and paternally dictatorial social organization"; Chu Chia-hua, vice-president of the Examination Yuan, "German educated, committed to the principle of rigid . . . one party control over all administrative activity and who is reliably reported as having said . . . that 'we must keep in mind that our friends of today may be our enemies of tomorrow and vice versa'"; and Tai Li, "head of the formidable secret political police system which has the Chinese, including even me and the G-mo worried."[44]

Representing the bankers and the landlords was H. H. Kung, minister of finance, and Chiang's brother-in-law, who, Vincent observed, "espouses no social program that is contrary to their interests." Then came the Political Science group, "a very loose grouping of Chinese officials whose common characteristic is distrust of foreign influence and an emphasis on 'China for the Chinese' and Chinese methods, measures and manners."

Here, then, was a "cross-section" of Chiang's allies within the government and party whose "common denominator [was] their determination to preserve party control." Ho Ying-chin, Vincent wrote in summary, "wants to conserve military strength to preserve party control. Chen Li-fu wants to control all social activity in order to maintain the party; Chu Chia-hua wants a rigid administrative system to insure party authority; and Tai Li shoots them or puts them in jail." This kind of politics was a violation of everything that Vincent believed in, and to support it without reservation would be nothing less than a personal tragedy.

"I am an advocate of no particular form of government," he wrote in explanation of his hostility toward the Kuomintang, "but I do believe that the primary function of government is to insure . . . that the people shall live in security and freedom. . . . The Kuomintang, as the governing party of China, has failed in its task. . . . It has been faced with difficulties but it has refused, and still refuses, to avail itself of the opportunities for assuming its responsibilities. And the character of the present government including its leader (who speaks of the masses but thinks of the classes) and his wife, is not such as to warrant hope for the future."[45] But the political problems of China were not totally devoid of solution, and it was here, Vincent believed, that the United States might play its most important role. For if Vincent's liberalism made him a natural enemy of the Kuomintang, it also made him eager to reconstruct it along lines that would make it more responsive to the Chinese people.

He considered the loan an "opportunity for us to influence the course of events out here in the right direction." With the United States government supporting domestic production and, above all, land reform, Chinese liberals, who had for years advocated such reforms, "would be given encouragement and be encouraged to demand more from the government." Unable to support a reactionary regime in China, Vincent was determined to create in its place that "society of dynamic possibility" of which he dreamed.[46]

These ideas were embodied in the final telegram that was sent to the secretary of state on January 8. Calling for an Anglo-American credit "of at most no more than a half billion dollars," Gauss urged that the money be spent on currency revision, industrial production, and agrarian reform. Vincent's recommendation that the loan be used as a political lever to bring about a reformation in the government was also accepted by the ambassador. To grant the Chinese a "free credit," Gauss told Hull, would be to support the "retrogressive, self-seeking, and . . . fickle elements in and intimately associated with the government"[47] at the cost of alienating the more progressive elements in the country who were sincerely interested in defeating the Japanese. The conservative ambassador from Connecticut and his liberal first secretary from Georgia were thus united in purpose against Chiang Kai-shek and the Kuomintang. Both men waited eagerly for Washington's response to the telegram.

President Roosevelt had no intentions of tying strings to the Chinese loan, or making the kind of demands Gauss and Vincent recommended. While his major goal was to win the war in Europe first, he was concerned that China might surrender and leave America without allies in the Far East. If granting Chiang a loan could prevent this calamity it was a small enough price to pay. Since most American military and economic assistance was going to the Russians and the British, no opportunity should be overlooked to reassure Chiang and thus convince him to remain in the war. For these reasons, and with Roosevelt's support, the aid bill passed easily through the Congress without reservations or restrictions.[48]

Roosevelt's rejection of Gauss's and Vincent's position on the loan was one more indication to the ambassador that his views counted for little in the State Department or the White House, and although he had never been a very cheerful man, it increased the gloom with which he usually approached his duties. "He'd give up this job and retire like a shot," Vincent had observed some months before, "if it hadn't been so recent that he took it. Now he can't quit; it would look like 'quitting.'"[49] In a sense, Gauss had already resigned, for by the spring of 1942 he had become even more withdrawn than before, avoiding almost all of the important social functions attached to his office. Despite his superior's personality, John Carter worked well, if not happily, at his side, but others who lacked Vincent's patience and compassion, were openly critical.[50]

"We have a misfire here as ambassador," one observer had informed President Roosevelt as early as October 1941. "Despite his thirty odd years in China, he has never lived among [the Chinese], does not understand them, and conceals very poorly his dislike of them. . . . He resents it if they invite him out (and has refused several dinners) but also resents if they don't invite him. . . . . Mainly he dislikes crossing the river at night and being with them."[51] Foreign Service officer John P. Davies, Jr. made similar comments in his diary after meeting the ambassador several months later. "I am told that Mr. G. does not enjoy social gatherings," Davies noted, "and that therefore he has not seen H.H. Kung since November . . . and that he has very few contacts with Chinese and British officials of any description. He will not consider opening an office in the city."[52] In contrast, Davies had nothing but praise for Gauss's first secretary: "John Carter is doing a magnificent job," he wrote Stanley Hornbeck in early 1942. "Everyone speaks of him in the highest terms. He has, despite considerable obstacles, maintained valuable contacts with the Chinese."[53] Even the normally modest Vincent was forced to agree: As Gauss declined to direct much of the embassy's important diplomatic and social functions, Vincent found himself assuming the responsibility and gaining more influence over the daily operations of the office.[54]

His average day was now especially crowded and busy. He would awake early in the morning when the first rays of the red sun struck the house, then rise to watch them creep down the side of the mountain until they reached the valley. After dressing and eating a hurried breakfast, he might put the finishing touches on a dispatch or telegram prepared the night before, show it to the ambassador for his approval, then deliver it to the code room for transmittal to Washington.

Crossing the Yangtze on the rickety ferry, he would begin the torturous climb up the slippery Wang Lung Men steps to make his rounds through the city. Riding in a sedan chair, he would have a few minutes to study papers or just observe the always fascinating Chinese scene. Every morning at a certain spot a small Chinese boy, dressed in a grey gown and black vest, his head shaved clean, would call to him: "Yang Hsien Sheng, Nin hao but hao"—"Foreign gentleman, how are you?" "Fine, fine," Vincent would reply in Chinese, laughing at what had now become a daily ritual. He would pass the vegetable market, crowded with Chinese women with babies on their backs. Along the narrow, crooked streets, he could see the tiny bamboo and wood shops where the Chinese worked and lived. He could smell bread being baked, hear sewing machines clatter as they turned out exquisite cloth, spy men "making funny things out of paper: animals, little houses, carriages." "Everybody seems very happy," he once told his daughter, "even though they are very poor."[55]

Whom he visited on a particular day depended upon his interest at the moment: If Chinese politics were on his mind, he might confer with T. F. Tsiang, executive director of the Political Affairs Section of the Executive Yuan; if it were economics, Minister Wong Wen-hao, or Dr. Solomon Adler representing the Department of the Treasury in Chungking; a question on foreign policy might take him to Chien Tai or Foo Ping-Sheung, vice-ministers of foreign affairs. If he were concerned about the military situation (as he almost always was) he might see General Magruder to swap rumors or ask for advice. In late afternoon, he would often drop in at the Foreign Press Hostel to "check on what American press correspondents were sending out," and to discuss the current situation with representatives of *Time* magazine or the United Press International. Then he would clamber down the steps and race for the ferry, "just as the last bit of light was fading from the sky." If no social events were scheduled for the evening, he would play a game of pinochle with the ambassador (who insisted on playing almost every night) or retire early to write Betty or read a book of special interest, from the serious *General Theory of Economic Relationships* to the trivial *Serenade* ("One cannot live on post-war, pre-war and present war problems continuously").[56]

Frequently an entire day might be spent planning a "monster Chinese dinner," a task which was often as complicated as preparing an important diplomatic dispatch. Vincent was usually in charge of organizing the menu ("eleven dollars a plate") and arranging the seating. To seat the Chiangs and himself was easy, he explained to Betty, "but two Generals with wives, two Ambassadors without wives, and a former foreign minister, made for difficulties." Vincent also assumed the role of social director and tried to maintain cordiality among the guests who sometimes disliked one another heartily. Ambassador Gauss, who, Vincent noted, "has no love for Madame and shows it," barely spoke to her throughout one dinner party, while the generalissimo observed the scene in stony silence. "Otherwise everything went along fine," Vincent wrote his wife; "at least nobody got hurt."[57]

At one evening's dinner Madame Chiang "was feeling coquettish and also appeared to have something on her mind." Previously, she had been cold to Vincent (whom she once described as "a very good and a very clever friend of China,")[58] but now as the new "assistant Ambassador" it was his turn to be the "object of the Mayling charm."

"I think Mr. Vincent looks particularly well tonight," Madame Chiang remarked to General John Magruder.

"It's probably that red polka dot bow tie he has on," Magruder replied with a grin.

"No, he looks very well," Madame Chiang insisted, "particularly his 'permanent wave,'" a reference to John Carter's wavy brown hair tinged with grey.

After dinner Madame Chiang continued to ply her wiles. Drawing Vincent aside, she whispered to him, "I want you to know that we understand and appreciate what you have done for us. I realize that it has been difficult but I know that you have done much."

"I have and always have had Chinese interests very much at heart," Vincent told her and then inquired if she had any special problems which she wished to discuss. She did indeed.

She spoke first about Colonel Claire Chennault of the Flying Tigers, her favorite American in China, and urged that the commander "be well taken care of. . . . I cannot let Colonel Chennault down," she said with a smile, "after all, we used to have breakfast together when I was head of the Air Force." Vincent assured her that Chennault's exploits were well known in Washington, but she abruptly shifted focus and expressed her desire to assist Vincent in any way that he desired. "Whenever you want to communicate in complete confidence with Dr. Currie," she told him, "you can do it through me." Vincent thanked her but explained that he always used normal embassy channels when communicating with Washington. "But you might wish to communicate with him," she repeated. He thanked her again, thinking, "that would be a swell way to tie knots in the ball of yarn," and changed the subject.

Vincent was not fooled. "It means that I am invited to doublecross the Ambassador. . . . But for what? I don't like General and Madame Chiang's government. To my sensitive nostrils it stinks," he wrote Betty in a burst of anger. "The General Chiang who sold the socially progressive elements down the river in 1927, selling out at the same time to the Shanghai bankers, is still the same Chiang, Methodism, bible and prayers notwithstanding and Madame is of the same material." His conclusion: "Do everything one can to hold them together during this war, and afterwards, to hell with Kuomintang!"[59]

To be flattered by Madame Chiang was one penalty to be paid by the first secretary of the American embassy in Chungking. But Vincent's burdens were soon to increase, for in late February Gauss recommended to the Department of State that he be made counselor of embassy. If Secretary Hull approved, Vincent would be the second highest ranking officer in the embassy in name as well as in fact.

He was not optimistic that he would be named counselor despite Gauss's encouragement. In early February he had been promoted to Class 3 which was itself a distinction, and he therefore did not expect to be promoted so soon again. Moreover, to his knowledge no one in Class 3 had ever become counselor of embassy, so tradition and precedent were also against him. "Personally," he didn't care, as he told Betty, "I get along very well as I am."[60]

Mostly, he longed to be with his family from whom he had not heard in nearly four months, their letters another casualty of the haphazard system that delivered equipment and material from the United States. Though blessed with a "disposition which . . . makes me try to make the best of it," their absence hurt him deeply. His "whole life" revolved around the activities of Sheila, and John Carter, Jr. (born in Peking in 1935), Betty had once observed. "He simply won't do anything on weekends but be with them." Unable to personally assist his wife in their rearing, he wrote his daughter and son letters which contained valuable suggestions and, on more than one occasion, wisdom. "You can learn this from the Chinese," he told ten-year-old Sheila in a letter written in 1942. "That you can be happy without having many 'things'; that you can learn to make the best of what you have got; and perhaps that just having many 'things' won't make you happy anyway. The Chinese have learned this without studying books. They have learned, too, that you can be happy by doing something useful, by plowing a field, or making a dress, or cooking a good meal. They do not ask that they get rich doing these things because getting rich usually means doing other people rather than doing something useful (you can ask your mother to explain this). But you don't have to ask your mother to explain to you that I love you more than any other 'lady' except her."[61]

His hopes of an early transfer to another post where he might be reunited with his family vanished in mid-March when he received "four large lovely letters" from Betty in which she described, among other things, her meetings with State Department officials regarding his return to Washington.

Her life without John Carter was as empty as his was without her. There was enough to keep her busy, especially the new farm in Fairfax, Virginia, that she had purchased with John Carter's approval last summer, and the problem of raising alone young Sheila and John Carter, Jr. There were also parties with her friends the Curries, the Thurmond Arnolds, the Raymond

Clappers, and the Robert LaFollettes, which filled an occasional evening, but all this seemed only to intensify her loneliness. Finally becoming "fed up" with the separation, she decided to do everything she could to bring him home. But her discussions with officers of the Far Eastern and Personnel Divisions did little to convince her that she might be successful.[62]

She found the State Department suffering its customary lassitude, and the Far Eastern Division isolated and ignored, as the War Department and the White House made foreign policy. "[Hornbeck] doesn't count for much of anything these days," she reported to her husband, "[he's] sort of an old man not registering so much anymore." Younger officers complained to Betty about how difficult it was to work for the hard-driving and irascible Hornbeck, and his protégé, Maxwell Hamilton, still chief of FE. Robert Smyth, an old friend, was "beside himself . . . he thinks he is getting stomach ulcers and going crazy both." Another officer resigned after inheriting sixty thousand dollars. "He paced the streets for a while," Betty was told, "and then wrote . . . a masterpiece. He gave his reasons for resigning: FE was not the kind of government he wanted to represent, [staffed] by the type of American who would pick the gold out of your teeth." She did not want her husband to return to the division, and told him so.

John G. Erhardt of the Personnel Division was even more discouraging. She learned that given Vincent's importance to the embassy he would probably have to remain in Chungking for at least another year. She took the news stoically, but thought: "There is nothing I can do. . . [;] my life is absolutely a blank with you not in it." "I am going to stop struggling," she told Vincent. "I shall try to make as easy a life for myself as possible this next year and keep the wrinkles from my face for your return."[63]

He received more definite word about his status a few days later when, to his surprise, he was informed by Under Secretary of State Sumner Welles that he had been appointed counselor of embassy. Now he was sure that Chungking would remain his home for at least another year, perhaps longer. It was not a prospect that he contemplated with much enjoyment, for the problem of maintaining friendly relations between China and the United States grew worse daily as the Japanese intensified their spring campaign to end Chinese resistance.

Nothing could stem the Japanese tide as it swept through East Asia: The key port of Rangoon fell on March 7; Java surrendered the following day; and in May, Burma was finally captured, sealing China off from the outside world on land and sea. The fall of Burma shocked the

Washington community as nothing had since Pearl Harbor, and to the men in the State Department it seemed only a matter of time until China followed too, unless the United States came to her rescue.[64]

Stanley Hornbeck, ever China's friend, urged the secretary of state and the president to reexamine the strategy of "Europe first": "Is there not something wrong about a strategy," he asked, " . . . which in theory or in practice would call for investing everything in several scattered theaters and investing absolutely nothing in a theater which, if occupied by the enemy, would mean the loss of a useful ally and the acquisition by the enemy of that prize which has been the major objective of political and military operations on his part for a period of nearly fifty years."[65] To Hornbeck and Hamilton[66] the answer was clear: "There is only one way by which we can make sure of maintaining China's confidence," they argued in several memorandums in late May, "we must deliver goods."

Vincent did not share the fears of his Washington colleagues. "Let Burma remain fallen. . . ," he wrote in his diary in early May, "and get on with the war. Let the Chinese continue to resist as they have . . . for the past five years—and get on with the war." Unlike Hornbeck, allied reversals in Asia did not alter his view that the real struggle was taking place in Europe, where "the war in both its positive and negative aspects is against Germany or what Germany stands for."[67] Still convinced of America's eventual victory against Japan, he worked to "assure the Chinese and other Allied representatives they were not alone," despite their isolation in Chungking.

His trips to the city were almost daily now and more purposeful. His mission, as he put it, was to spread his "doctrine of the three confidences. . . : that the Russians can hold the Germans this year and defeat them next winter; confidence that the United States . . . will be more than a match for Japan next spring; and confidence that China will, as she has for the past five years, carry on with her 'magnificent resistance.'"[68] British and Russian officials in Chungking were happy to see someone so confident of victory and they brightened when Vincent visited their offices. "Oh here's Mr. Vincent," the Russian ambassador remarked one afternoon. "I am always glad to see him because he looks like everything is all right."[69]

Surprisingly, he discovered that many Chinese, on both ends of the political spectrum, were not as discouraged as Hornbeck and Hamilton believed them to be. Chou En-lai, the representative of the Chinese Communist Party in Chungking, told him that while "defeat in Burma would have an adverse effect on morale . . . in official quarters . . . [he] did not think it would be serious." Chou dismissed the news of reported

Japanese peace overtures and "expressed confidence that General Chiang was determined to continue resistance, [as] there were not elements in the government with sufficient strength and influence to initiate an appeasement policy although there were some elements that might be inclined to do so."[70] He heard similar views expressed by Chou's political and ideological opposite, "a Chinese landlord businessman," named Dr. Wang. "All assistance possible should be given to Russia," Wang also told Vincent. "Nothing should be diverted to China which can be used in Russia." Surprisingly, for a Chinese businessman who was "no lover of Russia," Wang insisted that "the war is being fought in Russia. If Russia gives in to Germany there will not be [a] war anymore. If China gives in [to] Japan, the war can still be carried on to a successful conclusion but if Russia has to give in to Germany it will be hopeless. Therefore," Wang concluded, "help to Russia is of primary importance, irrespective of what professional pleaders for aid to China may say."[71]

It was one of few times that Vincent found himself in agreement with a member of the Chinese landlord class. For despite the continued Japanese invasion which threatened both New Delhi and Chungking, his attention was still captured by the conflict in Eastern Europe which was "stirring [his] blood and imagination as nothing else in this war has done." The Far Eastern theater, he wrote Betty in early summer, "is a holding operation for the time being. It would be better to lose the entire Far East and take Berlin than to win the Far East and lose Russia."[72] In the Ukraine, the Russians and the Germans were fighting at Kharkov, "one of the few places," he noted, "where I should like to be—*with a gun*. The outcome of the war . . . may be decided right now, right there."[73]

But for Chiang and his ruling circle, the outcome of the war would be decided in Asia, not in Europe, and the continued failure of the allies to recognize the importance of the Asian theater led to a new crisis. When the United States transferred bomber and transport aircraft from China to the British fighting Rommel's forces in the Middle East, in June 1942,[74] Generalissimo and Madame Chiang were furious. In a heated exchange with General Joesph Stilwell they demanded to know whether the British and the Americans still "considered [China] . . . one of the allied theatres." A few days later, Chiang notified Washington that unless certain conditions were satisfied he would consider the "liquidation" of the China theater. Included in Chiang's "Three Demands" were: "(1) Three American divisions to arrive in India between August and September to restore communication to China through Burma; (2) 500 combat airplanes to operate from China beginning in August and to be maintained continuously at that strength; (3) Delivery of 5,000 tons a month to be

79   Assistant Ambassador

maintained by the ATC [American Transport Command] beginning in August." To fulfill these demands in toto was impossible: To deliver a "minimum requirement" of 5,000 tons over the Himalayas required 304 planes, 275 men to fly and service them, and thousands more to support them on the ground.[75] Fearful that Washington would be frightened into capitulating to Chiang's demands, Vincent prepared a memorandum on June 29 designed specifically "to counteract pessimism in the State Department."

As he had since January, Vincent wrote the secretary of state that the likelihood of a cessation of Chinese resistance was "so remote . . . that it is hardly worth consideration." Internal factors, not the external circumstances the Chiangs had described, were the key to Chinese resistance. The generalissimo's political power and that of his associates was dependent on continued hostility toward Japan. Nor were there other competing groups powerful enough to seize power and make a separate peace, although he did not discount the possibility that provincial disintegration might weaken the Chinese further. Chiang would continue to fight—no matter how much aid was delivered.

American policy, Vincent insisted, should be based on a realistic assessment of Chinese capabilities and allied necessities, and nothing else. "The Embassy's view has been and . . . should remain that China should be given all practical assistance—practical from the standpoint of ability effectively to utilize such assistance in China, practical from the standpoint of transportation facilities, and practical from the standpoint of needs in other theaters of the war." As for Chiang's attempt at blackmail, he was as explicit as diplomatic language permitted: "Assistance should not be given because of a fear that the failure to do so would result in the Chinese authorities ceasing resistance and seeking peace with Japan."[76] Doubtful that his memorandum would influence the State Department or reach the White House, and fearing the worst, Vincent awaited Washington's response to Chiang's "Three Demands."

Vincent was not encouraged by Roosevelt's first reaction to the new crisis in China. Instead of telling the Chinese the truth, "that under the present circumstances we cannot give effective aid,"[77] Roosevelt informed Chiang that he would carefully examine his requests; and to facilitate communication between the two leaders, the president was again sending Lauchlin Currie to Chungking. Washington's policy remained the same despite the embassy's reports: If supplies could not be delivered, then a favorite emissary could. The thought of Currie acting as "special pleader for aid to China" was especially upsetting to Vincent. And for the first time, if not the last, Vincent was driven to real anger over Roosevelt's ignorance of the situation in Chungking. "I distrust—I detest this . . . attitude that we must keep everybody happy: the premier of Australia, Churchill, Chiang; the South Americans. It smacks too much [of] carrying 46 out of 48 states . . . and failing to do a good damned thing thereafter. Let's lose New Jersey, Ohio, Illinois, and even the solid South but let's carry our point by winning the war. We can't make everybody happy."[78]

Vincent's anger was something more than a momentary loss of poise: It was the reflection of emotional turmoil brought on by the difference between his own view of American policy in China and that of his government. In Mukden and Dairen, and later in the State Department, he had been adamant in his support for the Chinese, while his government, eager to avoid a confrontation with Japan, lagged far behind. Now in the summer of 1942, positions were reversed: Vincent was continually opposing requests and demands for assistance, while his government was supporting China unconditionally. Once again, he was out of step with Washington and it disturbed him greatly. What had caused this change? Why was the man who had once been China's warmest friend now her severest critic?[79]

The answer lay in the gulf that was growing between his love for the Chinese people and his hatred for their "reactionary" and "bankrupt government." How that government functioned was all too plain to see. "In downtown Chungking was the prison where Chinese were tortured," journalist Annalee Jacoby later recalled: "We went far out of our way to avoid hearing the screams. . . . College Professors talked intelligently about what must be done, and the next week vanished. A United Press messenger boy, a peasant, came to the Press Compound . . . with his tongue torn out, cigarette burns festering over all visible skin, and his mind gone."[80] This was the regime the United States supported in China, and it made Vincent sick. "You can be pro-Chinese," he finally concluded, "without being pro-Kuomintang."[81]

Despite his hopes for changes in government, the Kuomintang remained under the domination of the same conservative personalities he had described to Betty seven months before. Washington seemed blissfully unaware of the true nature of Chiang's government, describing it as "a mass movement of people led by a great leader [with] determination, persistence and [a] broad gauge outlook."[82] Still optimistic that he might be able to bring the president's views more in line with his own, Vincent prepared a long memorandum in late July devoted entirely to an analysis of the Chinese National (Kuomintang) government.

He began with a lesson in recent Chinese history, charting the decline and fall of the Kuomintang as a progressive political movement. "After sweeping north to the Yangtze on a revolutionary program [in 1927]," Vincent wrote, "[Chiang Kai-shek] made his peace in Shanghai with the bankers and landlords and took into his fold such reactionary warlords as he could attract to his camp. Thereafter commenced the long battle to subdue the communists and liquidate non-cooperative military and political elements." Even before the outbreak of the war between China and Japan in 1937, the Kuomintang "was suffering from a want of any applied idealism in its policies and undertakings. . . . The Party had become a sterile bureaucracy depending upon the monied interests and the military for its support."

Having failed to solve China's critical economic and political problems and faced with mounting opposition from a variety of dissident groups, the Kuomintang chose coercion instead of reform to maintain its authority. The result was "the adoption of repressive measures to control and eradicate opposition; to enforce party discipline and inculcate through educational and training systems loyalty to so-called party ideals. 'Party Tutelage,' the professed prelude to the institution of a democratic system, [became] an end in itself rather than a means toward the end of putting into effect Dr. Sun's ideal of socially and economically democratic government. Political unity, held out as a prerequisite to the accomplishment of social reform and the institution of democratic government [was] perverted into a means of achieving a high degree of centralized bureaucratic control."

The war with Japan brought a momentary lull in the struggle between the Left and the Right, but by 1942 it had become apparent that the Kuomintang was using resistance to Japan as yet another tool to command loyalty and eradicate opposition. "The communists are virtually outlawed," Vincent observed, "and other dissident elements are suppressed through control of the press and through the more direct method of secret service espionage and arrest. By these methods new blood, new thought, and new inspiration have been discouraged—prevented—from coming into the Party with the resultant bureaucratic sterility that now characterizes the Kuomintang Government."[83]

The "undisputed leader" of the Nationalist movement, "supreme in the Government, in the Army, and in the Party" was, of course, Generalissimo Chiang Kai-shek. For fifteen years Chiang had dominated Kuomintang politics, defeating rivals, subjugating warlords, and resisting Japanese encroachment. The general was no simple dictator in the European sense, Vincent argued, but a skilled manipulator of the "congeries of conservative political cliques" that made up the Kuomintang. Disorganized and without principle, these factions were tied together by nothing more than a "desire to maintain or increase their influence."

Vincent then described those leaders who served Chiang and whose interests were protected by him: the familial clique of Kungs and Soongs, the reactionary faction led by the Chens, the conservative, eastern Political Science clique, and the militarists known as the Whampoa clique. To control these groups required considerable political agility and this Chiang possessed—tied as he was matrimonially to his western-educated brothers-in-law, Kung and Soong, and temperamentally to the conservative easterners.[84]

What could this government contribute to the war effort? Very little, was Vincent's answer. To hope for "the active resistance which western military critics desire and western eulogizers portray" was sheer folly. Chiang would fight the Japanese but in a limited, conservative fashion, and this would probably be sufficient until the Americans closed in from the sea and air.

The future survival of the Kuomintang was less certain. Threatened by young liberal elements in the party, less conservative groups outside the party, and the Communists, Vincent thought it likely that Chiang and his associates would try to destroy their opponents rather than share power with them. Continued control of the Kuomintang by Chinese Nazis seemed assured unless dramatic efforts were made to reform the Nationalist regime.

Once again, Vincent urged that outside influence and pressure be applied to give liberal groups the opportunity to make the Kuomintang "a vital force for instituting social [and] political democracy in China." For the future well-being of China "the Chens and the Tai Lis must go, and the warlords and the landlords must be subordinated to the national interest." Then, a new progressive government could be created, one that did not exclude the participation of the Kungs, the Soongs, the Political Science clique, and the Communists. It would be "one of the major tasks of the post-war period," Vincent concluded, "to utilize our influence and support to the end that liberal elements are enabled to assume a position of leadership in the government of China."[85] Such a government would unify China, represent the people's interests and fulfill Roosevelt's and Vincent's hope that China might become "the strongest Far Eastern Nation in the post-war period."

Vincent's lengthy dispatch gave Washington a perceptive analysis of China's government and a strategy to reform the Kuomintang that would promote America's interests in the Far East. But Washington remained uninterested: The president's time and energy were consumed by events in Europe, not the present or future status of China. Choosing to believe the propaganda manufactured by Chiang's apologists, as well as that which emanated from his own office, Roosevelt failed to recognize the seriousness of China's problems and rejected any policy designed to pressure Chiang to reform his regime. Reflecting this attitude, the president ignored Vincent's recommendations and those of the War Department urging that the Chinese army be reformed in exchange for American lend lease assistance.[86] Instead, the president tried to fulfill Chiang's "Three Demands" of the previous June. While Roosevelt could not send the combat divisions that Chiang had requested, he did agree to increase the number of aircraft to be used in the China theater, as well as the amount of aid to be delivered over the Himalayas. The president asked for nothing in return, although he did inform Chiang that military reform "would be of the greatest importance in obtaining our mutual objectives."[87] Chiang's requests still carried more weight in the White House than did the embassy's recommendations. For the present, a diplomatic or military strategy of quid pro quo, whether suggested by General Stilwell or Counselor Vincent, found no support in the executive office.

Washington's habit of ignoring the realities of Chinese politics was again confirmed in October with the arrival in Chungking of former Republican presidential candidate, Wendell L. Willkie. Willkie had been Roosevelt's rival in 1940 but now went to China as the president's emissary, instructed to meet Chiang and his "good wife" for the purpose of improving Sino-American relations.[88] Vincent remained as skeptical as ever: "Chungking is getting into a flutter over the impending visit of Wendell Willkie," he informed Betty, ". . . I'm not impressed."[89]

Ambassador Gauss, on the other hand, looked forward to Willkie's visit with uncharacteristic eagerness. "This is no Roosevelt stooge," Vincent explained, "this is a Republican and a sound businessman."[90] In Willkie's honor, Gauss scheduled a special dinner and briefing during his first evening in Chungking and also invited him to stay at the embassy. Having a "sixth sense for trouble," Vincent stayed behind while the ambassador went to meet Willkie at the airport. Vincent's instincts were sound: Willkie's entrance into the city destroyed Gauss's hopes almost immediately.

Alighting from the airplane, Willkie "sensed" reporters and "with a scant how-do-you-do to the Ambassador"[91] invited the press to an unscheduled news conference. After a "triumphal" motorcade through the city, Willkie was driven to a beautiful house supplied by the Chinese for his convenience. Willkie decided to spend the night in these quarters and Gauss returned to the embassy "in a towering rage."[92] Vincent tried to soothe the angered ambassador but failed: "Ideas, China affairs, world affairs, touch him little," he noted, "but his prestige, Mon Dieu[;]

henceforth, Willkie can do no good—he stinks . . . with a stink that puts our bowels in an uproar."[93] To be ignored by the New Dealers was one thing—to be snubbed by a fellow Republican was Gauss's final indignity. Now it was up to John Carter to escort Willkie around Chungking.

Saturday, October 3, was an especially busy day for Counselor Vincent. Willkie's tour began early in the morning with a visit to the Foreign Office and discussions with General Ho Ying-chin and H. H. Kung, "who staged a cabinet meeting" for the visitors. In Willkie's honor, President Lin Sen gave a luncheon that lasted over two hours and consisted of fifteen courses, including a variety of wine, "bird's nest soup, little suckling pig, shark's fins, pigeon eggs, fish with sweet and sour sauce, deer's tendons, and champagne."[94]

In the afternoon, Vincent and Willkie had their first extended conversation. Surprised at Gauss's sensitivity, Willkie tried to explain "why he had not exerted himself to come across the river." He could not understand why ambassadors had to be "such God Damned sensitive fools always worried about their position and prestige."

The major event of the afternoon was Willkie's visit with Generalissimo and Madame Chiang Kai-shek. The Chiangs recognized that Willkie, "the titular leader of the opposition," as Roosevelt called him, might be exceedingly useful in gaining increased military and economic aid and, having failed to seduce Gauss and Vincent, turned their charms on their Republican guest. Willkie fell willingly under the spell cast by Madame Chiang. She "has taken him in completely," Vincent observed. "During the call on the Generalissimo . . . [Willkie] was barely polite. . . . directing most of his remarks . . . to Madame."[95] Returning her affection, Willkie invited Madame Chiang to visit the United States, as he put it, "to educate us about China. Madame would be the perfect Ambassador, we would listen to her as to no one else. With wit and charm, a generous and understanding heart, a gracious and beautiful manner and appearance, and a burning conviction, she is just what we need as a visitor."[96] Without further encouragement, Madame Chiang agreed to come to America as soon as arrangements could be made.

Even after the meeting had concluded, Willkie could not stop talking about Madame Chiang. "Bestirring himself from a paunchy haze," he remarked to Vincent that Madame "was the one thing that lived up to and surpassed all advance notices." "Ah me," Vincent thought, "it's a pity he really has not the authority to deliver all the airplanes that he promises. She knows it, but she figures that she might get a few."[97]

Willkie was not interested in hearing the embassy's view of the situation in China and Vincent could do little to penetrate the fog of pro-

Kuomintang propaganda that surrounded Willkie wherever he went. Willkie's visit, he concluded after a long day of meetings and a night of parties, was nothing more than a "publicity tour," a reflection of Washington's propensity for believing the fictions that passed for fact in Chungking. A few days later, his conceptions of China unsullied by reality, Willkie departed for home.

Had Willkie kept his views to himself, the damage would have been minimal; instead, he chose to share his experiences in China with the American people in a series of articles and a book called *One World,* which became an overnight bestseller. Willkie's China could not have been more different from Vincent's. "Military China," Willkie wrote in *One World,* "is united; its leaders are trained and able generals; its new armies are tough, fighting organizations of men who know both what they are fighting for and how to fight for it. . . . this is truly a people's war." The generalissimo was "bigger even than his legendary reputation": "scholarly" and "reflective" in manner, "poised," "sincere," and "imperturbable." For Willkie, signs of totalitarianism in government reflected only an interim period in Chinese politics, a "stage during which the people are being educated into new habits of living and thinking designed to make them good citizens of a complete democracy . . . at a later time." And above all, China was a valiant ally, a "warmhearted land filled with friends of America."[98]

While Vincent's analyses of the Kuomintang were ignored in Washington, Americans were digesting Willkie's report in massive doses: Two hundred thousand people bought *One World* in the first four days after publication; in eight weeks, over one million copies had been sold.[99] The China of Wendell Willkie (and Franklin Roosevelt) was now more firmly rooted in the American consciousness than ever before. Given public opinion, Vincent's proposals had no impact, and Washington did not have the courage to change its policy: The United States would stand behind Chiang Kai-shek and the Kuomintang without reservation, now and in the days to come.

Disgusted with officials in Washington who failed to realize the seriousness of the situation in China, and tired of the burdens of daily life in Chungking, Vincent longed for a new post where he might have more influence. He had been in Chungking nearly eighteen months and was beginning to feel the strain. The cost of living continued to skyrocket, raising the cost of running the embassy to over twelve thousands dollars a month: "ridiculous for what we get," Vincent noted, "food and service, nothing more."[100] Inflation "finally accomplished what moral and health arguments could not": He stopped smoking.[101] "Sometimes I feel like I have been here since the beginning of the world," he wrote Betty in mid-November. "The break and change since my arrival . . . has been so great that it is difficult to remember the past."[102] Now he thought more and more of the future and home. By late autumn he had concluded that his work in Chungking was done and that it was time to leave. "I must resume a life with my family," he remarked.[103]

In early December it appeared as if he might soon get his wish. Several people, including Madame H.H. Kung, had inquired whether it was true that he would be leaving soon, and one night he dreamed he was transferred to Guatemala City. Finally, there was Gauss's casual remark one morning that "it's about time that they cleared us out of here; I'm considered a sourpuss and you're looked on as a leftist."[104] The inquiries, the dream, the remark—all were "'good omens." A few weeks later he received confirmation from the State Department: He was going home, although, in typical bureaucratic fashion, the department failed to inform him exactly when.[105]

Bad news soon followed: His successor, George Atcheson, Jr., could not arrive until May. The thought of five more months in Chungking depressed him greatly and spoiled his Christmas holiday. "I presume you are your philosophical self," Betty wrote him after she was informed, "all I can get is mad!!"[106] Still, he was finally assured of an eventual homecoming and this realization (and the work yet to be done) helped the months pass swiftly.

The problems in Chinese politics that Vincent encountered during his last five months in Chungking were the same as those he had observed since his arrival in June 1941. The strength and vitality of the Kuomintang continued to decline and relations between the Communists and the Nationalists were still "unimproved" and "unimprovable."

In May 1943, the dominance of the Kuomintang reached one of its lowest points in recent years when peasant rebellions erupted in Kansu, Kweichow, and Ningsia. Coupled with the disastrous effects of famine and riots in Honan,[107] these "revolts against Central Government authority" were indicative, Vincent argued, not only of the influence of pro-Japanese sympathizers active in the area, but more importantly, of the "inefficiency and corruption of Central Government officials." Taken together, these recent developments in the provinces pointed "to the possibility of increasing lack of confidence in [the] Chungking Government."[108]

As the Nationalists grew weaker, the Communists grew stronger. Despite the presence of the Kuomintang blockade, the Communists were "solidly entrenched in most of North China;" Communist forces were also poised to occupy positions in Suiyuan, Jehol, and Manchuria as soon as Allied military successes forced the Japanese to withdraw. Even more distressing to Chiang was the news that the Communists had been able "to carry out some degree of popular mobilization" in the rural areas of northern China, making the likelihood of future Kuomintang control extremely unlikely. In short, the Communists were "far stronger" in the spring of 1943 "than they were when they stood off Kuomintang armies for ten years in Central China."[109] They were now undisputably a force with which the Nationalists (and the Americans) had to reckon.

But to Vincent's distress, the Nationalists were still unable to come to terms with the Communists, and most importantly, unwilling to "adopt . . . effective measures for agrarian reform, equitable taxation, and . . . promotion of home industries," which Vincent believed would "cut the ground from under the Communists."[110] Discussions between the Nationalists and Communists were at a "stalemate," Vincent reported to the State Department in early May, and no future accord seemed likely because the Kuomintang was more determined than ever to "liquidate the Communists." While Vincent did not believe open civil war to be imminent, it was certainly a future possibility: If Chiang could not eliminate the Communists through negotiations, "an attempt will be made when . . . a propitious moment arrives to effect it by force."[111] With the Kuomintang on the decline, and the Communists on the rise, there seemed no end to China's political ills without further bloodshed and tragedy.

The pleasure of his departure in mid-May was diminished by his continuing concern for China's complicated political and military problems. The situation was bleak, but he did not think it completely hopeless: If the Kuomintang could be persuaded to effect reform and if liberal elements could be given a greater role to play in Chinese government, then the Communist threat could be eradicated, political unity achieved, and the Japanese invasion halted and reversed. This had been his credo and his hope during his tour of duty in Chungking and would remain such in the years that followed.

Vincent would later receive a commendation from the State Department and a grade of "excellent"[112] for his service as counselor of embassy. It was an accolade that was well-deserved. By any standard, he had done an excellent job. As an administrator, he helped restore order and harmony to an embassy that was torn by disorganization and bureaucratic conflict. He established close personal relations with other American agencies and was able to reduce the hostility that existed among representatives of the State Department, the Treasury, and the Pentagon in Chungking.

He also served his chief with devotion and compassion, and Gauss was grateful for Vincent's assistance. In an efficiency report written in 1942 Gauss said: "He has a fine mind; he is acute and thorough in exploring sources of information and opinion; he is calmly objective in appraising situations and has a good sense of proportion. . . . He also has a talent for encouraging the younger officers of the staff to be appropriately inquiring but discreet in their contacts. He is courageous and independent in his opinions and judgments, testing them thoroughly and frankly in his consultations with the chief of mission. At the same time he is thoroughly loyal."[113]

Despite his administrative duties, Vincent was also a perceptive observer of Chinese politics and was the embassy's principal expert on the Kuomintang. His analyses of the Nationalist regime were well-researched and clearly written, and his warnings of future political deterioration proved to be prophetic. Not content merely to criticize, Vincent urged Washington to use its economic and military power to create a progressive government that would represent the interests of the Chinese people, defeat the Communists and the Japanese, and police the Far East in the postwar period. This was the major theme that ran through his reports and recommendations during his years in Chungking.

Unlike many Americans with an interest in China, Vincent was able to see the war in the Far East in a global context. For the present, the European theater demanded America's complete attention, and Vincent warned his government not to squander its resources in Asia when they were so desperately needed by the British and the Russians. The protection of American interests remained his constant preoccupation in the early 1940s as it had when he served in China in the 1920s and 1930s.

George Atcheson arrived in Chungking in mid-May, and after escorting him about the city and introducing him to Chiang and other Chinese officials, Vincent left China for what he thought would be the last time. He had no idea that he would return a year later in the company of the vice-president of the United States, on an urgent mission for Franklin D. Roosevelt.

3

A Catalytic Agent

It was a joyous homecoming. Betty and the children were at the airport to meet him and they drove immediately to the farm in Fairfax, Virginia, where Vincent could rest and recuperate from his ordeal in Chungking. "Little Spring Farm," as the property was called, was everything that Betty had described: Located on four acres of gently rolling farm land one-half hour's drive from Washington, D.C., the house was painted white and trimmed in dark green with four round columns going up in true southern colonial style. There were cherry, apple, and pear trees, a vegetable garden, and to Vincent's delight, a chicken house, where he could raise fowl as he had done when he was a boy in Macon. Above all, he was reunited with his family, from whom he vowed he would never again be separated.[1]

But as much as he enjoyed the life of a gentleman farmer, he soon became bored and his thoughts turned toward his next assignment. He knew that his tour of duty would be spent in Washington but he was determined not to return to the Far Eastern Division, unless there was a "radical change." The "thought of serving in the present FE gives me the creeps,"[2] he had written his wife from Chungking. His secret ambition, he told her on another occasion, was "to return to the halls of the Department as Chief of FE, seeing the tail end of some of my friends as they leave the place. This is not just personal desire," he added, because he believed that he had something positive to contribute and did not "see how those there now can contribute anything."[3]

The principal target of Vincent's hostility was Stanley K. Hornbeck, the man who continued to dominate the operations of the Far Eastern Division. During 1942 and 1943, Vincent (and the embassy staff in general) had been increasingly at odds with Hornbeck and his protégé, Maxwell Hamilton. Neither Hornbeck nor Hamilton had been to China in over a decade, and in Vincent's view, they were both dangerously out of touch with the situation there. "They clung so tenaciously to the idea that the future of China rested in the hands of Chiang Kai-shek," Vincent later recalled, and they ignored all reports that questioned the ability of Chiang and the Kuomintang to govern China.[4] American officials in Chungking had come to feel isolated from their superiors in Washington, and the result was a growing gulf between the embassy and the State Department. The distance between Washington and Chungking enabled Vincent to ignore Hornbeck's insistent orders, but that was a luxury that would be lost once Vincent returned to FE. So when Lauchlin Currie invited him in August to step out of the State Department, and join the staff of the Foreign Economic Administration as a consultant on China, he accepted with pleasure.[5]

While he worked at his new job on the Asian commodities desk at FEA, Vincent kept a close watch on developments in the State Department, where he began to notice the beginnings of an organized rebellion against Stanley Hornbeck. From discussions with his colleagues in FE, he learned that the differences in policy which separated the embassy from the Far Eastern Division were also present within the State Department bureaucracy itself.

Foreign Service officers serving in FE who had read reports from Gauss and Vincent on the precarious state of the Kuomintang could no longer tolerate Hornbeck's unconditional support of Chiang or his habit of withholding from the secretary of state cables that were critical of the generalissimo.[6] Hornbeck tried to discourage such reporting by attacking those who informed Washington of Chiang's weaknesses and the increasing strength of his political and military rivals. When the second secretary of embassy, John S. Service, reported on the growth of the Communist movement in January 1943, Hornbeck dismissed his views as "rash, exaggerated, and immature,"[7] and ordered his colleagues in FE to "maintain an attitude of intelligent skepticism with regard to reports emphasizing the strength of the 'Communist' forces in China."[8] Hornbeck detested the prospect of working with the Chinese Communists to defeat

Japan and "was almost fanatically opposed to . . . having any dealings whatever with the Communist regime," division officer Walter A. Adams later recalled.[9] The men in FE who did not share Hornbeck's views were isolated and ignored, while Hornbeck continued to give Secretary Hull and President Roosevelt optimistic reports of Chinese military and political progress.

Worse even than Hornbeck's convictions were his "frequent tongue lashings, tactlessness, and disregard of the feelings and sensibilities of the staff."[10] In an effort to force his associates to conform to his own peculiar bureaucratic code, Hornbeck would often inform them that "it would be appreciated if officers . . . would make sure that they understand the difference in meaning between the word 'particularly' and the word 'especially'; also between 'in regard to' and 'in respect to' and be guided accordingly."[11] (Not even the secretary of state was exempt from Hornbeck's lectures: "I query the use on page four, last line, of the word 'all,' and on page five, fourteenth line, the word 'therefore,'" he wrote Hull in reference to a memorandum just one month after Pearl Harbor.[12] Such "petty interference," one officer later complained, "increased the amount of paper work. . . and destroyed . . . initiative."[13]

Hornbeck's foremost critics in the department were assistant chiefs Laurence Salisbury and Edwin Stanton. When word reached them in early January 1944 that Hornbeck was to be appointed director of the newly organized Office of Far Eastern Affairs, Stanton and Salisbury decided to make their views known to the secretary of state. In a memorandum addressed to Under Secretary Edward Stettinius they described Hornbeck as "obstinate" and "opinionated" and accused him of withholding "important information from the top officers of the Department."[14] They also refused to become the chiefs of the Chinese and Japanese Divisions in the new office because "acceptance would mean perpetuation of the regime under Hornbeck, . . . a regime which prevented formulation and execution of intelligent policies based on facts and on views of officers in the field and at home."[15]

Vincent supported Stanton and Salisbury in their efforts and also declined appointment as chief of the China Division under Hornbeck. He informed Assistant Secretary Howland Shaw and Far Eastern Chief Joseph Ballantine in writing that he was "in sympathy with the viewpoint expressed by Salisbury and Stanton": If Hornbeck continued to run FE, then he would be happier serving in the department's Labor Division.[16]

On January 19, Vincent's letter and the Stanton-Salisbury memorandum were given to the secretary for consideration; the following day Ballantine informed them of Hull's reaction. Fearful that the revolt against Hornbeck might prove embarrassing to the department, Hull proposed a compromise: Joseph Ballantine would become his "chief advisor" on Far Eastern policy but Hornbeck would "retain his present office and title." Stanton and Salisbury rejected Hull's proposal. There would be no improvement in the division's efficiency or morale, they insisted, until Hornbeck was "out of FE." They urged Ballantine to continue to argue their case with the secretary.[17]

Five days passed without further word from Hull, and Hornbeck remained the appointed director of the Office of Far Eastern Affairs. Late on the afternoon of the twenty-fifth, Salisbury "took H[ornbeck]'s most recent irritating memo . . . to B[allantine] and said something definite had better be done soon."[18] Three days later Ballantine reported that a decision had been made: Hornbeck would become an assistant to the secretary of state (but without responsibility for Far Eastern policy); the appointment would be announced presently, "with some other changes in order to give it an appearance of normality."[19] One month later, Ballantine became the new acting director of FE and Hornbeck's fifteen-year reign in the department was ended.

Although the rebellion against Hornbeck was brief, it was not without its casualties. Salisbury believed that his effectiveness had been seriously impaired during the struggle against Hornbeck and he decided to retire from the Foreign Service. His resignation was accepted quickly by officials in personnel who informed him that it was a wise decision because he had "gone too far" in the Hornbeck affair, and was now "a dead goat."[20] Hornbeck never forgave Vincent for writing his letter to Howland Shaw and in 1950 told an agent of the Federal Bureau of Investigation that Vincent had been "disloyal." (Upon further reflection, Hornbeck admitted that he thought that Vincent had been "disloyal" to him and not to his country.)[21]

With the removal of Hornbeck from FE, and the transfer of Maxwell Hamilton to the American embassy in Moscow, Chiang Kai-shek lost two of his most important patrons in the State Department, and the China specialists in the embassy and the Far Eastern Division who were critical of the Kuomintang won a new chance to play a role in policy-making.[22] In early February, Ballantine again invited Vincent to become chief of China affairs (CA) and, in light of the recent changes within the department, he now agreed to accept the position.

A s head of CA, Vincent sat at the important junction where reports from the field entered the State Department for analysis and action. Cables emanating from the embassy in Chungking came first to Vincent's division, where it would be up to him to decide if the messages were important enough to bother the secretary or be passed on instead to the under secretary or one of his assistants. Vincent (or a member of his staff) would summarize a cable or point out a paragraph or two that the secretary might find interesting or significant. Having been at Hornbeck's mercy for two years in Chungking, Vincent was determined to see that Under Secretary Edward Stettinius and Secretary Hull received complete and informed reports on China,[23] where political and military developments seemed to be growing worse daily.

Vincent was accustomed to reading pessimistic reports from Chungking, but the cables that poured into the State Department in the winter and spring of 1944 seemed especially gloomy. Chiang and the Kuomintang were reported to be even more isolated than usual, and the chorus of criticism was now coming from all parts of the Chinese political spectrum. Attacks on Chiang's closest advisors, H. H. Kung, Ho Ying-chin, Tai Li, and the brothers Chen, were now coming from sections of Chiang's own army. "Younger officers" were openly critical, the embassy reported, because they believed that "the miserable condition of the Chinese Army . . . can be attributed to both Dr. Kung and General Ho."[24] In late 1943 dissatisfaction in the army flared into open rebellion when a group of young generals plotted to kidnap Chiang in order to force him to remove Kung, Ho, Tai, and the Chens from his cabinet. The conspiracy ended almost before it had begun, and the officers (estimated to number between two and six hundred) were arrested by Tai's agents; eventually, sixteen generals were charged with treason and executed. Although the plot was directed at Chiang's ruling circle and not at the generalissimo himself, it was symptomatic of the gradual disintegration of military forces which had once been loyal to the Kuomintang.[25]

Military dissidence was joined by geographical and political disunity. As Chiang's hold over free China grew weaker, the centrifugal forces of Chinese provincialism grew stronger. The old warlord Kwangsi-Kwangtung faction began to show new vitality under the leadership of Yu Han-mou and Chang Fa-kwei. Local strongmen in Szechwan and Yunnan were reported to be ready to join the Kwangsi-Kwangtung group if the Chinese government surrendered to the Japanese.[26] In Chungking, Chiang's political critics were growing bolder in their attacks: Madame Sun Yat-sen and Sun Fo, the "first family of the Chinese Revolution," now spoke freely to foreign reporters of the "fascist tendencies of the Kuomintang and Chinese Governments" and Chang Lan, the former governor of Szechwan Province and president of the Federation of Democratic Parties, "boldly published a pamphlet protesting Government dictatorship."[27]

Chiang remained publicly indifferent to the presence of a serious military and political crisis in Chinese life, and his every act seemed only to increase the likelihood of further criticism. Instead of dealing responsibly with the grievances of liberals and moderates, Chiang promoted the fortunes of his most conservative associates. At the twelfth plenary session of the Central Executive Committee of the Kuomintang, he engineered Chen Kuo-fu's election as minister of organization, "thus further strengthening the control of the CC Clique. Liberals both within and without the Party," Gauss reported, "viewed the results of the session as a defeat, for it had been expected that the need to offset recent foreign and domestic criticism of China and the Kuomintang by ostensible democratic reforms within the Party would result in some action which would outwardly give the appearance of liberalization of the Party. . . . The failure of the session to take any steps to meeting the mounting wave of criticism within the country [is] expected to increase political ferment among all liberal and dissident groups in the nation."[28]

As military and political conditions worsened, the Japanese intensified their campaign to destroy the Nationalist government. In April they launched a new offensive (code name ICHIGO)[29] designed to solidify their position on the Chinese mainland by opening a direct line of communication between Tientsin and Canton, while simultaneously destroying American Air Force bases in eastern China. The opening phases of ICHIGO were a brilliant success, and as the Chinese armies dissolved in defeat, American military observers feared that Chungking itself was doomed. American diplomatic officials felt equally helpless: "I confess that there is nothing that I can suggest at this time," a discouraged Ambassador Gauss informed the State Department.[30] The collapse of Chinese resistance seemed all but inevitable.

Vincent shared Gauss's concern but not his despair. Temperamentally, the two could not have been further apart: Where Gauss was sour and pessimistic, Vincent was perpetually hopeful. Where the ambassador saw only problems, Vincent saw opportunities. "Fortitude," "courage," and "intellectual resourcefulness" were the qualities he admired most.[31] "I must be . . . incurably optimistic," he once told Betty, . . . I look back at man's ascent from barbarism to his present state of intellectual development . . . and know that this has been accomplished through an exertion of will. . . . Man has not succeeded . . . through buckling under to circumstance."[32] With a confidence born of a belief in the power of human will, Vincent worked to find a way for the United States to save China before it was too late.

The way to rescue China, he still believed, was through reform of the Kuomintang. Roosevelt's policy of conciliation was a complete failure: The

$500 million loan, the visits of Currie and Willkie, the abolition of extra-territoriality, the meeting with Chiang at Cairo in 1943—all had failed to persuade the generalissimo to "put his house in order" and get on with the war against Japan. Now it was time for the United States to use the "stick" as well as the "carrot"; Chiang must be forced to liberalize his regime. Vincent was convinced that the hope of the future was still the amorphous group of moderates and liberals—the western-educated economists, businessmen, and academics whom he had known and admired when he was counselor in Chungking. If the T. V. Soongs, the K. P. Chens, and Quo Tai-chis, and the Chang Mon-lins were given a chance to govern China, they would bring energy to the war effort, transfuse new blood into the Kuomintang, and end the era of political discord with the Communists. The progressive elements must be given the chance to govern, Vincent argued, and that chance depended upon the influence of the United States. This was Vincent's recommendation in the spring of 1944, and although he did not know it at the time, the president was about to give him an opportunity to put his proposals into action.[33]

Although Roosevelt's attention remained focused on Europe (where the Allied invasion was scheduled to begin in June), he had grown deeply concerned about the military and political disintegration of free China.[34] He was not unaware of the revolts against Chiang's authority, but since there was no obvious successor whom the Americans could support, he saw no alternative to continuing his policy of comforting and conciliating the generalissimo. Unable (and unwilling) to go to China to reassure Chiang personally, the president decided to send Vice-President Henry A. Wallace in his place.

Wallace was instructed to inform Chiang Kai-shek that Roosevelt remained China's most loyal ally and that "the Generalissimo must . . . not let America down after America had pinned such faith and hope on China as a World Power."[35] Wallace was also to urge Chiang to improve his relations with the Soviet Union and the Chinese Communists in the interest of a united military effort against Japan.[36] "For the rest, Wallace was left to be guided by his perceptions. He had no authority to give promises or make decisions, only a chance to interpret and advise."[37]

The announcement that Vice-President Wallace would visit China (and Russian Siberia) was received with a mixture of surprise, concern, and amusement by officials in Washington.[38] Associates of Wallace believed that the president had decided to send the politically controversial vice-president to Asia in order to remove him from the public eye on the eve of the Democratic National Convention of 1944, leaving Roosevelt free to select a new candidate for the vice-presidency.[39] Others saw the trip as another presidential attempt to give Chiang "comfort in the absence of aid." "What is Wallace going to do?" John Pehle asked Treasury Secretary Henry Morgenthau, Jr. "Wallace is to go to China," Morgenthau replied. "In place of the goods?" Pehle inquired. "He is the goods!" Morgenthau answered.[40]

Secretary of State Hull and the men in FE were especially distressed to learn of Wallace's impending visit to Chungking. Hull remembered with displeasure the complications produced by the vice-president's tour of Latin America in 1943,[41] and Vincent feared that Wallace, like Currie and Willkie before him, would fall quickly under the spell of Madame Chiang and return to the United States as another agent of the Kuomintang.[42] To insure that the Wallace mission would not have an adverse effect on Chinese-American relations, Hull instructed Ballantine and Vincent to brief the vice-president on the critical situation in China.

Unlike Currie or Willkie, Wallace listened carefully to his State Department advisors and agreed "to be guarded in what he might say either publicly or in private conversation in China." He also offered "to have any statements which he might make carefully shroffed [sic] by the Department or by the Embassy in advance and his sojourn in China carefully programmed to minimize the possibility of difficulties."[43] At the same time, the vice-president informed Secretary Hull that he wished to have a Foreign Service officer accompany him on his Soviet-Asia mission, "someone with recent experience in China who knows the present Chinese scene and official personalities."[44]

In late April, Wallace asked Hull's permission to select Vincent as his State Department advisor on China,[45] and the secretary quickly consented. Hull ordered Vincent to keep a close watch on Wallace, lest the vice-president make "expansive" promises to the Chinese as he had to the Latin Americans the year before. "Vincent, don't let Wallace give everything away," Hull remarked. This was the only direction which Vincent received from the secretary of state before he left for Asia.[46]

Although Wallace's instructions from the president were vague, Vincent saw the mission as an opportunity for the vice-president to use the prestige of his office to persuade Chiang to reform the Kuomintang. As the symbolic leader of the liberal wing of the Democratic Party, Wallace's presence in Chungking would encourage liberal elements in their criticism of the generalissimo and such activity would persuade Chiang to make the political adjustments that Chinese progressives (and their American allies) thought essential. And to insure that Wallace would have a proper understanding of Chinese politics, Vincent started a campaign to educate the vice-president. In addition to oral briefings,[47] Vincent gave Wallace a series of memorandums that discussed the nature of Chiang's leadership, the problem of the Chinese Communists, and the future of Chinese-American relations.

The picture of Chiang Kai-shek that emerged from these reports was that of a "Chinese militarist" whose political philosophy was "the unintegrated product of his limited intelligence, his Japanese military education, his former close contact with German military advisors, his alliance with the usurious banker-landlord class and his reversion to the sterile moralisms of the Chinese classics."[48] Perched precariously at the apex of an unstable coalition of "residual warlords" and "provincial cliques" and threatened by political disunity and economic dislocation, Chiang's paramountcy in Chinese politics was described as "insecure and unsound."

The most important of Chiang's political rivals, according to Vincent and his colleagues, were the Chinese Communists. By the spring of 1944 it was estimated that the Communists controlled one hundred twenty thousand square miles of northern China and a population of over twenty-five million Chinese. Western observers who had been allowed to pass through the Kuomintang blockade into "Communist China" reported Communist military victories against the Japanese in Shantung, Hopeh, Shansi, and northern Kiangsu, as well as economic and political development in formerly primitive areas. "The policy of land confiscation has been given up," an American businessman reported in a memorandum that Vincent gave to Wallace, "and an effort has been made to organize the people into the most nearly democratic form of government that I have found in China."[49] Second Secretary of Embassy John P. Davies, Jr. heard similar reports from his contacts in Chungking, and Vincent passed the news on to Wallace. "Foreign observers (including American) who have recently visited the Communist area," Davies wrote, "agree that the Communist regime in present policy and practice is far removed from orthodox Communism; that it is administratively remarkably honest; that popular elections are held; that individual economic freedom is relatively uncurbed; that the regime appears to have strong popular support and that it is described less accurately as communist than as agrarian democratic."[50]

The reported strength of the Communist movement only made Chiang more determined to deal with the Communists on the battlefield. The generalissimo continued to demand that the Communists disband their army and incorporate their territory under the Nationalist banner, but the Communists considered Chiang's proposals an invitation to suicide and rejected them completely. An open civil war seemed inevitable. This development, Vincent told Wallace, was extremely dangerous to the

United States.[51] "Should Chiang attack the Communists," John Davies warned in another memorandum which Vincent gave to Wallace, "the [Communists] would turn for aid to . . . the Soviet Union. . . . A Central Government attack would . . . force the Communists into the willing arms of the Russians. . . . The present trend of the Chinese Communists toward democratic nationalism would thereby be reversed and they could be expected to retrogress to the position of a Russian satellite. . . . With Russian arms, with Russian technical assistance and with the popular appeal that they have, the Chinese Communists might be expected to defeat the Central Government and eventually to take over the control of most if not all of China." With the Americans committed unconditionally to Chiang Kai-shek and the Russians supporting the Communists, a civil war in China might lead to war between the United States and Russia.[52]

Because of the military and political significance of the Communist movement, Vincent and his colleagues recommended to President Roosevelt that an American observer group be dispatched to "Communist China."[53] The Communists would welcome such a mission, Chou En-lai had told Vincent in May 1943,[54] and American military and diplomatic officials were eager to explore a region that was considered crucial to the defeat of Japan. "In Communist China," John Davies had pointed out in a memorandum that was widely circulated within FE, "there is: (1) a base of military operations in and near Japan's largest military concentration and second largest industrial base, (2) perhaps the most abundant supply of intelligence on the Japanese enemy available to us anywhere, (3) the most cohesive, disciplined and aggressively anti-Japanese regime in China, (4) the greatest single challenge in China to the Chiang Kai-shek government, (5) the area which Russia will enter if it attacks Japan, and (6) the foundation for a rapprochement between a new China and the Soviet Union."[55] In the early months of 1944, Secretary of War Henry L. Stimson and Secretary Hull urged the president to persuade Chiang to permit the Americans to visit Mao Tse-tung's Communist capital at Yen-an,[56] but Roosevelt was unable to win the generalissimo's permission and decided not to press him further.[57]

Vincent was disappointed that the president had refused to fight for the observer mission and urged Wallace to discuss the subject with the generalissimo during their meetings in Chungking.[58] Although many of his colleagues (including the ambassador) remained doubtful that Chiang could be made to change his mind on this (and other) issues, Vincent was convinced that the generalissimo might come around if the Americans applied the proper pressure.[59]

99   A Catalytic Agent

On the morning of May 20, 1944, Vincent was driven by special limousine to Washington National Airport where he joined Henry Wallace and his staff (which included Owen Lattimore of the Office of War Information) on board the Skymaster that was to carry the vice-presidential party to Asia. Captain Richard T. Kight was directed to take off and soon the giant C-54 rose high into the clouds over the city. Three days later, after stopovers in Canada and Alaska, they landed in Soviet-Siberia.[60]

The next four weeks were spent touring towns and cities previously seen by only a few western travelers: Magadan, Yakutsk, Ulan-Ude, and Alma-Ata, among others. On June 21, Wallace and Vincent finally arrived in Chungking. Pei Shih Yi airfield was crowded with dignitaries: In addition to the generalissimo, Madame Chiang, and other important Chinese officials, all of the chiefs of the foreign missions in Chungking (save one) were present to greet the vice-president. Wallace, wearing a blue suit and carrying a Panama hat, alighted from the airplane and stepped forward to meet Chiang Kai-shek. Chiang introduced Wallace to Foreign Minister T. V. Soong, War Minister Ho Ying-chin, and the secretary consul of the Supreme National Defense Council, Wang Chung-hui. The generalissimo then led Wallace to the presidential limousine where Madame Chiang awaited the vice-president. At that moment, a white-gloved band began playing "The Star Spangled Banner," and Wallace stopped dead in his tracks. Chiang continued walking to the automobile, ignorant of the significance of the band's selection, and unaware that the vice-president was no longer following him. Suddenly a military aide "rushed up" and whispered in the generalissimo's ear and he came "stiffly to attention while the band finished the last strains of the National Anthem."[61] Having observed this charade with considerable amusement, Vincent concluded that "life in Chungking was as crazy as ever."[62]

Madame Chiang had invited Wallace to stay at the presidential villa during his entire visit in Chungking, but Vincent, remembering how upset Gauss had been when Wendell Willkie refused to meet with him at the embassy, persuaded the vice-president to spend his first night with the sensitive ambassador.[63]

Although Gauss usually disliked presidential emissaries, particularly if they were New Dealers, his meeting with Henry Wallace was a great success. After dinner, the vice-president conferred with Gauss, counselor of embassy, George Atcheson, Jr., and other officials of the American community in Chungking. "The Ambassador unfolds the story of . . . Chinese personalities," Wallace later wrote in his diary. "Madame Chiang has continually been knocking the U.S. . . . . While she was in the U.S. the Gen. took up with a young woman, very beautiful who is soon to have a child. The Gen. is infatuated with her. Some of his advisors urge him to divorce Madame Chiang. . . . Gauss says Madame Kung and Madame Chiang used the U.S. advance of $100,000,000 as a medium of speculation using stooges. . . . Kung took the stooges with him to the U.S. and it will be a long time before they venture back."[64]

Military officials told the vice-president that "the Chinese did not fight. They ran away and the peasants attacked them because they had robbed the peasants. . . . The situation [is] bad."[65] Vincent noticed that Wallace appeared moved by the briefings and he felt confident, as the evening drew to a close, that the vice-president was more than ready to begin formal discussions with Chiang Kai-shek.

The meetings during the next four days[66] were tense and often acrimonious, but they did result in one unexpected and important triumph for Wallace and Vincent.

With Madame Chiang translating, and Vincent taking notes, the generalissimo and the vice-president discussed Sino-Soviet relations, the Nationalist-Communist conflict, and the desperate military situation. Through most of the sessions Chiang sat rigid, the commanding general dressed in immaculate khaki uniform buttoned to the throat. As Madame Chiang spoke, he would grunt softly, and his foot would tap nervously. Vincent had seen these mannerisms before in private meetings and social gatherings, and knew that beneath the glacial exterior there existed a violent temper; at any time Chiang might explode into a rage, throwing cups and plates about the room, condemning men to beating or execution. The hidden side of Chiang began to surface as the meetings progressed, when he talked about those men he considered his enemies.

Some were Americans. With undisguised anger, he attacked General Stilwell and others in the army and the press who had criticized Chinese military prowess. Recent defeats were due to "loss of morale," Chiang claimed, brought about by Stilwell's refusal to follow his orders, and the president's failure to open an "all-out" campaign in Burma. "The Chinese people felt that they had been deserted," he said.[67]

The president, Wallace said, was troubled by Chinese military disunity, which he believed was caused by the split between the Nationalists and the Communists. In America, the Communists were working to defeat Germany and Japan. Why couldn't the Chinese Communists be enlisted in the same cause? Because the Communists were too dangerous, Chiang replied. He was well aware that "the United States army was anxious that all military power in China be utilized against the Japanese," but the

Americans, he argued, overestimated Communist military skill, and underestimated the threat they posed to him. Once the Communists accepted Kuomintang proposals (which he described as "support the President, support the Government, support the war effort") the army would be allowed to visit the Communists in Yen-an—although they would go under his government's "auspices." When Wallace and Vincent urged again that an observer mission be allowed to go, Chiang said: "Please do not press, please understand that the Communists are not good for the war effort."[68]

As the series of discussions drew to an end, Vincent feared that their visit was almost a complete failure and he sensed too that the vice-president was beginning to lose interest in his mission. How could you deal with such a regime, Wallace complained, when the minister of war was a rabid anti-Communist, the minister of education was a "leading reactionary," and the minister of agriculture was an admiral who "knows nothing about agriculture?"[69] And Chiang was no better: "I like him," Wallace noted in his diary, "but I do not give him one chance in five to save himself."[70] Vincent was afraid that Wallace would give up trying to influence Chiang and return to Washington without achieving anything of substance. The observer mission, in particular, seemed hopelessly dependent upon a settlement between Chiang and Mao, unless Chiang could be convinced to treat the two issues separately. Time was running out; only one full day remained to Wallace's visit to Chungking.

June 23, 1944, was to be the most important day in the history of the Wallace mission, although neither the vice-president nor his chief advisor were aware of it as they arose early and drove to Chiang's summer residence in the suburbs. From the start of the discussion, Wallace and Vincent fought for the observer mission. The Americans were not interested in the Chinese Communists, Wallace asserted, only "in the prosecution of the war." That truly was America's principal objective, Vincent added; a visit to northern China would give the army information vital to the defeat of the Japanese. He pleaded with Chiang to separate the political from the military, and let the group go.

For a moment there was silence as Madame Chiang finished translating Vincent's remarks. Then Chiang spoke in rapid Chinese and Vincent knew the answer immediately: "That can be done. The group could go as soon as it was organized," Chiang had said, but they must go under his government's authority and be accompanied by his officers. Why Chiang had reversed himself soon became clear. The United States had been pressuring his government to negotiate with the Communists, Chiang said, let the Americans now pressure the Communists to meet his demands. He asked Wallace to make a formal statement to that effect when he returned to Washington. Vincent was still concerned that the negotiation of a settlement might hold up the observer mission, so, for at least the third time, he stressed that it was not necessary to reach an accord before the group departed. Again, Chiang's answer came quickly: "The military observers would be permitted to go."[71]

Vincent left the meeting elated but wary; Chiang might again change his mind unless all the details were settled before they left Chungking.

The vice-president and his party went immediately to the embassy where Vincent told Gauss the remarkable news. Senior military and diplomatic officials in Chungking were alerted and an emergency meeting was called. For three hours Wallace was briefed about the objectives of the group and the vice-president invited General Benjamin Ferris and diplomat John S. Service to join him in his last formal meeting with Chiang. Service, a foreign service officer on loan to General Stilwell, was especially impressed by Wallace. He "was extremely good about all the details," Service later recalled, "and I gained a lot of respect for his general bureaucratic experience and ability. . . . He understood exactly what we wanted. . . . He was very cooperative and willing to comply." Apparently, the entire United States government was agreed upon the group's importance: Waiting for Wallace at the embassy was a telegram from President Roosevelt, reminding him to "press President Chiang" on the issue of the observer mission.[72]

Later that afternoon the Americans again faced Chiang Kai-shek. The vice-president read part of his telegram from President Roosevelt and recommended that they discuss the agreement and the conditions "which Chiang had laid down." Vincent and Ferris took over the meeting and fired questions at Chiang. His answers were so favorable that the Americans wondered if they had heard him correctly. Owen Lattimore, invited along to assist in translating, reassured them: The generalissimo "intended giving the group the most complete liberty of action." "There would be no delays," Chiang said again, "the group could leave as soon as assembled."[73]

"We have made some progress," Wallace wrote in his diary after the meeting.[74] It was, in fact, a major American victory: Perhaps the only time that the United States had been able to persuade Chiang to act as it requested. Because of Wallace's and Vincent's efforts, Americans would be going to Yen-an, to gather important military data, and to see first hand the Communist revolution in northern China.

That evening Wallace and Vincent dined with General and Madame Chiang: "strictly Chinese dinner," the vice-president later noted, "only chopsticks."[75] Vincent had no complaints—at least not until the next morning.

As the Americans were preparing to leave Chungking on Saturday morning, June 24, Madame Chiang took Wallace aside and invited him to ride to the airfield with her and the generalissimo. Vincent was "pointedly excluded" from the presidential company and watched with concern as they drove away. This was the first time that Vincent had been separated from his chief during their sojourn in the capital, and he wondered if the unprotected vice-president might finally succumb to the charms of China's first family.

Chiang wished to speak to Wallace privately, he explained, because he wanted the vice-president to give certain important information to the president. First, he wanted the president to know that he appreciated his "warmth," "character," and "views" as well as Wallace's own efforts to improve Sino-Soviet relations. Then he became more serious. The president must understand that "the conflict between the Communists and the Central Government [was] not like that between capitalism and labor in the United States. . . . The Communists are not men of good faith, their signature is no good." He thanked the president for his interest in Communist-Nationalist negotiations but warned of the dangers involved should the United States act as mediator between the two groups: "No matter what the Communists say they will do," Chiang pointed out, "it will not be carried out, in which case the president's prestige would suffer a great loss."[76]

The generalissimo also expressed his concern about his relationship with President Roosevelt. How could the two leaders have "closer cooperation and understanding?" Chiang asked. He was quick to suggest his own answer. Speaking openly of his dissatisfaction with the army and the embassy he wished that Roosevent would appoint "a personal representative" to "handle both political and military matters." There were simply "too many channels through the State Department."[77]

Finally, Chiang asked Wallace to reassure the president about the situation in China. "Things are not today as bad as . . . feared," he said. "The Generalissimo is shaping everything toward the democratic path."[78] On this optimistic note, the limousine arrived at the airfield. A few minutes later Wallace and Vincent bade their hosts farewell and boarded the Skymaster for their next destination—K'un-ming, the headquarters of General Claire L. Chennault and the Fourteenth Air Force.

As the airplane began its slow ascent and the cliffs of Chungking receded in the distance, Wallace informed Vincent of Chiang's message to the president. The vice-president had been impressed by the generalissimo's remarks. "It was very clear to me, from the tone and language of the Generalissimo, that he and Stilwell could not cooperate," Wallace later noted. "It seemed to me . . . that it was an unmanageable situation to have an American commander in China who did not enjoy the generalissimo's confidence and could not achieve friendly cooperation with him. The military situation in China was already critical. . . . Chiang . . . gave me the impression of not knowing which way to turn. This greatly increased the importance of having an American commander in China who could win the confidence that Stilwell had not won, and could genuinely help the generalissimo in the hard times through which he was passing. . . . I was deeply moved by the cry of a man in great trouble, and I was moved to start in and help him as soon as possible."[79] Vincent agreed with Wallace and they resolved to inform the president of Chiang's request for a new military advisor at the earliest possible moment.

In K'un-ming the Americans were once again involved in a frantic series of meetings and tours, which Wallace interrupted occasionally by coaxing American servicemen into volleyball games. General Chennault invited him to staff conferences and the two became fast friends: "He is a swell fellow," Wallace noted in his diary," and is looking forward to the day when he can retire on a Louisiana plantation." Chennault's flyers were just as eager to leave China, Wallace learned: "Chennault says after they have been here two years the probability of them drinking and sleeping with diseased native women increases. It seems that more than 95% of the native women of easy virtue are diseased."[80]

Chinese troops being trained by Americans looked fit and ready to fight, Wallace observed, causing him to reflect again on Chiang's system of governance. "The Generalissimo, the Secy. of War, etc. have not really supported the artillery schools, infantry schools, etc. staffed by army officers because they know these men will prove very superior to the Chinese trained. They fear the men will upset the static balance of power in China. I am beginning to think they would almost prefer to lose the war than see the old Chinese system upset in any way. Definitely the Chinese and Americans have not combined to do the job *that* could have been."[81]

Finally Wallace decided to act. On the night of June 26, during an informal meeting with Vincent and Chennault's close advisor, Joseph Alsop, Wallace concluded that the time had come to send Roosevelt an urgent telegram, "describing the crisis in China and suggesting corrective action."[82] Vincent was immediately enthusiastic. His "sharp features lighted up," Alsop noted; "he seemed to take fire at the opportunity of getting something done. Vincent's intervention convinced . . . Wallace" and with Alsop the three began to compose a telegram to the president.[83]

For hours, Wallace, Vincent, and Alsop "batted [ideas] back and forth. . . . This was continuous hard, sweating work," the vice-president later noted. "It was a serious thing, and we were determined to do everything possible for the war effort."[84] Certainly, General Stilwell should be removed from overall command of the China-Burma-India forces, but Wallace was reluctant to make such a recommendation because he had not met with the general, who was too busy in Burma to come to Chungking. During the course of the conversation, Wallace returned to this point several times until Alsop began "to fear that it would prevent action." Although he knew from an earlier discussion that Vincent shared his dislike for the cantankerous general,[85] Alsop did not expect that Vincent would try to influence the vice-president. "Vincent was a bureaucrat," he later observed, "[and] bureaucrats don't usually like drastic measures. . . . I [thought] . . . that . . . the usual feeling that if you don't do anything at least you haven't made a mistake might well prevail and [Vincent] would make a big issue of this matter of Mr. Wallace's inability to see General Stilwell." But Vincent was hardly a typical bureaucrat, as Alsop quickly learned. "Contrary to my fears," Alsop noted, "[Vincent] affirmatively participated . . . and encouraged Mr. Wallace in his inclination to send this message . . . recommending General Stilwell's dismissal."[86]

The group then went on to the choice of his successor. The vice-president's "first notion was to recommend General Chennault, in view of the generalissimo's avowed confidence in him and the impression he had made on" Wallace[87] during his visit to K'un-ming. Vincent also admired Chennault and remarked that the United States would "have had no trouble in China if Chennault had commanded there from the first."[88] But Alsop, the general's own advisor, persuaded the vice-president to select another candidate for two reasons:

First, "Chennault could not be spared from his job in K'un-ming of directing the air effort which was then the sole support of the hard-pressed Chinese armies, and [second] . . . Chennault was unpopular in the Pentagon [and] would never be approved by the Army staff. . . ."[89] "The recommendation to recall Stilwell was certain to make enough row all by itself," Alsop argued. "If this recommendation were coupled with a nomination of General Chennault, the roof was quite sure to blow off." Wallace and Vincent "accepted these practical arguments . . . as being compelling"[90] and Chennault's name was removed from contention. In his place, Alsop suggested General Albert C. Wedemeyer as "a man for whom the Generalissimo had expressed admiration and . . . a logical candidate in view of his record and position as deputy commander in the Southeast Asia theatre."[91] Wallace and Vincent were aware of Wedemeyer's achievements, though they had never met him and, after some discussion, the vice-president agreed to recommend the general to President Roosevelt. Together with Vincent and Alsop, he began a two-part telegram that encompassed all their views, including a description of Wallace's impressions of the generalissimo and a detailed presentation of Wallace's recommendations to the president.

Chiang had finally given his permission to the observer group, Wallace informed Roosevelt, and went on to say that he "found economic, political and military [conditions] in China extremely discouraging. Chinese morale is low and demoralization is a possibility with resultant disintegration of central authority. . . . The political situation is unstable and tense with rising lack of confidence in the G-mo [*sic*] and his reactionary entourage."[92] Wallace was also openly critical of Chiang, whom he described as "bewildered regarding [the] economic situation, and obviously distressed regarding military developments."

But there was still a chance to save China, Wallace argued, "if the right steps are taken . . . . With the right man to do the job it should be possible to induce the generalissimo to reform his regime and to establish at least the semblance of a united front, which are necessary to the restoration of Chinese morale." Stilwell had to be removed from his command because he did not "enjoy [Chiang's] confidence"; the man to replace him was Albert C. Wedemeyer, a general acceptable to Chiang. Wallace urged Roosevelt to appoint Wedemeyer (or anyone else the president might choose) but to act quickly before eastern China was "lost."[93]

For Vincent, the K'un-ming cable was both an achievement and an opportunity. He had played a significant role in the preparation of Wallace's recommendations and his influence on the vice-president was decisive. Now there was the possibility that Roosevelt might be forced by the telegram to focus his full attention on the crisis in Chinese politics and American policy. For the first time since the beginning of the Wallace mission, Vincent was hopeful that China might at last become a subject of major concern to the White House.

Their tour of K'un-ming completed, Wallace and Vincent flew on to Ch'eng-tu, Kuei-lin, and Lan-chou, their last stops in China, and in July returned to the United States. During the final moments of the trip, Wallace decided to write another, longer report to Roosevelt, to make certain that he fully understood the critical situation.

The summary report was perhaps the most critical analysis of Chiang ever written by a high-ranking United States official. Indeed, it long remained classified, and when the State Department finally published it twenty years later, it was significantly censored. "At best," Wallace wrote Roosevelt, Chiang Kai-shek "was a short term investment"; he had neither the "intelligence or political strength to run post-war China." American policy should "not be limited to support of Chiang."[94]

Like Vincent, Wallace argued that the United States should support, instead of Chiang, a "new coalition" of "progressive banking and commercial leaders . . . the large group of western trained men whose outlook is not limited to perpetuation of the old, landlord-dominated rural society of China, and the considerable group of Generals and other officers who are neither subservient to the landlords nor afraid of the peasantry."[95] If Chiang still possessed "the political sensitivity and ability to call the turn which originally brought him to power," and this Wallace doubted, then he might be able to "swing over to the new coalition and head it. If not, the new coalition will in the natural course of events produce its own leader."[96] This was Wallace's advice to the president as he and his party returned to Washington on July 10 after seven weeks and twenty-seven thousand miles of "exhaustive travel."[97]

Although Vincent and other Foreign Service officers had successfully persuaded Wallace to champion their cause, the choice of the vice-president as their spokesman proved to be unfortunate. During the previous four years, Wallace's complex personality and support of controversial policies had alienated important groups within the Democratic party, and, fearing a rebellion should Wallace be renominated, Roosevelt permitted the Democratic convention to select a new candidate for the vice-presidency. Eleven days after Wallace's return from China, Harry S. Truman became Roosevelt's running mate[98] and Vincent and his colleagues lost a sympathetic ally in their struggle to reform American China policy. The K'un-ming cable and Wallace's summary report now joined a score of other documents gathering dust in State Department and White House files.

Vincent nevertheless continued his efforts to educate Washington officials. In late July, Vincent and Wallace called on Secretary Hull and gave him a detailed report of their meetings with Chiang Kai-shek. "Hull listened vaguely to Wallace for fifteen minutes," Vincent later recalled, "then branched off into a discussion of his problems with the Russians and the Poles." Only once did Hull question the vice-president: "Tell me, Henry," Hull asked, "did you have a good time?"[99]

A month later, Vincent tried again to penetrate the veil of Hull's indifference. On August 28, he sent the secretary a copy of a pessimistic report on China written by John Service, and added his own views. Vincent urged that the United States (in Service's words) become "the catalytic agent in [the] process of China's democratization." "[Our] Government is confronted with the question, not *whether* it should do something, but *what* it should do," Vincent told Hull. "We cannot simply hope for improvement in China; we must work for it. We do not wish directly and actively to interfere in the internal affairs of China but we should overlook no opportunity to indicate to the Chinese Government the line of action we think it should take to strengthen itself and discharge its obligations now and in the post-war period. We should make clear our conception of the type of Chinese Government which we believe will make possible our close collaboration with China in military, political, and economic matters. In short," he concluded, "we should use our influence judiciously and consistently, . . . to guide China along democratic, cooperative paths."[100]

Secretary Hull was impressed by Vincent's memorandum and he passed it and Service's recommendations on to the president who unfortunately continued to display indifference toward news of a serious crisis in American policy toward China.

The president ignored the reports of his Foreign Service officers in part because he did not trust career diplomats. To Roosevelt, the men of the State Department and the Foreign Service were the "striped-pants boys," rich, eastern Republicans who were "unfriendly" to his foreign and domestic policies. "Those career diplomats . . . ," he complained to his son, Elliott, in 1943, "half the time I can't tell whether I should believe them or not. . . . Any number of times [they] have tried to conceal messages to me, delay them, hold them up somehow, just because some of those [men] aren't in accord with what they know I think. They should be working for Winston [Churchill]. . . . [A] lot of the time they *are*."[101]

While Roosevelt's picture of a pro-British, anti-New Deal State Department and Foreign Service officer may have characterized some career diplomats with whom he came into contact, it did not describe the members of either the Far Eastern Division or the American embassy in Chungking. Of the eighteen men who belonged to FE in mid-1944 (excluding clerks and messengers), only one fit the pattern of eastern-based wealth and education; the rest were born in the Midwest, South, and Far West and educated at large public institutions. Most of the prominent members of the Foreign Service in China[102] were also born in mid-America and the Far West, and went to school at the Universities of California, Oklahoma, Illinois, and the like. Roosevelt had little to fear (and much to learn) from the men of the China Service, the products of a pro-New Deal, middle-income America.[103]

But there was more involved in Roosevelt's rejection of the Foreign Service view of China than his dislike of career diplomats. For despite his sentimental attachment to China (he liked to tell visitors that, because of the Delano family's involvement in the early China trade, he too was an "old China hand"), Roosevelt believed that the security of Western Europe—and not the territorial integrity of China—was vital to American interests. His background and upbringing inclined him to look east to Europe rather than west to China. As a member of the eastern social class for whom Europe was the traditional playground and model of government and society, Roosevelt sailed across the Atlantic on holiday twenty-one times[104] before he was thirty-five years old and had more than a casual knowledge of the French and German languages. As a boy he wore Scottish and British clothing, was tutored by a Swiss governess, and "spoke English with something of a foreign accent."[105]

While Roosevelt did display a fascination for Chinese stamps and curios,[106] he never visited China or expressed more than a token interest in Chinese politics, philosophy, or history. And despite his anticolonial sentiments and his early support for the abolition of extraterritoriality, the president often spoke as if he were a "treaty-port old China hand": "There are forces [in China] which neither you nor I understand," he wrote to a friend in 1935, "but at least I know that they are almost incomprehensible to us Westerners. Do not let so-called facts or figures lead you to believe that any Western civilization's action can ever affect the people of China very deeply."[107] His later policy reflected this attitude: At Roosevelt's insistence, China was placed at the end of the American economic and military supply route while Western Europe remained the principal recipient of American attention and support. Thus personal prejudice toward career diplomats and membership in the "trans-Atlantic community" prevented the president from a serious consideration of the views and recommendations of his Foreign Service officers in the embassy and the Far Eastern Division. The result, as one Foreign Service officer complained in another day and age, "was . . . a divorce between the people who daily . . . had access to information . . . and the people who were making plans and policy decisions."[108]

The president again demonstrated his contempt for professional diplomats in late August when he appointed Major General Patrick J. Hurley and War Production Board Director Donald M. Nelson his "personal representatives" to Chiang Kai-shek.[109] Vincent, who knew Hurley as a vain and reckless Oklahoma millionaire who had once been Hoover's secretary of war, was horrified. Although Hurley was a Republican, his relations with the president were good and, during the war, Roosevelt had selected him for a number of special diplomatic missions, all of which in Vincent's opinion, the general had "thoroughly messed up."[110] His knowledge of Chinese history and politics was negligible (on one occasion Hurley asked the generalissimo to give his regards to "Madame Shek"),[111] and the general's recent experience of Chinese affairs was limited to a three-day visit to Chungking in late 1943. As for Donald Nelson, he had never been to China, and Vincent and other observers saw his selection as a convenient way for Roosevelt to remove him from the War Production Board where his public battle with Charles E. Wilson was causing the president considerable embarrassment.[112]

Since Vincent had urged the appointment of a new chief of staff to Chiang Kai-shek, he felt almost personally responsible for the Hurley-Nelson assignment, and he called the vice-president to see if the nominations could be withdrawn. Wallace's reaction was less critical than Vincent's. "Maybe they won't turn out to be as bad as you think," the vice-president responded as he rejected Vincent's request that Wallace ask the president to select new candidates for the job.[113] It was the last time that Vincent turned to Wallace for help and the end of a relationship that had moved Vincent to hope for concrete changes in American policy toward China.

4

Alternatives

The thought of Patrick J. Hurley as presidential emissary to China had been in the president's mind since the Allied conference at Cairo in 1943. Grateful for Hurley's assistance in arranging the meeting in the Middle East, the president twice told his son Elliott how much he admired the general. "I wish I had more men like Pat," Roosevelt remarked. "If anybody can straighten out the mess of internal Chinese politics, he's the man."[1]

Hurley thought so, too. When he was first offered the position by General Marshall, Hurley accepted eagerly and rushed off to the State Department, where he told Under Secretary Edward Stettinius that he wanted to be made ambassador.[2] Stettinius said that the job was filled, although later in the week it became public knowledge that Roosevelt was planning to replace Gauss with Hurley.[3]

Meeting twice to discuss the China mission, the general and the president surveyed the political scene and concluded that the United States had no choice but to support Chiang Kai-shek. Hurley assured Roosevelt that he could fulfill his directive "to promote efficient and harmonious relations between the Generalissimo and General Stilwell [and] to facilitate General Stilwell's exercise of command over the Chinese armies" as well as handle any other problems that arose. This meant trying to unify "all military forces in China"—a mandate to personally resolve the Communist-Kuomintang conflict.[4]

Hurley's mission was a disaster, as Vincent had feared. Soon after his arrival in Chungking in early September 1944, he met the generalissimo and assured him that the United States "stood behind Chiang personally all the way." Chiang liked Hurley immediately, *Time* correspondents Theodore H. White and Annalee Jacoby later noted, "and a great friendship was born." Chiang responded politely to nearly all of Hurley's recommendations, even implying that Stilwell's appointment to lead the Chinese army (which Chiang had resisted) could be easily and swiftly made. Hurley left Chiang's residence believing that his mission would be a complete success.[5]

In reality, Hurley's mission was undone the moment he assured Chiang of unconditional American support. What the general (and the president) did not understand was that such guarantees did not make Chiang compliant but, instead, more unwilling to enact reforms. And as Hurley's relationship with the generalissimo grew more intimate, Chiang became more self-confident and determined to force Stilwell's removal. Sent to China to "facilitate" Stilwell's appointment, Hurley's tactics assured that it would never be made.

Roosevelt and Chiang haggled about Stilwell without resolution through September and October. The president had always maintained that Stilwell's caustic approach was incorrect, a view now echoed by Hurley who told Roosevelt that Chiang "reacted favorably to logical persuasion" and not to "coercion or ultimatum." "There is no other issue between you and Chiang Kai-shek," Hurley argued, suggesting that once Stilwell was gone, Chinese-American relations would again be harmonious. Roosevelt needed little convincing, and in October finally removed Stillwell and appointed General Albert C. Wedemeyer to command American forces in China.[6]

Hurley, who had Chiang's support and Roosevelt's encouragement, then turned to the second phase of his mission: ending the conflict between the Nationalists and the Communists.

Rejecting Ambassador Gauss's offer of assistance,[7] the emissary met alone with representatives of each group and quickly discovered the wide gulf that separated the KMT from the CCP. The Communists called for an end to "one party rule," and the formation of a coalition government and a joint military command. Chiang's proposals were more limited: The Communist Party would be legalized and its forces merged with the national army, but it would play only a minor role in a government still dominated by the Kuomintang.[8]

In a style that would have pleased Franklin Roosevelt, Hurley combined all the proposals into a vague declaration of principles which he then decided to present personally to Mao Tse-tung.[9] He arrived in Yen-an on November 7, a six-foot-two-inch "bull in a China shop" to use Vincent's words. Towering over his Chinese hosts, and resplendent in a uniform that sparkled with medals, he let out suddenly with a Choctaw Indian "Yahoo!" startling both Mao and Chou En-lai. This was just the beginning of what was to be an extraordinary adventure for both Hurley and the Communists.[10]

Mao and Chou continued to be shocked by the behavior of this bizarre American during the next few days. Colonel David Barrett, leader of the American Observer Group, tried to translate Hurley's speech into intelligible Chinese but found it an impossible task "due," he later wrote, "to the saltiness of the General's remarks, and the unusual language in which he expressed himself." That—and the fact that "Hurley's discourse was by no means connected by any readily discernible pattern of thought."[11] His discussions with the Communists proceeded in this confusing manner. After studying Mao's proposals, Hurley declared them "entirely fair," then went on to broaden them. In the end, the general's plan encompassed all of the Communists' objectives, including a "coalition National Government." Mao was ecstatic and the accord was signed and celebrated in a special ceremony.[12]

Hurley left Yen-an in a triumphant mood. From the beginning of his mission, he had been told that it would be impossible to settle the Communist-Nationalist conflict; but now he was certain that an agreement was about to be made. He alone had succeeded where Roosevelt, Stilwell, Wallace, and Gauss had failed.

His joy was short-lived. Foreign Minister T.V. Soong told the general that he had been sold "a bill of goods" by the Communists, and that Chiang was sure to reject the proposals. Depressed and angry, Hurley spent the next several days in seclusion, only emerging to tell colleagues how much he despised the Nationalists and admired the Communists. Kuomintang officials were "crooks," he told Treasury representative Irving Friedman on November 15, while the Communists were "the only real democrats in China. They had a fine, liberal program to achieve unity . . . [and] were fully prepared to cooperate." Hurley was still confident, however, that a settlement would be forthcoming "in a month or so."[13]

Hurley passed this optimism on to the president who showed his gratitude by appointing Hurley to replace Clarence Gauss as ambassador to China.[14] The general-turned-diplomat accepted eagerly and returned to his work.[15] This time he urged the Communists to accept Chiang's program,[16] but Mao refused. "That turtle's egg Chiang!" Mao shouted. "If

Chiang were here I would curse him to his face!" Mao was confused by Hurley's change in position. "We find the attitude of the United States somewhat puzzling," he told Colonel Barrett. "General Hurley . . . asked on what terms we would cooperate with the Kuomintang. We offered a five-point proposal [recommending] establishment of a coalition government. General Hurley agreed that the terms were eminently fair and in fact a large part of the proposal was suggested by him. The Generalissimo has refused these terms. Now the United States . . . asks us to accept counter proposals which require us to sacrifice our liberty. This is difficult for us to understand."[17]

While both sides remained willing to discuss their differences through Hurley, it was obvious to almost every official in Chungking (except Hurley) that his mission had failed. "Hurley's contribution has been a major fiasco," Treasury representative Solomon Adler informed Under Secretary Harry Dexter White. "He enjoys the respect of neither party . . . and has badly bungled things . . . . The Gimo . . . referred to Hurley as a damned fool, while the Communists . . . invented the contemptuous nickname of 'Little Whiskers' for him."[18] Most Americans agreed with *Newsweek* correspondent Harold Isaacs that Hurley "had fallen among men whose brand of politics is a little too finely spun to compare with the Oklahoma frontier."[19] One journalist thought Hurley's erratic behavior was due to senility: "With increasing frequency," *Time*'s Annalee Jacoby later wrote, Hurley "forgot where he was, with whom he was, and even what he had just said."[20]

John Carter Vincent and other officers in FE knew nothing of Hurley's misadventures, until the ambassador finally cabled a report to the State Department on December 24. What Vincent read disturbed him: Hurley claimed important victories on the military and political fronts. The Chinese and the Americans were at last working happily together, he said, and the Communists and the Nationalists were close to agreement. There was "very little difference, if any, between the avowed principles [of] the Kuomintang and the Communist Party." The "most formidable opposition to political unification," Hurley argued, came not from the KMT or the CCP but "from European Imperialists (and some American military and diplomatic officials)."[21]

Skeptical of Hurley's optimism, Vincent expressed his reservations in a series of memorandums in December and January 1945. If Hurley's attempt to promote Chinese unity was "basically sound," nevertheless the general's close relationship with Chiang was unwise. While Hurley (and apparently Roosevelt) believed it necessary to "sustain Chiang Kai-shek as President of the Republic," Vincent thought the United States should "maintain sufficient flexibility in our attitude toward the political scene to avoid embarrassment in the . . . event that Chiang and his government are ousted," a possibility that grew more likely every day. "Sufficient flexibility" would enable the Americans to quickly "support the elements most likely to carry on resistance" should Chiang be deposed. Unlike Hurley and Roosevelt, Vincent did not believe that Chinese resistance depended solely on the existence of Chiang Kai-shek; to act under this assumption would only make Chiang more recalcitrant and commit America's fortunes to Chiang's crippled regime.[22]

The ambassador seemed especially unrealistic in his interpretation of the Communist movement and the likelihood of a settlement between the CCP and the KMT. "The gap between Chiang and the Communists is wide and fundamental," Vincent noted; "Chiang is prepared to grant the Communists representation in the government provided such representation has no controlling or directing influence. The Communists want a 'coalition government' in which they, the Kuomintang and the so-called 'third parties' group will have an equal say."[23] Given these "fundamental" differences, and Chiang's insistence on the retention of one-party rule, it was unwise to trust Chiang's assurances: "The past attitude and performances of Chiang do not encourage optimism," he wrote in contrast to Hurley.[24]

If the Hurley-Roosevelt effort seemed doomed to failure, what alternative policies remained available to the president?

Vincent believed that appointment of an American commander of all Chinese forces was still a worthwhile goal, despite Stilwell's failure to win the post, and recommended a continuation of the effort in two memorandums written during this period. To be sure, it would be immensely difficult to convince Chiang to accept American military leadership, but the task seemed less arduous than relying on Chiang's willingness to make peace with the Communists, and the benefits of a unified command would be as rich as those that might be gained through a political settlement. "Both Chiang and the Communists would agree to [having an American commander]," Vincent wrote the president on January 4. "Such a command would make possible limited supply of ammunition and demolition material to the Communists which . . . could be effectively used. It would obviate political difficulties in the event of coastal landings adjacent to the areas under Communist control. If Russia comes into the war in the Far East, it would be highly advantageous to have in China an overall American command, rather than a disunited Chinese command." And an American command could also "serve as a stabilizing political influence in the period immediately following the [war]."[25]

There was a third policy which was being urgently recommended to Vincent by John S. Service, a member of the American Observer Group in Yen-an: that the United States work with the Chinese Communists without first receiving Chiang's approval.

The first contingent of Americans had arrived in the Communist capital in north China on July 22, 1944, one month after Vincent and Wallace had convinced Chiang to approve the mission. (A second group of nine arrived on August 7, 1944.) Service lived in Yen-an from July through October 1944 and returned for a month's visit in March 1945. During this period, he wrote approximately seventy-seven memorandums, copies of which went first to Generals Stilwell and Wedemeyer (on whose staff Service was serving as political advisor) then to Ambassadors Gauss and Hurley for transmission to the State Department. In contrast to Hurley's sparse reports, Service's dispatches were in the great tradition of Foreign Service reporting: They were voluminous in scope and composition and covered nearly every aspect of the Communist movement in China.[26]

What Service and others found in Yen-an was not a guerrilla base but the center of an almost spiritual revolution in Chinese life. "There is an absence of show and formality both in speech and action," he reported. "Relations of the officials and people toward us, and of the Chinese among themselves, are open, direct, and friendly. . . . Bodyguards, gendarmes and the claptrap of Chungking officialdom are also completely lacking. To the casual eye, there are no police . . . and very few soldiers. . . . There are also no beggars, nor signs of desperate poverty." Morale was "very high" and the people were busy and purposeful. There was no "defeatism" or "warweariness." In contrast to the Kuomintang, which had "lost its early revolutionary character and . . . disintegrated, the Communist Party, . . . has grown to a healthy . . . maturity. . . . This movement is strong and successful," Service concluded, "and it will not easily be killed."[27]

Service was also impressed by the Communist leadership, especially Mao Tse-tung with whom he had a long conversation. He later remembered how he was "almost taken off [his] feet by the warmth and fervor and earnestness" with which Mao argued for "American support and sympathy."[28] The goals of China and America "were correlated and similar," Mao told Service. "They fit together economically and politically." The establishment of democratic capitalism (a precondition for the development of communism) would be accelerated through large scale foreign aid, and assistance of such magnitude, Mao argued, could only come from the United States. "We can and must work together," Mao said. "The United States will find us more cooperative than the Kuomintang. . . . We must cooperate and we must have American help."[29]

Service's visit to Yen-an convinced him that it was necessary for the United States to develop an independent policy toward the Communist movement. Red armies were in control of "most of North and part of Central China." They held "strategic positions along and in very close proximity to all the Japanese communication lines north of the Yangtze River" and they had access to the major cities and railways. The Communists were politically strong and popular and it appeared likely that they might eventually overthrow the Nationalist government. Because of their military and political significance, Service suggested that the United States open a direct channel to the Communists, furnish "basic military supplies, train Communist armies, and assist troops with air and ground forces."[30]

Such military assistance might also have a beneficial effect on Chinese domestic politics. This "boosting of the Communists might swing the balance of political forces in far enough so that the Kuomintang would be forced to reform its policies, . . . to change its present reactionary leadership, and thus move toward the cooperation which would lead toward unity, democracy and national strength," Service argued. And if the Kuomintang still opposed reform, then at least the United States would have some kind of relationship with the political movement that was destined sometime to win control of China. "Our influence in China will never be greater than it is now," Service told his government; he called upon it to act.[31]

Although Service was a member of General Stilwell's staff (he wore an army uniform while in Yen-an and also informed Mao that he was there in a "military capacity only")[32], he was still a career Foreign Service officer and his reports went first to ambassadors Gauss and Hurley before they were sent on to the State Department. Gauss knew Service well when he was a second secretary of embassy,[33] and in 1942 the ambassador called him the most "outstanding" young diplomat he had ever encountered. But Gauss and other embassy officials (like the more conservative Everett Drumright) were extremely critical of Service's view and his suggestions for American policy. These negative comments accompanied Service's reports as they flowed to Vincent in FE.

Gauss rejected any unilateral attempt to establish a relationship with Yen-an and also opposed arming the Chinese Communists without Chiang's permission. Yet he was also the first to recognize that not utilizing the Communists would "hamper the conduct of military operations against the Japanese and perhaps prolong the war."[34]

Between Service and Gauss lay the crux of the American dilemma: To arm the Chinese Communists might ultimately destroy Chiang Kai-shek, whom the American government recognized, and the American people revered; but to ignore the military potential of the Communists might also mean a longer, more costly war. Was there any solution to this tortuous problem? Could the Americans sustain Chiang but at the same time employ the Communists?

The American effort to reconcile the Communists and the Nationalists had been born of this puzzle, and Gauss still saw it as "the most satisfactory solution to the problem." A settlement between the two parties, Gauss argued,

> might be both political and military in character, or it might be military alone. It might involve participation of the Communists and perhaps other independent political groups in some way in the National Government; it might be limited to the formation of some kind of coalition military council to deal with military affairs and coordinate the activities of the Chinese armies.[35] Or it might involve some arrangement under which an allied field commander might be appointed to the control of the armies of the two factions.

Gauss was aware that prospects of agreement between the KMT and the CCP were "not at present bright," but he had not given up all hope. "The bringing to bear of American influence on both factions may even yet result in a harmonious solution," Gauss argued; "the only alternative was a continued and progressive disintegration of the situation in China, followed . . . by chaos and a consequent grave impediment to the prosecution of the war against Japan."[36]

The line between ambassadors Gauss and Hurley and John S. Service was thus clearly if finely drawn. Both ambassadors saw a settlement as the only diplomatic alternative to disaster but each pursued the prize in a different way: Hurley advised patient persuasion under his auspices, while Gauss recommended using American influence to prod Chiang. Service believed a settlement of any kind extremely unlikely and urged therefore that the United States not commit itself to Chiang, but instead deal openly and directly with the Communists.[37] Which position the American government ultimately chose was left to the State Department and the president to decide.

Vincent was critical of all the recommendations that entered FE from the field. He thought the reports of John Service and John Davies (who went to Yen-an briefly in November and December)[38] "basically sound" but "in the more conservative atmosphere of the State Department it seemed that they overstated their case. It seemed like they were special pleaders. . . . From the point of view of these things being received in the State Department, they overdid it," Vincent later recalled.[39] Having worked closely with both men when he was counselor in Chungking, his opinion of them influenced his response to their views. Service was "level-headed," "hardworking," "efficient," and "responsible" but not "brilliant;"[40] Davies was "sensitive, "unstable," "intelligent," but "not wise."[41] They were young and impatient, and perhaps unduly influenced by the openness and benevolence of Mao; he thought that, as a result, their interpretations of Communist behavior lacked balance and objectivity.[42]

His own personal view of the Chinese Communists differed from that of Hurley, Gauss, and Service. "The Communist problem in China is difficult of analysis," he told an audience of the Foreign Policy Association in December 1944. "Because of the shortcomings of the Kuomintang Government, some people have ascribed all virtue to the Communists. Others see in them a grave menace to future China." He thought "neither point of view . . . correct." "The Chinese Communists are Communists," he argued in contrast to Hurley; "the leaders are and they openly profess belief in Marxian ideology. They are not simply 'agrarian democrats,' although they have seen the wisdom of adopting a program of agrarian reform as the cornerstone of their policy. . . . The Communist regime is [also] not as democratic as some would have us think. . . . They are not democratic in our sense of the term. [And] the Communists look forward some day to getting control of the Chinese Government [although] at present they state that this is not their objective," he concluded in contrast to Service.[43]

This interpretation of Chinese communism reflected Vincent's liberal temperament and philosophy. He saw communism and fascism as historically similar phenomena—both developed because governments were too conservative to correct social inequities. Thus it was the failure of the Kuomintang to adopt agrarian reform and equitable taxation which explained the growth, popularity, and strength of the Communist movement.[44]

Reforming the Kuomintang and establishing a liberal China was still the best cure for China's ills, he felt. Vincent's continuing commitment to the liberal alternative is probably best explained by his background and experience. Vincent (as well as Service and other young diplomats in Chungking) were part of a new generation of China Service officers. In the late nineteenth and early twentieth century, young men went to China to live their lives in oriental comfort and to escape the boredom of conventional careers. Few were sincerely interested in learning Chinese or acquiring a knowledge of Chinese culture or history. Nor did these "old China hands" care very much about United States-China relations or America's world role.

Vincent and his colleagues were different, remembered Ambassador Nelson T. Johnson. "During the period that I served as Chief of Mission in Peking," he noted, "the young men attached to my office . . . . were older than [those] that I began my career with in 1907. . . . They were the product of the universities and colleges of the 20s and 30s. [They] had quite a different slant on world affairs . . . from the one that characterized [my] group. . . . In my period, it was generally felt that the United States had no business intervening in the political affairs of a nation with which we had relations. . . . [Vincent's] group . . . had a more positive attitude . . . , a belief that the United States had a position in the world which not only justified but demanded that it take a more positive point of view."[45]

As an admirer of both Wilson and Roosevelt, and a believer in the social responsibilities of government at home and abroad, Vincent typified the "new China hand" Johnson described.

But background does not alone explain why Vincent (and so many Americans) believed that liberalism might provide a solution for China's problems. Many Chinese thought so too, and it was those Chinese who looked to America for political guidance that Vincent—the senior China Service officer—dealt with on a regular basis and knew best. Both professionally and socially, Vincent had close relationships with those Chinese in Chungking and Washington whom he referred to as "the American returned student ('Christian,' 'YMCA,' 'Modern') type of Chinese": Western in education and outlook, advocates of "cooperation with America and England." "The list of American graduated Chinese in the government was endless," Theodore White later noted. "It ran from the National Health Administration to the Salt Administration to the Foreign Trade Commission." In the 1940s, White organized a Harvard Club of China and found that it "included a larger proportion of the high officials of Chiang Kai-shek's government than a Harvard Club would have in John F. Kennedy's Washington."[46] These Chinese New Dealers, so much like Vincent in age, outlook, and belief, convinced him that the liberal alternative was still viable and vital, and explains why he continued to hope that the liberal forces might triumph. Thus, by 1945, Vincent could only

121   Alternatives

recommend again that the United States use its military and economic aid "to induce Chiang to cooperate, reform the administration of his government, and put China's maximum effort into the prosecution of the war."[47] No matter how many times he suggested it, Vincent preferred this approach, rather than relying on Mao's offer to cooperate or Hurley's assurance that a settlement was near. China might still be saved, if only the president could be persuaded to adopt the liberal alternative.

As usual, the president's attention was focused elsewhere. In 1945 Roosevelt was totally absorbed by the problems of war and peace. In the Ardennes Forest, the Nazis launched a savage counteroffensive which succeeded in breaking through allied defenses; Roosevelt and his military advisors now feared that Hitler's armies were again on the march. At home, the president prepared for his fourth inaugural and worked on his new budget, legislative program, and State of the Union message. In February he was scheduled to travel to the Island of Malta for a meeting with Winston Churchill, to be followed a few days later by an important conference with Josef Stalin in the Crimea. Such presidential activity left Roosevelt little time to worry about China, a state of affairs which no doubt pleased him, for by the winter of 1944-1945, the president had given up all hope of achieving Chinese military or political unity.

"From the long range point of view . . . we can do very little at this time to keep China together,"[48] he had written. Admiral Leahy last December and in January he rejected Ambassador Hurley's request that he meet with Chiang in New Delhi.[49] In contrast, developments were somewhat brighter in the Pacific, where the Americans were making a major effort. Japan, the president noted, "was suffering losses in men and materials . . . that are many times greater than ours. . . . Even the almighty is helping," Roosevelt pointed out in a reference to a "magnificent earthquake and tidal wave" that was then ravaging the Japanese coast.[50]

American victories in the Pacific, planned or providential, increased Roosevelt's commitment to "island hop"; American planes would attack Japan from aircraft carriers off the Japanese coast and from the tiny islands like Iwo Jima, which were now falling to United States Marines. China was no longer seen as a base of American military operations, and as a consequence, the China theater languished from inattention; only Ambassador Hurley remained fully on the job, still believing that he alone would achieve a settlement between the Communists and the Nationalists.

Hurley's efforts to bring the two parties together were no more successful in the first months of 1945 than they had been in the last months of 1944.[51] "The Kuomintang and the Communists are as far apart as ever," Solomon Adler noted in February, "and there is no sign of improvement. . . . The Generalissimo [despite Hurley's assurances to the contrary] does not desire unity and is struggling to delay a settlement. . . . Chou En-lai is leaving Chungking . . . a clear indication of how much they expect from the negotiations at the moment."[52]

From Counselor of Embassy George Atcheson, Jr. Vincent learned of the outbreak of fighting between Communist and Nationalist armies at Ningkwo and Wu-hsing, as well as in other places in northern Chekiang. Communist forces were also reported to have recently crossed the Yangtze River where they were "gaining new recruits . . . and increased support from the people."[53] Communist military activity drove Chiang to a point of frenzy: At a meeting of the state council he attacked the Communists "and damned liberals in general," his face red with anger, his voice and hands shaking.[54]

Hurley was experiencing his own frustrations. Disappointed that his negotiations were at a stalemate and suffering from rotting teeth, "deteriorating" eyesight, and "splitting" headaches, the ambassador began to take out his anger on members of his diplomatic staff whom he blamed for the failure of his mission. He accused John Davies of "sneaking off to Yen-an . . . to wreck his negotiations," and in a heated argument, observed by General Wedemeyer, he called Davies "a Communist" and threatened "to have him kicked out of the State Department." At the ambassador's request, Davies was later transferred to the American embassy in Moscow.[55] At the same time, Hurley told John Service to stop formulating policy and confine himself strictly to reporting, or he would "break him."[56] As if all this were not enough to intimidate his subordinates, Hurley ordered the embassy house repainted and refurnished and then ejected Counselor Atcheson and other attachés on only a few hours' notice. "Then he moved in in solitary grandeur, to share the echoing space with only his army sergeant orderly and the Chinese domestic staff."[57]

Although Hurley picked fights with other prominent Americans in Chungking (including General Wedemeyer and his Chief of Staff Major General Robert McClure),[58] members of the embassy staff were convinced that the ambassador possessed a distinct prejudice against Foreign Service officers and professional diplomats in general.[59] They resented Hurley's refusal to share information with them regarding his negotiations with the Communists and disapproved of his habit of sending infrequent and incomplete reports to the State Department. It was no surprise therefore that when Hurley announced that he was leaving soon for Washington to consult with the president, American diplomats made it known that they were "hoping and praying" that he would not return since he made "their life miserable and their normal functioning impossible."[60]

Vincent, distressed by the deteriorating situation Atcheson described, acted to end the paralysis in policy-making that was afflicting both Chungking and Washington. On March 1, he summarized conditions in the field and recommended an extraordinary action that he himself had rejected four months earlier. "The prospects for early political and military unity in China are discouraging," he wrote FE Director Joseph Ballantine and Under Secretary Joseph Grew. Since Chiang still refused to relinquish one-party rule or offer the Communists more than token participation in his government, it was also extremely doubtful that "unity of command" would soon be achieved. Therefore, the United States should "seek an alternative solution to the problem of effective utilization of all forces in China capable of fighting the Japanese."[61]

Vincent's "alternative solution" called for the United States to supply "arms and ammunition" to the Chinese Communists, without first asking Chiang's permission. Indeed, he recommended specifically that Chiang be told that because he had "failed to effect military unity," he had "forefeited any claim to exclusive support." This did not mean Vincent accepted Service's general interpretation of the Chinese Communist movement, however. Vincent still believed if Chiang were faced for the first time "with a positive statement" of American purposes, the generalissimo "might actually be moved to effect on a military level, the unity of forces for which we have been striving."[62]

If Vincent's recommendation was hardly novel, he was the first person in a position of authority in the State Department to suggest in writing that the United States arm the Chinese Communists.[63] He was not alone for long, however; unexpectedly, he received additional support from the embassy in Chungking. There, a group of Foreign Service officers under the direction of Counselor Atcheson reached similar conclusions independently of Vincent and cabled a nearly identical recommendation to the State Department at almost the exact moment that Vincent was expressing his own view.[64]

Like most Foreign Service officers in Chungking, Atcheson believed that Washington had long been receiving "an incomplete and non-objective picture" from Ambassador Hurley and with the ambassador's departure on February 19, the counselor and his staff prepared a dispatch designed, as one observer noted, "to indicate their strong disapproval of the line [Hurley was] following."[65] John Service prepared the initial draft based on a longer memorandum which he had written with his colleague Raymond Ludden on February 14,[66] but "the telegram itself was a committee effort." "There was very broad unanimity from the start on the general content of the message and the nature of the recommendations we wished to make," Service later explained.[67] "We all saw [the situation] in the same light."[68]

The Atcheson telegram, like the Vincent memorandum, suggested that the United States arm the Communists so as to achieve both military unity and a reformation in Chinese domestic politics. "By such policy," the embassy concluded, "we could expect to secure the cooperation of all of China's forces in the war, to hold the Communists to our side rather than throw them into the arms of Russia . . . , to convince the KMT of the undesirability of its apparent present plans for eventual civil war, and to bring about some unification which, even though not immediately complete, would provide the basis for peaceful future development toward full democracy."[69] To underscore the "unanimity" of view in Chungking, the telegram was signed by every political officer in the embassy (in addition to Atcheson) and received the "hearty endorsement" of Brigadier General Melvin E. Gross, Wedemeyer's chief of staff.[70]

There was some concern in the field that the message might be suppressed by obstructionists in the State Department,[71] but the Atcheson telegram received widespread support in FE and was quickly adopted as the department's position.[72] Vincent was impressed by the dispatch and urged "that it . . . receive the most serious consideration."[73] He also wrote a memorandum for the secretary of state in which he commended Atcheson's report to the president.[74] This was sent, with the Atcheson telegram, to the White House where a presidential aide ordered that they be "given to the President when Gen[eral] Hurley comes in."[75]

Hurley exploded when word of this reached him.[76] The ambassador told Vincent and Ballantine that he "regarded the . . . telegram as an act of disloyalty on the part of his staff" and that Atcheson's recommendations meant the recognition of the Communists as "armed belligerents," a course that would "result in the speedy overthrow of the National Government."[77] They tried to reassure Hurley that such was not the case, but they failed to soothe the irate ambassador. Hurley accused them of not understanding America's role in China or the policy that he had been executing at the expressed order of the president of the United States. He alone "had talked with the Communists and . . . had broken the deadlock between [them] and the Kuomintang," Hurley claimed. "Neither Gauss nor Atcheson had ever seen the Communists [nor had] they [ever] brought the Communists and the Kuomintang together."[78] The Atcheson telegram left him no alternative but to demand the removal of those officers who had drafted it, and he promised to take his case directly to the White House.

Given the president's traditional hostility toward the Foreign Service and his habit of totally ignoring the recommendations of his State Department, it was to be expected that Roosevelt would be sympathetic to Hurley's tale of sabotage and betrayal. But by mid-March 1945, there were additional reasons for the president's reluctance to change either his ambassador or his policy toward China.

On the day that Vincent wrote his memorandum recommending that the United States give arms to the Communists, Roosevelt was reporting to the nation on his conference with Churchill and Stalin at Yalta. What the president did not make public was the Soviet-American agreement on China, which was the price that Roosevelt paid to assure Russian involvement in the war against Japan. The failure of the president's war-time effort to make China into a "great power" had led Roosevelt to choose his own alternative of defeating Japan at a minimum cost of American lives. Since it was clear that Chiang's armies were no match for Japan's superior forces, the president turned instead to the Soviets for support. In return for Russian agreement to recognize only the government of Chiang Kai-shek and to enter the war against Japan within three months after the defeat of Germany, Roosevelt accepted the restoration of Russian influence in Manchuria and the preservation of the status quo in Outer Mongolia. In addition, the president agreed "to use his influence to obtain the concurrence of Chiang Kai-shek to the provisions of the agreement."[79] Despite his decision to give up China as a military launching pad against Japan, Roosevelt still needed an ally in the Far East. Once he had hoped it would be China; now in early 1945 he had decided that it would have to be Russia.

A change in American policy such as that recommended by Vincent and Atcheson might have destroyed the edifice that Roosevelt had so carefully constructed at Yalta. The reforms in Chinese politics suggested by the embassy and FE might result in Chiang's removal from power, and the overthrow (or the abdication) of the generalissimo would free the Russians from their pledge to support only the Kuomintang; they could therefore join the Chinese Communists and seize control of China. Having gone to war to prevent the loss of China to Japan, the president could hardly acquiesce in China's loss to Russia—that prospect threatened Soviet-American cooperation, the most cherished of Roosevelt's postwar goals. When these risks were weighed against the military benefits of arming the Chinese Communists, they must have seemed to the president to have been small indeed. Thus, Hurley had won his case even before he first presented it to the president.[80]

The Yalta agreement salvaged Hurley's fortunes as well as Chiang's. In his discussions with the president on March 8 and 24 Hurley learned the details of the accord and was permitted to make a penciled copy of the document. The president instructed Hurley to visit London and Moscow before returning to Chungking, in order to obtain British and Russian support for American policy.[81] Since the ambassador's relations with Chiang were especially amicable (at least according to Hurley), Roosevelt depended on Hurley to persuade Chiang to support the understanding reached at Yalta. In Roosevelt's view there was no better man for the job than the former secretary of war. To have sided with the embassy staff on the now irrelevant issue of the Chinese Communists would have probably resulted in Hurley's resignation, leaving no one to sell Yalta to Chiang.[82] Thus, the ambassador's resignation (like Chiang's abdication) would have threatened the agreement made with the Russians and the successful conclusion of the war against Japan. Roosevelt seemed to have no choice but to support Hurley and reject Vincent's and Atcheson's recommendations.

His position affirmed, Hurley moved swiftly against his enemies. George Atcheson was recalled from Chungking and transferred to General MacArthur's staff where he became political advisor. Service was removed from the China theater with Stimson's and Wedemeyer's concurrence. Third Secretary of Embassy Fulton Freeman, language officer William E. Yuni, and Consul Arthur Ringwalt "were all variously reassigned." With the exception of Atcheson, who died shortly thereafter, the careers of all these men "were slowed or otherwise damaged to greater or less degree by this episode."[83] Although Hurley was critical of Vincent as well, the ambassador was apparently too busy rebuilding his shattered embassy staff to be bothered about his critics in the Far Eastern Division.[84]

Hurley's purge of the embassy staff had a significant effect on the conduct of American diplomacy in Chungking. Service, Davies, Atcheson, Ludden, and Freeman were all China Service officers: Service and Davies had been born in China; the others were equally proficient in the Chinese language and expert in Chinese history and politics. These gifted officers were replaced by a Virginia banker who came into the Foreign Service from the Foreign Economic Administration and a professional diplomat with twenty years service in Latin America.[85] Neither man had ever served in China before; both were eventually appointed counselors of embassy, the first time in the history of the China Service that a Foreign Service officer had ever been elevated to the second highest office in the embassy without benefit of previous experience.

"The Embassy's reporting [also] became more cautious and limited" after the Hurley affair. "Officers reporting bad news learned that their confidential reports might be shown to Chinese officials . . . thus endangering their Chinese sources," Service later observed. "Some were called on the mat to receive a lecture, in mule-skinner language, from the Ambassador." At Hurley's suggestion the ban on American travel to Yenan was reimposed and the military "agreed that it would transport no one . . . without [Hurley's] approval." The Army Observer Group was itself "reduced to the status of collecting routine enemy intelligence and weather reporting."[86] Any hope for an American-Chinese Communist rapprochement dissolved with the president's decision to sustain Hurley and Chiang. It was "the last important decision of Roosevelt's life."[87] A month later he was dead.

Roosevelt died without ever realizing that it was his own policy which had largely contributed to continued military and political disunity in China. Roosevelt's program was a simple one: "The job in China can be boiled down to one essential," he once told his son, "China must be kept in the war tying up Japanese soldiers." The collapse of Chinese resistance, he feared, would permit the Japanese to seize Australia, India, and even the Middle East, where "a giant pincer movement by the Japanese and the Nazis could cut off the Russians completely, slice off Egypt and slash all communication lines through the Mediterranean."[88] To avoid this catastrophe, Roosevelt was determined to support China with every material and rhetorical resource at his command.

For Roosevelt, this meant support of Chiang Kai-shek. The president was well aware of the "corruption and inefficiency" of the Kuomintang and Nationalist government, despite his own statements to the contrary, and he had "no patience with the regime's apparent lack of sympathy for the abject misery of the masses." But at the same time he wondered "who could take Chiang's place?" "There's just no other leader," he concluded; "with all their shortcomings, we've got to depend on the Chiangs."[89]

Roosevelt thus had to convince the Chiangs that they could depend on the United States. To compensate for a military strategy that delivered little in the way of military aid, the president offered the symbol if not the substance of assistance: the half-billion dollar loan in 1942; the end of extraterritoriality; the formal recognition of China as a member of the Big Four at the Moscow Conference; the promises made to Chiang at the Cairo Conference in 1943 (especially the offer to train and equip a ninety-division Chinese army); permission for the Chinese to participate in the major economic and diplomatic meetings at Bretton Woods, Dumbarton Oaks, and San Francisco in 1944-1945. In addition, there were the comforting visits of a host of presidential envoys including Lauchlin Currie (who went to Chungking three times during the period 1941-1942); Wendell Willkie (whose presence implied Republican as well as Democratic support); Henry Wallace (the second highest ranking elected official in the American government); and finally, and most significantly, Patrick Hurley and Donald Nelson (whose activities assured Chiang of Roosevelt's continued approval).

But the president's real or token assistance did not have the intended effect of increasing Chinese military and political unity. Aid toughened Chiang but weakened China. Encouraged by Nelson's plan to boost the Chinese economy, Hurley's assistance in removing Stilwell, plus his assurances that revitalized Nationalist armies could "walk over" Communist forces,[90] Chiang resisted American efforts to reform his government or settle his differences with all political parties who opposed the Japanese. It was Roosevelt who was partly responsible "for the state of mind of Chiang Kai-shek," Clarence Gauss later recalled in an interview with historian Herbert Feis. "Roosevelt went overboard [in] his promises of what the future would hold for China. This . . . turned Chiang's head. His thoughts soared into the sky and he took refuge in grandiose postwar plans for China as a Great Power in the Far East."[91] "The image of Chiang as a Chinese George Washington, publicly maintained in the face of the counter-current of criticism, weakened the generalissimo's sense of political reality," Adam Ulam has also noted. "Under American tutelage Chiang . . . lost his skills as a warlord without acquiring those of a democratic politician."[92]

As Chiang's exaggerated sense of his own power increased, so did his disinclination to deal realistically with China's grave social, economic, and political problems. His failure to reform increased domestic criticism from Communists and non-Communists alike and destroyed all hope of Chinese unity. A policy that reassured Chiang thus contributed to Chinese instability. Such was the tragedy of Roosevelt's policy: Designed to "assist in the development of a united, democratically progressive and cooperative China," the president's program helped instead to intensify disunity and make future civil war inevitable.

In a larger sense, the president's China policy revealed the damages that are done when American political techniques are applied to a foreign country. In China, Roosevelt was undone by those very qualities of flattery and cajolery which made him such a brilliant success at home.

Roosevelt's conduct of American China policy came to an end on April 12, 1945; it was left to Vincent and his colleagues to deal with its consequences.

5

Intervention and Involvement

Four months after the death of Franklin Roosevelt the war against Japan ended in a blinding flash over Hiroshima and Nagasaki. "The city of Hiroshima no longer exists," Vincent's brother-in-law, Rear Admiral Allen E. Smith, observed upon arrival in September 1945." It is a leveled off layer of rubble, all caused by one atomic bomb." Conditions in Nagasaki, he discovered, were even worse; there, the "sweet repulsive stench of death" was everywhere. In this one city alone, "20,000 were killed by the atomic bomb [and] another 50,000 injured." The "flash, the gamma ray, the intense heat, the tremendous pressure wave, [and] the noise" had nearly crushed the city flat—homes and factories looked to Smith like black skeletons. "Nagasaki is dead," he concluded after a brief visit.[1]

Japan's agonies were over, but China's had just begun. Roosevelt's vision of a strong, united, and democratic China did not conform to the reality of a country left weak and divided after fourteen years of war. Two million Japanese soldiers and nine hundred thousand puppet troops still roamed through northern China and Manchuria, provincial governors and military chieftains with their own private armies threatened to secede from Chiang's empire, and the Chinese Communists with a regular army of over half a million men and an equally large guerrilla force were dispersed throughout central, north, and even coastal China. Chiang Kai-shek was hardly the undisputed leader of what Roosevelt called one of the world's

130

"great democracies."[2] In fact, the Nationalist regime was barely dominant in southern China, Szechwan, and Yunnan, while the Japanese and the Communists ruled nearly everywhere else. It appeared that the China of Roosevelt's hopes had died with the president.

Unfortunately, neither Roosevelt's death, nor the end of the war against Japan, freed his successor from the commitments made to Chiang Kai-shek during the war-time period. By virtue of Roosevelt's policy (and nothing else), China was a member of the Big Four and the United Nations, and Chiang's regime was the recognized legal, if not actual, government of China. Under the provisions of the Allied agreements made at Cairo in 1943, and Yalta and Potsdam in 1945, as well as the unwritten pledges which Roosevelt gave to Chiang, the United States was committed to help the Chinese regain all of the territory lost to Japan since 1905 and to provide China with military and economic aid in the postwar period. In theory, Roosevelt's China policy promised to help China achieve unity and democracy; in reality, the president's course meant the support of a failing dictatorship whose survival depended upon American intervention and assistance. In 1941, John Carter Vincent had feared that the United States was fighting to "preserve and conserve" a system of government "that is already spoiled in half the world."[3] What he had feared then was about to come to pass in China. As for himself, he remained committed to social and political liberalism, and in the late summer of 1945 he was given a new opportunity to act on his ideas.

On August 16, 1945, Under Secretary of State Joseph C. Grew retired after fifty years' government service, and Assistant Secretary Dean G. Acheson was selected to take his place; a month later, Acheson appointed Vincent director of the Office of Far Eastern Affairs, a position that was later designated the assistant secretary of state for East Asia and the Pacific. Vincent was the first (and as it turned out, the last) China Service officer of his generation to be selected for the post, which then included responsibility for the development of American policy toward China, Japan, and the countries in the southwest Pacific (among them Thailand, Burma, Indochina, and Malaya). In 1946, the Philippines and Korea would also come under its jurisdiction. Ten years earlier, when Vincent had first served in the Division of Far Eastern Affairs, he was one of only seventeen employees; in 1946, he was directing an office which had eighty-six members. He let able subordinates run their own divisions without interference, while he handled Chinese affairs. He was a "very central and active . . . figure," one former colleague remembered, calling him as well the State Department's "chief producing scribe on policy toward China."[4] As director of FE, Vincent continued to urge his government to avoid unconditional support of Chiang Kai-shek and remain detached from the Chinese civil war that developed rapidly following the defeat of Japan.

The United States began fulfilling Roosevelt's promises to Chiang within days after the capitulation of Japan. According to directives of the War Department, the Japanese in China were required to surrender to Nationalist and American armies—and to no one else.[5] (The Russians were directed to receive the Japanese surrender in Manchuria.)[6] Chinese armies were confined largely to south and southwest China, so the decision was made by General Wedemeyer, the Joint Chiefs, and President Harry S. Truman to transport Nationalist troops into Japanese-held territories in central and north China, before these areas fell to the Chinese Communists.[7] Within a few days, two marine divisions were sent to China to accept the Japanese surrender "on behalf of the KMT" and to arrange for the repatriation of the Japanese army.[8] Chiang asked Wedemeyer on September 20 to dispatch American troops to Shanghai, Nanking, Peking, and Tientsin in order to "aid the Chinese in disarming the Japanese,"[9] and soon eighteen thousand Chinese were moved from Chih-chiang to Nanking.[10] Marines and Nationalist forces arrived in Peking on October 5, and American military officials announced that they would transport four additional Chinese armies into northern China in the next few weeks.[11] Thus slowly, and without fully understanding it, the United States was rescuing Chiang not just from the Japanese but from the Communists, who were not included in the surrender arrangements. Civil war, with the United States backing Chiang, was now inevitable.

Vincent was extremely troubled by America's military alliance with Chiang Kai-shek, and when he heard that arrangements were being made for marines to occupy Peking, Shanghai, Tientsin, and Foochow in order "to maintain order and facilitate the control of the Central Chinese Government," he wrote an urgent memorandum to Under Secretary Acheson. "If American troops occupy Chinese cities to maintain order until conditions are 'stabilized,'" Vincent warned, "it stands to reason or at least it must be anticipated, that they would be prepared to put down disorder. There could be civil disorder, or there could be disorder arising from an attempt by non-National Government forces (Communist or otherwise) attempting to assume control of a city or cities. The picture of American troops putting down civil disorder in China is not . . . a pretty one." To avoid this "alarming" possibility, he recommended that "Chinese troops, transported to the cities by General Wedemeyer's planes . . . be used" to maintain order, rather than American forces. He also urged Acheson to ask Assistant Secretary of War John J. McCloy for a "precise" statement of the army's plans, and "if they do envisage occupation of Chinese cities . . . by American troops 'to maintain order,'" he suggested "that the matter be [immediately] placed before the President."[12]

Five days later, on September 25, Vincent learned that his fears were well-grounded. He again urged Acheson to discuss the matter with officials of the War Department, including General Wedemeyer who was now in Washington. Vincent thought the subject important enough to discuss with the president, and he recommended that Acheson tell Truman that "unless there are over-riding military reasons for carrying out these dispositions of American Marines, the plan should be abandoned in favor of occupation by Chinese troops."[13]

Acheson's response was quick in coming. McCloy told Acheson that General Wedemeyer believed the use of marines essential for the purpose of repatriating the Japanese. "The General had stressed that there were in China somewhere in the neighborhood of 4,000,000 Japanese, 2,000,000 of whom were armed. . . ," Acheson wrote Vincent on September 28. "The General thought that the principal evacuation would take place through the ports at which it was now proposed to have American troops." Since "the ports in question were those in the neighborhood of which trouble was most likely to start . . . the presence of American troops would strengthen the position of the Nationalist Government." Such assistance, Wedemeyer added, "was desired by the Generalissimo."[14]

Wedemeyer's explanation did not satisfy Vincent, and he remained critical of all Pentagon plans designed to enlarge or perpetuate the American military presence in China. One such project, which had the support of Ambassador Hurley and the Joint Chiefs of Staff, was the creation of an American Military Assistance Advisory Group for China, numbering forty-five hundred army, navy, and air force personnel.[15] Vincent was astonished to learn of the "size and character" of the group and told Secretary of State James F. Byrnes that the War Department scheme had many of the "characteristics of a de facto protectorate with a semi-colonial Chinese army under our direction." Since Chiang's past record had "shown a decided preference for military methods, rather than political methods, in seeking a solution of internal difficulties in China," Vincent thought it "not unreasonable to anticipate that American military assistance on the scale contemplated might encourage Chiang along this line . . . and discourage attempts at unity by peaceful means."[16]

In criticizing the recommendations of the Joint Chiefs, Vincent also stated his opposition to the Pentagon policy of trying to achieve Chinese unity by military force. It was his "general conviction," he informed the secretary, that "interference in the internal affairs of China would not pay dividends and involvement in civil strife in China would occasion serious difficulties . . . without compensatory advantages." War Department projects such as the proposed Military Assistance Advisory Group would, "unless restraint and judgment are used," propel the United States "into the field of intervention and involvement in China's internal affairs," and that would place the United States in an "unenviable and perhaps untenable position."[17]

Vincent's prediction that American military intervention in China would produce "serious difficulties" proved to be correct. United States efforts to unify China by military means in September, October, and November, failed either to disarm and repatriate the Japanese or insure Nationalist dominance in northern China: Indeed, military support of the Nationalists created the exact opposite. As soon as KMT forces arrived in liberated areas they attacked the Communists instead of receiving the surrender of Japanese troops. And the generalissimo was so encouraged by the American presence that he embarked on an ambitious campaign to reoccupy Manchuria, despite Wedemeyer's advice that the generalissimo "should first consolidate his political and military hold on North China as a base of operations."[18]

As the situation in China continued to deteriorate through the fall of 1945, American policy-makers began to reexamine the United States role in the Chinese civil war. General Wedemeyer suggested that either "all United States forces be removed from China as soon as possible, or . . . American policies under which they were being employed be clarified to justify involvement in fratricidal strife." Wedemeyer left it to Washington to decide which alternative was to be followed, but he believed that "unequivocal assistance" to Chiang Kai-shek in his war against the Communists was the only way to preserve American interests and those of the "free world" in China.[19] "If China were to become a puppet of the Soviet which is exactly what a Chinese Communist victory would mean," Wedemeyer wrote Army Chief of Staff Dwight D. Eisenhower in late November, "then Soviet Russia would practically control the continents of Europe and Asia. Domination of so great an expanse, particularly by a totalitarian power, would jeopardize world peace. We were determined to prevent Japan from making China a puppet power. It is believed even more important . . . that Russia not be permitted to do so." He therefore urged his government to "continue to provide encouragement and material aid to the recognized Government of China."[20]

Wedemeyer was not alone in his fear of international communism. The end of the Soviet-American alliance against Germany and Japan and the outbreak of the cold war had a significant impact on the development of American China policy during this period. Many agreed with Wedemeyer that the United States should support Chiang Kai-shek in order to prevent Russian expansion in the Far East. Assistant Secretary of War John J. McCloy (who had long been concerned about the "locust-like" presence of the "Soviet Colossus")[21] told a meeting of the State-War-Navy Coordinating Committee on November 6 that it was time for the president to decide "how far we should back Chiang in his efforts to unify the country." McCloy believed that the United States had a "considerable investment" in Chiang and argued that "Chiang's prestige would suffer" if the marines were withdrawn. "The Kuomintang must have our support," McCloy proclaimed, lest the Russians come to dominate north China as had the Japanese.[22]

Secretary of the Navy James F. Forrestal joined his colleague in the War Department in recommending additional aid to Nationalist forces. Forrestal believed that a Soviet-American confrontation was "unavoidable" and therefore did not wish to see the Americans withdraw from China "as a result of Russian pressure."[23] In late November, Forrestal and Secretary of War Robert Patterson drew up a long, detailed memorandum[24] describing the views of the War and Navy departments. They argued that "it was impossible to support Chiang against the Japanese without supporting him against the Chinese Communists" and the secretaries "firmly elected to accept the risks of the latter case." They urged that the marines be kept in China for the foreseeable future, "in spite of the admitted danger of involvement in 'fratricidal strife.'"[25]

Unlike much of official Washington, Vincent remained relatively unexcited by the cold war, whose beginnings he had personally observed. The previous July, he had been a member of the American delegation at the Potsdam Conference, the first time Harry Truman, as president of the United States, met Winston Churchill and Joseph Stalin. The Russians were "like people from across the tracks whose manners were very bad," Truman remarked before leaving for Germany. "Like bulls in a china shop, we've got to teach them how to behave."[26] To Vincent, Truman at Potsdam appeared both "defensive and sensitive that he would be slighted." Truman entered the conference room "preceded by a wedge of secret service people" that pushed Vincent against the wall. Churchill and Stalin, confident masters of the diplomatic art, "just strolled in by themselves."[27] Later Vincent heard that Truman "got very snappy with Stalin," lecturing him as if he were a schoolboy. It was clear to Vincent that the Soviet-American alliance was over and the cold war had begun.

He continued to have grave doubts about the new president in the months that followed. To Henry Wallace (now secretary of commerce) he said that Truman seemed "to use the right words" but did not do "anything effective."[28] In particular, he thought Truman wrong to challenge the Soviets in Eastern Europe, an area of vital strategic importance to the Russians and one in which they were temporarily predominant. Given the presence of an Eastern European *cordon sanitaire* against the Soviet Union after World War I, he thought it entirely logical that the Russians should wish to create a security band in that same area after World War II. He therefore did not think the Russian control of Poland, Hungary, and Rumania indicated a Soviet plan to conquer Western Europe.

Nor did he share the view of McCloy, Patterson, and Forrestal that Soviet Russia wished to dominate China. "The real question in Chinese-Russian relations," he noted in early 1945, "is not so much 'territorial' as political." What concerned the Russians was the political nature of the Nationalist regime and its hostility toward the Chinese Communists. If Chiang continued to persecute the Communists and threaten the Russians, he thought it likely that Moscow might intervene in the Chinese civil war to "seek security in fostering a satellite Chinese regime in north China and Manchuria."[29] Issues of security and national interest were to Vincent stronger than ideology; Russian history was a better guide to Russian behavior than Marxism-Leninism. A liberal Chinese government which was acceptable to both the Russians and the Americans was his answer to the Sino-Soviet riddle, as it was to much else. Just as he opposed unconditional support of Chiang to contain Japan during World War II, so did he reject any proposal that called for cold war alliance with Chiang to contain Russia and maintain postwar stability in Asia.

He also objected to Patterson's and Forrestal's recommendation that the marines be maintained in China, as Wedemeyer put it, to insure "peace" and achieve "world order."[30] "What is reasonable stability?" he asked in a memorandum to Under Secretary Acheson in mid-November. "Will American assistance be effective in bringing about stablity? What is the military estimate as to the size and character of assistance needed to bring about stability?" He had his own answers to these questions: He was very "skeptical of our willingness to utilize American military assistance to the extent which I fear will be needed to bring about 'reasonable stability' in north China and Manchuria." He believed that "reasonable security [could] only be brought about by the Chinese themselves, preferably through agreement between the National Government and the Chinese Communists." The marines might be able to maintain order but they could "not produce stability of any lasting character." Indeed, he thought that

General Wedemeyer's own pessimistic reports (which he was sure to bring to the attention of the secretary) cast "considerable doubt on the long-term efficacy of our present 'program' of military assistance to China."[31]

Byrnes and Acheson also had their doubts about the desirability of increased military assistance to Chiang Kai-shek. The American military presence in China had created a "flood" of critical comment in the press[32] and in the month of November alone, seven separate joint resolutions were introduced in the Congress calling for withdrawal of the marines.[33] Acheson finally concluded that the recommendations of the Joint Chiefs were "inadequate as a basis for judgment" and he asked Vincent "to prepare a more comprehensive analysis and alternative recommendations."[34]

The result was a long memorandum entitled "Our Military Position in China," which listed the pros and cons of four possible policy choices. Choice A called for the complete evacuation of American marines; Choice B, a continuation of present policy; Choice C, an enlargement of American military assistance to the Chinese Nationalist government, and, Choice D, a more determined American effort to bring an end to the Chinese civil war.

Of these alternative recommendations, Vincent preferred Choice D,[35] his decision reflecting his background and experience as a career China Service officer. He had become convinced through the years that Chinese political unity was of strategic importance to the United States, and he had been critical of his government when it had not acted in accordance with this principal. A politically disunited China had invited Japanese expansion between 1931 and 1945; now disunity threatened to draw the United States and Russia into confrontation over north China and Manchuria. Despite his own reluctance to involve the United States in Chinese domestic politics, he believed that America had an obligation to assist the Chinese in achieving a liberal, progressive government which could provide both political unity and economic justice for the Chinese people. "China [is] not a country where we [can] hope that conditions [will] improve and be stabilized," he told Congressman Michael Mansfield in October 1944, "we must use our best efforts to bring this about."[36] The "negative" policies of the past, the Open Door Policy and the Nine-Power Treaty had not prevented war. It was therefore time "for more positive measures" and he thought that the "most logical and reasonable" means to protect China and the United States from future aggression was "for us positively to [help] China achieve political unity."[37]

Choice D recommended that Chiang be told

> (1) that we consider it advisable for us to act more directly and effectively in disarming and getting the Japanese back to Japan; (2)

that, in order for us to do this, it is essential that there be at least a truce between the National Government and the Chinese Communist forces providing for a temporary fixing of troop dispositions in north China; (3) that we intend to communicate these views to the Chinese Communists in north China as well as to the Chinese Government; (4) that we expect Chiang and the Communists to utilize this period of truce to negotiate a firm and realistic agreement providing for fair representation of all political elements in the Chinese Government and for cessation of hostilities; (5) that we, or Chiang . . . will notify the other signatories to the Potsdam Declaration of our plans to act directly and effectively to bring about the early disarming and repatriation of Japanese troops in north China; (6) that we shall . . . speed up plans for shipping facilities out of North China . . . ; (7) that care will be taken in carrying out our plan to avoid benefit to either National Government or Communist forces in so far as territorial occupation is concerned; (8) that upon completion of the plan we shall withdraw in the hope that a political settlement if not already reached, will be speedily effected; and finally (9) that, if agreement is not obtained to our proposal, we shall withdraw the Marines from North China, deactivate the U.S. China theater and suspend any action on contemplated military, economic or financial assistance to China until a solution of its difficulties has been achieved.[38]

Vincent's memorandum and other reports submitted by the armed services were discussed at meetings of the secretaries of state, war, and navy on November 20 and 27. At the end of the latter meeting, Acheson formed "certain conclusions" which he summarized for the cabinet group and which contained elements of both Vincent's view that Chinese unity could only be achieved through a political settlement and the military view that geographical unity could be achieved by force. Acheson argued that "the Marines must be kept in China" and the United States should "prepare to move other Chinese Nationalist armies north and support them." At the same time, he recommended that the United States "should seek to arrange a truce" between the KMT and the CCP and "continue to support the efforts . . . conducted by the Nationalists and the Communists to bring about a political settlement."[39]

Acheson's exposition differed significantly from Vincent's Choice D. Where Vincent had argued that repatriation of the Japanese depended upon a truce and political settlement, Acheson believed that both could be arranged simultaneously. In Vincent's view, it was impossible to combine the military and the political approaches because the one affected the other. He thought it "illogical to arrange for a cessation of hostilities" and also "assist the National Government in introducing more troops into north China."[40] Vincent recognized that the movement of Chiang's troops into north China would encourage Chiang to continue his military efforts to

138   CHINA SCAPEGOAT

defeat the Communists and destroy any hope of a peaceful settlement; only later did Acheson acknowledge that his proposal contained this contradiction.[41]

The November 27 meeting adjourned without a final decision on American China policy. Byrnes and Acheson believed that there was still time to consider a number of possible alternatives before sending their recommendations to the president. Unfortunately, their time had run out. That same day, Patrick J. Hurley resigned as ambassador to China and in the turmoil that followed, the Truman administration was forced at last to define American policy toward China.

Although Hurley had been victorious in the Atcheson affair the previous February, he remained suspicious of Vincent and other officials in the Far Eastern Division who he believed were still working to subvert his mission to China.[42] By the fall of 1945 he was convinced that his government had "decided not to continue what President Roosevelt outlined as the long range policy of the United States in . . . China,"[43] and he returned to Washington to do battle with his "enemies." Secretary Byrnes attempted to reassure the excitable ambassador that the State Department supported his efforts, but Hurley remained unconvinced. He charged that career diplomats in Chungking and Washington had betrayed the United States by serving the cause of the Chinese Communists.[44]

President Truman was furious when word reached him of Hurley's resignation: "See what a son-of-a-bitch did to me," he told a cabinet luncheon, then showed his colleagues the story which had come over the White House wire service ticker. The scheduled agenda was canceled and the Hurley affair and United States China policy became the principal topics of discussion.[45]

The participants were divided in their concerns: The president, obsessed by the cold war, was worried that the Chinese Communists were receiving Russian arms. Something had to be done, Truman argued; unless the United States "took a strong stand . . . Russia would take the place of Japan in the Far East." Secretary of State Byrnes was more concerned about the unfinished business of World War II: There were still more than seven hundred thousand Japanese soldiers and one hundred thousand civilians wandering through northern China. He felt that the United States was obligated to disarm the Japanese and assist the Nationalists in taking control. But once that was accomplished, Byrnes said, the United States "should stand pat and not give Chiang anything whatsoever until he agreed to come to terms with the Chinese Communists." Clearly, Vincent's memorandums on the dangers of American involvement in the Chinese civil war had made an impression on the secretary.[46]

What should be done about Hurley? someone asked. Secretary of Agriculture Clinton P. Anderson suggested that a dramatic appointment would "steal the thunder away from Hurley" and urged Truman to send General George C. Marshall "on a fact-finding mission to China."[47] Truman agreed to ask the general and a short time later he agreed.[48] Just what the general was to do in China became the subject of intense debate between the State and War departments during the next two weeks.

The diplomats and the soldiers disagreed about the seriousness of the cold war and how it affected Chinese affairs. Vincent and his colleagues in FE did not expect the Russians to move into China on the backs of the Communists. Therefore he prepared a memorandum based on Choice D: It called for a truce between Nationalist and Communist forces and the convocation of a national conference to negotiate "a peaceful solution." If a representative government was established, he wrote further, the United States was prepared to help rebuild the war-torn nation.[49]

Marshall, on the other hand, believed that the Chinese Communists were a "Trojan horse" which would allow the Soviet Union to dominate China. The Japanese must be repatriated quickly and the Nationalists reestablished in north China and Manchuria. Chiang's troops should be moved now, Marshall argued, a political conference could come later. This was the reverse of Vincent's recommendation.[50]

Vincent saw this immediately and inserted into the Pentagon memorandum an amendment which would prevent the transport of Nationalist troops into areas (like north China) if their presence should jeopardize the negotiation of a political settlement. He knew full well that Chiang would never negotiate so long as the United States supported his troops against the Communists. Acheson and Byrnes approved the changes Vincent made and returned the document to the War Department.[51]

But Marshall again rejected Vincent's proposals. He deleted Vincent's amendment entirely, on the grounds that any delay in moving Chiang's troops would only aid the Communists. Then, in blistering language, he and his aides called United States policy "vague" and "indecisive" and called for the creation of a policy that was "firm and unequivocal."[52]

The differences between the State and War Department versions of the Marshall directive were finally "resolved" during discussions between Byrnes and Marshall (and their advisors) on December 9, 11, and 14. Despite Vincent's warnings about the effect of troop movements on the negotiations, it was agreed that the United States would transport Chinese troops into Manchuria "to take control of that area" and that "arrangements should go forward to move additional forces as needed into North China in order that the Japanese can be removed and stability established." The actual movement of these last forces would "await negotiations" between Marshall and Nationalist and Communist representatives.[53] In the latter, the general agreed to "do his best to influence the Generalissimo to make reasonable concessions" in the hope that a united government might be established.[54]

One final problem remained. What should the government do, if a reasonable political settlement was accepted by the Communists but rejected by the Nationalists? Was the United States prepared to deal directly with the Communists?

Byrnes and Vincent had discussed this possibility, and Vincent recommended that if the discussions should break down "due to the stubbornness of Chiang Kai-shek" then the United States should "proceed as rapidly as possible with the evacuation of Japanese troops," despite the fact that such a course would mean that Chinese Communist troops would occupy the areas from which the Japanese had withdrawn.[55]

Marshall also rejected this proposal. If the United States abandoned the generalissimo, the general argued, China would remain "divided," and Manchuria would become a Russian satellite: These "tragic" developments would mean the "defeat" of America's war-time objectives. Therefore, "it would still be necessary for the U.S. Government to continue to back the National Government . . . [and] the Generalissimo."[56] Truman and Byrnes finally accepted the general's position, and Marshall was assured that he had the president's confidence and support. Marshall was satisfied at last.

The creation of the Marshall directive was a triumph for the American military and the general himself. Marshall had asked for and received the kind of specific military instructions which had long been requested by Wedemeyer and the Joint Chiefs of Staff. The marines were to stay in China indefinitely (as McCloy, Patterson, and Forrestal had recommended) and the Americans were to continue to transport Nationalist forces into Manchuria and north China (subject to the general's orders). Marshall could now give Chiang "sufficiently definite data on which to calculate the troops available to him" to take control of those parts of China still held by the Japanese.[57]

In addition to receiving absolute control over the disposition of United States forces, the general was also granted unlimited authority in the conduct of political negotiations. All previous discussions between

American and Chinese officials were suspended and the president ordered that hereafter "all discussions and negotiations with the Chinese in this country . . . [must] be initiated . . . and carried on only in complete coordination" with Marshall and his representatives.[58] The general was also given the right to bypass the State Department in communicating with Truman: As the president's special emissary, Marshall's message would be sent directly to Under Secretary Acheson (instead of going first to FE). Acheson would then pass the reports on to the White House.[59] Thus, by the eve of his departure, Marshall had nearly total dominion over the American military and diplomatic establishment in China.

Unfortunately, the general's understanding of American policy was not as great as his control over its instruments. Marshall did not yet understand that American military and political efforts in China were incompatible. Returning Manchuria and north China to Nationalist control (if one can call Chiang's tenuous prewar hold on these areas "control") did not contribute to unity and stability in China: On the contrary, it only made Chiang more eager to wage war against the Communists. "Transporting troops to north China . . . will not be a satisfactory solution," Vincent warned on December 9, "because it will not prevent civil war."[60] Indeed, the transportation of Nationalist troops made permanent civil war inevitable. Truman and Marshall were still committed to Roosevelt's goal of a geographically united China under Chiang Kai-shek (directed now against Russia instead of Japan). They did not realize that their program would only contribute to further disorder and disunity. Only later, after nearly seven months in China, would Marshall come to understand the contradictions in American policy and act to contain their effects—but by then it was too late to prevent the outbreak of the national civil war which the United States had inadvertently helped to precipitate.

General Marshall's education in Chinese politics began on December 18, 1945, when he arrived in Chungking. The general set up his center of operations in a western-style villa called "Happiness Gardens"[61] and began a series of discussions with representatives of China's major political groups.

The name of his residence was a good omen: Within a few days Marshall had arranged an armistice between the Nationalists and the Communists and established an agency (the Executive Headquarters) to enforce the truce. He next persuaded Chiang to permit the convocation of the Political Consultative Conference (PCC) which had been called to draft recommendations for government reorganization. After only a brief period in China, it appeared that Marshall's mission had been successful: Civil war had been averted and the Chinese seemed to be on the verge of establishing a new political democracy. Proud of his accomplishments, Marshall returned to Washington in March to arrange for economic and military assistance for Chiang's government.[62]

Unfortunately, Marshall's achievements were more nominal than real. Although Chiang agreed to respect and support the resolutions of the PCC he was unable (or unwilling) to control the powerful conservative clique within the Kuomintang. While the Central Executive Committee of the Kuomintang met to discuss the PCC program, reactionary forces led by the brothers Chen "denounced the agreements and refused their assent to a new democratic government."[63] Even more ominous were a series of riots and demonstrations that erupted throughout February: At the order of Tai Li and the Chens, Nationalist secret police broke into Communist Party headquarters in Chungking, disrupted meetings held to celebrate the work of the PCC, and assaulted members of the liberal Democratic League. The generalissimo displayed indifference toward the activities of his gestapo and during one especially violent episode actually left the capital for a visit to Nanking.[64] The Central Executive Committee later approved the PCC resolutions but with such significant modifications that the Communists and the Democratic League publicly expressed doubt that government reorganization would ever take place.[65]

The American effort to end civil strife in China received its most critical setback in the spring of 1946 when fighting broke out again in Manchuria. The gradual withdrawal of Russian forces and the arrival of Nationalist troops on American transport planes led Chiang to renew his campaign to destroy the Communists on the battlefield. American economic and military assistance during the previous months was also a significant factor in the generalissimo's decision. Between August 1945 and March 1946, the United States gave the Nationalist Government over $600 million in lend lease aid and transported more than 145,000 Kuomintang troops into Manchuria.[66] In February and March, Washington announced that it would establish an American Military Assistance Advisory Group in China and also transfer 271 naval craft (and other surplus property) to the Chinese. At the same time, Chiang learned that Marshall was arranging for the continuation of lend lease and grants for agriculture, transportation, and telecommunications. The Export-Import Bank was also considering loaning China $500 million.[67] "Under these circumstances and with this backing," Joyce and Gabriel Kolko have noted, "it is not surprising that Chiang opted for a military solution to his internal problems."[68]

Marshall returned to China in mid-April to find the political and military edifice he had constructed in January and February a shambles. Once again, the general tried to bring a halt to the fighting. The Communists, in retreat after a series of defeats at the hands of Chiang's American-trained New First and New Sixth Armies, agreed to reopen discussions with the Nationalists but Chiang refused, on the grounds that he could not command his own generals.[69] Hoping to get "control of the situation," Chiang announced that he would go to Manchuria to stop the fighting. Marshall was encouraged by what he thought were Chiang's peaceful intentions and offered him the use of his own airplane to make the trip. What resulted was a personal disaster for the American envoy.

In spite of Chiang's statements to Marshall, the generalissimo took no action to stop the advance of his troops in Manchuria. On the contrary, his presence in Mukden at the time of the capture of the Communist stronghold at Changchun "made it appear that his journey was timed to coincide with a previously planned military triumph [and] his use of Marshall's official plane for his flight to Manchuria conveyed the impression of Marshall's close connection with the trip."[70] The fighting continued for two more months until June 7, 1946, when Marshall was able to get both sides to agree to another cease-fire.[71] This truce lasted only twenty-three days.

Marshall's failure left him "deathly tired" and discouraged.[72] Both sides now viewed him with suspicion and mistrust: Nationalist officials believed that his "advice regarding cooperation with the Communists had proved unworkable," and the Communists were publicly attacking the general because of America's assistance to Chiang Kai-shek.[73] Neither Marshall, nor John Leighton Stuart, the respected president of Yenching University who was assisting Marshall in his discussions with the generalissimo,[74] could persuade Chiang to end hostilities against the Communists. They warned that the United States would not support the Nationalists in a "great war" and that only through a political settlement could Chiang's predominance be assured.[75] But their efforts were futile: The "irreconcilable members" of the Kuomintang who believed that "the Communists could be destroyed with very little difficulty" were still "firmly in the saddle" and Chiang apparently shared their views; in June, he told Marshall to be patient: In time victory like a "ripe apple will fall into our laps."[76]

By July, Marshall had concluded that his "resources" were "exhausted," and fearing a loss of "perspective," asked Acheson and Vincent for a "frank" appraisal of "present developments" and future problems.[77] It was the first time in eight months that the general had turned to the State

Department for advice. "Never since the days of the Roman pro-Consuls had a single man held . . . such personal responsibility. . . ," Theodore White later noted. "All relations between the U.S. and China existed in the vest pocket of George Marshall."[78] Cut off from a full flow of information, Acheson and Vincent could tell Marshall little that he had not already learned for himself.

"The basic difficulty," they cabled Marshall on July 4, "is the absence of mutual trust, not only . . . between the Kuomintang and the Communists but also . . . between the two parties and the Chinese people who . . . are distrustful of the motives of both parties." The way to restore "trust," Acheson and Vincent suggested, was to revive the negotiations which Marshall had been sponsoring; the general should "obtain agreement to [a] meeting of a high level group to discuss [a] political solution" based on the PCC resolutions. Both still believed that each faction was susceptible to American pressure: The Communists, because they were "over-extended militarily," the Nationalists, because they "wished to avoid responsibility for jeopardizing the success of [Marshall's] mission." The reopening of discussions would "calm those who fear [an] early outbreak of civil war and also act as a brake on [the] actions of diehards in each [group]."[79] Nevertheless, the general should prepare himself for one of two eventualities: "a stalemate without civil war" or "a breakdown resulting in civil war."[80]

If a "stalemate" should develop, they recommended that Marshall "maintain contact with both groups but relax for a time our efforts at bringing them together for agreement." A pause in the discussions might "bring wiser counsels to the fore. . . ." But "if the stalemate is clearly due to Kuomintang intransigence" then American "material support" might be withheld. In the case of civil war, the United States should continue to recognize the Nationalist government but "consider withholding support and withdrawing American forces."[81]

Vincent's cable to Marshall was again a restatement of the view of Chinese politics and American policy which he had held long before the general went to China and which he was to hold long after Marshall's mission ended. Despite the outbreak of civil war in the summer of 1946, Vincent believed the effort to create political unity in China to be the best alternative available to the United States. Giving substantial material support to a Chinese government engaged in large-scale civil war meant only "trouble, trouble, trouble" for the United States, but leaving China in a state of chaos was also a threat to America's vital interests in the Far East.[82] Therefore, Vincent would "still rather have [his] money on General Marshall. . . ." The general's "very presence in China, he told Under

Secretary of State Will Clayton, "irrespective of the progress being made in negotiations, [was] a moderating, if not stabilizing influence. What he can't accomplish today he may be able to accomplish tomorrow or next week." He recommended that his government "bear and stay with the situation, trying to avoid seeing it as all black and white" until it was "possible for an advancement of General Marshall's mission."[83]

Vincent now worked to limit United States military involvement in the Chinese civil war and at the same time tried to convince the Nationalist government to settle its differences with the Communists. It was a mission that he frankly enjoyed. "I admit [that] I should have been an evangelist," he once wrote Betty, "I love 'bringing people around.'"[84] Ironically it earned him some powerful enemies who would later come to haunt him.

The first group of adversaries he confronted were his colleagues in the military bureaucracy. President Truman had agreed in principle to the creation of a Military Assitance Advisory Group in China (MAGIC)[85] and the Pentagon hoped to establish a large and ambitious organization, despite Vincent's warning that their program might "propel" the United States "into the field of intervention and involvement in China's internal affairs." What was the group's real purpose? Vincent once asked Acheson. "Is it going out solely to please the Chinese? . . . is it going out . . . to reinforce our security by creating for ourselves a military position in China? or . . . is it going out . . . to assist in the creation of a unified, peaceful, and relatively strong China?" He preferred "the latter conception of the Group" and in early January he was able to persuade Secretary Byrnes to adopt his view as the official State Department position toward MAGIC.[86]

The State Department opposed the creation of a military advisory group of approximately forty-five hundred Americans, Vincent wrote to the State-War-Navy Coordinating Committee on behalf of Secretary Byrnes on January 3, 1946, "because the size and contemplated activities of the Group [were] not in conformity with its 'advisory' character." The Joint Chiefs of Staff were not creating an "advisory group" but a "military training group which would permeate throughout the Chinese Army on an operational level." If the War Department truly wished to create an advisory group, Vincent suggested, the group should consist of a few hundred individuals and should function only on a "military staff level." The State Department recommended therefore that the Joint Chiefs of Staff revise their program because "the present plan might be construed as a projection of U.S. military power onto the Asiatic continent rather than as simply an aid to China in modernizing its army."[87]

Because of these State Department reservations, the Pentagon paper proposing MAGIC was returned to the War Department for reexamination. General Wedemeyer rejected Vincent's view that the group would be a "projection of U.S. military power on the Asiatic continent" by pointing out that generalissimo himself supported the establishment of MAGIC and favored "complete cooperation with the U.S." (It was for this very reason that Vincent questioned the creation of the group.) Nevertheless, the general agreed to a reduction in the size of MAGIC provided that a "nucleus" of from three hundred to seven hundred and fifty officers and men (which could be increased depending upon developments) was created at once.[88] Wedemeyer's recommendations, supported by General Marshall and Secretary of War Patterson, were sent to Washington in late January, and quickly became the new position of the Joint Chiefs of Staff.

The revised Pentagon proposal, which Vincent received on February 19, called for "an initial authorization of 750 Army personnel and 165 Navy personnel or a total of 915 [Americans]." The "ultimate size and organization of the Advisory Group," the JCS report concluded, "[could] be re-examined when the pattern of political and military organization of China is more clear."[89] Although the War Department had agreed temporarily to reduce the size of the group and limit its function "to the military staff level," Vincent was still not satisfied. He was especially "concerned over the implications in the JCS paper that the Group may be further expanded" and to prevent this he inserted into the Pentagon version of the presidential directive authorizing MAGIC the statement that the "strength of the Advisory Group shall not exceed one thousand officers and men except as authorized by [the president] in the light of possible future political and military developments."[90] President Truman agreed with Vincent and signed this version of the enabling directive. On February 25, a limited MAGIC was born.[91]

Vincent's victories over the Joint Chiefs were only temporary, however; they did not prevent the War Department from further attempts to gain control of MAGIC for the purpose of expanding American military influence in China. Vincent remained equally determined that this should not occur and continued to cast a watchful eye on the activities of Wedemeyer and his associates in the Pentagon.[92] For these efforts, Vincent earned the enmity of certain officials in the military establishment who refused to permit him to see "sensitive information" because they considered him a "Communist." [93]

With similar evangelical fervor and with much the same success, Vincent worked to persuade the Nationalists to renounce their own military ambitions. Chiang and his associates resented the "pressure" being brought on them "to reach an agreement with the Communists and attributed it to the presence of Communist sympathizers in the State Department."[94] Wellington Koo, the Chinese ambassador to the United States and his minister-counselor, Dr. Tan Shao-hau, registered similar complaints with Vincent who tried to "bring them around" to his own view.

It was impossible to achieve a settlement with the Communists, Koo and Tan told Vincent on two occasions during the summer of 1946, "because of their untrustworthiness, their ambition to gain control of the Chinese Government, and their subservience to Moscow." Their "attitude towards the National Government's sharing its monopolistic control of China was completely defeatist," Vincent noted on August 13; neither Chinese diplomat would "envisage that the Government would be able to share its present authority with the Chinese Communists even on a limited basis without seriously endangering the governmental structure in China."[95]

Vincent did not share their "fears that a coalition government would mean the end of the Kuomintang as the principal party and political influence" provided, of course, that the Kuomintang was "alive to its own responsibilities." Indeed, "a reduction in the influence of the Communists might be more readily achieved," he told Dr. Tan on September 9, "if the Government 'took them in' (in more sense than one) on a minority basis rather than to try and shoot them all. . . . A National Government moving ahead with American support in the job of rehabilitation and reconstruction would have a better chance to cut the ground out from under the Communists, even though they were in the Government, than it would have of doing so by keeping them out of the Government and endeavoring to eliminate them by force."[96]

These lectures on the benefits of political liberalism were lost on the Chinese, for by the summer of 1946 Chiang was determined to exterminate the Communists once and for all. In late July hostilities spread throughout China and the "efforts of the Executive Headquarters and its field teams to stop the fighting were futile. . . . Diplomatic and other qualified sources conceded privately that the United States had failed in her prolonged effort to bring peace to China."[97]

With characteristic determination, Marshall continued his effort to bring a halt to the fighting. On the general's recommendation, the United States imposed an embargo on the shipment of arms and ammunition to the Chinese on July 29,[98] and President Truman sent Chiang a personal message (drafted by Vincent and his colleagues in FE)[99] warning the generalissimo that "unless convincing proof is shortly forthcoming that genuine progress is being made toward a peaceful settlement" the president might be forced to "redefine" American policy toward China.

Neither the arms embargo nor the stern presidential message had much effect. On August 13, the generalissimo issued a public statement holding the Communists solely responsible for the breakdown of negotiations, and demanding that they withdraw from areas "where they threatened the peace and obstruct[ed] communications." And to add insult to injury, Chiang did not respond to Truman's message for nearly three weeks.[100]

Despite these discouraging developments, Marshall continued to work for a revival of discussions between the Nationalists and the Communists. The general found the position of each "confused" and "maddening." The Communists were demanding a meeting of the original Three Man Truce Committee (which Marshall had created the previous December) and a government-issued cease-fire before they would agree to join Ambassador John Leighton Stuart in a discussion of political questions. The Nationalists were equally stubborn: Before declaring a cease-fire, Chiang demanded that the Communists meet with Ambassador Stuart and government representatives as a sign of their sincere desire to reach a peaceful accord.[101]

"Underlying these mechanistic differences," Vincent noted on September 26, were "two fundamentals. One is the lack of confidence on the part of either party in the word or intentions of the other party. . . . The other is the question of whether either party actually or sincerely desires a political and military settlement." Although a settlement appeared unlikely, Vincent remained optimistic, encouraged by the general's own statement that he could still "pull this chestnut out of the cross fire which rages around us."[102]

But Vincent's hopes were not to be realized: In October, the situation took a turn for the worse when a new Nationalist military adventure threatened to destroy the Marshall mission. On October 15, Marshall learned that Chiang intended to attack Kalgan, a Communist stronghold in Inner Mongolia, in spite of his previous declarations to the contrary and Communist warnings that such action would result in "a total national split."

Marshall was furious. If the Nationalists moved on Kalgan, Marshall told Chiang, then nothing would be served by further discussions; if a formula for ending the fighting was not found without delay, he would ask the president to terminate American mediation. And to prove to Chiang that he was not bluffing, Marshall cabled the State Department that he intended to ask Truman to end his mission.[103]

The general's ploy was temporarily successful. Chiang did declare a three-day truce in the Kalgan area and announced that his representatives would return to the conference table to discuss outstanding political and military issues with the Communists. Marshall responded by withdrawing his request to be recalled.[104]

But American hopes were again quickly dashed. Chiang's cease-fire offer was "rejected by the Communists on the ground that there should be no time limit to the truce and that they would not negotiate under military pressure."[105] Probably pleased by the Communist decision, Chiang ordered his armies to continue their operations against Kalgan and Chihfeng. Both cities were captured on October 10, making the Nationalists supreme in Jehol province. A few weeks later, after further victories in northern Kiangsu, Chiang halted his troops and declared a new cease-fire. This offer and an earlier announcement that the National Assembly would be permitted to meet in mid-November were, in Chiang's words, "evidence of the sincere desire of the Government to achieve a lasting peace."[106]

The Communists declared such assurances worthless and chose not to participate in the National Assembly, a decision also supported by the liberal Democratic League. The National Assembly began its deliberations on November 15; four days later, Chou En-lai returned to Yen-an, ending the long period of negotiations which had begun eleven months earlier. And on December 4, Marshall received a final communication from the Communists ignoring his offer to continue working to bring both sides together. With this rejection, American mediation came to an end.[107]

Marshall remained in China for a few more weeks "waiting and watching" for some sign from either party that discussions might be resumed. It was his hope that if the National Assembly passed a "sound democratic constitution," and the State Council and Executive Yuan were thoroughly reorganized, the "door" might be "left open" for the Communists to join the new government. To the general's surprise, the National Assembly did produce a "reasonably democratic constitution," but Marshall, now as cynical as any old China hand, was reserving judgment: The "prime question," he told a representative of the Nationalist government, was the "degree and manner" in which the new charter was enforced.[108]

Despite its "democratic" quality, the Communists rejected what they called "Chiang Kai-shek's fake constitution" and called for the convocation of a new National Assembly consisting of "all parties and groups" not "hand-picked by the KMT dictatorship."[109] The door leading to further negotiations now seemed firmly shut.

Having concluded that it would now be "necessary for the Chinese themselves" to achieve political unity, Marshall decided to return to

Washington to tell the president and the American people what he had learned after a year in China. Like Vincent and other Americans who had observed Chinese affairs in the 1940s, Marshall had come to the conclusion that China's salvation depended upon the development of "a highly organized, liberal party . . . devoted to peace, genuine democratic government and maintaining the rights of the people."[110] Through the creation of a new liberal party, Marshall told Chiang during their last extended conversation, the generalissimo could check the influence of reactionary groups in the party and army and "move in to the position of the father of the country. . . . I emphasized this in every way within my power," Marshall cabled the president on December 28, "because I am convinced that this is the key to the immediate future in China." [111] Believing that he could better "strengthen the position and influence of [liberal] elements by coming home, rather than remaining in China," Marshall formally asked Truman to end his mission.[112]

Vincent found Marshall's telegram of December 28 "a very fine statement of the situation" and supported the general's decision to return to Washington. By the end of 1946, even Vincent's "indomitable optimism" had been shattered by the continuation of the Chinese civil war, and like Marshall, he had reached the conclusion that the United States could do little to prevent further hostilities. He therefore recommended that we get "out of the negotiation business" entirely in order to permit the Chinese themselves to find their own solution "without a 'middleman.'" Sino-American relations, he told Acheson on December 31, should now "get back into a normal groove." Ambassador J. L. Stuart should "concentrate his attention on furthering and strengthening our diplomatic and economic relations with China in a manner regardful of our own interests and of our desire to aid China in non-political ways."[113] Acheson agreed with Vincent's view and, with Byrnes's and Truman's approval, General Marshall was informed that he could return home "at [his] earliest convenience."[114]

Marshall left China on January 8, 1947, "tired," "angry," and "frustrated"[115] but much more knowledgeable about Chiang Kai-shek and the Kuomintang than when he had first arrived. He had gone to China in December 1945, as the executor of Roosevelt's Asian estate, determined to achieve "the major purpose of our war in the Pacific," a unified China under Chiang Kai-shek. But like Vincent and the others who had preceded him, Marshall came to realize that unconditional economic and military support of the generalissimo (through the transportation of fourteen Nationalist armies into Manchuria, the assistance provided by 113,000 sailors and marines, the continuation of lend lease and United Nations

Relief and Rehabilitation (UNRRA) aid, and the promise of additional supplies, loans, and credits) only encouraged Chiang and his generals to fight rather than to negotiate and thus accelerated the process of civil war and political disintegration.

Marshall's final conclusion that the "salvation of the situation" in China lay in the creation of a new liberal party was hardly original: Vincent and other Foreign Service officers had recommended this program since 1942. Nevertheless, Marshall's view was of great importance to Vincent and his colleagues in FE because it signified that the general (who would shortly replace James F. Byrnes as secretary of state) had come to share the China Service opinion about Chiang Kai-shek and the Kuomintang. Marshall's effort to end the Chinese civil war failed, but in the process the general attained something more important than success: an understanding of Chinese politics and an appreciation of America's limited ability to resolve China's complex economic and political problems. This was the great achievement of the Marshall mission.

6

The Paths of Vengeance

In July 1946, when the situation in China was rapidly deteriorating, General Marshall told James Forrestal that if his efforts to achieve a peaceful settlement failed "he would recommend a period of withdrawal so that the United States could take two or three months for reappraisal and reevaluation of her policy toward China."[1] Shortly after becoming secretary of state in January 1947, Marshall put this policy into effect. The Committee of Three and the Executive Headquarters were terminated and the marines removed from Peking, Tientsin, and Tangku.[2] (A small contingent was left at Tsingtao.) The embargo on arms and ammunition also continued. The general then asked Vincent and his colleagues in FE to review past policy and recommend future action. His request marked the beginning of a period of intense debate that was to have an important effect on both the development of American China policy and Vincent's career.

After several weeks of discussion with his associates in the Division of Chinese Affairs, Vincent outlined his views on America's role in China for the new secretary of state. Despite the failure of the Marshall mission and the continuation of civil war, Vincent believed that the United States should seek a "united, democratically inclined China," because neither a "Communist China" nor a "feudal fascist China" could contribute "toward peace and progress in the Far East." The United States should therefore use

153

its influence in helping the Chinese to achieve "unity by democratic methods" rather than through military force. Aid should be given to encourage political reforms such as the inclusion of liberals and non-Kuomintang Chinese in a reorganized Nationalist government. "Genuine reform in the government," Vincent emphasized, "was the only practical method of combatting the challenge of Communism."[3]

Large-scale military and economic assistance to Chiang Kai-shek would only "contribute to and encourage civil war" so Vincent also recommended that the United States continue to withhold arms and ammunition from the Nationalists and maintain a modest Military Assistance Advisory Group in China. This policy of limited assistance could be reversed if the Russians decided to actively aid the Chinese Communists (a course Vincent thought unlikely), or if the embargo threatened to weaken government forces to the point of "military anemia."[4]

General Marshall found Vincent's memorandum persuasive[5] and forwarded a summary of its major points[6] to Secretary of the Navy Forrestal and Secretary of War Patterson. The military chiefs, still as critical of a limited policy toward China as they had been in 1945 and 1946, warned again that withdrawing support from the Nationalists would "increase the influence of the U.S.S.R. in China."[7] Patterson thought it unwise to insist that Chiang negotiate with the Communists (whom he characterized as having "a continuing community of interest with Soviet-inspired international Communism") and he urged his government to revise its policy and help the Kuomintang in the interest of preventing the Russian domination of China. Given the seriousness of the situation and what he saw as the inadequacy of the State Department's recommendations, the secretary of war also suggested that the Joint Chiefs of Staff be directed to prepare an official study of American China policy for the State-War-Navy Coordinating Committee.[8]

In a memorandum written by Vincent, Marshall rejected the Pentagon recommendation that the United States increase its military commitment to Chiang Kai-shek. "There is a strong doubt in my mind," Marshall wrote Patterson on March 4, "that, even if the United States were willing to give a large amount of munitions and support to the Chinese . . . it would be unable . . . to crush the Chinese Communist armies and Party. Limited amounts of munitions would encourage the Kuomintang military leaders to continue their inconclusive war which . . . for economic reasons, will lead . . . to the disintegration of the National Government." And although it seemed unlikely that the Nationalists and the Communists would soon come together in a coalition government, the United States should not be "deterred" from its "policy of encouraging the Chinese to achieve unity and democracy by peaceful methods."[9] The general did agree to permit the Joint Chiefs to begin their examination of American policy toward China but the State Department was able to use this concession to the military to block further Pentagon initiatives on the ground that the United States should not consider altering its fundamental policy until the Joint Chiefs completed their report.[10]

With Marshall's report, Vincent and his colleagues were able to win the first round in the struggle between the State Department and the Pentagon for control of American China policy. But as the months passed and winter gave way to spring, developments abroad and at home began to make it progressively more difficult for the United States to limit its involvement in the Chinese civil war.

In April and May economic and military conditions in China took a sharp turn for the worse. The rate of inflation, which had risen steadily since the end of the war, took a spectacular leap: The cost of flour, rice, and coal, for instance, rose fifty to one hundred percent over previous figures. Black marketeers and financial speculators tripled the price of American dollars, while a series of "dollar exchange explosions" cut the value of Chinese currency to less than one third of its original value. "From the present look of things," the embassy's assistant military attaché noted, "the time . . . is not far off when a larger percentage of the population will no longer be able to [afford] to eat, and come winter may freeze to death."[11]

Meanwhile, Chiang's armies suffered new and significant military defeats. In late April, Mao's forces brilliantly outmaneuvered Chiang's troops in Shantung and in mid-May they launched a summer offensive throughout Manchuria. The victories of the Communists spread "fear" and "defeatism" throughout Nationalist military ranks, the American consul general at Mukden reported on May 30, warning at the same time that a "sudden debacle" might soon lay "all Manchuria open to the [reds] whenever they choose to take it."[12]

The economic and military chaos bred social and political unrest in China's largest cities. Students in Shanghai organized a movement against "hunger" and "civil war," and demonstrations quickly spread to Peking and Nanking. The government retaliated by banning strikes and public meetings, and Kuomintang secret police attacked students and political dissidents. But official repression could not quench the fire of rebellion raging throughout China; soon even the People's Political Council and the Legislative Yuan were calling for an end to civil war and a revival of discussions between the Communists and the Nationalists.[13]

As China's military and political crisis worsened, Chiang and his associates turned once again to the United States for assistance. "China was like a man who needed a blood transfusion," the president of the Executive Yuan told Ambassador Stuart at this time, "and . . . the transfusion had to come from the U.S."[14] In late May, the Chinese ambassador, Wellington Koo, informed Secretary Marshall that his government would soon request $1 billion in aid for industrial and agricultural rehabilitation.[15]

Although the Chinese expected that Marshall might reject their request, they had reason to believe that the political climate in Washington favored the success of their mission.[16] By the summer of 1947, the Nationalist government had concluded that it could count on the support of the Republican Party in its quest for additional military and economic assistance. Although most Republican politicians supported General Marshall in his effort to end the Chinese civil war in 1945-1946, many GOP legislators were becoming increasingly critical of American China policy in 1947. Republicans dominated both houses of Congress, and it was widely anticipated that their presidential candidate would defeat Harry S. Truman in 1948. America's problems in China seemed to be one attractive issue (among many) on which to build a case against the Democrats, and Republicans now took every opportunity to use it. Throughout the first half of 1947, Republican Senators Arthur Vandenberg (the chairman of the prestigious Foreign Relations Committee) and Styles Bridges (the chairman of the powerful Appropriations Committee) called repeatedly for increased aid to Chiang Kai-shek. These statements were not overlooked by the Chinese.[17]

The president's own conduct of foreign policy contributed to the Chinese expectation that assistance would definitely be forthcoming. In response to the continued deterioration of Soviet-American relations and what his administration saw as a Russian bid to seize control of Greece and Turkey (and perhaps western Europe as well), the president announced on March 12 what later became known as the Truman Doctrine. The heart of the president's speech was the assertion that the American way of life was being threatened by an organization of totalitarian aggressors bent on world conquest and that "it must be the policy of the United States to support free people who are resisting attempted subjugation by armed minorities or outside pressure."[18] It was to this general threat, the president argued, "that the U.S. had to respond."[19]

Many officials in Washington were shocked by the president's speech. Vincent agreed with Marshall that Truman "was overstating the case" when he held the Communists responsible for Europe's grave economic and political crisis. Former Secretary of State James F. Byrnes thought the speech "nervous because . . . some of the reasons given for the assistance [to Greece and Turkey] seemed to imply . . . that we would oppose the efforts of Communists in any country to gain control of the government." Summing up the fears of Vincent, Marshall, and Byrnes, Bernard Baruch noted that the Truman Doctrine "was tantamount to a declaration of . . . an ideological or religious war."[20]

Truman's global rhetoric encouraged the Chinese. Administration spokemen were hard pressed to explain why the United States was helping King George defeat the Communists in Greece "while urging Chiang Kai-shek to embrace them" in China, and Republicans in the Congress refused to approve financial assistance for the British and the French until the government gave equal amounts of aid to China. The insistent demands of the Nationalists and their Republican allies, plus the president's growing political vulnerability on the China issue, increased the likelihood that Secretary Marshall would have to reverse his earlier course and increase American support to Chiang Kai-shek.[21]

The strongest call for additional aid to the Nationalists came in June with the appearance of the Pentagon study of American China policy. In a long and carefully argued memorandum, the Joint Chiefs of Staff warned that China, like Europe and the Middle East, was on the verge of being conquered by Soviet imperialism. In their view, the Chinese Communists were "Moscow inspired and . . . motivated by the same basic totalitarian and antidemocratic policies as are the Communist parties in other countries of the world. Accordingly, they should be regarded as tools of Soviet policy." Chinese Communist domination of Manchuria and northern China would pave the way for the "continued expansion of Soviet power in Asia . . . towards Indo-China, Malaysia, and India."[22]

The American response to this Asian crisis had been "piecemeal and uncoordinated," the Pentagon argued, in obvious disapproval of the State Department's policy. To attempt to achieve a politically unified China by means of a coalition government was not only unwise, it was itself a threat to American interests. "Regardless of the corruption and the political shortcomings of the present National Government," the Joint Chiefs noted, "recent events have proven conclusively that under present circumstances the Chinese Communists will only accept a solution which would assure their early control of the government and ultimate communist domination of China," a development "which would jeopardize the military security of the United States."[23]

Instead of continuing this self-defeating policy, the generals recommended that the United States renounce its pledge of noninterference in the Chinese civil war and furnish the Nationalists with "selective and well-supervised assistance." Large supplies of ammunition and equipment

157   The Paths of Vengeance

would be enough to halt Soviet expansion in China until the time when "the Western, concept of democracy" was able to prove to the Chinese "its practical and ideological superiority over Communism."[24]

While the Pentagon called for increased assistance, Vincent argued vigorously for continuation of a limited policy toward China. "The fundamental difference in viewpoint" between the Joint Chiefs of Staff and the Far Eastern Office, Vincent wrote Secretary Marshall on June 20, was "the answer each would give to the following question: Is it good and feasible American policy to give direct and substantial military assistance to Chiang Kai-shek in his attempt to eliminate Communism from China by force?" Vincent and his colleagues believed the answer to be "no," for the following reasons. First, large-scale aid "would lead inevitably to direct intervention in China's civil war." Second, it "would provoke the USSR to similar intervention on the side of the Chinese Communists." Third, it "would be inconclusive unless [the United States] were prepared to take over direction of Chinese military operations and administration and remain in China for an indefinite period." Fourth, it would "invite formidable opposition among the Chinese people." And fifth, a commitment of this kind would be inconsistent with earlier Pentagon memorandums which had placed China "very low on the list of countries which should be given such assistance."[25]

Vincent also rejected the military's argument that "failure to assist Chiang would result in the [Russian] domination of China." After considering "the administrative inefficiencies of the Chinese . . . , the magnitude of the task of dominating China, the easily aroused Chinese resentment of foreign interference, the lack of industrial development and material resources, and the inability of the Russians to make China a going concern," Vincent believed that a Soviet-controlled China was "not a danger of sufficient immediacy or probability to warrant committing ourselves to the far-reaching consequences which would ensue from our involvement in the Chinese civil war on the side of the National Government."[26]

Although Vincent was doubtful that Chiang could defeat the Communists (with or without American aid) he *was* troubled[27] by the growing disintegration of Chinese military morale and for that reason recommended limited assistance designed to prevent the "collapse of the .. . National armies." Specifically, he urged Marshall to lift the embargo on arms and ammunition.[28] But even as he made this recommendation (which he did reluctantly), he emphasized that it would not eliminate the Communists and "that in the final analysis the Chinese themselves must find a more fundamental solution" to their national problems.[29]

Vincent also opposed substantial increases in economic aid, rejecting the

Chinese request for a grant of $1 billion[30] and recommending instead limited support for specific industrial or agricultural projects. By "pacing" American assistance to steps Chiang took toward reforming his government, Vincent believed that the United States could encourage the Kuomintang "along the lines we want."[31] Not until Chiang reorganized his cabinet and established a new State Council should the president ask the Export-Import Bank to extend credits approximating $130 million to assist in the rehabilitation of Chinese mines, railroads, and harbors. Such conditional aid would help the Nationalists in a "practicable way," Vincent informed Marshall, without impairing the basic American position "that large scale support should not be forthcoming until there was some degree of real improvement in conditions in China."[32]

Secretary Marshall shared Vincent's critical view of the requests of the Chinese and their American allies. He was of course distressed to learn of the deterioration of the Chinese military position in the spring of 1947 (and for that reason agreed to lift the embargo), but the general was more angry at Chiang and his advisors than he was concerned about their future prospects. The generalissimo, whose armies "were overextended and were expending their military strength," was "the worst advised military commander in history," Marshall told Wellington Koo on May 8.[33] Koo nevertheless asked about the likelihood of substantial increases in military aid and the general responded with an "icy stare" and a tart reply. "Chiang is faced with a unique problem of logistics," Vincent remembered Marshall telling Koo. "He is losing about forty percent of his supplies to the enemy. If the percentage should reach fifty percent he will have to decide whether it is wise to continue to supply his own troops." ("This is the only time I ever heard General Marshall indulge in irony," Vincent later commented.)[34] Marshall's hatred of Nationalist generals explains in part why he joined Vincent in opposing Pentagon requests for large-scale military assistance to the Chinese.

Ineptness in military affairs was matched by lack of progress in the areas of political reform and government reorganization. Marshall welcomed the appointment of the distinguished liberal Chang Chun as premier and the establishment of a new State Council in May, but these minimal advances seemed to be wiped out by the simultaneous creation of a Kuomintang Political Council led by Chen Li-fu. Since the same reactionary generals and politicians continued to control Chinese affairs, Marshall saw little point in granting economic assistance which would only be used to promote civil war. He therefore rejected the Nationalist request for a billion dollar loan, accepting instead Vincent's proposal that short-term credits be granted on a project-by-project basis.[35]

General Marshall remained resistant to foreign and domestic pressures pushing the United States toward direct involvement in the Chinese civil war. Although Chiang's supporters in the press, the Congress, and the Pentagon continued to request substantial aid in the period from 1947 to 1949, Marshall refused to reverse the limited policy he established during the first six months of his service as secretary of state. To be sure, he remained concerned about developments in China (and for that reason sent General Wedemeyer to Nanking on a fact-finding mission in July 1947[36] and seven months later approved a one year congressional appropriation of $570 million for economic aid),[37] but he never lost his determination to avoid direct intervention. His policy of limited assistance was continued until Chiang fled the Chinese mainland in 1949.

John Carter Vincent played a crucial role in defeating efforts that would have involved the United States more deeply in the Chinese civil war. At every turn, he countered Pentagon arguments that it was in the American interest to support the Nationalist regime. His memorandums during these years reflected what one scholar later called "a calm realpolitik" toward the crisis in China.[38]

Advocating realpolitik, in a Washington torn by bureaucratic conflict and suffering from the fevers of the cold war, turned out to be very dangerous indeed. Vincent was accustomed to *foreign* situations that had threatened his life: He had faced down angry Chinese in Ch'ang-sha, turned aside Japanese bayonets in Mukden, and dodged Japanese bombs in Chungking, but nothing in his past prepared him for the *American* ordeal he was about to experience.

In January 1947 Vincent was promoted to the rank of career minister, and it was expected that he would be given an important new assignment abroad. But when his name was submitted to the Senate Foreign Relations Committee for approval, he found himself suddenly under attack and his future in jeopardy.[39]

His nomination was held up at the request of Republican Senator Styles Bridges of New Hampshire, who told Foreign Relations Committee Chairman Arthur Vandenberg that he had received reports that Vincent was "leftist to an extreme" and had "notoriously and harmfully distorted the American position" in the Far East.[40]

Bridges received this information from Alfred Kohlberg, the New York businessman who had despised Vincent since 1941, when the two had clashed over international politics while en route to Shanghai. Contemporary critics called Kohlberg the evil genius behind the China Lobby,[41] an informal organization of lobbyists, former Communists turned conservative, and businessmen, missionaries, and journalists with financial or sentimental ties to China. Kohlberg was the leader of this group: He had been active in the China trade for over thirty years, and his work (chiefly the import of Chinese embroidery) had made him a millionaire.[42] To his foes, Kohlberg's financial stake in China was explanation enough for his support of Chiang Kai-shek.[43]

But Kohlberg had other motives besides this economic one: His view of American China policy was the reflection of a personal political philosophy. To Kohlberg, the major issue in the twentieth century was not (as Vincent believed) the relationship between man and the social-industrial order; it was instead the conflict between two faiths, freedom and communism.

Kohlberg came late to an appreciation of communism. "I never took Communists seriously until [1943]," he later admitted. "Some people act according to ideas, but the businessman always looks at results. I went to Russia in 1926, 1932, and 1935. I looked at what they were doing . . . and decided we didn't have to worry. . . . I wasn't at home in the world of ideas. I didn't realize that people could be moved by ideas."[44]

Aware of his intellectual shortcomings, Kohlberg became an enthusiastic student of communism—and moved forever into "the world of ideas." He studied the resolutions of the Comintern, read the *Daily Worker*, attended Communist Party functions, and developed friendships with ex-Communists like Louis Budenz, Benjamin Mandel, Freda Utley, and Max Eastman. Many of these ex-Communists later served on the Board of Directors of the American China Policy Association, an organization dedicated to the support of Chiang Kai-shek, which Kohlberg helped to establish and later directed.[45]

Like the Communists (whose ideas he followed closely) and the ex-Communists (with whom he mostly associated) Kohlberg came to abhor liberals, whom both groups saw as their major adversary. To the Communists, liberalism was "an attitude in the service of the bourgeoisie," to the ex-Communists it was "an ally of communism"; to both it was a philosophy to be despised.[46] From these sources came Kohlberg's own antiliberal faith.

Eventually, Kohlberg developed his own antidote for both liberalism and communism, a program he called "offensive counter-subversion." Its international aim was "the destruction of the Communist dictatorship that now enslaves one-third of mankind." Specifically, Kohlberg recommended

161   The Paths of Vengeance

that the United States "break off diplomatic relations with the Communist world," "aid all nations fighting Communism or willing to fight it," "arm and direct the underground behind the iron curtain," and "permit free trade only with [our] allies."[47]

His program also had its domestic counterpart. It was "to clean our own house [and] separate the traitors in our midst from the dupes and the well meaning people who don't know what it's all about. The timid, the weak, the fellow travelers," all must be exposed and removed from those public or private agencies to which they belonged. Of special importance to the "housecleaners" were the group of men who had "misled our . . . government about [communism], betrayed our anti-Communist allies in Eastern Europe and the Far East," and had caused the deaths "of millions of Poles, Russians, Yugoslavs . . . and Chinese."[48]

Kohlberg was not, then, simply a businessman with Chinese connections: He was an ideologist and propagandist for a new political faith. Given his perspective and views, it is not surprising that he sought to destroy men like John Carter Vincent, who symbolized the liberal philosophy he hated.

In his crusade against liberalism and communism, Kohlberg had the important assistance of two other major groups. The first were conservative publishers and journalists who shared his faith and had vehicles to propagate its gospel: These included a number of magazines—
Life, Time, U.S. News and World Report, the American Mercury, the Reader's Digest, the New Leader, Human Events, Colliers, the Saturday Evening Post, and Plain Talk and the Freeman, publications financed by Kohlberg; newspapers like the New York Journal American, the Washington Times Herald, the Los Angeles and San Francisco Examiner, the Oakland Tribune, and the Manchester N.H. Union Leader; and two publishing houses, Henry Regnery and Devin-Adair.[49]

The second group were certain Republican politicians who, if they did not completely share Kohlberg's extremist views, were willing to use his help in developing issues that would oust the Democrats from power. Some scholars have labeled this group "the Congressional China Bloc"[50] because of their support for Chiang Kai-shek, but like Kohlberg their view of American Far Eastern policy was the reflection of a rabid conservatism and their major goal, as historian Athan Theoharis has noted, "was to discredit the New Deal."[51] These included Styles Bridges, Kenneth Wherry, George Malone, Homer Ferguson, and Democrat Pat McCarran in the Senate, and Fred Busbey, Lawrence Smith, George Dondero, and ex-China missionary Walter Judd in the House. This informal organization of congressional politicians and ideological propagandists deserves an appellation more precise than the China Lobby, for their interests were global, and their objectives both political and philosophical. Perhaps a more accurate name is the conservative coalition. John Carter Vincent was one of their first targets.

When word reached Kohlberg early in 1947 that Vincent was to be promoted to career minister, he hurried to Washington, determined, as he later put it, "to do his part to check the slimy traitors who are playing the game of our enemies." There he met with Senator Bridges, Congressman Judd, General Hurley and General Wedemeyer, and Parker La Moore of the Scripps-Howard Newspapers; after several discussions it was decided that Bridges would pressure the Foreign Relations Committee to reject Vincent's nomination.[52]

As a courtesy to his colleague, Vandenberg agreed to postpone Vincent's confirmation pending his own private investigation into the diplomat's record. His review disclosed nothing of a subversive nature. "The record is clear," Vandenberg informed Bridges, "therefore the case against him depends entirely upon the character of the work he has done"—a question of personal opinion which, Vandenberg noted, "made a challenge difficult to sustain." Nevertheless, Vandenberg told Bridges that he would continue to investigate Vincent and invited the senator to appear as "a personal witness" or give the committee a written memorandum detailing his accusations.[53]

Bridges responded quickly to Vandenberg's request for more information on Vincent and sent the senator a report which he believed indicated the need for a thorough examination of Vincent's views and activities.

The Bridges memorandum was a condensed version of a long essay on Vincent which Kohlberg wrote earlier that year. It implied strongly that Vincent's "actions, advice and recommendations" had been coordinated with the steps outlined in two official Communist documents: *The Program of the Communist International and Its Constitution* and "The Revolutionary Movement in the Colonies and Semi-colonies," a resolution adopted by the Comintern in 1928. The memorandum contained eleven other accusations charging that Vincent had "expressed dislike" for Clarence Gauss and the Chinese, and was anti-Japanese as well as pro-Communist. It also said that Vincent tried to undermine the efforts of Ambassador Hurley, destroy the government of Chiang Kai-shek, and further "the extension of Russian influence" in China. Bridges called his report "a danger signal" indicating that the "approval of John Carter Vincent as Career Minister would be inimical to the interests of the United States and dangerous to an effective, intelligent and truly American foreign policy."[54]

Bridges's evidence was sent by the Foreign Relations Committee to Under Secretary of State Dean Acheson, who gave the report to Vincent for comment. "I have never seen a document so thoroughly characterized by misstatement, misrepresentation and prejudice," he informed Acheson. "I have never read the two [Communist] documents mentioned. . . . Therefore, the inference drawn that my 'advice and recommendations' have been intentionally coordinated with the steps outlined in those documents is not correct. I do not know what advice and recommendations the author has in mind, but I am quite certain whatever it was, it was not coordinated, either intentionally or coincidentally, with [these] documents."[55]

Vincent found the other charges equally absurd. "I lived with Ambassador Gauss for two years in Chungking. Our association was close and amicable. As his Counselor I supported the policy and line of action advocated by Mr. Gauss and continued to do so after my return to Washington." There was also "no basis of truth whatsoever for the statement that I have expressed 'a general dislike for the Chinese.' On the contrary, my record of over twenty years in the Service, the larger portion of which was spent in China, will demonstrate that I have been a friend of the Chinese in far greater than the average sense and that I have associated with them on an intimate and very friendly basis."[56]

The Bridges memorandum was correct in only one respect: He *had* been anti-Japanese in the years leading up to Pearl Harbor and was proud of it: "I am quite pleased to admit that during the years 1936-39 when I served in the Department I was keenly aware of the aggressively dangerous activities of the Japanese and advocated through my superiors . . . measures to meet and counteract this danger."[57] The rest of the statements contained in the memorandum had "no factual basis," Vincent argued, "or where they do, the facts are maliciously misconstrued. . . . My record will show that nothing I have done with regard to China, or any other place, has 'contributed to extension of Russian influence' and also that nothing in my record will show that I 'favor the Communist line.' On the contrary, . . . I have worked consistently to further policies the objective of which was to minimize the influence of Communists in China."[58]

Acheson, who had worked closely with Vincent on China policy, needed little convincing that the allegations were "wholly groundless," so on April 18 he sent the Foreign Relations Committee his own detailed analysis of each specific charge. Acheson labeled the various accusations "unfair," "wholly untrue," "without foundation," "entirely false," "absurd," and "inaccurate." "I have known Mr. Vincent well throughout my service in the State Department," he wrote Senator Walter George, the senior Democrat on the committee. "I recommended him for his present post and have worked intimately with him during my service as Under Secretary during which period he has reported directly to me. Increasing knowledge has brought increasing respect for his judgment and admiration for him as a gentleman and a disinterested and loyal servant of our republic. He is a man of the finest intellectual quality and the highest character."[59]

Despite this strong endorsement, the Vincent nomination remained lodged in committee, principally because of the objections of Senators Bridges and Vandenberg.

In May, Vincent's chances of receiving Senate confirmation received a new setback when the once secret accusations against him became public. On Monday, May 12, the "antitotalitarian monthly" *Plain Talk* announced that its current issue contained an article charging that John Carter Vincent had "sabotaged the traditional American policy in China and has been fronting for the Soviet viewpoint." The title of the article was "The State Department's Left Hand"[60] (its earlier title had been "Kremlin Agent in the State Department");[61] its author was Alfred Kohlberg. "Mr. Kohlberg," the statement noted, "accuses John Carter Vincent of being the head of a Red 'cell' in our diplomatic service and demands a thorough investigation by the Senate of Mr. Vincent's conduct of our Far Eastern Affairs before his pending nomination as Minister Plenipotentiary is confirmed."[62] A press release and Kohlberg's six-page article were sent immediately to the Foreign Relations Committee, where they were added to the growing file on Vincent.[63] And Congressman Fred Busbey of Illinois placed a copy of "The State Department's Left Hand" in the *Congressional Record.*[64]

By summer, Vincent had become the subject of both public and private debate, and his promotion was in real jeopardy. So long as Vandenberg remained opposed it seemed likely that his nomination would die in committee, unless Vincent made some effort to overcome Republican objections. Realizing finally that his career might be permanently damaged if Kohlberg's vicious polemics were not discredited, Vincent turned to former Secretary of State James F. Byrnes for help.[65]

Byrnes, a veteran of political wars in South Carolina and Washington, advised Vincent that it would take some vigorous personal lobbying to free his nomination and offered to accompany him on visits to important members of the Senate. Together the two southerners met with most of the men who would vote on Vincent's confirmation, telling them, as Vincent later remembered, that the charges were "all a bunch of crap; that it all came out of Kohlberg and Hurley."[66] Senator Walter George, who had originally assisted him in joining the Consular Service twenty-three years earlier, was especially helpful in convincing doubting colleagues. He told fellow members of the Foreign Relations Committee that "he would hate to see [Vincent] held up if . . . other [nominations] are reported. [I have] known him for some time and [do] not know what objections could be raised to this simple promotion."[67] The senators seemed to respond favorably to the arguments of Byrnes and George, and Vincent began to feel confident once more that his nomination would be approved, eventually.

Vincent was finally confirmed in late July, but only after Republicans were assured that he would not be sent to an important post in the Far East (Kohlberg feared that Vincent might be named ambassador to China),[68] or Europe (Vincent had expressed interest in going to Czechoslovakia).[69] Switzerland was chosen, and his nomination was approved two days after the Senate was officially informed of his destination.[70] Senator Vandenberg was still not pleased with the outcome; before casting his vote in committee he told his colleagues: "I am not enthusiastic about this one."[71]

The struggle over Vincent's nomination in 1947 demonstrated the growing influence of the conservative coalition in Washington. Through Bridges in the Senate and Judd in the House, Alfred Kohlberg had instruments to express his own special views and complicate the administrative procedures of the Foreign Service and the State Department. Vandenberg's role in postponing Vincent's confirmation revealed the extent to which the moderate wing of the Republican party was willing to accept Kohlberg's help in forcing the Truman administration to make political and diplomatic concessions. But it also showed that the moderates were beginning to lose control over the extremists within the conservative bloc. While Vandenberg did not like Vincent's record, he was "quite sure," he told a constituent, that Vincent was "not a 'Red'" and was satisfied—if not enthusiastic—with the compromise that sent Vincent to Switzerland.[72] Kohlberg, on the other hand, rejected the normal give-and-take of domestic politics: He was interested only in destroying Vincent's career. Despite the fact that Vandenberg had lately been his ally, he turned on the senator, telling him that his "so-called bi-partisan approach" to American foreign policy was actually working to the advantage of the "conspiratorial group" in the State Department.[73] Such attacks suggest that Kohlberg's movement was itself oddly bipartisan: It threatened both the Republican and Democratic Parties as well as those responsible for the development of American China Policy in the 1940s.

For Vincent, the whole affair had been acutely distressing, but at least it now appeared to be over. He was at last a career minister (at the age of forty-six) and chief of his own diplomatic mission in a country which he

dearly loved. He felt enormous pride and not a little relief, along with the
satisfaction of knowing that in the end he had defeated Alfred Kohlberg.
Vincent had no idea, as he and his family prepared to leave for Bern, that
his troubles with Kohlberg were far from over. Switzerland was destined
to be not the first important post he was to hold as minister, but the last.

Vincent's move to Switzerland was only one in a series
designed to appease Republican critics of Truman's foreign and domestic
policies. In May, the embargo restricting arms to Nationalist China was
lifted; in June, 130 million rounds of ammunition were sold to the Chinese
at a discount, and in July the president announced that General
Wedemeyer, a Republican favorite, was going to China on a fact-finding
mission. Toward the end of that same month, it was publicly revealed that
Vincent was leaving the State Department ("to remove him," Acheson later
wrote, "from the direct path of Republican vengeance").[74] These steps were
partially successful in quieting Republican criticism that the United States
was giving aid to Europe while ignoring China.[75] The Vincent and
Wedemeyer appointments, Vandenberg informed Kohlberg, indicated that
Truman's administration was "now making progress in the right direction"
toward the establishment of "an appropriate China policy."[76]

Truman's attempt to combat criticism of his domestic policies did not
succeed. By 1947 it was apparent that fear of Communist subversion could
be exploited for political gain; the Republicans had won a significant
victory in the congressional elections of 1946, winning control of both the
Senate and House, after skillfully using the "Communist-in-government"
issue. When the newly elected Eightieth Congress convened in January,
1947, the Republican Speaker of the House, Joseph W. Martin, Jr.,
announced that a major goal of the Congress would be to seek out and
destroy subversives who threatened the "American way of life."[77] During
the next two years, twenty-two hearings were held on communism by six
separate congressional committees.[78]

Hoping to protect his administration from charges that it was ignorant
of the domestic threat posed by international communism, President
Truman established, in the spring of 1947, the Federal Employee Loyalty
Program, "an unprecedentedly broad program of background investigations and screening procedures for all incumbent and prospective
employees." But instead of calling off Republican investigators, the new
program spurred them on. Truman's action helped legitimize the efforts of

Kohlberg and his allies in the Congress, and they took full advantage of the new opportunity which the President unintentionally gave them.

In 1948, Republican Congressman Karl Stefan of Nebraska, chairman of the House Appropriations Subcommittee, persuaded President Truman to permit Robert E. Lee and a group of House investigators to examine the loyalty files of State Department employees. These files contained all sorts of derogatory information, including "false or unconfirmed statements and allegations," which had turned up during the course of the Loyalty Program's required security check. Because the files contained unanalyzed material emanating from the FBI and other agencies, they were dangerously unreliable as a means of determining an employee's loyalty. But this did not deter the House investigators. After spending several weeks combing through the files, Lee and his aides developed a list of approximately 108 "past, present, or prospective employees" whose loyalty appeared questionable. The "Lee List," as it came to be known, was passed back and forth between Republicans in the House and Senate, and State Department officials were forced to explain why these 108 still worked for the government.[79]

Case Number 52 on the Lee List was John Carter Vincent. "Is Number 52 still employed?" Stefan asked State Department Security Chief Hamilton Robinson during a hearing on January 28, 1948. "Yes sir, he is employed," Hamilton answered. Without waiting for an explanation, Stefan began to read the contents of Vincent's loyalty file into the subcommittee's record:

> A raincoat believed to be the subject's was found on September 28, 1946, by guards in the men's room of the State Department Building. In the pocket were papers which were believed to be those of a Russian language student. The subject does not know Russian and is not studying Russian and there was apparently no explanation for the papers found in the coat pocket.

The next statement Stefan read was more serious. An anonymous informant told a State Department investigator a "most incriminating" story regarding Case Number 52. In April 1945 the informant said, an American ambassador was preparing to leave London for Teheran when he was approached by a top agent of the OSS, America's wartime espionage organization. The man from OSS told the ambassador "that a telegram which had been prepared by President Roosevelt to send to Chungking . . . had been 'picked up at Moscow'; that an investigation had precluded the possibility that the leak of information could have occurred in Washington, because the information in the telegram reached Moscow before the actual telegram left Washington. Case Number 52 had been observed contacting a man in Washington, and this man . . . had been followed to the Sovet Embassy. [The agent] was clearly disturbed by this occurrence," the informant stated, and "warned [the ambassador] against divulging information of a secret nature which might reach [the suspect]." What this complicated tale meant was that Vincent was suspected of espionage by the OSS. Stefan was therefore extremely interested in Robinson's reaction to the story.[80]

The informant's report was no mystery to the State Department, which had investigated the matter thoroughly. The ambassador was in reality Patrick J. Hurley; the OSS agent, Director William J. Donovan. Agent Daniel H. Clare, Jr., of the department's New York Office of Security, had originally heard the story in August 1947, probably from the ubiquitous Alfred Kohlberg.[81] He wrote it up as Kohlberg described it and gave it to his superior who immediately informed Washington. The department studied the memorandum, then ordered Clare to interview Donovan regarding Vincent.

Donovan's version of his meeting with Hurley differed significantly from that reported by Kohlberg. The general remembered seeing Hurley in April 1945, just prior to the ambassador's departure for an international conference. They spoke for "about five minutes." Donovan told Hurley that secret government documents had recently been leaked to Philip J. Jaffe, pro-Communist editor of *Amerasia* magazine.[82] Among those arrested and charged with espionage was Vincent's friend, John S. Service. No doubt it was Service's involvement in the case that led Donovan to warn Hurley that he had heard that "John Carter Vincent is overly friendly with the Reds." (Service had indiscreetly loaned copies of his reports to Jaffe but was not indicted by the grand jury that looked into the incident.) But Donovan was certain, Clare later wrote, "that he had not told General Hurley nor did he know anything about a telegram. . . . , nor did he tell General Hurley anything about Mr. Vincent having been observed contacting a man . . . . later followed to the Soviet Embassy." (Apparently both Kohlberg and Hurley confused the "telegram" with the *Amerasia* documents.) As far as the State Department was concerned, "there was no basis for allegation." "It now appears that the informant was mistaken," Robinson told the committee.[83]

An examination of the remaining contents of Vincent's file also turned up no other "incriminating" evidence. The information in the file, Robinson said, "consists in large part of quotations from various publications pertaining to the subject. It also lists the names of certain persons with whom the subject is alleged to have or may have had contact. However, it is not indicated in this report, nor is there any evidence in departmental files that any of these alleged contacts were made for other than official purposes." The department was satisfied that Case Number 52 was absolutely loyal to the United States and therefore no further investigation was necessary. Stefan listened attentively to Robinson's explanation then shifted his attention to another "questionable" State Department employee.[84]

The incident involving Case No. 52 demonstrated the weaknesses of Truman's loyalty program and showed how easily material developed by it could be exploited by the president's political enemies. The "quotations from various publications" pertaining to Vincent which filled his loyalty file were drawn generally from articles written by Alfred Kohlberg and other critics of American China policy. Kohlberg was hardly an objective source and it was unfair to Vincent to have his loyalty questioned on the basis of charges leveled by the man who proudly called himself "the China Lobby." Loyalty files contained mostly damaging material; there was nothing to indicate that Vincent's work in Chungking and Washington had won him high praise from Ambassador Clarence Gauss and Under Secretary of State Joseph C. Grew, both life-long conservative Republicans. Robinson summed up the problem concisely when he told still another congressional committee inquiring about Case No. 52: "Investigator's allegations are placed in security files, the Department's statement to the effect that [they are] not . . . fact[s] has been left out." It was therefore the president's own loyalty program which provided the Republicans with the material they were seeking to damage Truman's credibility and remove him from the White House.

Kohlberg's charge that a Soviet clique existed in the State Department and the evidence (such as it was) produced by the House investigators came together in 1950 when they fell into the hands of still another Republican legislator, Senator Joseph McCarthy of Wisconsin. But by this time certain domestic and foreign events had conspired to lend an air of credibility to the allegations which Kohlberg had been circulating. In August 1948 (eight months after Stefan had interrogated Robinson about Case Number 52), Alger Hiss, a former State Department official, was accused by ex-Communist Whittaker Chambers of belonging to a Soviet spy ring which had been active in Washington during the 1930s. Hiss denied the charges and sued Chambers for libel but was later indicted for perjury and convicted. "Here at last was meat and substance for the Republican charge of Communism in government," historian Robert Griffith has noted. "Here was confirmation of their worst suspicions and their fondest hopes. Here was proof positive of treason in high places and perfidy at the vitals of government."[85]

The Hiss case made hunting for subversives a legitimate enterprise and in the presidential campaign of 1948 both Republicans and Democrats fought to make the issue their own. Governor Harold E. Stassen of Minnesota, a candidate for the Republican presidential nomination, urged that Congress make it unlawful for Americans to belong to the Communist Party of the United States.[86] Nominees Thomas E. Dewey and Earl Warren accused the president of "coddling the Communists." And not to be outdone, President Truman and Democratic strategists (like Clark Clifford) labeled Henry Wallace's Progressive Party a tool of the international Communist conspiracy.

Despite Truman's surprising victory in 1948, he remained on the defensive when challenged by Republicans on the Communist issue, and events in 1949 and 1950 gave him little opportunity to mount a counter-attack. First came the unexpected news that the Soviet Union was in possession of the atomic bomb. Two months later, in October 1949, the forces of Mao Tse-tung finally defeated Chiang Kai-shek's government and drove it into exile on Formosa. The Communists seemed to be everywhere: Half of Europe was theirs and all of China. In the United States, eleven American Communists were convicted of sedition; Justice Department aide Judith Coplon went on trial for espionage; and Ethel and Julius Rosenberg, Morton Sobel, David Greenglass, and Harry Gold were arrested and charged with giving America's atomic secrets to the Russians. International communism appeared to be omnipotent and invincible. Against this background, the myths of Alfred Kohlberg and the realities of Soviet subversion merged until it became difficult to separate fiction from fact. The fall of China, the Russian bomb, the Hiss, Coplon, and Rosenberg cases—all breathed new life into Kohlberg's charges, which lay in government loyalty files waiting to be exhumed. In February 1950, they became the property of the junior senator from Wisconsin. Many men had used the fear of domestic subversion to attack the Democrats before Joseph McCarthy. But McCarthy's activities, beginning in February 1950, proved that he was the most unscrupulous and dangerous of them all.[87]

McCarthy first unveiled his charges against Vincent in a speech before the Senate on the night of February 20. During the previous week his shocking speeches on Communists in government had made him a national celebrity. Now he was taking his crusade directly to his colleagues.[88] Removing reams of documents from his overstuffed briefcase and placing them in piles atop his desk, he turned and addressed the chair. "Mr. President," he said, "I wish to discuss a subject tonight which concerns me more than any other subject I have ever discussed before this body. . . . It not only concerns me . . it disturbs and frightens me."

McCarthy's subject was the Soviet "Fifth Column" which he believed existed in the State Department. While Democrats angrily disputed

McCarthy's claims, the senator asked that he be granted the opportunity to give detailed descriptions of "approximately 81 cases" which, he said, would substantiate his charges. The most important cases were Nos. 1, 2, and 81: "Three big Communists . . . who are tremendously important and of great value to Russia." McCarthy argued that, "if we can get rid of those big three, we will have done something to break the back of the espionage ring within the State Department."[89]

The biggest of the big three, McCarthy claimed, was Case No. 2. "This is a case to which I particularly invite the Senate's attention:

> I am inclined to think that this individual's name may be known for the information which I shall give here.
> The file shows two things. It shows, first, that this individual had some of his clothing picked up, with unusual material in it, and second,—and this is important—it shows that the State Department and the President had prepared material which was to be sent to a foreign government. The file shows that before the material left the State Department it was in the hands of the Kremlin in Moscow. Do [the] Senators follow me? The State Department's own investigative file shows that some secret material, which was being transmitted to another nation, before it even left this country for the other country, showed up in Moscow. So far, that is not too significant. However, the file shows that this particular individual, who has held one of the most important positions at one of the listening posts in Europe, was shadowed, that he was found to have contacted a Soviet agent, and that the Soviet agent was then followed to the Soviet Embassy, where the agent turned the material over to the Soviet Embassy. Do [the] Senators follow me? This is what the secret State Department file shows: First, the papers get to Moscow in some mysterious manner, and second, this individual, who is now one of our foreign ministers, contacts a Russian espionage agent, and that agent is followed to the Russian Embassy, where the material is handed over. This is no secret to the State Department.

McCarthy believed that the charges against Case No. 2 were so serious that he "should not only be discharged but should be immediately prosecuted."[90]

Case No. 2 was John Carter Vincent, and the dossier from which McCarthy read was the same loyalty file unearthed two years earlier by Robert E. Lee and his team of investigators. That McCarthy was reading from the Lee List was apparent to several of his colleagues who had their own copies. Republican Senator Homer Ferguson, unable to keep up with McCarthy, interrupted to ask "why the Senator had taken them out of order." Not surprised by Ferguson's question, McCarthy replied "I get the impression that the Senator may have a file of his own."[91]

Actually, Ferguson had good reason to be confused, because McCarthy not only chose to read certain cases from the Lee List while ignoring others, he also exaggerated the old allegations and invented new tales more wild than the old ones. In Vincent's case, he wove disparate strands of information together to fashion a story that would have piqued anyone's imagination. Where the Lee team reported that a memorandum was simply missing from Vincent's file, McCarthy said: "Upon contact with the keeper of the records, he stated that, to the best of his knowledge, the major portion of the file had been removed." Then he noted that a piece of Vincent's clothing containing "unusual material" was "picked up." Next, "secret material" (the same or different material from that found on the clothing?) arrives in Moscow before it ever leaves Washington. How? The mystery is quickly solved: The acccused has been "shadowed," seen contacting a Soviet agent who is "followed to the Soviet Embassy, where the agent turned the material over to the Soviet Embassy." By merging events that allegedly occurred separately and ignoring evidence to the contrary, McCarthy involved Vincent in a crime that was punishable by death.

For nearly six hours McCarthy droned on, leaping from case to case with great verbal dexterity, if not accuracy. (He never said a word about cases 15, 27, 37, and 59; failed to recognize that cases 3 and 4, like 9 and 7, were identical and did not know that cases 13 and 78 were never employed by the federal government.)[92] Shortly before midnight he finished his remarks, the Senate chamber almost empty. Despite McCarthy's failure to hold his audience, he did win still another opportunity to present his case, this time in a larger forum. Senate Republicans demanded that a special congressional committee be appointed to investigate whether there were Communists in the State Department, and Democrats, once more on the defensive, reluctantly agreed. "I guarantee that a committee will be formed at once," Democratic Majority Leader Scott Lucas stated, "and the Senator from Wisconsin will have an opportunity to come before the committee to tell who these persons are. Before the Committee, he will not be able to hide behind numbers. He will have to tell the facts and disclose the names of the persons within the State Department who are Communists. It ought to be done. . . . [I]t . . . is absolutely necessary to clear this matter up as soon as possible."[93]

A few days later, Dean Acheson came to his department's defense. "In all the recent discussions of the Department's employees no one has yet supplied us with the names," the secretary told a news conference. "There is no one in the Department who has been found to be disloyal . . . or . . . a bad security risk."[94] On February 25, Dorothy Thompson gave Acheson the name behind Case No. 2. "McCarthy's Charges Are No Red Herring," she declared in the *Washington Star*. "This column is willing to name [the] man who 'holds an important listening post in Europe' and whose presence has caused some uneasy feeling—John Carter Vincent."[95]

M cCarthy's charges and the publicity they were receiving also had an impact on J. Edgar Hoover, who was responsible for investigating government employees under the President's Loyalty Program. The director of the FBI had long been suspicious of Vincent, and on April 21, 1950, asked the Attorney General's Office if a "full field loyalty investigation" should be conducted.[96] Ten days later the State and Justice Departments formally requested that such an inquiry begin. In February 1946, Vincent's FBI file contained barely two pages of information regarding his life and career; by August 1951, when the bureau completed its investigation, the file was filled with hundreds of pages.

Hoover's interest in Vincent had originated in October 1947, when Vincent began his service as minister to Switzerland. On October 31, Hoover informed the legal attaché in the London embassy (a member of the FBI) that since Vincent had been associated with persons Hoover considered suspect, Vincent should "not be contacted . . . in connection with Russian and Communist matters."[97] During the months that followed, the director's aides kept Hoover aware of Vincent's activities and how they were reported in the press. On May 22, 1948, a memorandum was prepared summarizing current "derogatory information": Hoover was reminded that Vincent had accompanied Henry Wallace on his Soviet-Asia mission; that Patrick Hurley had accused Vincent (and others) of "trying to destroy the Chinese National Government"; and that most recently the House Appropriations Committee had uncovered evidence indicating that Vincent might be "a Red Spy." After reading the report, Hoover scrawled on the bottom of the page: "What about a loyalty investigation of Vincent?"[98] D. M. Ladd, Hoover's chief assistant, told the director that the "facts" on Vincent had been sent to the attorney general along with a letter asking if he thought an investigation was necessary.[99] So far, Ladd reported, there had been no reply (only nine days had elapsed since the bureau's original letter).[100] Hoover again marked the paper with his comments—which were terse but direct: "Follow up."[101] Another letter was drafted and delivered to the attorney general.

Hoover received an answer from the Attorney General's Office on June 8, but it was probably not the one he had hoped for. The Justice Department informed Hoover that his memorandums had been sent to the

State Department to determine whether an investigation should be launched. Assistant Secretary of State John E. Peurifoy replied that virtually all of the information was in the possession of the department when Vincent was appointed minister and that "a review of his full record convinced the Department of his loyalty to the United States." As for the accusation that Vincent was a red spy, "this information," Peurifoy noted, "was originally reported . . . by an informant who, we have subsequently learned, was either grossly mistaken or misinformed." He invited the bureau to examine the department's files to decide if an investigation was warranted.[102] Assistant Attorney General Peyton Ford recommended to Hoover that the FBI examine the State Department's files but added that if it did not produce "leads which would seem to require additional investigation I do not believe that it is necessary to undertake a[n] investigation . . . at the present time."[103] Agents reviewed Vincent's security file and found in it no new information; Hoover therefore decided not to ask permission to conduct an investigation.[104] But he was quick to point out that the final verdict had not been rendered by the bureau. He ordered that a notation be placed in Vincent's Loyalty File explaining that information had been sent to the State Department but due to the "absence of a specific request" no investigation was being conducted. In short, Hoover was insisting that the record clearly show that it was the State Department which was ultimately responsible for the decision not to investigate John Carter Vincent.[105]

Although the FBI had not been authorized to investigate Vincent, it continued to watch him, updating his file whenever Vincent's name appeared in the press. A memorandum written in May 1949 noted that Senator Styles Bridges had recently asked the State Department for Vincent's loyalty file, believing that it would help him learn who was "responsible for the tragedy of China." Also of interest was an article in Kohlberg's *Plain Talk* which accused Vincent of being "a member of a pro-Communist China group in the State Department." Both the article and a news clipping covering Bridges's charges were added to Vincent's file.[106]

Hoover renewed his effort to have Vincent investigated following McCarthy's speech to the Senate in February 1950. On February 24, the director received a lengthy report summarizing each of McCarthy's cases and identifying the individuals behind the numbers. The "High-Ranking Diplomat" McCarthy called a spy was "probably identical with John Carter Vincent," Hoover learned. When the senator repeated his charges against Vincent on March 19, Hoover wrote an assistant: "What are the facts on this?" The next day a copy of McCarthy's statement (which now appeared as part of Vincent's file) was sent to the director, with the reminder that Vincent had never been investigated.[107] After studying the most recent information, Hoover again contacted the assistant attorney general. "As you are aware," Hoover wrote Ford on April 21, "Vincent's name appears among those . . . cases recently mentioned by Senator Joseph R. McCarthy in the United States Senate. . . . Charges have [also] been made in the public press that Vincent is . . . pro-Communist. . . . For an example, . . . *Plain Talk* magazine for May 1947, carries an article by Alfred Kohlberg, in which John Carter Vincent is described as the 'chief figure in the pro-Soviet clique in the State Department.' In view of the above, it will be appreciated if you will advise whether . . . a full field loyalty investigation . . . should be conducted at this time."[108] On May 1, after consulting with the State Department, Ford gave his consent.[109]

The director wasted little time in setting the bureau's machinery in motion. On May 10, by "special messenger," the FBI's fifty-nine district offices were ordered to begin their investigation. Accompanying the order was a ten-page report describing the "facts" in the Vincent case: Included were extracts from McCarthy's Senate speech ("Case No. 2"), the 1948 House Appropriations Subcommittee hearing ("Case No. 52"), and articles on Vincent which had appeared in the right-wing *Washington Times-Herald* and *Plain Talk*. "This case should be assigned to experienced agent[s]," Hoover told his lieutenants, "and should be given very prompt attention." A deadline of May 30, 1950, twenty days hence, was set for the completion of the inquiry.[110] Hoover also contacted the State Department's Division of Security requesting that it conduct an overseas investigation of Vincent.[111] (The State Department, much to Hoover's annoyance,[112] was responsible for conducting investigations of American citizens living outside the western hemisphere.) At the same time, the director asked the department to furnish a list of persons who knew Vincent and could report on his loyalty to the United States. S. D. Boykin, of the Division of Security, sent Hoover the names of nine foreign service officers who had worked with Vincent; and each time the bureau asked for an interview abroad, State Department security agents were promptly sent where Hoover directed.[113] During the next eighteen months officers interviewed friends and associates of Vincent's in eleven countries around the world: England, France, Italy, Switzerland, Czechoslovakia, the Philippines, Hong Kong, Singapore, Thailand, Japan, and India.[114] FBI agents were also permitted to again examine Vincent's file in the Department of State. "Set out necessary leads at once [after] review of this file," Hoover told the special agent in charge of the bureau's Washington office. "Investigation in this case must be very thorough and all logical leads covered."[115] Finally, Hoover ordered his representative in Paris to interview Vincent himself: on the Wallace mission, in particular, and his own career in general, if the minister wished to volunteer such information.[116]

The investigation of Vincent at home was as extensive as it was abroad. The FBI conducted interviews in twenty states, the District of Columbia, and the territory of Hawaii. Agents began their work in Kansas, where Vincent was born fifty years earlier. Their first stop was the Topeka Bureau of Vital Statistics where they searched for a record certifying Vincent's birth. When none was found, they moved on to Seneca, Vincent's native home. There they checked school records, again finding no listing for John Carter Vincent. A birth announcement was finally found in the files of the Seneca *Courier Democrat*. Having established that Vincent had in fact been born, agents then combed the town looking for people who remembered Frank and Beulah Vincent and their four children, Ned, Frank, John Carter, and Margaret. "Mr. and Mrs. Vincent had a good reputation in Seneca and were considered loyal citizens," the agents later told Hoover. But as for the subject of the investigation, all those questioned found it difficult evaluating Vincent's loyalty since he had been"an infant when he resided in Seneca." There was nothing more for the agents to report: During their inquiry they discovered that the family had moved to Macon, Georgia, sometime between 1905 and 1907; therefore, they informed the bureau's Atlanta office on May 19 that it was now their responsibility to examine the next chapter in Vincent's life story.[117]

Three days later, agents from Atlanta arrived in Macon. They checked first with the chief of police to determine whether Vincent had a criminal record and the credit bureau to see if he had any debts. Agents visited Mercer University and questioned officials, former classmates, and neighbors who stated that Vincent "was regarded as [a] loyal American while living in Macon." But at least one-third of those interrogated pointed out that they had not seen Vincent since the early 1920s and were "therefore not in a position to comment on his loyalty since that time."[118] The results of the investigations were forwarded to bureau headquarters in Washington.

(Hoover also sent his agents to Clemson College to examine Vincent's life from September 1920 to June 1921. A number of his former professors were interviewed but none could remember Vincent. The FBI again tried to evaluate Vincent's financial probity at the age of twenty but discovered that the town had no credit agency.)[119]

While the bureau was studying Vincent's past, the State Department was investigating his present activities. On May 13, Chief of Security Donald L. Nicholson (a former FBI agent), wired Regional Security Offices overseas that the "FBI has requested urgent investigation . . . of John Carter Vincent . . . based on allegations he possesses pro-Communist sympathies. . . . Obtain discreetly all possible information concerning this allegation."[120] Special instructions were sent to William H. Hussey, regional security supervisor for Western Europe, who would investigate Vincent's office. "Due to Vincent's position dept. [*sic*] cannot make the usual request that investigation be conducted by chief of mission," Hussey was told. "[P] roceed to Switzerland for interviews with those members mission staff that may be able to clarify the allegations. . . . Initiative should be used to develop new leads."[121]

Hussey flew to Bern and spent two weeks questioning Vincent's closest aides. "No derogatory information developed," Secretary Acheson was informed by telegram on June 6. "Answers to questions depict individual typical man in the street who enjoys baseball, bowling, tennis, and is deeply fond of his wife and children. Statements also indicate he regards all foreigners from an American viewpoint and has not strayed away from his Southern Baptist upbringing. Characterized by all . . . as very intelligent, high-minded, absolutely objective and truthful. No leads concerning possible disloyalty or pro-Communist viewpoints. . . . Eight individuals questioned . . . outspoken in support of him as fine representative American citizen who cherishes his country and all it stands for."[122]

Hussey's finding were of little help to Vincent: The loyalty machinery ground on. State Department and FBI investigators continued their work under the watchful eyes of their superiors. When the deadline set for completion of the bureau's investigation was not met, Hoover fired off an angry letter to the special agent in charge of the Washington field office. The Vincent case was "delinquent," Hoover stated. "The Bureau is holding you personally responsible for [its] immediate completion."[123]

The subject of this controversy wanted to make his own public statement but was denied authorization by the State Department. As early as March 7, two weeks after McCarthy's Senate speech, Vincent sent a long letter to Assistant Secretary of State John E. Peurifoy, explaining his position, and requesting that it be made known to the press. "A friend has sent me a copy of the Congressional *Record* of February 20," Vincent wrote. "I gather that I have been "identified' in the press as Senator McCarthy's Case No. 2. I am, in fact, one of our 'foreign ministers,' although the job is hardly what I would call 'high brass.' I did misplace a piece of clothing sometime in 1946 but I must profess myself amazed that the incident became a matter of record. . . . It was not my piece of clothing. It was a raincoat which some visitor left behind in the Far Eastern Office . . . and which hung there for weeks." Vincent continued:

One rainy day, having no coat with me, I put this raincoat on to go to lunch. Returning, I stopped at a Department wash room and forgot to take the raincoat when I left. Some days later, I recalled the oversight and called the Building Guard Office, where I learned that the coat had been found and turned over to the Department's Security . . . Office. [T]hat office . . . informed me that there was a piece of paper in the inside breast pocket containing writing in what looked like Russian. I explained the history of the coat and asked whether the writing gave a clue to ownership. [They] did not know, but subsequent examination showed the writing . . . to be a practise or exercise in Russian word endings. . . , presumably the work of someone studying Russian. The coat was returned to the Far Eastern Office. When we moved to [the] New State [Department Building] in 1947, I appropriated the coat and still have it.

Vincent assured Peurifoy that he would be happy to "return the raincoat to the real owner, should his memory . . . be revived by Senator McCarthy's story."[124]

He was completely mystified by McCarthy's charge of espionage. "I have never acted directly or indirectly to provide espionage agents of Russia or any other country with information in the State Department or from any other governmental source," he stated. "The Senator's story is simply not true. . . . I do not believe there were people in the Far Eastern Office capable of such action. No case of the kind came or was brought to my attention."[125]

He continued his message with a brief autobiographical sketch which he hoped the department would release to enquiring reporters. There was certainly nothing subversive about his background, he argued. His father had been a real estate agent in Macon, Georgia, who, with Vincent's stepmother, had been active in no more radical an organization than the Baptist Church. His surviving brother was a banker in South Carolina; his sister was married to a rear admiral and his wife's two brothers were insurance brokers, "respected and sturdy Republicans."[126]

In words that would later become tragically familiar, Vincent reaffirmed his loyalty to the United States. "I have never joined any political organization, 'front,' or . . . political party," he told Peurifoy. "I am a Jeffersonian democrat, a Lincolnian republican, and an admirer since youth of Woodrow Wilson. I am a member of the Cosmos Club. . . , the Sigma Alpha Epsilon fraternity, and the Baptist Church. . . . I have never knowingly associated with American Communists or Communist sympathizers. I say 'American' because my official duties have . . . caused me to be in contact with foreign Communists. Chou En-lai, for instance (the Foreign Minister of the Chinese Communist Regime), I met in the house of Chiang Kai-shek. He was head of a Liaison Ministry to

Chungking during the war. Here and in Washington . . . I have met foreign Communists at official or social functions. Our relationships have been perfunctory, except where official business had to be transacted."[127]

"Any American, in public or private life, has a right to criticize our policies toward China and the Far East. . . ," Vincent concluded "but he does not have the right to impugn, simply on the basis of disagreeing with the policies themselves, the motives or character of those who are charged with the duty of implementing them. One is free to question my ability; but they cannot, in truth, question my loyalty. My record of public service is clear and so is my conscience. I regret very much the circumstances that have caused me to make this protest of innocence and loyalty but it is my belief that you, and if you approve, the public, have a right to expect a statement from me."[128]

This letter received no answer from the State Department, and ever conscientious, Vincent refused to comment on McCarthy's charges without the department's prior approval. On May 12, he asked again for permission to defend himself: "United Press, Associated Press and *Times* have indicated desire to have statement from me re McCarthy campaign," Vincent cabled Peurifoy. "I have declined saying that department will make statement when warranted. I have no desire to feed the press but am prepared to make statement if you would consider it would be useful. As you know, If McCarthy is inferring as he clearly seems to be that I have or ever have had any leanings in any direction other than firmly toward democracy and my own country then he is wrong again and malicious."[129] Peurifoy wired back, "Suggest you sit tight for time being. If we need statement will get in touch with you. Sorry you are being subjected this type treatment."[130] Ironically, at the exact moment this expression of sympathy was transmitted to Bern, the department ordered its overseas investigation of Vincent.[131]

The Senate was also busy with its own inquest. A foreign relations subcommittee, chaired by Senator Millard Tydings, began its hearings on State Department loyalty in March. Vincent expected that McCarthy would use this new forum to continue his attack but, surprisingly, the senator shifted the spotlight to other personalities.[132] Why McCarthy chose to focus his attention elsewhere is still not clear: Some contemporary observers believed that "McCarthy hesitated about pressing his charges against Vincent because he received word . . . that General George C. Marshall [was] ready to come to Vincent's defense."[133] An even more likely explanation is that the reports he received from Alfred Kohlberg[134] convinced him that there were other more important suspects to pursue, specifically the man who finally became McCarthy's principal target, Professor Owen Lattimore of Johns Hopkins University.[135] Then, as now, it is difficult to understand the senator's behavior: "One never knows what Senator McCarthy may come up with at any hour of any day," one newspaper noted at the time.[136]

After four months of angry hearings, the Tydings committee filed its final report on McCarthy's charges against the State Department. The Democratic majority accused him of "perpetrating 'a fraud and a hoax' upon the American people . . . [and] charged him with deliberate and willful falsehood."[137] A major source of the senator's accusations against Owen Lattimore and others, the report stated, was Alfred Kohlberg, who was described as a "New York importer whose wealth appears to have stemmed from contacts with . . . the Nationalist Government of China."[138]

The senators also noted that the charges originally made against John Carter Vincent were "absurd" and that an examination of his loyalty file did "not show him to be disloyal or a security risk."[139]

To Vincent, the Tydings committee's vote of confidence seemed to indicate that his troubles were now finally over. But Switzerland was too far from Washington for Vincent to appreciate the political passions aroused by McCarthy's speeches. McCarthy called the committee's report "a green light to the Red Fifth Column in the United States," and the Senate as a whole adopted the report on "a straight party line vote," after one of the bitterest debates in its history. More harassment was in store for those whom McCarthy and his allies had singled out for destruction. "No matter how much McCarthy bleeds in this procedure," the senator told a cheering audience in May 1950, "the job will continue until we have a thorough house cleaning."[140]

McCarthy and his associates apparently agreed with the Tydings committee that Vincent's file contained nothing indicating procommunism because next they began to invent the evidence they so desperately needed to prove their charges. In May, two months before the committee rendered its verdict, Robert Morris, the counsel for the Republican minority and a friend of McCarthy's, tried "to load Vincent's loyalty file" by telling Naval Intelligence that he had received information "that Vincent was a Communist."[141] McCarthy was also corresponding with Charles Davis, a young American living in Europe, who claimed to have damaging information on Vincent. In August, McCarthy informed Davis that he would be contacted by John Farrand, a friend of Robert Morris, whom the senator had hired to act as his "lawyer" in Europe. "Any arrangements

181   The Paths of Vengeance

made with Farrand," McCarthy told Davis, "will be satisfactory to me."[142] This communication led to the strangest attempt yet made by McCarthy to wreck Vincent's career.

The true identity of Charles Davis is difficult to determine. Given the number of different roles that he played during his brief but colorful political career probably not even Davis himself was certain. At various times he claimed to be an actor, a singer, a Communist journalist, an FBI agent, and an official of the State Department. He was some of these and more; in an effort to ruin Vincent he also became a forger and a spy.

Born in Dallas in 1927, Davis grew up in Los Angeles where he joined the Communist Party sometime before his twentieth birthday. In 1947 he enlisted in the United States Navy, "for the purpose," he later stated, "of propagandizing service personnel." Within a year he was dishonorably discharged because he admitted being a homosexual. He then returned to California to become a correspondent for the *People's World,* the *Daily Worker* of the West Coast.[143]

Late in September 1949, he boarded the SS *Washington* bound for Le Havre, France; his mission: "to effect closer liaison between the European and American Communist parties." Five days after his arrival he made the first of what were to be several visits to the American embassy in Paris, asking for money; this time to cover the cost of traveling to Antwerp where he claimed to know someone "who would help him work his way home."[144] His next stop was not Antwerp but Lausanne where he was picked up by Swiss police and charged with stealing an overcoat. Somehow he still found time for his political activities: He contacted several Communist groups, attended meetings, and gave speeches in a number of cities.[145]

In 1950, Davis assumed a new role—counterspy in the employ of the United States government. On January 16, he visited the American consulate in Geneva, admitted his Communist affiliations, and offered to provide information on his "local Communist contacts." The consulate was apparently impressed by Davis because in June he was put on a train to Paris and told to contact the embassy, which was informed that Davis "might be of help." During the next three months American officials gave Davis nine thousand francs in return for information about his experiences in the Communist movement.[146]

Such rewards barely covered his weekly expenses and by mid-summer Davis was "broke" and "stranded." (In July he urgently cabled a relative asking for an immediate loan of forty-five dollars.) It was at this time that Davis first wrote Joe McCarthy. McCarthy replied on August 15, thanking him for his "interest in my efforts to expose Communists and subversives" and expressing curiosity about the records Davis claimed to have. The senator said he was "very much interested" in Davis's papers and offered to arrange a meeting between Davis and his "personal representative."[147]

"I am overjoyed to get your letter," Davis wrote McCarthy. "At this moment I have been in Paris contacting all delegates to Prague from America and Americans in Paris who are Communists. . . . The documents are copies sent to the top CP man in Switzerland, also some papers on atomic theory and American troop movements in Germany. These papers are top rank materials and can sink all persons underground in the CP of the USA." Davis asked McCarthy for a press card to facilitate entry into political meetings, fifty thousand francs to pay off various informants, and the agent McCarthy promised to send. "I hope to have the pleasure to work with you and getting material [sic] to you," Davis told the senator. McCarthy, always eager to receive potentially valuable information, responded quickly to Davis's letter, assuring him that he would soon be contacted by John Farrand, the man *Newsweek* later called McCarthy's European detective.[148]

Farrand met Davis in Paris, received the documents, and told him that Senator McCarthy was especially interested in "getting evidence" on John Carter Vincent. Davis was given one hundred fifty dollars to obtain information concerning Vincent. (The money, Farrand explained mysteriously, had come from New York.) Eventually, the two conceived the idea of sending Vincent a fake telegram signed by Swiss Communist Emil Stampfli. Davis composed the text of the wire, signed Stampfli's name and sent it to Vincent. A copy was mailed to Senator McCarthy to be used to prove that Vincent was linked to the Communists. Davis also mentioned the telegram to his contacts at the embassy and gave them a photostat of the receipt Stampfli was supposed to have received after sending the wire.[149]

In the weeks that followed, Davis developed another elaborate scheme to discredit Vincent. Learning that Vincent was scheduled to visit Geneva in late November for a series of meetings, Davis immediately wrote to the minister and invited him to use his apartment during the trip. For some reason Davis felt confident that Vincent would accept the invitation of an unknown twenty-three-year-old American of doubtful background, so he informed McCarthy that he had arranged to have "the flat wired and all talk on tape to you." He asked McCarthy to send additional funds to pay for the installation of the listening devices (he promised to keep the receipts). "I think we have Vincent for good if he lives at my place," Davis assured the senator.[150]

But September and October came and went without word from either Vincent or McCarthy, and Davis began to panic. On the afternoon of

November 16 he again visited the Geneva consulate, this time to request its help in leaving Switzerland. "Things were getting too 'hot' for him in this country," Davis told Consul Randolph Dickens, Jr. "He said he was . . . caught between the Swiss political police on one hand and members of the local Communist Party on the other," Dickens noted, "and that his situation was so precarious that he desired the consulate to issue him a set of orders, together with money for transportation, to Marseilles and then to Tangier where he would like to 'hole up' for several months." Davis also admitted that he had been paid by Senator McCarthy to investigate John Carter Vincent, but he "now thought that . . . McCarthy had gone too far and he wished to get away from his control."[151]

Dickens, and other officials, dismissed Davis's testimony as the rantings of a man who was "not mentally normal." "Mr. Davis freely admitted to playing all ends toward the middle and so contradicted himself that little of what he said appeared to be founded on any truth," concluded Dickens. "His ability to continually contradict himself and then calmly wriggle himself out by some vague explanation . . . leads one to believe that he is a pathological liar." For once, however, Davis's statements came close to the truth. The Swiss police were searching for the author of the telegram received by Vincent in October, and McCarthy was dissociating himself from his European informant. The Senator and his staff had examined the documents Davis considered so important and determined that they were worthless. Davis, McCarthy now concluded, was "completely irresponsible" and he directed his assistant Donald Surine to inform the young man that his services were no longer required. By the time Davis received this letter he was in jail, charged with mail fraud and espionage.[152]

During Davis's trial, his relationship with Farrand and McCarthy was made public but the senator denied that he had ever hired Davis. He did admit that Davis sent him "some information" on Vincent, which he gave to the FBI; Farrand had also done some "work" for him but he declined to discuss further the nature of Farrand's work.[153] (Never one to let opportunity go by, McCarthy told investigators that Vincent knew Davis intimately and owned a diary which referred "to acts which Vincent attempted to get Davis himself to do."[154])

Although McCarthy's accusations and the antics of Davis and Farrand were exposed as a hoax, these attacks on Vincent were publicly embarrassing, and they soon began to do serious damage to his career.

In March 1951, Vincent was almost appointed ambassador to

Costa Rica when the State Department, fearing a Senate battle over his nomination, abruptly shifted him to Tangier, Morocco, a post not requiring Senate confirmation. News of the appointment,[155] which Vincent heard first from the *New York Herald Tribune* reporter Bert Andrews, came as no surprise. In December, Vincent had received a transatlantic telephone call from Elbridge Durbrow, chief of Foreign Service Personnel, notifying him that he was soon to be transferred to Costa Rica, perhaps elsewhere should Vincent's nomination as ambassador create problems for Truman's administration. He was not especially happy about going to Costa Rica, but Vincent told Durbrow that he preferred to face "the issue squarely and fight through . . . to [a] win or lose decision in the Senate."[156]

The State Department was "sympathetic to my point of view," Vincent later wrote his mother, "but stated that larger issues than my confirmation were involved and that it [might] be best to take a post which would not require going to the Senate." Vincent understood the department's position and in January wrote Durbrow: "If you are worried about an unfriendly section of the Senate ganging up on me, please don't. If they don't like the cut of my trousers, I shall be perfectly willing to take some non-honorable but useful job." When Tangier was suggested, Vincent "accepted, considering 'team interest' superior to my own."[157]

At one o'clock on the morning of March 3, Bert Andrews called to get his reaction to the State Department's decision. Vincent told him he would accept the new assignment. "Why?" Andrews asked, since he believed Tangiers "a terrific comedown." "Don't you remember the old Baptist Sunday School Song?" Vincent replied with a laugh. "It goes 'I'll go where you want me to go, Dear Lord.'" Then, in a more serious vein, he added: "I'll take the Tangiers appointment because I am in no position to fight this thing financially" (that is, he was not prepared to retire from the Foreign Service), "although I could fight it morally."[158]

Personally, Vincent did not consider his transfer "a terrific comedown"[159] but it did entail a twenty-five-hundred-dollar-a-year cut in salary[160] and was widely interpreted as a demotion. The announcement produced a heated debate in Washington, as Vincent's critics and supporters rushed to comment on the news. As expected, McCarthy and Kohlberg were ecstatic and cited the State Department's action as evidence to support their view that Vincent was a security risk.[161] *Time*, a longtime foe of Vincent, used the incident to repeat the charges that Vincent "assiduously promoted an anti-Chiang policy that played right into Mao's hands." The "Vincent Case had already grown so hot," *Time* said, "that the White House was reluctant just to leave him in Switzerland, a major listening post for the meeting of East and West. Finally, the State

Department hit on a slick way out. It appointed Vincent diplomatic agent and U.S. Counsul General to Tangier." Accompanying the article was a picture of Vincent captioned: "Some Hiss, Some Steam."[162]

Vincent's friends came just as quickly to his defense. "Mr. Vincent is a first-rate foreign service officer," the *Washington Post* editorialized, "and in diverting him more or less off the diplomatic map, the State Department has toadied outrageously to McCarthyism. Experience, surely, should have taught the executive branch that such timidity, to use no stronger word, merely puts a premium on McCarthyism. It boosts his stock, exaggerates his ego and whets his appetite. That Secretary Acheson, who himself has suffered at the hands of Senator McCarthy, concurred in this frightened deal is a sad commentary."[163]

Some urged Vincent to refuse his new assignment and take his case directly to the Senate and the American people. James McHugh informed Vincent that he knew several distinguished Washington attorneys who would happily represent him without charge in court or before congressional committee just for the opportunity to fight McCarthy. "The point at issue is you as an individual and loyal servant of the Foreign Service," McHugh insisted, "and your right to be cleared of this slander against your name."[164]

Vincent chose to go to Tangier. He was not insensitive to the issues raised by McHugh but, like the State Department, preferred to "avoid a full scale debate on Far Eastern policy which request for my confirmation would have provoked and which would have involved many besides myself. I might have won," Vincent later noted, "but an infinite amount of trouble would have been stirred up in the process which is just what the Republicans want."[165] Moreover, he was a firm believer in "one of the cardinal points of the Foreign Service—that a Career Minister should go willingly where he is sent without regard to prestige."[166] In the final analysis, he had quoted Baptist scripture to Bert Andrews only half in jest: He was a veteran Foreign Service officer who would go where his government (and his God) sent him.[167]

Had Vincent decided to fight for confirmation he probably would have been defeated. In the spring of 1951 the Korean War was dragging on, seemingly without end; the previous December, the Chinese Communists had crossed the Yalu River and inflicted serious casualties on American forces. And, just one month after the announcement of Vincent's Tangier appointment, President Truman dismissed General Douglas MacArthur from his Asian command. The membrane of political civility—already strained by partisanship—now broke apart completely. McCarthy publicly called the president a "son of a bitch,"[168] and Senator William Jenner urged that Truman be impeached.[169] MacArthur received a hero's welcome upon his return to the United States, and the Senate launched a special investigation into his dismissal which lasted nine weeks; during the hearings Republicans once again attacked Truman's Far Eastern policy which they said began with the "loss" of China and now led to disaster in Korea. Against this background, Vincent's nomination as ambassador probably would have been defeated.

Now, no one was immune from Republican attack. In June, McCarthy took on General George C. Marshall. His lengthy Senate speech on Marshall's career, McCarthy told reporters, gave documented proof of "a conspiracy so immense and an infamy so black as to dwarf any previous such venture in the history of man."[170] But McCarthy did not linger long on Marshall; after his assault he moved on to other personalities, some new, others already familiar.

He returned to John Carter Vincent on August 9. This time he claimed to be reading to the Senate fresh reports never heard before. "Please keep in mind that these 'letters of charges' were not prepared by me," McCarthy told his colleagues, "they were prepared as the result of investigations by the FBI or State Department investigators." Vincent (whom the Senator labeled "an individual well known to all of us") was now accused of "being a member of the Communist Party" and "also charged with espionage activities while in Switzerland." And there was more: McCarthy noted that during Vice-President Wallace's Soviet-Asia mission Owen Lattimore and Vincent had actually been praised publicly by "a high official of the Soviet Government." During a dinner party in Siberia, "a top representative of the Soviet" had proposed a toast to Lattimore and Vincent which in McCarthy's mind proved that the two were Communists. "To Owen Lattimore and John Carter Vincent," the toast went "America's experts on China on whom rests great responsibility for China's future." "So much for John Carter Vincent," McCarthy concluded.[171]

Word of McCarthy's latest attack reached Vincent as he was settling into his new residence in Tangier. "Weary" and "disgusted," he prepared another statement for the press giving his view of the personal and national consequences of McCarthyism. "For myself," Vincent said, "the fact that the [State Department] Loyalty Board may be conducting an investigation on my behalf causes me no concern whatever. I am proud of my 27 years of service. It will stand the test of malicious representation regardless of the source or character." More serious, Vincent believed, was the way that "anonymous accusers" could question his loyalty without identifying themselves, a practice that ran counter to American judicial tradition. "This is a dangerous state of affairs, for the interests of our country in general and for the government service in particular. . . . McCarthy's nefarious campaign . . . against loyal State Department officials . . . has caused untold harm and embarrassment in the conduct of our foreign affairs."[172]

Vincent's restrained and dignified responses to McCarthy's scurrilous charges (the farthest he ever went in personally attacking McCarthy was once telling reporters that McCarthy was "like a bad tooth that should be extracted")[173] frequently mystified his friends and even angered his own wife. They wondered how he could remain so "calm," so "detached," so "objective" when confronted by such outrageous provocations.[174] It was his "equable and philosophical temperament," his "Chinese philosophy," and his faith in "ultimate justice" which sustained and comforted him, he would tell them repeatedly: "Being sure that I am right while I am being wronged gives me strength in the future."[175]

Elizabeth Vincent, "very impatient by nature" and especially "impatient of injustice,"[176] found it more difficult controlling her temper. "Several days ago the Paris *Herald Tribune* carried a story on the front page about McCarthy again accusing. . . John Carter Vincent of being communist . . . or communist inclined," she wrote her children after McCarthy's speech.

> This is the Hitler technique of repeating the big lie often enough with the hope, finally, of making your point seem true; and making McCarthy's point means to discredit the Democratic administration and get his brand of Republicans in . . . God help us! (My family having been staunch Republicans for years, I look upon his espousing of that party's future with fear and horror. . . . WHAT KIND of Republicans are they???)
>
> All of this is deeply disturbing to me, first because I am an American citizen and that is a big responsibility for anyone; second because all forms of injustice burn me up, and this is such a flagrant case and in such cowardly form (McCarthy will never make these accusations where he can be challenged. He will not expose himself to a fair court of law to prove any of his charges, but takes advantage of the immunity of the Senate floor to deliver his false accusations) that I am often consumed with rage, mostly because your Father says there is nothing to do and if there were, HE would not do it. He has the aristocratic viewpoint, how COULD he stoop to answer a swine like McCarthy who . . . said even worse things of General Marshall who of course did not even waste his breath to answer or deny any of them.
>
> . . . This is a difficult period for all of us. I don't know how much your comrades in school believe "the big lie" if repeated often enough and I don't know how much ammunition you would like to have in your guns to shoot back at them. But there is one undeniable fact, that not ONE—not one single accusation that McCarthy has made has been proved to be correct. The FBI would certainly lean backwards to give the harsh facts about any communist or past communist they investigated. They have investigated your father's case . . . ad nauseum. Everyone of our friends has been written to, every associate,

every connection, a painful experience I find for a free-born New England Congregational militantly democratic citizen like your Ma, and equally so your deeply religious-grounded, super-honorable, wise and tolerant Pa . . . but in no instance has a compromising fact been unearthed.

. . . McCarthy is not only a bad man but a cowardly man and below our notice personally, but not from the notice of an American Citizen who cherishes the institutions of his Republic. Ours is a daring experiment—Democracy WITH freedom and we must never let demagogues endanger either. In my position I cannot fight—some day you both may be called upon to fight just such inimical forces and with your background and heritage, you will be able to. Now you can only bear any social discomforts that may come your way with equanimity and even pride; I think it is a small price to pay to be the son and daughter of your Father and citizens of the United States of America. Both are real privileges.[177]

As Mrs. Vincent wrote these words developments occurred in Washington that would test every ounce of faith and tolerance both Vincents possessed. The painful events of the past four years—the obstructed promotion, McCarthy's charges, the FBI and State Department investigations, the Davis affair, and the transfer to Tangier—all were but a prelude to a more horrifying nightmare still to come.

7

Bearing False Witness

Two weeks after McCarthy's Senate speech, John Carter Vincent was once again the subject of national controversy. On August 23, 1951, counsel for the Senate Subcommittee on Internal Security asked the witness Louis F. Budenz, ex-Communist and former editor of the *Daily Worker:* "Was John Carter Vincent a member of the Communist Party?"

Budenz replied: "From official reports that I have received he was."[1]

Elaborating further, Budenz affirmed that in 1944 he had "heard in official Communist Party circles that John Carter Vincent and Owen Lattimore were members of the Communist Party traveling with Henry Wallace. . . . The trip by Wallace to China was followed by the Communists with a great deal of interest . . . ," Budenz told the subcommittee. "In those discussions [in the Politburo] it was pointed out that Mr. Wallace was . . . under good influence from the Communist viewpoint, . . . that he had on the one hand Mr. Lattimore and on the other hand John Carter Vincent, both of whom were described as being in line with the Communist viewpoint, seeing eye to eye with it, and that they would guide Mr. Wallace largely along those lines."[2] "The Communists were eager that Mr. Vincent advance and that he obtain a place in the State Department where he could get rid of [Ambassador] Hurley and . . . also influence policy."[3]

Budenz's charges against Vincent were the most serious yet made;

190

Vincent now became the first top State Department official to be seriously charged with actual Communist Party membership since the conviction of Alger Hiss.[4]

News of Budenz's testimony reached Vincent almost immediately. The Associated Press telegraphed its Spanish correspondent, requesting him to contact the American minister to learn his reaction to Budenz's charges. After reading the telegram containing Budenz's statement, Vincent snapped angrily: "No comment! Except that . . . son of a bitch should be in jail or hell!" The reporter asked for "something printable" so Vincent composed himself and drafted a statement for the press: "I do not know Budenz but he is manifestly either a misinformed fool or a vicious and subversive liar. In the serious business that confronts us we cannot afford the diversion of testimony of the kind he is giving."[5]

L ouis Francis Budenz was no stranger to jail or even to hell, if one accepts the sincerity of his much-publicized religious convictions. "White haired, palefaced, looking like a conservative elderly lawyer," Budenz had traveled a long road to his confrontation with John Carter Vincent. Born in Indiana in 1891, Budenz grew up in a "simple Catholic family" and attended parochial schools in Indianapolis. He was trained in the law and admitted to the bar in 1913 but practiced only briefly. Just a few months after becoming a lawyer he became involved in the politics of radical labor. During the 1920s he edited *Labor Age,* a leftist publication, and was active in organizing workers and picketing industrial plants, efforts which led to his arrest twenty-one times. For a decade he belonged to a succession of radical or socialist groups, before joining the Communist Party in 1935. Budenz was active in journalistic and political circles, becoming managing editor of the *Daily Worker* in 1941. Four years later he renounced his allegiance to communism and returned to the Catholic Church. His life as a Communist was over but a new life and career as a professional anti-Communist quickly began.[6]

In 1946, Budenz was contacted by the FBI and during the next five years became the most celebrated informer in the bureau's history. According to Budenz's own calculations, he spent a total of over three thousand hours, "the staggering equivalent of 375 eight hour days,"[7] telling government agents everything he knew about Communist operations.[8] He begged to be believed, on the grounds that former Communists were "the most truthful people in the world . . . : they have learned how utterly incorrect is the morality of Lenin, the morality of deceiving for a cause. They have learned in pain and suffering. . . . they have [had] a resurrection within themselves."[9] In the feverish atmosphere of the postwar years, the inner resurrection of ex-Communists like Louis Budenz became, for many Americans, a substitute for evidence and due process of law.[10] The more Budenz accused, the more popular and wealthy a public figure he became: By 1953, his activities as anti-Communist polemicist, lecturer, and congressional witness were earning him seventy thousand dollars a year.[11]

Budenz had the important help of Alfred Kohlberg in winning such wealth and status. Not long after Budenz left the Communist Party, Kohlberg rushed to his home in Crestwood, New Jersey, and the two became close friends. "We went to lunch together at least once a week," Budenz later told Kohlberg's biographer, "and oftener if something interesting was doing."[12] Kohlberg made available to Budenz his voluminous files on China and with the help of Congressman Walter Judd, introduced Budenz to Senator McCarthy and his aide Robert Morris. In 1950, Morris had tried to "load" Vincent's loyalty file; later, he had recommended that McCarthy hire John Farrand to act as his European agent; now he was counsel to the Senate Internal Security Subcommittee, before which Budenz testified that Vincent was a Communist. By August 1951, the chain connecting Kohlberg, Budenz, and Morris was solidly linked.

Budenz's testimony also shocked Henry Wallace and Joseph Alsop, who with Vincent had earlier called for the changes in American China policy that were now being labeled pro-Communist. The former vice-president wrote immediately to Senator Patrick McCarran, the chairman of the subcommittee, to inform him of the "erroneous nature of what Budenz had claimed."[13] Alsop, now one of the nation's most respected journalists, planned to answer Budenz's charges in his syndicated newspaper column. He spent a full week analyzing Budenz's charges in the *New York Herald Tribune*. His first piece contained the section of the K'un-ming cable which called for the replacement of General Stilwell by Albert C. Wedemeyer, an officer more acceptable to Chiang Kai-shek. Since Stilwell despised the Nationalists and admired the martial skills of the Communists, his removal, Alsop argued, was a definite setback for their cause. The Wallace-Vincent-Alsop recommendation was therefore "one of the really striking and decisive anti-Communist acts of the war."[14]

In two other pieces, Alsop raised serious questions about Budenz's honesty and that of McCarran and his staff. He pointed out that when

Budenz testified before the Tydings subcommittee he refused to state that Vincent was a Communist; but now, barely a year later, he did so confidently. How could Budenz reconcile such conflicting testimony, Alsop asked, especially in light of the important role Vincent played in preparing the K'un-ming cable? "There is only one answer to all these questions," Alsop wrote. "The contemporary documentary evidence refutes Budenz's late-remembered verbal evidence in implication and in detail. Every word he said about Vincent would surely be thrown out in any court of law in the land." In short, Alsop accused Budenz of committing perjury.[15]

The charge was then extended to include Robert Morris, McCarran's counsel. Alsop noted that it was Morris ("a specialist in leading questions") who directed Budenz "to testify as he did." Why was Morris unaware of the K'un-ming cable when "the document . . . was always available to the McCarran Subcommittee, either from Wallace's files or the Government file"? In fact, "Wallace communicated its substance to the McCarran Committee's close collaborator, Alfred Kohlberg, some months ago and then wrote about it . . . to Senator Pat McCarran himself, as soon as the Wallace trip of 1944 began to be discussed." At issue in the Budenz affair was not just the loyalty of John Carter Vincent, Alsop concluded, but more importantly the committe's "selective system of dealing with the documentary evidence" and its "effort to build an obviously false case around the Wallace [Mission]. This sort of thing, if permitted and approved for very much longer, can threaten the common liberties of any ordinary citizen."[16]

Alsop's columns had immediate political repercussions. On September 14, New York's Democratic Senator Herbert Lehman brought the journalist's charges to the attention of the Senate and asked permission to insert the three articles in the *Congressional Record* by unanimous consent. But Republican Senator Owen Brewster, an ally of McCarthy and McCarran, rose in protest, defeating Lehman's request. When word of the Democrat's effort reached McCarran, he became furious. "Shaking with rage," his "thin voice" cracking, the senator from Nevada accused Lehman of sponsoring "a columnist who charges a committee of the Senate [with] . . . subornation of perjury. . . . So far as I am concerned," McCarran told reporters, "the committee is not going to be bulldozed. . . . Let someone dispute [the charges] under oath when the time comes." "Senate observers cannot recall when McCarran so openly lost his temper," reporter William V. Shannon noted.[17]

Nine days later the conflict erupted anew when President Truman released to the public copies of Henry Wallace's reports from China.[18] The former vice-president had suggested this action to Truman in a letter on September 19:

> During the last three weeks [Wallace wrote Truman], there has been considerable newspaper and radio controversy as to what part John Carter Vincent and Owen Lattimore played in my trip to the Far East in 1944. . . . There has been testimony before the Senate Internal Security Committee that Messrs. Vincent and Lattimore were members of the Communist Party at that time and were relied on by the party leadership to "guide" me along the party line. Hence it is important to specify the parts that these two men took in the recommendations that I presented to President Roosevelt. As to Mr. Lattimore, he had no part whatever.
> Mr. Vincent, as the designated representative of the State Department, was naturally consulted by me when we were travelling together. [His] most important part was his assistance in the preparation of the [K'un-ming] cable. . . . Mr. Vincent joined in the advance discussions of the projected cable, was present while it was drafted and concurred in the result.[19]

To Wallace, the K'un-ming cable was "the most important contribution I made while in China." "History suggests that if my recommendation had been followed when made, the generalissimo would have avoided the disasters resulting from the Japanese offensive in East China later that summer. And if Chiang's government had thus been spared the terrible enfeeblement resulting from these disasters, the chances are good the generalissimo would have been ruling China today."[20]

With the publication of the Wallace papers the battle was now fully joined. On one side was McCarran's committee and its ex-Communist star witness whose evidence consisted of verbal statements based on vague "official" Communist reports; on the other was the Truman administration supported by Wallace's documents and Alsop's commentary. For once the Democrats seemed to be ascendent: "Mr. Henry Wallace's letter to the President . . . would seem to go far toward sustaining . . . Mr. Joseph Alsop," the New York Herald Tribune editorialized. "Mr. Alsop's basic point seems to stand—which is, that if the McCarran subcommittee is to throw any real light on the origins of past Far Eastern policy, it must do so by getting the evidence, rather than by repeating unsupported allegations."[21] The editors of the New Republic agreed, adding that Wallace's report "substantiates the grave and important charge of Joseph Alsop that Budenz perjured himself . . . in accusing Vincent and that the Committee, presided over by Pat McCarran, is guilty of subornation."[22]

Emboldened by the release of the Wallace reports, Senator Lehman tried again to insert the Alsop articles in the Congressional Record by unanimous consent. But again he was blocked by Brewster and other Republicans. This time Lehman would not be stopped; unable to win a ruling of unanimous consent, he spent the next hour "literally reading the Alsop articles into the records."[23]

While the debate raged in Washington, Vincent busied himself with his official duties and prepared to return to the United States for his first "home leave" in four years. His wife, son, and daughter had already left Tangier in late August; Sheila, twenty, was scheduled to enter Goucher College in Baltimore, while Jack, sixteen, planned to study at Phillips Exeter Academy in New Hampshire. Both had previously attended schools in Switzerland while their father was minister but decided to return to America to complete their education. The departure of his family saddened Vincent: "This is the god-damndest house to get lonesome in that I ever got lonesome in," he wrote Betty on August 21. "There isn't a thing in its curious roominess that I can get sentimental about or attach myself to. . . . The place and the people [here] are without meaning to me with you and the children gone." Knowing that she would be arriving in Washington "with the reverberations of the Budenz testimony ringing in your ears," he counseled patience and recommended silence should people inquire about it. "Concentrate on the children," he told her. "Don't let yourself be drawn, even by friends, into emotionally exhausting and inconclusive debates, or even mutual admiration discussions. . . . Tell them that your husband, who is a taciturn relic of the New Deal, will do the talking, when necessary."[24]

Vincent's own reaction to the statements of Budenz, Wallace, and Alsop was characteristic detachment, mixed with concern and surprise over the way ex-Communist and anti-Communist zealots had come to dominate American life. Although he "found it hard to get mad when I have a clear conscience," he was indignant because "a man like Budenz, who was one of Stalin's miserable stooges . . . can . . . damage the reputation of those who have devoted their lives to public service." "Every time I think of Budenz calling me a Communist agent, my old Baptist blood begins to boil," Vincent told journalist William Atwood in late September. "What can be done about men like Budenz? . . . He's just a damn liar. Can't the Committee try him for perjury?"[25]

Vincent also wrote directly to Senator McCarran: "I should appreciate knowing whether [Budenz] was asked to show the so-called 'official reports,' or to produce any other evidence to back up his statement. I know, as I know my own name and record, that he could not produce anything that could even bear the semblance of evidence. . . . To me, the conclusion seems inescapable that irresponsible testimony such as Budenz is wont to give is itself subversive to the interests of our country and democracy. . . . I do not think I have to reassure you that I am not and never have been a Communist," Vincent said. "If I do, I wish you would call me home to appear before your committee." In closing, he respectfully requested that the senator "find time to give me a brief answer to my inquiry." McCarran never replied.[26]

Vincent was as troubled by Wallace's and Alsop's "defense" as he was by Budenz's lies and McCarran's silence. He appreciated their statements, he told Betty, "but instead of pleasing me it makes me very uneasy. It is all so utterly distorted—out of focus." Wallace and Alsop were not "being dishonest," he wrote his brother Frank, "but the truth does not appear." The China story was far too complex to be discussed strictly in terms of actions and recommendations deemed pro- or anti-Communist, the standard by which all past behavior was now being judged. "Prompt White House response to [the K'un-ming cable] would no more have saved Chiang Kai-shek than a reinforced Swiss palace guard would have saved Louis XVI in [1789]," Vincent argued, in sharp contrast to Wallace and Alsop. "There never was a time when we could have saved China for Chiang Kai-shek without going into the country with a large army and literally establishing a protectorate. The historical tragedy is that the rise of Communism coincided with the complete deterioration of the Nationalist Government. Revolution there would have been. We tried to make it a liberal one but the odds were against us." In Vincent's mind, this interpretation was closer to the truth than the "calculated lies of Budenz" or the "defensive attitude" assumed by Wallace and Alsop. Why this explanation did not satisfy McCarran's committee and the American people puzzled him frequently in the late summer of 1951.[27]

In early October, Vincent boarded the American export liner S.S. *Constitution* bound for New York. He was tired, anxious, and above all, reluctant to degrade himself by directly challenging the McCarthyites. "I am about ready to go back to peach packing," he wrote Betty on the eve of his departure. ". . . I've had enough of 'foreign service.' . . . We'll find clear water to bathe in and fresh air to breathe somewhere. . . . You and I and the children . . . make life significant."[28]

Clear water and fresh air were not characteristic of the American political topography to which Vincent was returning. Like a cancer, anti-Communist hysteria had metastisized throughout the American body politic. "Never in the history of the world was one people as completely dominated, intellectually and morally, by another as the people of the United States by the people of Russia," observed Archibald MacLeish in 1949. "American foreign policy was a mirror image of Russian foreign policy: whatever the Russians did, we did in reverse. American domestic politics were conducted under a kind of upside down Russian veto: no man could be elected to public office unless he was on record as detesting the Russians, and no proposal could be erected, from a peace plan at one end to a military budget on the other, unless it could be demonstrated that the Russians wouldn't like it."[29]

The fall of China, Russian possession of the atomic bomb, the conviction of Alger Hiss, McCarthy's charges, the Korean war—all added fuel to the fires of extremist discontent. Within a short time, twenty-six states forbade Communists from seeking public office; twenty-eight states prohibited Communists from holding city or state civil service positions; more than two-thirds of the states required that men and women swear their allegiance to the United States before they were allowed to teach in local schools. Actors and actresses, and writers and directors, who had once belonged to the Communist Party or, just as typically, to liberal organizations now labeled Communist by the attorney general's list or the House Committee on Un-American Activities, found themselves out of work or in jail because they refused to cooperate with congressional committees. Some fled to Europe; others were forced to take up new occupations, and a few committed suicide.[30]

The China Service was suffering its own casualties. Blamed for the Communist conquest of China and the outbreak of the Sino-American war in Korea, several of Vincent's colleagues were being brought up on charges before the State Department's Loyalty-Security Board. O. Edmund Clubb and John Paton Davies, Jr., were suspended from duty in June 1951; both were judged innocent of procommunism a few months later, but Clubb believed that the damage done to his career was irreparable and resigned from the Foreign Service. John Service, long the target of Kohlberg and Company, also ran the security gauntlet in 1950 and 1951. In December 1951, the Civil Service Loyalty Review Board would declare him a security risk, a verdict which brought about his dismissal by Secretary Acheson. John Carter Vincent was soon to join their ranks.[31]

The attempt to ruin Vincent's career intensified on October 5, 1951, when Louis Budenz made his second appearance before the Senate Internal Security Subcommittee.

"Primly," "a little nervously yet with voluble assurance," Budenz repeated his charge that Vincent was a Communist who had directed Henry

Wallace toward a "Communist objective." Although Budenz had been accused of perjury, the committee continued to treat him courteously, even respectfully. They gave him every opportunity to reconcile his earlier testimony with the history Alsop had recounted in his columns. They believed that only Budenz, the ex-Communist, could define what acts were truly "pro-" or "anti-Communist."

"The contention has been made that [the K'un-ming] cables are demonstrably anti-Communist," Counsel Morris told Budenz. Did he agree? According to his understanding of the "Communist line" in the 1940s, Budenz replied, the cables "were in accord with the Communist policies at that time." Budenz also dismissed as untrue Alsop's belief that the appointment of General Wedemeyer was an anti-Communist act: "General Wedemeyer . . . was not opposed by the Communists. The Communists were very much opposed to General Chennault and didn't want him in the picture at all. They thought Wedemeyer was a better choice." Having satisfied the committee that he, rather than Alsop or Wallace, was correct in his interpretation of events that occurred seven years before, Budenz "left the witness stand in a little buzz of congratulations."[32]

To Joseph Alsop, Budenz's testimony was "altogether sensational." "Listening to Budenz' words in the stuffy little hearing room," Alsop later wrote, "I felt myself almost physically transported, over many years and half way 'round the world, to the little house among the rice paddies where Wallace, Vincent and I talked." He remembered that Wallace and Vincent's first choice to succeed Stilwell was not Wedemeyer, but Chennault, the man Budenz said the Communists did not want "in the picture at all." Instead of resolving the questions raised by his previous statements, Budenz's second appearance before the committee, Alsop noted, "caused [him] to sink deeper in the mire of conflict with historic fact."[33]

Enraged, Alsop wrote McCarran an open letter which appeared in the nation's newspapers on Sunday, October 7. He accused Budenz of telling the committee "a tissue of half truths," "a farrago of misrepresentation," and "three demonstrable lies." "It is hard to know which is more shocking—," Alsop declared, "Budenz' free and easy way with the reputations of American citizens, or his fantastic distortion of already recorded history." He asked McCarran to call him to testify before his committee.[34]

Reluctant to confront Alsop, McCarran informed the journalist that he would be heard "in due course" and in a surprise move ordered Henry Wallace to appear before the committee.[35] "Although Wallace had never refused to provide information to any investigating committee," note historians Edward and Frederick Schapsmeir, "Senator Pat McCarran... took it upon himself to issue the former Vice President a subpoena..., the first such calculated insult ever dealt him."[36] Additional insults quickly followed. Wallace was given less than a day's notice to prepare himself for the hearing which was to be held behind closed doors, its time and place a guarded secret. The committee gave him an unfriendly reception when he appeared on October 9: By formal motion, it denied Wallace's request that his statement be placed in the record and also refused him the right to be heard in an open session.[37]

To McCarran's dismay, Wallace released his statement to the press[38] and indicated how he had been treated by the committee. The *Washington Post* and the *New Republic*, longtime foes of McCarran, denounced the senator and his committee. "It seems to be the settled doctrine of the McCarran Subcommittee that accusations concerning the loyalty of reputable citizens may be made at open hearings but that refutations may be offered only in executive session," said the *Post*. "Why does the McCarran Subcommittee seem so eager to publicize Louis Budenz' sensational charges and so reluctant to publicize any rebuttal of them?" William Atwood suggested an answer to these questions in the *New Republic:* "The ruthless attempt to deny Wallace a chance to get his side of the story before the public should permanently destroy the illusion that the McCarran Committee is conducting an impartial and judicious investigation of our Far Eastern policy.... McCarran has never been interested in getting the whole truth. From the outset, he and his colleagues set out by hook or by crook to prove McCarthy's case against ... the State Department."[39]

McCarran, stung by such criticism, decided to permit both Wallace and Alsop to testify in open session. Wallace appeared first, on Wednesday, October 17.

For five and a half hours, the former vice-president answered questions about his China mission in a committee room crowded with interested spectators. This time he was allowed to read a statement, and he used the opportunity to speak directly to the charges leveled by Budenz. "I refuse to believe that members of a great and powerful body, the most distinguished legislative body in the entire world, can possibly fall for testimony that it was following the Communist line to recommend that Stilwell be replaced by Wedemeyer in 1944," Wallace said. "Never have I seen such unmitigated gall as that of this man [Budenz] ... coming before a committee of the United States Senate to utter such nonsense. I say it is an affront to the dignity of a great and honorable body, over which I had the honor of presiding for 4 years."[40]

McCarran and his staff could not allow such criticism of their star witness to go unchallenged, so to destroy Wallace's credibility they began to dissect his testimony bit by bit. They demanded that Wallace remember minute details about events which occurred nearly a decade earlier, and when he had difficulty answering their questions they would use it to impeach his testimony generally. For example, there was Committee Counsel J. G. Sourwine's attempt to reconstruct the origins of Wallace's report to President Roosevelt:

"You remember the notes that you took. What did you do with the notes as you took them?"

"I can't say," Wallace answered.

"Did you stuff them in a pocket, or hand them to somebody to put away? You kept your notes?"

"I did until I got this out of my system."

"Do you know where you kept them?"

Wallace did not.

"Did you have any particular place where you accumulated your notes?"

"I stuffed them away in a bag I had with me," Wallace said.

"Do you remember at any time taking them out of that bag?"

"I have no recollection at all."

"You must have taken them out if at some time you used them."

Wallace began to grow weary under the pressure of this persistent (and irrelevant) questioning: "Sir, I just don't know. That is all I have to say. Your questions, no matter how they are phrased, will get no other answer, because I don't know."

"I believe you, sir," said Sourwine, "but pardon me if I keep trying. You will recognize that you must have taken the notes out of that bag at some time."

"The answer to that is obvious," snapped Wallace.

"Obviously you did? Is that true?"

Wallace finally lost his patience: "What are you really getting at," he demanded, "what are you trying to do?"

Sourwine replied quietly: "I am trying to find out if we cannot recapture one fragment of your memory. . . ."

Sourwine found it "incredible" that Wallace could not remember such details.

"I do not think it is incredible in the slightest, . . ." Wallace countered. "I have been so active over so many years that with regard to a minor matter of this sort, I see nothing incredible about it. I would say it would be remarkable if I did remember."[41]

When the committee thought it was not receiving enough information, as in Wallace's case, it was quick to register its displeasure. But *too* much information also upset the senators, as Joseph Alsop learned when he testified on October 18. "In a metallic baritone voice and in a most precise and authoritative manner, Alsop lectured the committee on the intricacies of the Chinese situation. It was as if a nuclear physicist had taken over a class in second grade arithmetic," one reporter observed. Alsop "showed an amazing memory for small detail at the same time as he conveyed the drama and urgency of the wartime period and the larger historical issues involved."[42] The journalist's answers to the committee's questions were so sophisticated, so verbose, that at one point Counsel Sourwine told him to keep his replies "down to a minimum." When Alsop refused, an irritated Sourwine asked if he had "an aversion to using the simple Anglo-Saxon negative."[43]

Alsop, having observed the committee's treatment of Wallace, was ready for the encounter and went immediately on the offensive. Budenz was "guilty of three untruths," Alsop testified: that the Wallace mission "carried out a Communist objective"; that John Carter Vincent "guided Wallace toward any Communist objective"; and that Vincent was a Communist. "The weight of the contrary evidence," he said, "is such as to make this undoubtedly unsupported allegation inherently incredible."[44]

Despite the length and complexity of Alsop's testimony, the committee remained unpersuaded that Vincent was not a Communist, even if he had participated in what Alsop called "the most profoundly anti-Communist act that could have been attempted in China at that time."[45]

"I cannot say what you said contradicts what [Budenz] has told us," Republican Senator Arthur Watkins insisted. "The mere fact [Vincent] did some things that would be contrary to the Communist line would be some evidence, but it might not be the controlling evidence in the end that he was anti-Communist because spies and people who are working that way, of course, will perform many things to mislead the people with whom they are working."[46] For Watkins, as for so many others, only ex-Communists like Budenz who were familiar with the "secret inner workings of the Politburo" could be trusted to determine what was truly subversive. Guided by this principle, there was no way for Alsop to convince the committee that Vincent (or anyone else so accused) was not a Communist.

Toward the end of the session, Senator Willis Smith asked Alsop: "Is Mr. Vincent still living?"

"I believe he has just returned from Tangier," a startled Alsop replied.

"[Then] I do not see any need of us fussing about whether he was or was not a Communist. . . ," Smith asserted. "I think it is up to Mr. Vincent if he wants to come here to give us testimony. . . . We will certainly investigate it."[47]

Vincent was willing (if not exactly eager) to appear before the committee. He had arrived from Tangier on the afternoon of October 15, discovering immediately that he was something of a celebrity. Waiting to meet him as the SS *Constitution* docked at New York's Pier 84 were a group of reporters and photographers as well as Charles Owsley, a Foreign Service officer representing the State Department's legal advisor. Before he had an opportunity to speak with the press, Vincent and Owsley conferred privately for over twenty minutes. Owsley, who had served as second secretary of legation at Bern when Vincent was minister, spoke frankly about the madness afflicting American politics and explained to his former chief "how seriously the whole matter had to be taken." "I wasn't very successful in this," he later recalled, "because Vincent knew perfectly well that there was no substantive basis for the uproar and his understanding of the mood and atmosphere in Washington was somewhat imperfect ... because he hadn't been directly exposed to it." Owsley's final suggestion was that Vincent hire an attorney.[48]

Troubled by the grim picture painted by his friend, Vincent decided not to hold a formal press conference and, after posing briefly for photographers, began to leave the ship. Reporters pursued him anyway, firing questions along the way. "I am in no defensive position," yelled Vincent. He would stand by his earlier statement that Budenz was a liar who should be prosecuted for perjury.[49]

It was hardly the homecoming Vincent had hoped for. "I find the whole dirty business very wearysome [sic]," he wrote his brother shortly after arriving. "It would be easier if I had a natural bent for publicity."[50] But despite his desire not to stir "up any more bitterness at home," he could not permit Budenz's accusations to go unchallenged, so on November 9 he wrote once again to Senator McCarran, this time requesting an opportunity "to testify publicly under oath." "I am now home on vacation and have had an opportunity to read the Budenz testimony," Vincent said. "I am shocked at the devious manner in which he attempted to support his false testimony.... Believe me, this is not simply a matter of self-defense. The issue far transcends personal considerations. We cannot defend democracy with perfidy or defeat Communism with lies."[51] To ensure that the senator received his letter, copies were hand-delivered by a State

Department courier to the offices of McCarran and the Internal Security Subcommittee. Again, Vincent's letter went unanswered.

When more than a week elapsed without a reply, the State Department, on Vincent's recommendation, made public the text of his letter.[52] The story of McCarran's apparent refusal to grant Vincent a hearing received prominent attention in the national press: "Chance For Denial Asked By Vincent," "Vincent Pleads In Vain To Testify," "Vincent Demands Senate Hearing," proclaimed headlines in the *New York Times* and *Daily Compass*, and the *Philadelphia Inquirer*.[53] A few days later, McCarran informed him that he "would be happy" to hear his testimony; a mutually convenient date for the hearing would be arranged.[54]

Some observers believed that the State Department's decision to publish the Vincent letter signified that the department was at last ready to fight McCarthyism. "If the State Department follows through on the Vincent affair," Nancy Shannon wrote in the *New York Daily Compass*, "Budenz' usefulness to the Congressional Red hunters may be impaired considerably more than it already has been by Alsop and Wallace."[55] The *Washington Post* also hoped that the development meant an end to the State Department's "spineless stand." "When Senator McCarthy began making charges against Mr. Vincent the department hustled him off . . . to Tangier rather than let him face his accusers. This refusal to permit Mr. Vincent to fight back hurt him as well as the State Department."[56]

These hopes were never realized. The State Department was incapable of mounting an aggressive campaign against McCarthyism because of politcal and administrative factors. First the pressure of foreign and domestic events—the Korean stalemate, McArthur's dismissal, McCarthy's perpetual charges—kept Acheson and his associates constantly on the defensive. But just as important was the effect of the president's loyalty program on the department and its employees. Executive Order 9835 had created a special board composed of twenty-eight members to examine loyalty and security cases in the State Department. The Loyalty-Security Board considered itself a judicial rather than an investigative body; the latter function was assumed by the FBI in conjunction with department security agents. FBI and department reports were "exceedingly complete in most cases," Brigadier General Conrad E. Snow, chairman of the board, testified in 1950. They cover "the life history of the employee, from his college days and in some cases high school days to the present. Everyone who remembers the employee, and many who don't, has been contacted,—neighbors, teachers, friends, enemies and associates. Everything they say is put down.... The reports make no attempt to evaluate the information, derogatory or otherwise, and draw no conclusions on the evidence." Thus malicious gossip had the same evidentiary value as factual information, although the former was invariably more provocative and proved more damaging to the employee. General Snow (like J. Edgar Hoover) considered this investigative process "objective" because files contained both positive and negative evaluations. But this was not true; the raw data was itself highly subjective and without an independent analysis of the evidence the board member had no way to separate fact from fantasy. Such an analysis would have been advantageous to the board (easing their heavy workload) and helpful to those falsely accused.[57]

The completed reports were sent unanalyzed to the Loyalty-Security Board legal officer who would select three members to examine the evidence and determine the employee's status. An employee might be cleared at the outset; the panel might ask for additional information from the FBI or, if the information was particularly derogatory, it could propose "removal action," which required that charges be stated explicitly and the employee granted the right to respond, either in writing or personally during a full administrative hearing. Thus the background and personalities of the members—the judges—were as important as the material—the evidence—on which their decisions were based.

In 1951, the men responsible for operating the State Department's loaylty-security system did not inspire confidence in the judiciousness of the system. Directing the program was Deputy Under Secretary of State Carlisle H. Humelsine, a former military officer who had joined the department in 1946. Conrad E. Snow, the chairman of the Loyalty-Security Board, was a lawyer who had been director of the Signal Corps' Legal Division and a member of the War Department's Clemency Board, but he had no personal diplomatic experience and had served in the State Department for only five years. Assisting Snow as legal officers were John W. Sipes and Lawson A. Moyer, both young and new to the board, having been appointed in 1950 and 1951 respectively. Sometimes a career diplomat would serve on the panel, but just as frequently, according to one Foreign Service officer who was interrogated by the board, "other ... members were outright amateurs at a task requiring the services of the finest professionals." These men, without knowledge of either diplomatic procedures or Chinese-American relations, were responsible for judging the activities of those who had spent decades in the China Service.[58]

The Loyalty-Security Board operated independently of its parent organization; as a consequence, the State Department often found itself trying to defend employees against charges emanating from its own agency.

This made it difficult, if not impossible, for the secretary of state to protect one of his beleaguered diplomats while he was being accused of procommunism by the Loyalty-Security Board. This is exactly what happened to John Carter Vincent: Only one day after the State Department issued Vincent's letter to McCarran, Vincent was informed that the Loyalty-Security Board had found it necessary to formulate charges against him. In this way, Truman's loyalty program inadvertently played a major role in preventing the State Department from responding confidently to its critics. Worse—it helped to destroy the careers of those who worked in the president's own service.

In a five-page letter from Conrad E. Snow, Vincent learned the exact nature of the case against him: "You are hereby informed that the specific charges against you . . . are as follows:"

(1) *You were pro-Communist in your views and sympathies in the period 1940-1947.* According to the allegations of numerous informants, you had the reputation of being favorable to the Communist regime in China; were too prone to criticize destructively and extremely the Nationalist Government of China and Chiang Kai-shek at a time when it was the policy of the United States to support the Chinese Nationalist Government and Chiang Kai-shek; were oblivious to the dangers of the Communist regime in China and never considered the consequences of a China controlled by the Communists; sacrificed the best interests of the United States Government by supporting and aiding the Chinese Communist forces; attempted to convince Chinese Communist leaders that support of the Communist regime was the official policy of the United States; were more concerned with insuring and considered it more important to insure United States cooperation and collaboration with Russia after the war than with furthering and preserving the policies and interests of the United States in the Far East; recommended approval for the appointment of Owen Lattimore as an advisor to the State Department at a time when Lattimore was advancing policies favorable to the Communists; were the "chief figure" in a "pro-Soviet China clique" in the State Department; advocated policies favorable to the Chinese Communists which were detrimental to the interest and security of the United States and contrary to the established and expressed policy of the United States; were "in line with the Communist viewpoint and saw eye-to-eye with it"; were regarded as being "overly friendly with the Reds"; and were favorably disposed to Communism.

(2) *You were a member of the Communist Party.* According to the allegations of several informants, you went into the Institute of Pacific Relations as a secret member of the Communist Party; were under

Communist Party discipline during 1943-1944; were regarded as a member of the Communist Party on the basis of official Party communications and conversations; and told someone in 1940 that you had been a member of the Communist Party.

(3) *You have or have had contact or association with individuals concerning whom the Board has certain derogatory information.* According to the allegations of various informants you are or have been in association or contact with the following named individuals:
(a) Owen Lattimore
(b) Solomon Adler
(c) Edward C. Carter
(d) T. A. Bisson
(e) Frederick V. Field
(f) Lawrence K. Rosinger
(g) Julian R. Friedman
(h) Laughlin Currie [*sic*]
(i) Anna Louise Strong

Vincent was further informed that the board was considering these charges "with a view to making a recommendation to the Secretary of State as to whether you should be removed from employment." Though he was not required to appear in person to answer the charges, the board had taken the liberty of scheduling a personal hearing on December 19, one month hence.[59]

The charges had been drawn from material collected by the FBI and State Department during their investigation of Vincent. The bureau's two main field offices, New York and Washington, prepared packages containing interviews with informants (whose identities were confidential) and exhibits consisting of extracts from speeches and articles pertaining to Vincent and American China policy. Hoover kept a close watch over the case, at times alerting both offices to pieces of evidence he considered significant. When the director came across Kohlberg's article, "The State Department's Left Hand," he notified New York asking the office to make seven copies which were to be included in its final report. He also ordered the inclusion of "pertinent portions" of "America Betrayed," a pamphlet written by Joseph Kamp, a notorious anti-Semite and neo-fascist.[60]

The New York office submitted its report on July 13, 1950. The forty-eight-page document revealed that agents interviewed approximately twenty-five people and had searched for references to Vincent in the files of the New York Public Library, the *New York Daily Worker,* and the clipping morgue of the *New York Times* and *Newsweek.* The "Synopsis of Facts" found on page 1 stated that Alfred Kohlberg and Joseph Kamp alleged that Vincent "promoted [the] cause of the Chinese Communists" and "play[ed] ball with Soviet Russia." The FBI apparently thought Kamp and Kohlberg more reliable than their ex-Communist informants Elizabeth Bentley, Michael Crouch, Whittaker Chambers, and Samuel Adams Darcy who stated that they did not know Vincent; their views were relegated to page 32. A copy of the report was forwarded to the State Department.[61]

The Washington field office reported the results of its inquiry on July 28, 1950. Agents there examined the records of the House Committee on Un-American Activities, the Department of State and Civil Service Commission and had also exchanged notes on Vincent with their counterparts in the CIA, and Army and Navy Intelligence. A check of the bureau's own files was made to determine whether Vincent had a criminal record. Approximately forty people were also interviewed including one Republican congressman (Walter Judd), one admiral (Milton Miles), one general (Albert C. Wedemeyer), two former ambassadors to China (Nelson T. Johnson and Patrick J. Hurley) and two ex-secretaries of state (James F. Byrnes and George C. Marshall). Byrnes told agents that "since Vincent was reared in the state of Georgia, he could not be expected to have any Communist tendencies."[62]

Washington's "Synopsis of Facts" stated that Vincent was "recently cited by Senator McCarthy concerning his charges of Communism in the State Department. . . . [Congressional] Hearings [in 1949] charged [Vincent] with leaking State secrets to the Soviet Union. Vincent also charged by segments of American press as being a 'Communist apologist' and member of pro-Soviet clique in State Department." The report noted without comment that "Communist informants . . . do not know Vincent, . . . other former associates do not question his loyalty."[63]

Though the New York and Washington offices formally ended their investigation of Vincent in August 1950, Hoover continued to study him and, whenever an anti-Vincent article appeared in the press sent copies to the State Department and Civil Service Commission. By the fall of 1951, Vincent's loyalty file contained several hundred pages of FBI interviews and exhibits.

When these materials arrived at the State Department they were sent to the Loyalty-Security Board where they were examined by its staff and the three men selected to serve on Vincent's panel, General Conrad Snow (the chairman), Ambassador Arnold A. Nufer (a Latin American specialist), and Arthur Kimball, a lawyer who had worked for several federal agencies before joining the State Department in 1947.[64] Predictably, it was the derogatory information that caught the attention of these men. The FBI interviews they found especially significant were those held with Congressman Judd, General Wedemeyer, Alfred Kohlberg, Louis Budenz, and another ex-Communist, Joseph Zack Kornfeder.

Congressman Judd, who had helped to block Vincent's promotion in 1947, told agents that while he had never heard Vincent "make any pro-Communist statements, . . . likewise had never heard Vincent make any statements damning the Communists. . . . [T]he natural assumption is that Vincent must have favored the Communists. . . . In my opinion," Judd concluded, "Vincent has for some time been advocating policies detrimental to the interests and security of the United States. . . . I believe Vincent's ideas as to possible compromise arrangements between the National Government and the Chinese Communists were foolish and mistaken. . . . I personally think that a man who has been that wrong on important issues ought not to be given a position of trust. Vincent's interests have always worked out to the best interests of the Communists."[65]

General Wedemeyer was even more critical of Vincent. Their differences over China policy had convinced the general that Vincent was "a weak character with very little moral courage. . . . In all his conversations with Vincent," the bureau reported, "[Wedemeyer] was impressed with the fact that Vincent always emphasized . . . the mal-administration and corruption of the Chinese National Government, but never referred to or considered the consequences of a China dominated and controlled by Communists. . . . 'Vincent,' the General said, 'is favorably disposed toward Communism and is a dangerous man to be holding a public office.'"[66]

Information given the FBI by Admiral Miles originated with Tai Li, the chief of Chiang's secret police. During the war, Miles had worked closely with Tai in organizing SACO, a Chinese-American version of the OSS. The group was feared by the Japanese and Chiang's political rivals and became an acute embarrassment to American officials in Chungking. ("If the American public ever learned that we poured supplies into a questionable organization such as Tai Li operates . . . it would be unfortunate," Wedemeyer informed the War Department in 1945.) In return for aid, Tai gave Miles entree to his secret files which revealed that Chinese agents were "intensely interested in Vincent's comings and goings while in China." Chiang's gestapo routinely followed Vincent, noted whom he visited, and, on at least one occasion, "rifled his files" and stole embassy documents.[67]

Tai's reports became property of the FBI in 1951. Vincent (and others) were accused of trying to "discourage cordial relations" between Chiang and Donald Nelson, director of the War Production Board; of sending "derogatory information" regarding Chiang to Owen Lattimore "who fed it back to China through the Office of War Information"; and of "convincing Chinese Communist leaders that the official policy of the Government . . . was to support the Chinese Communists." Miles was certain, "after a review of Dai-Li's [sic] intelligence files," that Vincent and his colleagues "were sacrificing the Chinese Nationalists and were not acting in the best interests of . . . the United States."[68]

The statements of Judd, Wedemeyer, and Miles were paraphrased in the State Department's letter of charges; Kohlberg, Kornfeder, and Budenz were quoted almost exactly. References to Vincent as the "chief figure" in a "pro-Soviet China clique" came from "The State Department's Left Hand." Kohlberg's article had received wide circulation by November 1951. It had appeared in the *Congressional Record,* was sent to the State Department and Senate Foreign Relations Committee, and on Hoover's order was included in Vincent's loyalty file. It proved to be the most damaging piece of "journalism" ever written about Vincent.[69]

Kohlberg was not content to simply label Vincent "pro-Soviet" in a journal he personally financed. He also told the FBI that Vincent had expressed "pro-Communist views" as early as 1941, when both men were passengers aboard the SS *Pierce* bound for Shanghai.

In fact, Vincent had called himself a "Bolshevik" during a student strike at Clemson College in 1919, Kohlberg said. What further proof was required? Kohlberg's story sent the FBI on a search for other passengers who could verify his testimony; at least four were found but all confessed that they did not know Vincent "well enough . . . to express an opinion concerning [his] loyalty."[70] Kohlberg had no such reservations.

Neither did ex-Communist Joseph Zack Kornfeder who supported Louis Budenz's testimony that Vincent was a "secret" member of the Communist Party. Kornfeder had joined the party in 1919 and eventually became the top Comintern agent in Latin America. He left the party in 1934 after a dispute over "labor policy." Like Budenz, he later testified before congressional committees, wrote and lectured, and gave information to the FBI.[71] Kornfeder told agents that Vincent was a Communist who had been sent by the party into the Institute of Pacific Relations.[72] The Loyalty-

Security Board was impressed by Kornfeder's statement and included it in their letter of charges. Only later, when General Snow asked Kornfeder to appear as a witness "on behalf of the Board" did he admit to being uncertain about Vincent's identity. "I do not recall that I ever stated knowing Mr. John Carter Vincent personally, or having any direct knowledge of his activities," Kornfeder wrote Snow on December 8, 1951; "after all these years I am confused on the 'two Carters,' namely Edward C. Carter, . . . the Secretary of the Institute of Pacific Relations, and, John Carter Vincent, whose role in the Institute . . . is vague in my mind. . . . To the best of my recollection, I never met either of the Carters [sic] at a Communist Party meeting, and have no direct first-hand knowledge of their membership in the Party. . . . In view of my uncertainty. . . , my appearance before your Board seems to me worthless."[73] By then it was too late for the board to retract its charge that Vincent "went into the Institute of Pacific Relations as a secret member of the Communist Party."

Louis Budenz was the source of the most serious charges: that Vincent was "under Communist Party discipline," was "regarded as a member of the Communist Party," and "was in line with the Communist viewpoint." The board incorporated his statements verbatim into its letter, not realizing that the evidence supporting them was at best second-hand, at worst, nonexistent. Confronted by a mass of FBI material and pressed for time, Snow and his colleagues apparently did not examine Budenz's statements with the care they deserved. They did not notice how they evolved over time, changing subtly but significantly under the skillful direction of McCarran and his staff.

It appears that, from 1946 to 1949, Budenz never heard of John Carter Vincent. During his celebrated three thousand hours with the FBI, he never once mentioned Vincent. When this fact was made public by Joseph Alsop in 1951 a disbelieving J. Edgar Hoover asked an aide whether this assertion was correct. "Alsop's statements . . . are correct," Hoover was informed.[74] When Budenz finally mentioned the diplomat's name he told agents that he was not personally acquainted with Vincent but "thought" he was "under Communist Party discipline" because, during the Wallace mission, Budenz was instructed to give Vincent a "proper press" in the *Daily Worker*, and to "treat Vincent as a Communist." Budenz told the FBI that "he was not able to recall any other details concerning Vincent's connection with the Communist Party, nor any other instances in which such connection was mentioned, discussed or inferred in his presence." He had no concrete evidence to prove that Vincent was a Communist beyond this vague conversation with his associates on the *Daily Worker*.[75]

That Budenz's evidence was weak became immediately apparent during his appearance before the McCarran committee. At first, he refused to state that Vincent was a Communist, and would say only that he was described by party officials as being "a good influence." Journalist I. F. Stone, who observed Budenz testifying, noted that it was "as if Budenz were slipping away into the fog of what he really remembered." Counsel Robert Morris moved in where Budenz feared to tread: "Mr. Budenz, is it your testimony that it was an official Communist Party secret shared by a few people that ... John Carter Vincent was a member of the Communist Party?"

"Yes, sir," Budenz answered.

"This was putting words in the witness' mouth," wrote Stone in the *New York Daily Compass*. "This is the testimony of a witness who was being coaxed and coached to say more than he really wanted to say and more than he knew could be supported by his own recollection."[76] The board, seemingly unaware of the history of Budenz's testimony and that his words were really those of Robert Morris, made his accusations their own. Not until December did Snow, Kimball, and Nufer begin to realize that perhaps Budenz was not the reliable witness he appeared to be. When they invited the usually loquacious Budenz to testify before the board he declined,[77] leaving the panel without a single witness willing to state that Vincent was in fact a Communist. Instead of solid evidence, all the board had were the opinions of Judd, Wedemeyer, Miles, and other rabid supporters of Chiang Kai-shek. Support of Chiang was no longer simply a choice of policy; by 1951 it had become a test of loyalty.

Vincent was not permitted to examine the evidence collected by the president's loyalty system—he was only given a list of its charges and they looked formidable. He was horrified; Charles Owsley had not exaggerated his troubles after all: He would need a lawyer and quickly, for he had less than thirty days in which to prepare a defense.

For legal advice and assistance Vincent turned to Adrian S. Fisher, the State Department legal advisor. Fisher, a big, burly former Princeton football player who had once clerked for Supreme Court justices Brandeis and Frankfurther, was deeply concerned about what was happening to Vincent and his colleagues in the China Service. The Office of the Legal Advisor was poorly equipped to deal with the flood of loyalty cases which had poured forth since 1947; its principal work, Dean Acheson once noted, "dealt largely with claims by or against the United States. . . , treaty drafting, and the legal dialectics of an international imbroglio."[78] Nevertheless, Fisher did all he could to prepare Foreign Service officers for their appearances before congressional committees or the department's

Loyalty-Security Board. He made certain that diplomats received the help of competent counsel and had a place in the State Department where they could examine old memorandums and write their statements of defense. (Not everyone in the State Department was happy to see Vincent, Clubb, Service, or Davies working in the files; "State was a gutless place" Fisher later recalled. "People with loyalty problems were treated like they had the plague.")[79]

Fisher also examined individual loyalty files (which he believed the FBI leaked to administration enemies) and gave the accused "informal quizzes" so they would not be caught off guard by unfriendly congressional interrogators. Vincent had first come to his attention in February 1950, when McCarthy claimed he was a spy. Fisher studied Vincent's file and concluded that the charge was ridiculous. Subsequent attacks on Vincent did not change his initial view that there was "nothing wrong" with the diplomat. In other cases, Fisher could find something, however intangible or insignificant, on which Republican witch-hunters could seize: John Service had foolishly loaned copies of his reports to the pro-Communist editors of *Amerasia* and had been arrested and charged with espionage; although not indicted and quickly freed, his connection with the celebrated *Amerasia* affair made him vulnerable to McCarthy's charges. John Davies's arguments with Patrick Hurley left him open to charges of disloyalty to the ambassador (though technically Davies served under General Stilwell not Hurley). Edmund Clubb had once visited the office of the *New Masses* and chanced to meet Whittaker Chambers, with whom he had a brief and unimportant conversation. Nineteen years later this harmless incident was considered one reason to doubt Clubb's loyalty to the United States. But Fisher could find *nothing* in Vincent's file to equal even these harmless indiscretions: "There was not a damn thing," he later stated. Fisher saw "no way for any reasonable man not to clear Vincent."[80]

But the legal advisor was well aware that McCarthy and McCarran were not reasonable men, so he suggested that Vincent contact Walter S. Surrey, once a member of the Legal Division, and now a prominent Washington attorney. He had already spoken with Surrey, who agreed to represent Vincent without charge. "Dink" Surrey was "hard-hitting," "aggressive," and "unafraid," Fisher told Vincent. These qualities were hard to find among Democrats in 1951. He also told Vincent what to expect during his hearing before the McCarran committee, now scheduled tentatively for late January. Henry Wallace and Joseph Alsop had been treated brutally, Vincent learned; he should anticipate an even worse grilling. The committee would "heckle him," "try to catch him in a slip of the tongue," and then indict him for perjury. He instructed Vincent to be "careful, very careful" when he answered the senators' questions.[81]

Like Owsley, Fisher came away from his meeting with Vincent believing that he did not fully appreciate the seriousness of the crisis; Vincent seemed "too detached," "too objective." Still, he did succeed in introducing Vincent to the man who was to become his lawyer and close friend during the trials that lay ahead.

8

Taking the Blow

Vincent spent the next twenty-eight days preparing for his appearance before the Loyalty-Security Board. The office of lawyers Walter Surrey and Monroe Karasik became a kind of command headquarters: Junior staff members rushed about getting documents from the State Department, secretaries typed drafts of his opening statement of defense (the final version numbered fifty-four pages) and Vincent, his coat off, tie askew, lounged in a deep leather chair while he and his attorneys examined evidence and debated strategy.

Surrey and Karasik were an interesting team: "Dink" Surrey was a small, intense man, while Monroe Karasik was his physical and emotional opposite—tall, husky, and gregarious. The attorneys had handled such loyalty cases before and understood well what Vincent was only slowly coming to appreciate: The cold war had profoundly altered the way past events were currently perceived. Vincent's hearing would begin shortly after the tenth anniversary of Pearl Harbor, yet the issue which dominated the war-time period—the challenge of German and Japanese fascism—was all but forgotten. Now America was obsessed by international communism, which had worried few men at a time when Germany and Japan controlled half the globe and Russia was America's ally. Anticommunism had replaced antifascism as the national faith and standard used to evaluate past and present behavior. The only way to defend Vincent,

214

Surrey concluded, was to demonstrate that he was and always had been what Vincent called a "Sunday School blue eyed boy."[1]

"We had to document a man's lifetime behavior," Surrey later recalled, "to prove a negative—that Vincent's character and personality were inconsistent with pro-Communism." Evidence was collected from several sources to contradict the main allegations: Forty-one exhibits—cables, memorandums, and speeches written by Vincent between 1941 and 1947—were selected as proof of his hostility toward communism. Eight colleagues were asked to testify before the board on Vincent's behalf. And to four others Vincent telegrammed:

> You may be aware I am to appear before McCarran committee . . . at my request to refute charges that I am Communist tainted. I am also . . . appearing before State Department Loyalty Board at my request so that thorough investigation and testing of these charges may be had . . . My counsel insists I produce evidence demonstrating my character is such that in minds of reasonable men knowing me it is improbable that I am Communist sympathetic or disloyal to the United States. . . . It would be helpful if you could find it convenient to telegraph me . . . short statement giving your views my character generally and . . . stating facts which qualify you to express such views.

All four, Ambassador Clarence Gauss, Senator William Benton, Under Secretary of State William Clayton, and General John Hilldring, responded without hesitation. For Vincent, gathering documents and soliciting affidavits to demonstrate his Americanism were as painful as being charged with procommunism. Partisan politics and the loyalty system were forcing him to emulate the McCarthyites, and he was ashamed and embarrassed.[2]

Vincent made his first formal appearance before the Loyalty-Security Board on the afternoon of December 17, 1951.[3] The meeting place was Room 3268 in the New State Department Building, one of the "dignified and convenient suites of rooms" assigned to the board for its hearings. The members of the board, General Conrad Snow, Ambassador Arnold Nufer, Arthur Kimball, and the two legal officers, John W. Sipes and Lawson A. Moyer, sat on one side of a long, black table facing Vincent and Surrey "in accepted tribunal fashion." Four court reporters were ready to record the testimony. The witness and his counsel confronted the group from "a lonely position well across the room." Doubtless Vincent was thinking the same thoughts that passed through

Edmund Clubb's mind when he appeared before the board in July: "I had confronted various tests before but with factors that could be calculated. . . . This time I found myself in an encounter with the imponderable, a mystery created of elements outside my knowledge; and at issue were high stakes—my career, my reputation, and the happiness of my family."[4]

General Snow opened the session by reading the letter of charges, the source of which, he said, would remain secret: "The transcript of the hearing will not include all material in the file of the case. It will not include reports of investigation conducted by the Federal Bureau of Investigation, which are confidential; . . . the transcript will *not* contain information concerning the identity of confidential informants or information which will reveal the source of confidential evidence." Having robbed Vincent of the constitutional right to face his accusers and examine their evidence, Snow abruptly turned the proceedings over to Walter Surrey and invited him "to develop the defense in your own way." In effect, as Clubb later noted, "the LSB sat in joint capacity of accuser, prosecutor, judge, and jury in a matter where the accused was not enabled to know what it was all about." In a regular court of law, the burden of proof belonged to the prosecution, but in General Snow's courtroom the process was reversed: It was up to Surrey to produce evidence to prove Vincent innocent.[5]

Surrey had Vincent sworn in, then directed him to read his statement of defense. "Mr. Chairman," Vincent read, "I would like to have been brief but the charges against me are of such a serious nature that I think I am warranted in making a full report." For the next three hours Vincent told the board the story of his personal and professional life. He described his family's history which he believed typical, unexceptional, and thoroughly American. His youth was orthodox: a normal education in the Macon public schools, traditional extracurricular activities, "sand-lot baseball, hunting in the . . . nearby woods, working on my uncle's farm in the summer and attending church services with great regularity. Mine was a very religious family." He told them about his brief army service and his years at Clemson and Mercer University. He had paid for his education himself, by working in his father's real estate office and packing peaches from Georgia to Virginia. "In this way," Vincent noted, "I early developed the habit of paying my own way—of relying on my own resources, spiritual as well as financial." These biographical details were not trivial, Vincent argued; they were evidence that he "was not then, and am not now, the conspiratorial type that one generally associates with Communism."

Inheritance and experience had combined to produce a personality for whom communism was politically, spiritually, and intellectually abhorrent. "Very serious charges have been made against me," Vincent said,

> the most serious of which is that I have been a Communist sympathizer and a member of the Communist Party. Now I am not and never have been a member of the Communist Party, I have never sympathized with the aims of Communism, and, on the positive side, I have worked loyally throughout my career in the interests of our own Government and people. I am strongly attached to the principle of representative democracy and to the system of free enterprise.
>
> I am not by nature a "joiner." . . . I do not identify myself with cliques, despite the comment of one of my detractors. I am in fact prone to hoe my own row and to resent dogmatic leadership. Since my youth I have pretty much done my own thinking.
>
> My interests outside my work are normal American ones. I have played baseball from China to Switzerland to Morocco. I have won bowling and tennis cups in China. I am not asocial, but I do not like social entertainment for its own sake. My wife and I enjoy music and are regular attendants at concerts. I read an average amount, largely on matters having a relation to my work.
>
> I have never taken part in politics or political activity. . . . I endeavor to follow the teachings of Jesus Christ. In short, I am not a Communist.

He also considered his career in the China Service further proof that he was not pro-Communist. Since the Mukden Incident in 1931, he had "wholeheartedly favored all practical support for China and firmness with Japan. I was to use the parlance of the time 'pro-Chinese' and still am." During the war, he explained, his chief objective had been to strengthen Chinese resistance:

> We were critical of the Chinese Government at times, almost everyone in Chungking was but the criticism was constructive, made with a view to determining the best way to improve conditions to aid China, and to support the authority of the Chiang Kai-shek government. The question of utilizing the forces of the Chinese Communists entered very little into our thinking at this time. It was the National Chinese who were obsessed with the problem, brought it up in conversation, and were seeking a means of establishing a unified front. It was only later, when the possibility of our making landings on the Chinese coast arose where Communist guerrillas were operating in force, that the use of these forces became important to us. Also, we anticipated the entrance of Russia into the war in the Far East, and it seemed to us of great importance that a united Chinese command be firmly established, and political differences settled, in order to forestall separate use by the Russians of Chinese Communist troops.

217   Taking the Blow

His service in the State Department coincided with the beginning and end of the Marshall mission, and Vincent supported the general's policy of aiding the Nationalist government while avoiding large-scale involvement in the Chinese civil war. He believed that his complete record, as evidenced by the documents he was submitting to the board, constituted "an impressive denial to the charges made against me."[6]

Then he analyzed each specific charge laid out in Snow's letter. He again denied ever being pro-Communist or a member of the Communist Party. "My whole life, my thinking and my principles, constitute a refutation of any suggestion of my membership in a Communist Party at any time." Of the nine individuals listed in charge # 3, Vincent admitted knowing well only Owen Lattimore, Solomon Adler, Julian Friedman, and Lauchlin Currie, and he had no reason to doubt their loyalty to the United States. Finally, Vincent discussed those accusations made in public by Budenz and McCarthy—none of which, he argued, was related to loyalty or security. "The common factor of each of these allegations," Vincent said, "is that something I said or did—or something I am supposed to have said or done—either pleased or is assumed to have necessarily pleased the Chinese or Russian or American Communists. Whether or not these things in fact pleased the Communists, everything I actually said or did was in pursuance of the then existing policies of the United States, and what my accusers . . . are actually attacking are those policies. . . . Whether in the light of history [they] were or are right or wrong is not in issue here. My loyalty is in issue [and] I was loyal to those policies."[7]

By the end of the afternoon Vincent was physically and emotionally exhausted; he had spoken for hours almost without interruption, and his throat hurt and his back ached. But his ordeal was far from over: At 4:30 General Snow adjourned the hearing until the following day, when the board would begin its cross-examination.

That interrogation lasted six hours. There was little organization or continuity in the board's questioning: The panelists and their staff moved quickly from issue to issue, revealing in the process their ignorance of Chinese-American relations and their preoccupation with cold war anticommunism. The board was primarily interested in Vincent's repeated concern, expressed in his memorandums, that there be "mutual understanding" between China and Russia, and Russia and the United States. "What understanding did you have in mind," asked Legal Officer John Sipes, "and just what was the importance of that understanding?"[8]

In the 1950s, anyone who had once recommended an "understanding" with Russia was immediately suspect. Vincent had to remind the young lawyer that the era they were discussing was different from the one in which they were now living. "The idea at the time," Vincent explained, ". . . was that Russia would probably be coming into the war in the Far East, that it would have been better for the Chinese to have sat down with the Russians and tried to work out some understanding as to how they would avoid any conflict or to arrange for a joint operation against the Japanese. We are speaking of war, understand."

But Sipes did not understand. He pointed to a section of the K'un-ming cable which called for a united front. United front and popular front were terms frequently used by Communists. "What was the context of . . . the phrase 'united front,'" Sipes wondered. "It was a military front," Vincent replied.

"Between the—" Sipes groped for the correct answer.

"Between the National Armies and the Chinese Communist Armies," Vincent said.[9]

Sino-Soviet cooperation may have been necessary during the war, Sipes granted, but was it not also true that Vincent had stated that peace in general depended on harmonious relations between China and Russia? Having first given Sipes a lesson in history, Vincent proceeded to give him one in geography. "The boundary between Russia and China is . . . over three thousand miles," Vincent noted. "It was essential to peace in the Far East that there be some kind of mutual understanding between those two countries which had a common frontier."[10]

Why had Soviet-American cooperation been so important to him? the board asked. Again he explained "the frame of reference," the historical context in which he had lived and worked. General Marshall was in China when Vincent had publicly expressed the hope that Russia "might support our efforts to bring about peace in China." "We were trying to get an arrangement where the threat of civil war would cease," Vincent said; ". . . the only power that could have any influence on the Communists in China was the Soviet Union. Therefore, if we could get Russian influence brought to bear for the common objective of stopping the civil war and getting the Chinese to settle their internal difficulties we would certainly have strengthened General Marshall's hand."[11]

Having done no independent investigation on its own, the board was dependent on two sources for its questions: Vincent's exhibits and the FBI's reports. Once they were finished discussing the exhibits they turned to the reports. More information was requested about Vincent's relations with those whose names had appeared at the top of McCarthy's various lists: Alger Hiss, Owen Lattimore, and Lauchlin Currie.[12] The board also asked about the men who (unbeknownst to Vincent) had supplied the bureau with the most damaging accusations: General Wedemeyer ("We did not always see eye to eye")[13]; Admiral Miles ("I knew what his general objective out there was . . . but he never discussed it with me nor I with him");[14] Congressman Judd ("Judd's views . . . with regard to the Marshall mission were not those of mine. I don't think Mr. Judd ever quite could swallow it");[15] and Alfred Kohlberg (". . . After I came back from China Kohlberg . . . and I had lunch together. At that time I considered Mr. Kohlberg a man interested in China and interested in getting facts. I may have been naive about it.")[16]

The second session ended as the first had begun, with a discussion of Vincent's politics. "This question may be difficult for you to answer," Arthur Kimball told Vincent, "but I think it would be sort of interesting . . . to get your reaction: In the course of the testimony and the various . . . statements which have come to the attention of the Board . . . there have been quite a few people . . . who have described you as being very Leftist. . . . The fact that such a large number of people have classified you as that raises a question in my mind. . . ."

"That is a difficult question," Vincent agreed.

"I knew it would be," Kimball said.

Vincent thought he was vulnerable to attack because he had inherited two groups of enemies, one opposed to the New Deal, the other to China policy. There were many who were against the New Deal, Vincent told Kimball, and "I was for it. [People] don't make their judgments in half ways; I became immediately a left winger because I am in favor of the New Deal." That he had also been the public spokesman for Truman's China policy explained why he had become the chief target of partisan criticism: "The attacks on me started long before Budenz had ever thought of me, when I took over the Far Eastern Office and I foresaw that myself. . . . China policy was not going to be popular, had hardly ever been popular. And the Scripps-Howard papers were the first ones to take it up in the fall of 1946 . . . during the [congressional] election campaign. . . . General Marshall was not subject to any kind of attack; therefore, if you are going to attack China policy through a personality I was the obvious target. I remember telling [Secretary] Byrnes—one time he asked me: 'what do you think these people have got against you. . . ?' and I said: 'Mr. Byrnes, Roy Howard hasn't got anything against me, but China policy is going to be a headache for you, and I am going to be for sometime the fellow who is going to have to take the blow.'"[17] That he was still taking the blow was evidenced by the fact that he was appearing before them that day.

General Snow closed the session a short time later. During the next two days the board would continue its consideration of Vincent's character and views, as it questioned those witnesses who had volunteered to testify on Vincent's behalf.

Eight men appeared separately before the board on December 20 and 21. Together they represented a cross section of American personalities and professions: There were three retired military officers (Brigadier General John Magruder, and Colonels William Mayer and James McHugh); two career diplomats (Nelson T. Johnson and Maxwell Hamilton); a United Nations lawyer (Herbert F. May); a businessman (Hugo F. Seitz); and a journalist (Demaree Bess). All had known Vincent for over twenty years and had observed him at work in Europe and Asia. Each was asked first to classify Vincent politically and then to comment on his honesty, integrity, loyalty, and competency. Generally, Vincent was described as being a "liberal," although one friend placed him "right of center."[18] When asked about Vincent's character Demaree Bess snapped: "I think that's an insulting question. . . . I haven't the remotest doubt of his integrity or honesty." Neither did the other witnesses. Vincent was "an intelligent fellow, always terribly keen," said General John Magruder, former head of the United States military mission to China. Maxwell Hamilton, former chief of the Far Eastern Division called Vincent "a thorough going American . . . desirous of advancing the interests of the United States at all times." "He is Americanism," Herbert May noted. "I have known many dozens of Foreign Service officers and I think his Americanism is more deeply rooted in the soil of this country than almost anyone I know."[19]

Had Vincent been "too prone to criticize destructively" the government of Chiang Kai-shek? the board asked. No, said those men who had known him best during his China service: "It would have been exceptional that an American at that time wasn't critical of the regime," said Bess, who had covered China for the *Christian Science Monitor*. "All of us were critical of the regime." Among Chiang's most severe critics were American businessmen, noted Seitz, who had represented the Standard Vacuum Company in China for over two decades: "They were very critical of the Nationalist Government because of the corruption and the hardships that were worked on the Chinese people." Just as dissatisfied were America's soldiers: "I think it was the consensus . . . that the Chinese Communists were . . . trying to give [the peasantry] a better break . . . ," testified Colonel Mayer, the embassy military attaché from 1939 to 1942. "Everybody wondered why the hell Chiang Kai-shek didn't take a few little leaves from the Communist book and do the same thing."[20]

Had they ever heard that Vincent "was or is pro-Communist?" All said no, except Bess. "I have heard it from only one person," he told the board.

That is Alfred Kohlberg. A year and a half ago . . . I interviewed Mr. Kohlberg . . . who told me . . . that he knew John Carter Vincent was a member of the Communist Party.

I said, "How do you know that, Mr. Kohlberg?" He said, "I know it because a former member of the Communist Party told me so."

He obviously was referring to Budenz. . . . So I said to Mr. Kohlberg, "I have known John Carter Vincent since he was a young Vice Consul in China. We have been on very intimate social and business terms. I have seen him in many parts of the world. And I have never seen the faintest trace of any evidence. I worked four years in Russia myself as a correspondent so I know a lot of Communists. . . . Do you take your ex-Communist's word for it rather than mine?" He said, "I certainly do. . . . You don't know about these people."

So what do you do? I mean I left it at that.

Vincent never took such criticism "seriously," Bess recalled. "He thought it was rather a joke. Well, I'm older than he is, and I remember . . . after the first World War . . . what was happening in this country under A. Mitchell Palmer's 'benign' influence. Something of the same sort might very well happen. I thought he should take it much more seriously than he did. But I can well understand how he wouldn't take it seriously. If I had been in his position I probably wouldn't either, if I didn't have those memories."[21]

By the time the hearings ended, on December 21, no one could again accuse Vincent of not taking Kohlberg's charges seriously. They had led him to this appearance before the Loyalty-Security Board, resulting in fifteen hours of testimony which eventually filled five volumes totaling over four hundred pages. Having presented his case as best he could, it was now up to Snow, Kimball, and Nufer to study the evidence, to take an imaginative leap into the past, and to determine whether there was reason to doubt Vincent's loyalty to the United States. If they found him suspect, they were required to recommend his dismissal from the Foreign Service.

Vincent had no time to ponder his fate; there was more work to be done, other hearings to prepare for. On January 10 he was to appear before the House Committee on Un-American Activities, then two weeks later he would meet with Senator Pat McCarran's Internal Security Subcommittee. This encounter was expected to be the most difficult Vincent had so far experienced. Indeed, his public criticism of the senator's reluctance to give him a hearing had already caused problems. McCarran sent him a subpoena demanding that when he appeared he bring with him his loyalty file and thirty-two categories of official documents. Included among the latter were "drafts of all memos prepared for Henry A. Wallace, or correspondence with him"; "all memoranda and correspondence with or dealing with Owen Lattimore, Lauchlin Currie, and Solomon Adler"; "drafts of all statements prepared by Vincent for General Marshall" and countless other records.[22] Vincent informed McCarran that he was personally willing to accede to the request but could not without State Department and presidential authorization. (Authorization was later denied by President Truman on grounds of executive privilege.) Surrey expected this rejection to further anger the senator, who would then use the hearing as a forum in which to humiliate his client. He therefore prepared Vincent for the confrontation with meticulous and exhaustive care.[23]

While Vincent worked on another opening statement, Surrey and his staff drew up an outline entitled "Issues Which May Be Raised in Hearing of John Carter Vincent before McCarran Committee." It was divided into six sections, each with its own subdivision: "Issues Previously Raised in McCarran Committee"; "McCarthy Charges"; "Charges in Loyalty Proceedings"; "Tydings Hearings"; "House Un-American Activities Committee Hearing"; "McCarran Committee's Letter of January 2, 1952." The published record of the McCarran committee was also studied and a list made of twenty-nine persons who had been "named in conjunction with Vincent." Leaving nothing to chance, a second list of sixty-nine names was compiled, men and women who were supposedly associates of Vincent's associates.[24] With these outlines and lists as a guide, Vincent prepared short essays on each subject and personality who Surrey expected would be discussed during the hearing. Vincent also studied the list of documents McCarran requested and wrote brief descriptions of all thirty-two categories. These papers were collected together in a briefing book that Vincent would take with him to Capitol Hill. With the invaluable help of Surrey and his aides, Vincent had amassed a wealth of information about American China policy and the men who made it. He was ready for almost any reasonable question that could be asked.

His first congressional appearance—before the House Committee on Un-American Activities—was brief and uneventful but it did not help him clear his name. The committee was investigating the activities of American Communists in China during the 1930s and asked Vincent to testify about his knowledge of Max Granich, one of the committee's prime suspects. In 1936, Granich had published *Voice of China*, a leftist magazine considered so inflammatory by the Chinese that Shanghai police were ordered to confiscate its first issue. The committee wanted to know why Vincent, then serving on the China desk in Washington, had ordered the consul general to contest the Chinese action. Vincent explained that the treaty of extraterritoriality required the State Department to lodge such protests, regardless of the character or views of the Americans involved. The department had no love for Granich (Vincent's telegram stated that his activities "should not receive support or encouragement from this Government") but felt duty bound "to protect Granich's property as an American citizen."[25]

The congressmen were generally satisfied with Vincent's explanation but the fact that he appeared before the committee proved to be damaging. Once again he was associated in the public mind with Communists. "VINCENT HELPED RED PUBLISHERS," noted the *Chicago Daily Tribune* in its coverage of the committee's hearing. "QUIZ VINCENT ON SUPPORT OF COMMIE PAPER," read the headline in the *Washington Times Herald*. This was not a very comfortable position for Vincent to be in less than two weeks before he was to testify before the McCarran committee.[26]

Of that experience Elizabeth Vincent was later to say: "John Carter had faced death in Mukden and terrible danger in Changsha, and had been cool as a cucumber. But this almost killed him. And the McCarran Committee was the worst experience of my life, too. Childbirth was fun compared to that."[27] Journalists who covered Vincent's appearance before the McCarran committee were shocked by the way he was treated. "During [the] days of interrogation . . . Vincent all but had a light shined in his eyes and was beaten by a rubber hose," observed Joseph and Stewart Alsop. "An offensive spectacle," said the *Washington Star*'s Lowell Mellett: "One got the impression that the Committee intended to make an object lesson of Mr. Vincent; a warning to any other persons accused by Budenz or McCarthy that it was better to let the accusations stand." And the *Louisville Courier-Journal*, in a long editorial, commented: "It was such as to shame any American who still believes in justice for all and a decent objectivity in judges. . . . The Internal Security Subcommittee . . . turned in a performance worthy of any Communist-controlled court of justice. It presumed the witness guilty and set out by every cheap trick and bullying tactic to . . . trap and snare him in confusion. . . . There was never any pretense that this was a hearing to establish truth or to permit a man to defend his reputation."[28]

Responsible for this "travesty" were the members and staff of the Senate Internal Security Subcommittee. The chairman was seventy-four-year-old Patrick Anthony McCarran, Democrat of Nevada. "Silver haired" and "barrel chested," McCarran was a senatorial baron who had the reputation of being "one of the most shrewd, petty, ruthless and arrogant men ever to descend upon Washington." He was also one of the most powerful: In January 1952 he was sixth in seniority in the Senate, chairman of the important Judiciary Committee, and unofficial leader of a coalition of conservative Republicans and Democrats. To question Vincent, McCarran selected men of similar ability and views: Indiana's William Jenner, Mississippi's James Eastland, and Michigan's Homer Ferguson.[29]

Equally irresponsible was the subcommittee staff: ex-Communist Benjamin Mandel (director of research) and the counsels J. G. Sourwine and Robert Morris. Sourwine, known in congressional circles as "a master of the elastic innuendo" was a Nevadan whom McCarran had come to admire, a feeling Sourwine reciprocated. When McCarran took over the Judiciary Committee, Sourwine became its chief counsel. Robert Morris was appointed the subcommittee's "special counsel" at McCarthy's request and through Morris, McCarthy used the subcommittee as a clearinghouse for every bit of malicious rumor and gossip which came his way. Mandel, Sourwine, and Morris were primarily responsible for developing the questions that members of the subcommittee asked Vincent. Their chief sources of information were the Bridges memorandum and other articles by Alfred Kohlberg; McCarthy's speeches; and reports which originated with Chiang Kai-shek's secret police.[30] Every public and private accusation that had been made against Vincent since 1946 was grist for their mill. "At occasions through this hearing," Sourwine told Vincent, "questions are asked which may to the witness seem preposterous. . . . we are throwing . . . everything that we have found that has been thrown, and giving [you] an opportunity to answer."[31]

The ordeal lasted six and a half days. Vincent testified for over twenty-eight hours, fifteen behind closed doors, thirteen in public session. He *was* permitted to read a voluntary statement proclaiming his loyalty, but it had little effect on the committee. "Mr. Chairman, and members of the Committee," Vincent said:

> I have requested an opportunity to meet with you for two reasons. First, to repudiate under oath certain irresponsible but very grave allegations made against me before this Committee, and secondly, to give the Committee whatever other assistance I may in the conduct of its investigation. . . . Gentlemen, anyone, including, [Louis] Budenz, who before this Subcommittee or anywhere else, testifies that I was at any time a member of the Communist Party is bearing false witness; he is to put it bluntly, lying. I do not pretend to *know* what motives guide Mr. Budenz. In my own case, his motives seem to be clearly malicious. He has endeavored before this Subcommittee to support his allegations by strained suggestion and devious insinuation.
>
> I am not a Communist and have never been a member of the Communist Party. I have never sympathized with the aims of Communism, on the contrary, I have worked loyally throughout the twenty-seven years of my foreign service career in the interest of our

own Government and people. I am strongly attached to the principle of representative democracy and to our system of free enterprise. These being the facts, the members of the Committee will appreciate, I am sure, how disagreeable it is for me to find it necessary to affirm my devotion to our democratic institutions because of unfounded allegations made by Budenz or anyone else.

We cannot dismiss the Budenz testimony as a "mistake." Any attempt through malicious testimony to cause the American people to lose confidence in their officials, or in each other, is in itself subversive to the interests and security of our country. When, as in my case, the official represents his country abroad, the effect may be doubly harmful.

I am in full accord with the objectives of this Subcommittee. The internal security of the United States, now probably more than ever before in our history, is vitally important to all of us. Our American way of life is threatened from within as well as from without. But we . . . cannot defend democracy with perfidy or defeat Communism with lies. And I wish to state, not as an official of our Government who has been falsely accused, but as a citizen who is deeply concerned for the welfare and security of his country, that irresponsible testimony, such as Mr. Budenz is wont to give, might have its use in a totalitarian state but has no place in our American democracy.

. . . But, Gentlemen, my main purpose in seeking an opportunity to come before you has been accomplished. At the Subcommittee hearings of October 5, 1951, Senator Smith is reported as saying: "Mr. Vincent should come here and challenge Mr. Budenz' statement and say "I am not a Communist." That draws the issue.

Mr. Chairman and members of the Committee, I now solemnly repeat:

I am not and never have been a Communist. I so draw the issue.[32]

As soon as he had finished reading his statement, McCarran fired off the first in an endless series of hostile questions: "Let me say to you, Mr. Vincent, that it is not alone membership in the Communist Party that constitutes a threat to the internal security of this country; it is sympathy with the Communist movement that raises one of the gravest threats that we have."

"Mr. Chairman," Vincent replied, "I think I said . . . that I had no sympathy with the aims of the Communists."[33]

Throughout the course of the hearings McCarran and his associates attempted to "shake" Vincent's denial. The committee's style, one writer noted, was to "break down" the witness, "twist him, collapse him, transform him into a weakened hulk beating his breast and crying mea culpa."[34] Literally hundreds of questions were asked regarding Vincent's role in the Wallace and Marshall missions, his relationships with Owen Lattimore, John Service, John Davies, and approximately ninety other individuals; his membership in the Institute of Pacific Relations, and the development of American policy toward China, Japan, and Korea. These questions Vincent and Surrey had anticipated and prepared for; others were totally unexpected and inexplicable:

Sourwine on January 25: "Sir, has it been reported to you at any time that your name has been mentioned in connection with the disappearance of three C.I.A. agents in Bulgaria?"

"No, Sir," Vincent replied.[35]

And on January 26: "I have been asked to ask you this question. Sir, do you own a home in Sarasota, Florida?"

"No, Sir," answered Vincent.

"Are you buying a home there?"

"No, Sir."

"Do you plan to live there?"

"No, Sir."

"Maybe the Florida Chamber of Commerce has an interest in you," Sourwine said.

"I find that is the most curious question that has been asked here," Vincent noted.[36]

As with Wallace and Alsop, Vincent was required to remember and discuss minute (and irrelevant) details about memorandums, meetings, and conversations which occurred a decade earlier. When he had difficulty answering, the senators were furious. For example, the committee was extremely interested in a brief visit by Wallace and Vincent with Madam Sun Yat-sen in June 1944:

"Do you recall the nature of the meeting?" Sourwine asked.

"Yes," said Vincent.

"Do you recall anything about the dwellings in which it took place?" Vincent could not.

"Can you recall anything about the room in which it took place? Was it a room with small windows?"

"It probably did have," Vincent guessed.

"Was she seated or standing during the conference?"

"I would think that she was seated. . . ."

"Was she behind a desk, or in a chair, or on a divan?"

"I don't recall whether she was on a chair or on a divan," Vincent said.

"And you don't recall your own position, what you sat on?"

"I would certainly remember it if I stood the whole time, but I must have sat."[37]

When Vincent was unable to recall other meaningless details about his visit with Madame Sun, Senator Ferguson asked in consternation: "Mr.

Vincent, do you have the same difficulty in your work in the State Department. . . , remembering things that have happened, as you have here on the witness stand? . . . Are you as uncertain in your work there . . . as you are here?"

"Senator, this all happened 7 or 8 years ago," Vincent explained.

"Can you answer that question?" Ferguson insisted.

"You better answer that question," McCarran demanded.

"Are you in as much doubt in conferring with State officials on things that have happened as you are before this Committee?" Ferguson repeated.

"Senator, it is a matter of recalling what I think now as details."

Ferguson became angry: "I am asking are you usually in as much doubt?" "I think that is a simple question," cried McCarran. "Why do you not answer it?"[38]

On another occasion when Vincent's memory failed him, Counsel Morris asked, "Do you think it is possible you may have been a member of the Communist Party in 1945 and now have forgotten it?"

"No, Sir," replied Vincent firmly.[39]

This heckling was clearly designed to exhaust and confuse Vincent, to force him into a contradiction in testimony which could later lead to an indictment for perjury. That this was in fact the committee's goal was expressed openly by Senator Ferguson who, during a committee recess, told a group (which happened to include Mrs. Vincent): "Come along to the hearing, today. We're going to get Vincent on perjury."[40]

Throughout the hearing Vincent remained calm, his voice kept to a "low pitch" as he "softly but steadfastly" maintained his innocence. When it might have been wiser to equivocate, he staunchly defended American China policy even though the committee called it "pro-Communist." "It was a matter of alternatives," Vincent insisted. "I thought and the President thought and the Secretary of State thought that the best alternative was to try to bring about a cessation of civil war . . . through some kind of political settlement. . . . [The] outbreak of civil war, after the Chinese had already been undergoing 8 years of war, would make conditions in China even worse . . . and would be conducive, even, to the future spread of turmoil from which the Communists themselves could take advantage."

"So the cure for that situation," Senator Eastland said, "was to take those Communists into the government and form a united front between Chiang and the Communists."

"I think that is an oversimplification . . . ," Vincent responded. "They were already discussing the matter of some kind of peaceful solution of a political difficulty. There had been a . . . conference at which the Communists were already present . . . when General Marshall went to

China. . . . [T]aking the Chinese Communists into the government on a minority basis, for the time being, was a better solution and gave a better chance of putting them in a subordinate position than carrying on civil war. . . . In the light of the situation . . . at that time, I still think it was the most feasible . . . policy. . . . [I]t was not the perfect solution, but . . . it was better than civil war."

Eastland disagreed. "It has always wound up that way," he said. Coalition "is a Communist stepping stone to take a country over. That was an identical system that Communists used all over Europe. . . . Why is it that you had adopted that Communist tactic and was [sic] pressuring it on Chiang Kai Shek [sic]?"[41]

Only once, toward the end of the hearings, did Vincent lose his patience and "bitterly" accuse the committee of deliberate distortion. This heated exchange occurred on February 1, during a discussion of American policy toward Japan. In late 1945, Vincent had stated in a broadcast over NBC radio that "all democratic parties" would be assured the right to participate in Japanese politics—and since he had not explicitly excluded the Japanese Communist Party from this group, he was guilty, Sourwine suggested, of encouraging the Communists to seize power.

"That is a wrong inference," cried Vincent, "and you know it!"

"Mr. Vincent, I do not know that is wrong, or I would not be urging it here," Sourwine said.

"I can tell you flatly then, that irrespective of the language . . . , it was not the intention . . . to in any way permit the Communist Party to take over control of Japan, or to operate in a manner which would be inimical to the occupation of Japan. . . ."

"Then why did you not exclude the Communists. . . ?" asked Ferguson.[42]

As that session ended, Ferguson predicted that perhaps only two more hours of testimony were required to complete the hearing. "I have great confidence in Mr. Sourwine," said Vincent wryly, "but he has made those 2-hour promises [before]."

"Mr. Vincent, I have made no promises as to 2 hours or when we could conclude," Sourwine replied sharply. "Why did you say that I had made a promise of 2 hours?"

"I correct the statement," Vincent said wearily. "You have not made a promise. You have said at times you would hope to get through in 2 hours."

"And I have expressed that hope with the utmost sincerity, sir."

Ferguson then added: "I might suggest, [Mr. Vincent], that if you get a good night's rest and then answer these questions a little more directly we might save some time."[43]

Vincent's hearing ended the next day, Saturday, February 2. "Have you had a full hearing?" asked Ferguson, just before dismissing him.

"I have had full hearing," Vincent agreed, " . . . a very full hearing."

"Do you believe it was a fair hearing?" the Senator asked.

"Yes, Sir, in all intents and purposes." This was the first time that Vincent had not been completely honest in his answers. "I knew that if I'd said 'No,'" he later told his wife, "they'd have started in all over again."[44]

Vincent left the committee room "grim and unsmiling," according to the reporters who gathered around him in search of a statement. When asked if he thought the hearings had "cleared his name,"Vincent said: "Certainly," and walked away. Senator Ferguson was quick to tell the press that he did not share the diplomat's view. Vincent's testimony, he said, was not "conclusive."[45]

While Vincent was recovering from his ordeal before the McCarran committee, the State Department Loyalty-Security Board was reaching its final decision in his case. Snow, Kimball, and Nufer had studied Vincent's testimony and the documents submitted in his defense and concluded that he was innocent of all the charges. There "is not in the file a shred of evidence supporting the Budenz allegation," the board noted in a private memorandum. "It is clear that the Wallace Mission, far from supporting the Chinese Communist cause, took action, with Vincent's approval and connivance, directly contrary to Communist interests."[46] On February 6, Snow informed the secretary of state that Vincent had been cleared and "recommended that the case be closed."[47]

Vincent received official notification of the happy news twelve days later from Carlisle Humelsine, the man in charge of the State Department's loyalty program. "The favorable decision . . . will be referred to the Loyalty-Review Board of the Civil Service Commission for postaudit review," Humelsine wrote. "The Department's security decision, however, is final. The Secretary has asked me to reaffirm the Department's full confidence in you and to tell you that, as you return to your duties as American Diplomatic Agent and Minister to Tangier, you take with you the Department's appreciation for your twenty-seven years of conscientious service and best wishes for the future."[48] These words seemed to Vincent little compensation for the troubles he had experienced, but at least the matter was behind him and he could return to his work in Tangier. As far as the Civil Service Loyalty Review Board was concerned, such postaudit reviews were routine; since the inception of the Loyalty Program in 1947, a favorable decision by the Loyalty-Security Board had been reversed only once. Surrey and Vincent thought this a good omen.

Still, there were disturbing signs that all was not yet well. When the State Deparment made Humelsine's letter public, McCarran reacted with characteristic fury. With "all the information our Committee has before it," the senator told reporters, "it is difficult . . . to see . . . how the State Department could arrive at the conclusion and especially how the Secretary of State could congratulate Mr. Vincent." Ominously, McCarran noted that the committee's records were "not yet closed" on Vincent and that "the clearance process is not completed. The action of the State Department is subject to review of the Loyalty Review Board. . . . I've nothing more to say except I understand he is about to take leave for a foreign post, which might be regarded as unusual and peculiar in view of all the circumstances."[49]

McCarran's statement, though predictable, left Vincent feeling uneasy. As he waited for the SS *Constitution* to sail for Europe on the morning of February 20, he looked nervously about the crowded deck, expecting that as he read a farewell statement[50] to the press the "damned committee would present a subpoena" and he would be hustled off the ship with flashbulbs popping and reporters yelling. But nothing disturbed his reading but the quiet whirring of the Movietone cameras and the sound of the waves slapping against the ship. "Well, it's over," he wrote to his wife later that day, "and I didn't get drunk when we cast off."[51]

He spent his first week in Tangier recuperating: sleeping ten hours a day, eating "heartily," taking long walks on the beach, and reading Carl Sandburg's *Abraham Lincoln*. "I have put the recent unpleasantness out of my mind for the time being," he told Betty, who was still in America. "I know that I was inadequate to the situation no matter how unfair the situation was. Letters keep coming in. A lovely one from Mama as usual. A very good one from Bishop Larned. . . . [Senator] Bill Benton writes that he had a talk with Senator [Willis] Smith of North Carolina who 'seemingly doesn't attach any importance to the issue.' It may be about time he did. . . . The weather is beautiful. The sun, the ocean, the wind, and the sand are a lovely comfort. . . . Soon you will be with me and I don't care much about anything else just now."[52]

In the beginning he had felt spiritually empty, not up to answering the mail, both good[53] and bad. (One correspondent told Vincent that as far as he was concerned the diplomat was a liar, a perjurer, and a traitor. He urged Vincent to either join Alger Hiss in prison, or kill himself.)[54] But slowly he began to recover enough to reflect with humor, anger, and concern on "the past months' travesty."

"Writing to sob sisters and sympathetic friends has been child's play in comparison to writing to you two," he told his attorneys in a letter on March 2. "No, don't get alarmed; I'm not going to become sentimental. But the relation of client to counsel is a new one for me, and I realize now that I should have started at the bottom and worked up rather than starting off in the rarified atmosphere . . . that characterizes the partnership of Surrey and Karasik. You deserved a better client and with that idea in mind I'm now preparing the Moroccan case in advance; that is, getting all the testimony in advance of the charges, drawing up the charges myself—or planting them, and, with the able guidance of counsel, pulling off a committee scene that will end all committees."

He also had some thoughts about striking back at his enemies. Before leaving Washington, he and Surrey had discussed the possibility of having William Benton (perhaps the first senator courageous enough to publicly denounce McCarthy)[55] make a statement defending Vincent. But after doing "quite a bit of thinking," Vincent decided against it. "Walter, I don't think much of the [idea]. McCarthy has been covered in my statements. Kohlberg is the origin of 90% of the slander against me, but answering his article ["The State Department's Left Hand"] by reading something into the Congressional *Record* doesn't seem to me the way to handle the matter. Kohlberg ought to be gotten but I don't know quite how."[56] He just did not have the stomach to engage in a McCarthy-like attack even if it was directed against McCarthy or Kohlberg.

To relatives and friends, he argued that what was happening to the nation was more important than what was happening to him. "So far as the 'events' are concerned they have been unpleasantly past for me," he wrote his brother and sister-in-law, "but they have not been past, or are not past, for our public. For we the public must decide whether our public servants shall be judged impartially and fairly or whether they shall be judged for the benefit of partisan and selfish politics. We must decide whether ex-post facto disagreement as to how something should have been done can be used as a basis for questioning a public servant's loyalty. We must decide whether we can continue to permit anonymous and false witnesses to undermine confidence in our public servants. . . . The decision on these questions seems clear to me; and urgent. . . ."[57] "These are parlous times," he wrote to Professor Woodbridge Bingham, an old friend from Ch'ang-sha whose father was chairman of the Loyalty Review Board which would soon examine his case. "I can readily sympathize with the public concern over what has transpired since the war. What is most disturbing is the advantage that is being taken of this public concern to undermine confidence in our public servants and in our intellectuals. . . . And in trying to get at the root of the matter, I do not find completely satisfactory the explanation of partisan politics although it obviously accounts for a lot. Perhaps it is that the poison of Russian Communism produces or calls forth a vicious antidote almost as dangerous to our institutions as the poison itself. Thus carpet-bag politics in the South brought out the Ku Klux Klan, and Napoleon's excesses inspired the Holy Alliance. These are not very good analogies. I should be more content, in my present frame of mind, if I could cite the Inquisition. Well," he concluded in the end, "I have confidence that our democracy is healthy enough to slough off the scrofulous growth; [and] I hope there will not be too many casualties in the process."[58]

As the memory of his trial faded, Vincent's detachment and sense of humor began to reappear. By late March he found himself able to write parodies of Congressional hearings, like the one that had recently treated him so cruelly:

"Mrs. Vincent, where were you on the night of December 31st, 1929?"

"Senator, I do not recall. I have a poor memory but I assume—"

"You are not here to make assumptions but to help the Committee establish facts. Do you know John Carter Vincent?"

"Yes, Sir, more or less."

"Let me refresh your memory. Did you pass the night of December 31, 1929, with John Carter Vincent?"

"Senator, I have testified that I don't recall where I passed the night of December 31, 1929, and therefore I cannot recall whom I passed it with but it may be that I passed it with Vincent."

"Do you mean that it would be logical to assume that you passed the night with him or simply that it was a possibility?"

(Mrs. Vincent mumbles.)

Senator X (reading): "'My love, I stole this bit of jade from the Japanese Embassy. Take it in remembrance of me.' Is that a pro-Communist or anti-Communist statement?"

"Senator, it doesn't seem to me—"

"Mrs. Vincent, did you ever have Vincent's security checked?"

"Senator, it never occurred to me to—"

"Mrs. Vincent, you're being evasive again. How long did you live in Chicago?"

"Off and on for twenty years."

"And you never thought it necessary to check on a State Department official—incredible!"

"Well, not in the way you mean, Senator, but—"

"There you go 'butting' again. Would you say that the night you spent with Vincent, December 31, 1929, was pro- or anti-Communist?"

"No—to both questions. Now that you have refreshed my memory I would say that it was free-enterprise in the best sense of the term."

"Congratulations, Mrs. Vincent; you have been a very helpful witness. Won't you have a glass of sourwine?"

"Senator, these hearings remind me of—"

(BELL RINGS)

"Gentlemen, we are expected on the floor to vote for Senator Nitwit's bill outlawing Un-American sexual activity. Thank you, Mrs. Vincent; members of the Committee may want to see you individually. . . ."[59]

This parody and a similar one sent to Surrey and Karasik, was evidence that by spring the depression Vincent experienced following the hearings had begun to lift. The sun and the sea, and most important, his wife's return, had raised his spirits. So too did an incident which occurred while he was in Paris for a meeting with the American ambassador. At a luncheon sponsored by the American Club of Paris (a businessman's organization), Vincent found himself the recipient of a vast outpouring of support and affection. "I, along with some visiting firemen, was at the speaker's table," he later told Walter Surrey. "The visitors (Ambassadors Flake and Ravndal, and a general or so) were introduced by the President of the Club and there was the usual polite applause. My turn came. I don't suppose I knew personally 20 people out of the 500 present, but there was a most 'shocking' and sustained burst of applause. I had to stand twice before it subsided. The President then said: 'You see, Mr. Vincent, what we think of you.' As you know," he reminded Surrey, "the American Club in Paris is not composed of New Dealers." In describing the "ovation" to relatives he noted, with typical modesty: "It wasn't personal. It was protest against [McCarthyism]."[60]

Surrey was pleased to hear the news and had his own story to tell: His secretary had mailed Vincent a copy of *Reporter* magazine's exposé of the China Lobby without adequate postage but the Post Office informed the lawyer that the clerks themselves placed additional stamps on the envelope simply because it was addressed to John Carter Vincent. "So now you have the wealthy American businessmen in Paris, and the poor hard working post office in Washington on your side," Surrey wrote.[61] Vincent's troubles did indeed appear to be over.

This happy interlude was not to last. The Federal Loyalty System was like an immense and intricate spiderweb; once imprisoned in its sticky strands there was no release. The more the victim struggled to escape, the tighter he was held. Even as Vincent celebrated his clearance by the Loyalty-Security Board, he was still being investigated by the State Department and the FBI.

On April 1, State Department Security Chief Donald L. Nicholson informed his New York office that allegations had been made concerning Vincent's departure for Europe aboard the S.S. *Constitution*. An "anonymous source" claimed that just before Vincent gave his passport to the ship's clerk, he tore two pages from it and stuffed them in his pocket. The clerk reportedly told Vincent that such behavior was highly irregular and he would have to inform his superior. Nicholson asked Agent R.D. Clark to investigate. Clark went directly to the office of the American Export Line and interviewed the man who had checked Vincent aboard on the morning of February 20. Irving Fisher "clearly" recalled that both Vincent's ticket and passport had been in perfect order and stated that none of the events Clark described ever took place. Clark also questioned other officials who said that "nothing came to their attention regarding Mr. Vincent and his passport; they had no contact with him and no complaints, no unpleasantness, no incidents of any kind." As was customary, a record of the allegations and a copy of Clark's dispatch were placed in Vincent's loyalty file.[62]

Other rumors proved more difficult to dispel. Although J. Edgar Hoover had supposedly ended his investigation of Vincent in 1951, the bureau was still watching the diplomat and recording his activities. When Vincent appeared before the House Un-American Activities Committee in January, the Washington field office obtained a transcript of his testimony and sent it to the director. Three FBI offices—the Loyalty Unit, the Espionage Unit, and the McCarran Special Squad—reviewed this testimony as well as his testimony before the McCarran committee. One memorandum noted that during the latter hearing "Vincent professed a general lack of knowledge of the principles of Communism and was unable to identify any person with whom he had contact as Communists."[63] In February, March, April, and July, Hoover sent additional reports to the Civil Service Commission,[64] which in turn ordered the State Department Loyalty-Security Board to reopen Vincent's case.[65] The board examined the FBI interviews and cleared Vincent three more times: on March 14, May 23, and August 5. "It is recommended that the case be closed," the board stated in its fourth, and final, report.[66]

But the case would not stay closed. By August, Vincent had received two new shocks: one from the McCarran committee, the other from the Civil Service Loyalty Review Board.

On July 2, the Senate Internal Security Subcommittee presented its findings, after an eighteen-month investigation of the Institute of Pacific Relations. McCarran's staff claimed to have interviewed over 600 witnesses and informants in public and private meetings; examined 22,000 documents and printed 6,000 pages of testimony and exhibits. Its final report, alone, numbered 234 pages.[67] Speaking to the Senate, McCarran said: "I am convinced, from the evidence developed in this inquiry, that but for the machinations of the small group that controlled and activated the Institute of Pacific Relations, China today would be free and a bulwark against a further advance of the Red hordes into the Far East. . . . Our Government agencies have been infiltrated by persons whose allegiance is with Communist Russia."[68]

Such conclusions were a distortion of reality: The Institute of Pacific Relations was basically a private scholarly organization which played no active role in developing American China policy.[69] "The McCarran Subcommittee has given us not a report but a revision of history," noted the *Washington Post,* "a revision compounded out of McCarthian bigotry, McCarranesque spleen and MacArthurian legend. It is an attempt to perpetuate another fraud and hoax on the American people."[70]

Vincent figured prominently in "this extravagant nonsense." The committee's report mentioned his name over thirty times, and its conclusions stated that "over a period of years John Carter Vincent was the principle [*sic*] fulcrum of IPR pressures and influence in the State Department" and was also "influential," with Owen Lattimore, "in bringing about a change in United States policy in 1945 favorable to the Chinese Communists."[71] Among the committee's final recommendations was that a grand jury should determine whether Lattimore and Vincent's colleague, John Davies, were guilty of perjury.[72]

Vincent first learned of the committee's report in a wire from his attorneys: "Believe you will find it not nearly so bad as we expected. All in all you were a much better witness than you thought."[73] An eight-page letter soon followed in which Surrey appraised the report. He continued to be moderately optimistic:

> I do not contend that the report . . . is good. However, all things are relative. The report did not in its conclusions accept Budenz' testimony that you are a Communist, . . . That obviously was too much for the committee to swallow. While it also does cite the testimony . . . that you were a member of the Communist Party, it does print your denial and this fact is contained along with the reports and all other accusations made before the Committee. . . . The report does not say that you were a dupe of the Communists, that you did not understand Communism, or many of the other vicious things which the Committee tried to bring out. The most damaging part of the report is the conclusion [concerning] you and Owen Lattimore."

But this statement had received little mention in the press, Surrey stated: ". . . The main attention is on Lattimore and Davies." He had also "checked with people around town . . . and the reaction is that you came off very well. They all contend that the Committee's report is slanted badly and considering that factor you did very well." Surrey ended his letter on a positive note: "I think the basic conclusion I draw from all this is that you were a good witness. . . . I believe that your persistence in sticking to the facts as you remembered them, in refusing to recall events which the Committee tried to get you to recall and your dogmatic insistence on facts which you knew, all helped in making it more difficult for the Committee to go too far in reaching a strongly adverse position against you. I remain pleased at having had you as a client." Jokingly he added: "Someday I would like to know how it feels to be a 'fulcrum.' The reaction to that conclusion has caused considerable amount of amusement. Somehow its seems to have a dirty connotation but I can't figure it out."[74]

Vincent found Surrey's letter "comforting,"[75] but as events soon proved, the attorney had underestimated the seriousness of the situation. Six days after Surrey's letter arrived, Vincent received a message from the Under Secretary Humelsine marked "Personal-Confidential (Eyes-only the Minister)," a designation reserved for only the most urgent communications. "Dear John Carter," Humelsine wrote, "I regret exceedingly to have to inform you that the Department was advised in a letter dated July 2, signed by Senator [Hiram] Bingham, Chairman of the Loyalty Review Board, that the Board had reached a decision, based on its post-audit authority, to rehear your case and make its own determination. This decision will, of course, mean that it will be necessary for you to return to Washington for the hearing. . . . I realize, of course, that this will be unwelcome news to you, but in the circumstances there is nothing we can do except to make the arrangements for you to be here at the appointed time." The department wished to keep this development "strictly confidential" to avoid publicity, so Humelsine asked Vincent to suggest a reason the secretary could use to order him home for consultation and in this way hide the fact that he was returning to face another loyalty hearing.[76]

As usual, Vincent's first thought was institutional, not personal: to make certain he did nothing to embarass the department or harm the Foreign Service. "I am sorry for your sake as well as mine that [this] situation . . . has arisen," he wrote Humelsine, almost apologetically, on July 17. "I have no idea what the Board has in mind other than a review of the ground that has already been covered, I thought thoroughly and satisfactorily." He believed there was "ample justification" to return to Washington to discuss the Moroccan situation with Secretary Acheson. Walter Surrey should be kept fully informed, Vincent told Humelsine, but "to make sure there are no over-riding considerations in your mind which would make such a step unwise" he was enclosing a letter to Surrey with the request that it be delivered only if the State Department had "no objections." "It is a wearysome [sic] business," Vincent said. "I trust some day it will close."[77]

The State Department decided that keeping Surrey informed would not violate the security it had invoked in the Vincent case, so on July 23, Under Secretary John Peurifoy telephoned the attorney and told him that his client's loyalty was once again at issue. The next day Surrey received the letter Vincent sent through Humelsine.[78] "To say that I find this news displeasing would easily qualify me for the under-statement-of-the-year prize," Vincent told Surrey. "At the same time my equable and philosophical temperament, plus my reliance on ultimate justice, keep me from getting excited over the matter." What reasons lay behind the review board's decision? Vincent asked. "I have no idea of what is at the bottom of the thing unless it is a desire on the part of the Board to act directly in my case [because] the McCarran . . . report was issued after my clearance from State. The timing of the Board's request would seem to indicate as much." Would it be necessary to write still another statement of defense? "Do you have any words of wisdom as to what I might do . . . to prepare myself? . . . What specifically is troubling the Review Board?"[79]

There was little Surrey could tell Vincent; he was as mystified as his client. He did suspect that Vincent was correct in assuming that the board felt the need to render its own verdict, because of McCarran's speeches and his committee's report. He recommended that Vincent study thoroughly the McCarran committee testimony, and told him to arrive in Washington no later than the first week in September, one month before Vincent was scheduled to appear before the board. "I believe that you should return [then] in order that we can have four weeks to prepare whatever the ordeal might hold for us," Surrey said. "I really believe that not only should I counsel you to follow this schedule, I shall order you to do so. I so do."[80]

"I accept your orders," Vincent replied with a new note of bitterness.

> I must say I am deeply resentful over the whole matter. When one knows that there should be no question of one's loyalty it is disgusting, to state it mildly, to be placed in the position of a defendant by irresponsible and malicious accusers. That is my say; now I shall do what you want me to do which I gather is to prepare a defense. [But] how do we go about removing doubts from people's minds (if they exist) when there is no real basis for their existence? . . . I am not in the least doubtful of my 'complete and unswerving loyalty' but that very fact makes it difficult for me to disabuse minds of a non-existent situation arising out of the wholly prejudicial testimony. Maybe you . . . have the answer![81]

On September 8, Vincent left Tangier for his appointment with the Loyalty Review Board.[82]

9

More Damn Trouble

This time there were no reporters waiting to greet Vincent as his plane landed at New York's Idlewild Airport. His presence in the United States was a secret known only to his family, his closest friends, and a few colleagues in the State Department. From New York, he took a train to Washington and the home of Maxine and Jim McHugh, where he would stay until his hearing was over. Why the review board had decided to call him home was still a mystery. His attorneys had "set out lines" and made "soundings" but learned nothing that they had not already surmised: that the board, in Monroe Karasik's words, "has the problem of correlating the Committee's findings (if you can call them findings) with the Loyalty-Security Board's report."[1]

Karasik's suspicions soon proved correct. For over five years Vincent's career had been a pawn in the savage political chess game played by the administration and its critics: His promotion to career minister had been blocked for over six months; he had been accused of being a spy and a Communist; he had been transferred to Tangier to avoid a Senate row; the State Department had leveled charges, cleared him, then had him reinvestigated; the McCarran committee had tried to force him to commit perjury. Now the Civil Service Commission's Loyalty Review Board was beginning a new chapter in this ultimately tragic story. How the board handled Vincent's case and reached its final decision would be even more incredible than what had gone before. A friend, John Creighton, did not realize how right he was when he wrote Vincent in 1951: "For a nice man, an intelligent man, a capable man, a useful and good one, you have more damn trouble than anyone I ever saw."[2]

The Civil Service Loyalty Review Board, now examining Vincent's case, had been established in 1947, as part of the Federal Employee Loyalty Program. It consisted of a permanent chairman, staff, and approximately twenty-eight members (businessmen, academics, and lawyers) who served on a voluntary, part-time basis. Originally, the board was to act as a custodian, guarding against procedural irregularities within the system and coordinating the activities of the various national and regional loyalty agencies. Its major responsibility was to review cases submitted on appeal by employees who had been found disloyal by their departments. But soon the board began to extend its jurisdiction and, regardless of a department's decision, it would return cases for reinvestigation or hear them itself.[3] The board's more active role in trying to ferret out Communists won it few friends in the Congress; although it (and the system of which it was part) had been created as a concession to Republicans, conservatives regarded it with suspicion and charged repeatedly that not enough Communists or Communist sympathizers were being removed from federal service.[4] "To counter charges that the Loyalty Review Board was soft on Communists,"[5] President Truman, in January 1951, removed the chairman (whom McCarthy said was doing "an extremely foul job")[6] and appointed in his place an arch-conservative Republican, former senator Hiram Bingham of Connecticut.

But this alone did not satisfy the McCarthyites; pressure soon mounted in Congress for revision of the regulations which governed the Loyalty Program. The Republicans demanded that the standard used to dismiss government employees be changed from one that required "reasonable grounds" to prove disloyalty, to the World War II standard that required only "reasonable doubt" of an employee's loyalty. This was a violation of civil liberties and for a time, President Truman resisted making the change.[7]

In Hiram Bingham the McCarthyites found a valuable ally. Like them, Bingham believed that the best way to evaluate the effectiveness of the loyalty program was to calculate how many employees had been dismissed, not how many had been investigated and cleared. "The State Department has the worst record" of any federal department, Bingham told a meeting of the board in February 1951. "It has not found anyone disloyal." Convinced that the recommended change would "double the number of [employees] that [could] be thrown out," Bingham (and a majority of his colleagues on the board) asked Truman to establish the new standard of "reasonable doubt." In April, the president complied. When word of Truman's action reached Bingham, he remarked: "It's the best news I've heard in months."[8]

Bingham's activities were praised by the men who had attacked his predecessor. When Bingham spoke before the American Bar Association in September 1951, Senator McCarran called his address "one of the finest that it has been my privilege to read," and had it inserted in the *Congressional Record.*[9] Senator McCarthy said that Bingham was doing "the best job anyone could do under the circumstances";[10] and after the board recommended John Service's dismissal in January 1952,[11] Congressman Fred Busbey told the House that "Mr. Bingham has accomplished more in 1 year than [the previous Chairman] did in four years. Saddled with a crew who have for four long years sat idly by, watching a parade of questionable characters infiltrate the Government service and doing nothing about it, Mr. Bingham has labored hard to create some order out of chaos. He therefore deserves to be aided by every member of Congress." In that spirit, Busbey urged Bingham and the review board to turn their attention "to another John and . . . release a similar decision on John Carter Vincent."[12]

The chairman needed little coaxing from the Congress: Bingham's conduct throughout Vincent's hearing demonstrates that he was more interested in satisfying congressional opinion than honestly evaluating Vincent's loyalty. This is surprising given Bingham's background: A noted historian and explorer before entering politics, he was, like many in the China Service, the son of American missionaries; he had even dated John Service's mother. He also knew Vincent, having met him first in 1927 during a tour of Hankow. At that time, Senator Bingham had thanked Vincent for helping his son Woodbridge, a teacher at Yale-in-China, leave Ch'ang-sha during the antiforeign riots. But such relationships meant little in 1952, when the hot spotlight of congressional witch-hunters focused on Vincent and Bingham alike.

Vincent's case received unusual treatment almost from the moment it arrived at the office of the Loyalty Review Board in late February 1952.[13] The voluminous files were sent first to the board's "inspection section," where they were studied by Weldon D. Hartsfield, one of Bingham's examiners. The examiner's "first duty," Bingham told a journalist in 1951, "is to see whether the lower board followed the procedure correctly in issuing the interrogatory, in taking testimony under oath, [etc]. If the case has been properly handled the Examiner clears [it] right way without referring it to a panel [of the Board]."[14] This was the way the system was supposed to function, according to its chairman; but in Vincent's case it did not. Examiner Hartsfield either ignored this instruction or interpreted his authority more broadly, because he objected to the State Department's decision on Vincent not on procedural grounds (he never criticized them), but solely on his own interpretation of the evidence in the record. After a two-month study of the files (which included FBI reports, and Vincent's testimony before the Loyalty-Security Board and McCarran committee), Hartsfield wrote a forty-two-page report recommending that the review board reopen the case, hold its own hearing, and "enter new findings." His report covered all the significant aspects of the Vincent case: the derogatory information given the FBI by Congressman Judd, Admiral Miles, General Wedemeyer, and Louis Budenz, among others; the Wallace and Marshall missions; Vincent's association with organizations and individuals considered Communist or pro-Communist; the suspicions of espionage, and the "raincoat" and Charles Davis incidents. Hartsfield's findings were shocking:

> A review of Vincent's record chronologically shows that he has been pro-Chinese Communist and very definitely anti-Chiang Kai-shek since he first became associated with young Chinese revolutionists and young American liberals in Peking in . . . 1939; that he advocated recognition of Russia in 1932 and took the side of Max and Grace Granich when they were attempting to propagate Communist propaganda in Shanghai in 1936; that in the early 1940s he aided or led others in a campaign to convince the American people that the Chinese Communists were democratic reformers and that Chiang was weak, inefficient, reactionary, and corrupt.
>
> In 1945 and 1946, [Hartsfield continued], Vincent [intensified] his defense of the Chinese Communists and also appears to have followed the Communist Party line regarding . . . Japan. . . . Vincent was closely associated with [Owen] Lattimore and other members of [a] pro-Communist group [in the IPR]. . . . Vincent admits having made a contribution of $40 or $50 to John Stewart Service's defense fund and has had an unusually large number of associates whose loyalty has been questioned. . . . All the items of evidence . . . are indications of Communistic beliefs and sympathies, but if there were no other damaging evidence in the file, they might be considered merely as incidents of poor judgment and . . . lack of knowledge. . . . However, there is evidence of a much more serious nature in the case file. [Louis] Budenz states that in 1943 and 1944, Vincent was a 'non card-carrying

member' of the Communist Party. . . . While Budenz' allegation is not directly substantiated by the testimony of a witness, it is substantiated . . . by Vincent's record. Also, very few persons have been in a position to know the secret members of the Communist Party as Budenz knew them.

On the basis of all the evidence [Hartsfield concluded], it is believed that Vincent knowingly aided and abetted the Chinese Communists to the detriment of the interests of the United States, that he has followed the Communist Party line, that he has associated with pro-Communists by choice, and that he was, in 1943 and 1944, a secret member of the Communist Party. Therefore. . . , there is a reasonable doubt as to his loyalty to the Government of the United States.[15]

Not even the McCarran committee had reached such extreme conclusions.

The examiner's report was supposed to be (in Bingham's words) the "result of a careful study of all [the] evidence,"[16] but in Vincent's case it was not. Despite its length and detail, Hartsfield's report simply summarized and accepted the evidence; it did not analyze or evaluate it. Even as a summary it was superficial, incomplete, ignorant, and as one board member said, "biased."[17] For example, when Hartsfield quoted from Walter Judd's interview with the FBI he omitted the fact that the congressman also said: "I would never make even a suggestion that Vincent is a Communist." Similarly, in quoting Admiral Miles, Hartsfield failed to mention an important caveat that even the FBI emphasized in its report: "Admiral Miles was clear to point out that he is not in a position to testify to [his] evaluations of Vincent . . . He pointed out that [his] information was rather an evaluation based upon his knowledge of the contents of Dai-Li's [sic]" files. In short, Hartsfield discussed only part of what the FBI had learned and left out any statements which might impeach the credibility of damaging information.

Hartsfield's discussion of the Wallace mission also reflected an absence of "careful study." He did not examine the specific, historical events which led to the drafting of the K'un-ming cable; instead, he evaluated past, factual reports only in light of present preoccupations. It was as if World War II had never happened: There was no longer even a common language to bridge the gap that separated the age of Roosevelt from the age of McCarthy. Believing only the testimony of an ex-Communist, Hartsfield argued that "the so-called Wallace Reports were definitely pro-Chinese Communist, were anti-Chiang Kai-shek, and followed the Communist Party line."[18]

Finally, Hartsfield ignored almost completely the evidence presented in Vincent's defense. He devoted less than two pages to a discussion of Vincent's fifty-four-page statement before the Loyalty-Security Board, noting that "to summarize each of the 41 'selected exhibits' does not appear to be advisable at this time." He even went so far as to point out that "in spite of the fact that these exhibits were selected by Vincent to show that he is not pro-Communist, they contain statements disparaging to Chiang Kai-shek and the Chinese Nationalist Government." And, there were only seven short paragraphs (five were one sentence long) which Hartsfield classified as "favorable information."[19]

The board's records do not indicate whether Hartsfield's report was the product of carelessness or conviction. But they do reveal that he was impressed by the views of Robert Welch, the ultraconservative founder of the John Birch Society. Hartsfield collected reviews of Welch's books and sent them (and other anti-Communist polemics) to members of the review board. Perhaps this explains why his analysis was so distorted.[20]

Hartsfield completed his work in mid-April 1952, and gave copies of his report to the three board members Bingham selected to review the Vincent case. The chairman of the panel was Dr. Burton L. French, a seventy-seven-year-old former Republican congressman from Indiana, renowned as a lawyer, lecturer, and writer. Despite his age, he led an active life, both as a member of the board and as professor of government at Ohio's Miami University. Second was Harry W. Blair, seventy-five, a Missouri Democrat who had served as an assistant United States attorney general during Franklin Roosevelt's first administration. He liked to call himself a simple "country lawyer" but he was more than that; he had a sharp, retentive memory and extensive legal knowledge. In 1952, he was practicing law in an influential Washington firm which bore his name. Last was John Harlan Amen, youngest of the three, but just as able. Educated at Princeton and the Harvard Law School, he was, at fifty-three, nationally famous as a tenacious prosecutor. His investigation of municipal misconduct in New York City in the 1930s and 1940s resulted in the disbarment of three assistant district attorneys and the mass retirement of one hundred policemen. During World War II he served as a colonel in the United States Army and was later one of the chief Allied prosecutors at the Nazi war trials. His fellow board members continued to call him "Colonel" in the 1950s when he was one of the most important lawyers in New York State.[21]

When the three met for the first time on April 15, Dr. French argued for postponing the case: Word had reached him that supplemental information from the FBI would require the Loyalty-Security Board to reopen the case. Their own group could not make a decision until the State Department had acted. Also, French thought they should wait until they had an opportunity to study the pending McCarran committee report. The meeting thus adjourned without even a "tentative conclusion."[22]

Bingham apparently had no doubt that the panel should consider the case: As soon as he was notified that Vincent had again been cleared by the State Department, he wrote to both French and Amen, asking them to sign the "Memorandum of Decision" that would authorize the review board to order Vincent home for a new hearing. French replied that the panel had not yet progressed far enough to take that step, but he, personally, had read Hartsfield's analysis and hoped that the matter might be handled without further delay. He planned to compare notes with Harry Blair on June 17, when they would be together to hear another case in the board's southern region.[23]

During their meeting in Atlanta, French and Blair found time to "go over many aspects of the [Vincent] Case." They discussed Hartsfield's report, the FBI records, and Vincent's statements and testimony. To their surprise, the two old gentlemen, one a Republican, the other a Democrat, found themselves in virtual agreement: first, that Hartsfield's summary was "prejudiced, one-sided . . . , overlooking everything favorable to Vincent"; and second, that "there was nothing in the record to justify further action." The Vincent case should be closed. Surely Colonel Amen must have reached the same conclusion. Now that the Loyalty-Security Board had again cleared Vincent, French thought it appropriate to call the panel together for what he felt would be its final meeting. Both men returned home convinced that their work on the Vincent case was almost over.[24]

In reality, their work was just beginning, as both men learned during their meeting with Colonel Amen on July 1. Of their discussion that morning Harry Blair later recalled: "Both Dr. French and I [thought] that Mr. Vincent should not be asked to come to Washington, as the file we had read did not seem to us to justify [another] hearing." There was "nothing in the record to indicate disloyalty or the possibility of disloyalty." But then Amen "raised a new point": A friend, a businessman who had "for years" dealt with the Zaibatsu, the organization of families which dominated Japanese economic life before and during World War II, had told Amen that John Carter Vincent had been "instrumental" in "breaking up" that "business group." There were rumors that the "Communists had something to do with [it]." Amen was "upset" that his friend had been inconvenienced by Vincent and thought he should be questioned "about the Japanese situation," Blair said. "Neither Dr. French nor I had ever heard of such a situation in Japan or of Mr. Vincent's connection with it. But both of us finally agreed to [Amen's] request that Vincent be called back to Washington. . . . [I]t was . . . a matter of courtesy on our part to comply with the request and insistence of our fellow Panel member."[25] So primarily "out of deference to Amen," French and Blair agreed to sign the "Memorandum of Decision" which would reopen the Vincent case.

As it turned out, Amen had to wait three months to question Vincent about Japan. On July 2, the Civil Service Commission received still another FBI report that required the board to cancel its decision and return the case to the State Department.[26] Actually, the supplemental material was nothing more than recently published transcripts of Vincent's testimony before the McCarran committee. "The information is not new," one State Department official complained to another, ". . . we informally obtained Vincent's testimony . . . before we made our final adjudication of Vincent's case and submitted it to the Review Board. Nevertheless," E. K. Meade, Jr., noted, "under present procedures the case will have to come back to the Department for readjudication."[27] The Loyalty-Security Board met again on August 5, and for the fourth time cleared Vincent.[28] Thirteen days later, the State Department sent the case back to the Loyalty Review Board, which reaffirmed its previous decision to hold a hearing.[29]

Chairman Bingham was pleased that the panel could finally get on with its work: The Vincent case was "very important," he told Harry Blair, "the McCarran Committee has passed on it." He then asked Blair what he thought about expanding the panel from the usual three to five members. "Five heads were better than 3," Blair replied, "5 or 500," whatever the chairman desired. Bingham appointed Marion Wade Doyle, a Washington civic leader, to the panel and then to everyone's surprise asked French to step aside as chairman and assumed the role himself. Blair considered this an "unusual step."[30] He was correct. The regulations of the board did not prohibit the chairman from directing the work of an individual panel but neither did they state that it was his function to do so. Indeed, the rules suggested otherwise: Section 8 of the "Regulations For The Operations of the Loyalty Review Board" stated that it was the responsibility of the chairman to appoint at least three members to a panel, one of whom would preside, be known as the chairman of the panel, and "make due report to the Board of all acts and proceedings of said panel."[31] Bingham also implied in speeches and interviews he gave during his tenure as chairman that he played no active role in individual cases. When a case came to the review board, Bingham told the American Bar Association in 1951, "it then becomes my duty to appoint a panel to hear the case. . . . I appoint a panel of 3 from among the 25 members of the Loyalty Review Board and [eventually] the panel . . . presents me with a signed statement of its decision. It then becomes my duty to inform the individual of this decision."[32] Bingham also gave the same explanation to his son: He never intervened in the affairs of the panel, Dr. Woodbridge Bingham remembers him saying, he simply checked procedures and reported the final decision without change or comment.[33] All this suggests that Bingham's action in the Vincent case was not just "unusual" but perhaps improper and a violation of the spirit, if not the letter, of the laws which governed the review board.

State Department officials were troubled by Bingham's decision to enlarge the Vincent panel. When E. K. Meade, Jr., an assistant to Carlisle Humelsine, learned the identities of the panelists, he listed their names and descriptions on a piece of office stationery, and then in the corner casually drew a doodle—a sketch of a grave, complete with cross; the deceased was obviously meant to be John Carter Vincent. As a prediction of events, Meade's drawing turned out to be extraordinarily accurate.[34]

The new review board panel began its interrogation of Vincent on October 7, 1952.[35] For six hours that day, and two the next, Vincent again discussed his views on communism, the Wallace and Marshall missions, his brief honorary membership in the Institute of Pacific Relations, his contribution to John Service's defense fund, and relationships with Owen Lattimore, Lauchlin Currie, and Alger Hiss, among others. Like the Loyalty-Security Board and McCarran committee, the panelists had difficulty understanding how Vincent had been so seemingly unaware of the "Red Menace." This charge was incorrect, Vincent again argued. He had been aware of the Communist threat, though he stressed, again, that fascism—not communism—was the issue which dominated the war years. The American goal was, first, military unity to defeat Japan, then, political unity to avoid a divided China which might tempt Russia as it had Japan. From Ambassador Gauss through Hurley and Marshall, American objectives had remained constant.[36]

Vincent insisted on being historically accurate even if it might hurt his own case. Instead of simply emphasizing his anticommunism (as his attorneys recommended) he explained to the panel how communism looked in the 1940s, when Mao was fighting the Japanese in northern China, and Stalin was America's ally. The nature of Chinese communism was always a complex and controversial subject, Vincent told the panel. Just as the Kuomintang had its eastern and western branches so did China's Communist Party. "In those days we used to . . . divide the Communists . . . into what we called 'Russian Chinese Communists' and 'Chinese Chinese Communists.' Russian Chinese Communists were those who were supposed to have a tie-in with Russia by past training or something else, and the 'Chinese Chinese Communists' were not Moscow trained and . . . took more of a Chinese point of view." Evidence available during the war (superficial at best until the observer mission in June 1944) suggested that Stalin did not control the Chinese. But by late 1945, Vincent said, he was convinced that the Communists were "getting direction from Moscow."[37] He was aware that such candor was dangerous but it was not in his nature to dissemble. Nothing would deter him from telling his story thoroughly, objectively, and in the end, truthfully.

For the most part, the board listened respectfully to Vincent's testimony in a pleasant contrast to the badgering he had received from the McCarran committee. Only John Harlan Amen gave Vincent some trying moments, when he questioned him about his role in formulating United States policy toward Japan.

Amen had read FBI reports in Hartsfield's summary that seemed to confirm what he had learned from his friend: Vincent had been a major architect of pro-Communist policies toward Japan. The principal source of these accusations was Eugene H. Dooman, one of Vincent's rivals in the State Department.

Dooman was a veteran of the Japanese Service whose thirty-year career was spent in the Tokyo embassy and on the Japan Desk in the State Department. In 1937 he was appointed counselor to Ambassador Joseph C. Grew and he remained Grew's loyal assistant and close friend when both men returned to Washington following Pearl Harbor. During the 1930s and 1940s Dooman (like Grew) was more sympathetic toward Japan than Vincent, who had seen the Japanese at their worst in Mukden, Dairen, and Chungking. Dooman wanted to preserve as much of the political and economic structure of prewar Japan as the war allowed, while Vincent (and countless others) hoped to establish a constitutional monarchy and a more liberal Japan by dissolving the Zaibatsu, the group of family-controlled monopolies which had supported Japanese aggression. These differences in viewpoint frequently led to bitter words between Dooman and Vincent. Later, Vincent recalled Dooman's face twisted in a "perpetual scowl" and described him as being "psychologically diseased. He loved to know the names of the big boys, Baron Shinewawa and the like. He was an ultraconservative, suspicious, anti-Communist and had the FBI outlook on anybody who adopted an attitude not openly condemnatory of Russia."[38] By 1945, Grew and Dooman (and the policies they represented) were being attacked not only by their colleagues in the State Department and military services but by many newspapers and magazines which held them responsible for Pearl Harbor and accused them (correctly) of advocating a "soft peace" in the Far East.[39]

Such criticism hurt Dooman profoundly[40] and he soon began to blame

China Service officers along with the "leftist press" for his troubles. When John Service was arrested in the *Amerasia* affair, Dooman told Vincent how pleased he was and expressed his hope that other enemies might soon follow Service to jail.[41] He also charged Julian Friedman, a clerk in Vincent's China Division, with leaking confidential information to his enemies.[42] The turning point came in August when Joseph Grew retired, and Dean Acheson became under secretary of state. Dooman despised Acheson: "I had had so many unpleasant experiences with Mr. Acheson," he told the State Department Loyalty-Security Board in 1951, "some of them over Japan, while he was Assistant Secretary that the moment I heard he was [becoming] Under Secretary . . . I went down to the Department and put in for retirement. I went to [Joseph] Ballantine [Director of the Far Eastern Office] and I said 'Joe, you're going to get it in the neck. I'm quite certain that things are in trend for your replacement by Vincent and I'm retiring under my own steam and I now advise you to do so.'"[43] When Acheson appointed Vincent to replace Dooman as chairman of the State-War-Navy Far Eastern Subcommittee, Dooman was equally enraged: How dare he be replaced by "a man who had had no experience in Japan, who knew nothing about Japan except from second hand." The hatred Dooman felt for Acheson he now directed at Vincent. As he cleaned out his desk and packed his files, he told colleagues that he had been betrayed by Vincent and his patron Acheson.[44]

Dooman's anger grew in the years after he left government service. In 1947, he told *Newsweek* editor Harry F. Kearn that Vincent had inserted radical clauses in the directive which guided General Douglas MacArthur in reconstructing Japan, and that Vincent was also responsible for formulating "FEC-230," a program which, Dooman claimed, would destroy Japanese industry. Kearn publicized Dooman's accusations in two stories which appeared in *Newsweek* in 1947 and 1948.[45] Two years later, when the FBI began its full field investigation of Vincent they included summaries of Kearn's articles in their reports and also interviewed the editor, who identified Dooman as one of his sources.[46] Dooman repeated his charges to the FBI, and in 1951, testified under oath before both the McCarran committee and the State Department Loyalty-Security Board.[47] His statements received prominent attention in Hartsfield's report, from which John Harlan Amen drew his questions.

Amen cross-examined Vincent as if he were a Nazi war criminal: "I want you to think carefully before you answer this," he told Vincent. "Is it your testimony that at no time from . . . when you assumed your position with the State, War and Navy [Far Eastern Subcommittee] . . . did you have anything to do with drafting, redrafting, or changing the plan or the policy paper known as the 'Initial Post-Surrender Policy' for Japan. . . ?"

"I can show you here what the testimony was at the time," Vincent offered.

"I am asking you a question and I want an answer, please," demanded Amen.

"My testimony was—"

Amen interrupted: "I am not asking what your testimony was; I am asking what it is today."

"My testimony today is there were changes made in this paper."

Amen interrupted again and asked the reporter to read back the question.

And again Vincent said: "My testimony was, there were minor changes made in the—"

Amen shot back: "Sir, I am not asking you that and you know I am not asking you that. . . . Will [the reporter] read the question again?"

The reporter repeated the question.

"I don't know what your difficulty is," Vincent said, "but my testimony is I did have something to do as Chairman of the FE [Subcommittee] with making minor changes in the—"

"Now we are getting somewhere," said Amen, satisfied at last.

"If you will let me, I will show you what the minor changes were."[48]

According to Dooman's testimony, the final version of the "Initial Post-Surrender Policy for Japan" was approved by the State-War-Navy Coordinating Committee (SWINCC) on August 28 or 29, 1945, two days before he retired. When the State Department published the paper on September 22, he found new paragraphs which authorized programs he had originally opposed because he thought they would "atomize" Japan and lead to a Communist take-over. And since Vincent became chairman of the FE subcommittee on September 1, no one but he could have been responsible for recommending such changes. This, in brief, is what Dooman had told *Newsweek*, the FBI, the McCarran committee, and the Loyalty-Security Board.[49]

Vincent denied Dooman's charges: His study of State Department records showed that the "Initial Post-Surrender Policy" was approved by SWINCC not on August 28 or 29 but on August 31, at a meeting Dooman himself attended. Moreover, that document, adopted in his presence, was the same one (except for some minor changes in phraseology) later published by the State Department. As for the minor changes, Vincent was ordered to make them by the Joint Chiefs of Staff and SWINCC. The final draft of the directive Dooman considered subversive was approved by

SWINCC, the military chiefs, the president, and Dooman's own sub-committee.[50]

This is what Vincent told the Loyalty-Security Board and the McCarran committee—and the original State Department records support his version of the story. But Amen, convinced that Dooman's version was correct, did not give Vincent an opportunity to make a full explanation to the review board. Indeed, when Vincent offered to give Amen a chronology of the events, Amen (as he had throughout most of the questioning) shut Vincent off, saying: "Never mind that." Instead of discussing the conflicts in testimony or evaluating each man's evidence, Amen, once more the crusading prosecutor, tried to force Vincent to accept full responsibility for the major changes Dooman said had been made.[51]

Amen also tried to hold Vincent responsible for the creation of FEC-230, although, in fact, he played no active role in its formulation. This program, which recommended major changes in Japan's economic system, had many fathers, both in Washington and Tokyo. In its original form it was a report prepared by economist Corwin D. Edwards and a group of Justice Department antitrust experts who had visited Japan in 1946. A special committee of economists assigned to Vincent's FE subcommittee worked on it next, revising it according to suggestions made by their counterparts in General MacArthur's headquarters. The final version, approved by the assistant secretaries of state, war, and navy on behalf of their chiefs, and sent to General MacArthur for implementation, was an amalgam of the recommendations made by the Corwin Group and State Department economists. MacArthur endorsed it and tried vigorously to enforce it. Later, when the program met resistance in Japan and was criticized by American businessmen (like Amen's friend), it was withdrawn and scrapped.[52] Dozens of men had contributed more than Vincent to FEC-230's creation, yet five years after its death, he alone was being held responsible for its birth.

Vincent tried in vain to persuade Amen that this notion was not correct. "It's your document," Amen said sarcastically after a rapid exchange of questions and answers regarding the history of FEC-230.

"I . . . had nothing personally to do with the preparation of it," Vincent insisted. " . . . It is my document only in the sense that I was the titular head of the Far Eastern [Sub]committee. This was prepared by technicians. It was prepared as a result of a commission that went [to Japan]."[53] That Vincent chaired a subcommittee which worked on FEC-230 was enough to convince Amen that he should be held fully responsible for the program.

Had Amen carefully read Dooman's testimony before the Loyalty-

Security Board (instead of just studying Hartsfield's summary of it) he would have seen how weak was the evidence supporting Dooman's charge. When Dooman was asked repeatedly by General Snow and Legal Advisor John Sipes what he knew personally and specifically about Vincent's views on Japan, Dooman replied: "practically nothing."[54]

"Mr. Vincent and I had very few contacts," Dooman testified on December 6, 1951. "What contacts there were were limited largely to meetings of [the Far Eastern] Area Committee, and in those . . . meetings, . . . he had very little to say."[55] Ambassador Nufer asked Dooman whether, during these meetings, Vincent had ever advocated the changes in policy which he later said were adopted. "Not to my knowledge," was Dooman's reply; "[he] participated very little in the discussions. . . . Mr. Vincent was very reserved."[56] It seems that Dooman selected Vincent as his chief target through a curious process of elimination:

> I was conscious that there were certain elements in the State Department who were trying to indoctrinate the higher officers of other departments in ideas quite contrary to those that I was maintaining. . . . On a certain occasion when the State, War and Navy Coordinating Committee had a meeting I found . . . that Mr. Acheson was present. . . . After I made [a] statement . . . Mr. Acheson said . . . "I don't go along with what we have heard." And then he expressed his own view. . . . [I]t was almost word for word out of [Owen Lattimore's] *Solution in Asia.* . . . He either read it on the recommendation of somebody or . . . the ideas set forth in that book had been communicated to him orally by somebody. He [later] testified . . . that he had never met Mr. Lattimore. . . . Now taking that fact into consideration and the fact that no time was lost by Mr. Acheson in replacing me with Mr. Vincent, I would assume that it was Mr. Vincent.[57]

General Snow then noted that during Dooman's appearance before the McCarran committee he admitted having never heard Vincent express views similar to Lattimore's. Was that correct? Snow asked. "That's right," replied Dooman.[58]

Could Dooman "connect" Vincent with FEC-230? Sipes inquired. "Mr. Sipes, I was not [then] in the Department," Dooman answered. "I'm in no position to say that I know that he was responsible." The only proof Dooman had was that Vincent was chairman of the Far Eastern Subcommittee during the period that postwar policies toward Japan were developed. On the basis of this one assumption, Dooman had concluded that Vincent was "responsible for the formulation of United States policy."[59]

Apparently Dooman's anger and resentment prevented him from understanding Vincent's real role. Two other theories have been presented to explain Dooman's quixotic behavior. Vincent believed that Dooman resigned "in a huff" because President Truman refused to appoint him chief of his own foreign mission.[60] And Monroe Karasik told the Loyalty Review Board that Dooman "suffered from and was treated for a condition of mental ill health at about this period."[61] Dooman's recovery was less than complete: Twenty years after leaving the Foreign Service he was still complaining to friends that in 1945 he had been the victim of a conspiracy led by John Carter Vincent.[62]

Amen's motives for attacking Vincent are more difficult to determine. Mrs. Vincent recalls Harry Blair telling her that Amen represented the Zaibatsu in New York, although Blair later stated that he "did not know" or had never "understood" that Amen was their legal counsel. Instead, he emphasized that Amen was close to businessmen who did have such connections and "heard their complaints as one lawyer hears of other lawyers' troubles."[63] Perhaps it was simply that Amen was a man too busy with his own career and his work with the board to give the Vincent case careful attention. He seems to have depended almost entirely on Hartsfield's report for his information, not realizing that the examiner's summary, like the FBI records on which much of it was based, was not an objective analysis of facts but the regurgitation of rumors, half-truths, and errors. Whatever the reason, Amen's easy acceptance of Dooman's claims casts doubt on his professional ethics and abilities. In any court of law, Dooman's testimony would have been immediately rejected as hearsay.

Hartsfield's own abilities became a major issue during the closing minutes of Vincent's hearing. The day before, Dr. French had asked Vincent about a comment he was supposed to have made regarding Ambassador Gauss's evaluation of one of John Service's Yen-an reports. Gauss had disagreed with Service's view that the Communists were following a cautious, limited program. Vincent, according to a charge contained in Hartsfield's summary, told the secretary of state "to pay no attention to [Gauss], that Service was right." Vincent told French that he did not remember seeing the memorandum and asked if he might examine it. Hartsfield interrupted to say that no one had actually *seen* the document in question; the charge was based on "a statement made by a confidential FBI witness [who] didn't give the exact date and title."[64] Monroe Karasik was not satisfied with this answer and asked that the document be identified.

During the luncheon recess following this exchange, Karasik did some investigating of his own and reported his findings the next day, after

Bingham announced that the board was finished questioning Vincent. The attorney said that he had called the State Department and asked for a copy of Gauss's dispatch. "I assumed it was unclassified," said Karasik wryly, "since Mr. Hartsfield undoubtedly would not have read me classified information since I am not qualified to receive [it]." The document was found, removed from the files, and delivered to Karasik. He waved it in the air, as Joe McCarthy liked to do with his lists of Communists in government. It was as Hartsfield described, Karasik said, except for "a most curious discrepancy": The comment critical of Gauss had not been written by Vincent at all, but by another China Service officer. Karasik then asked Hartsfield if *he* had any questions about the dispatch.[65]

Obviously embarrassed, Hartsfield turned to Bingham and said, "Mr. Chairman, as I stated yesterday, my questions were based on information in the file I received from a confidential informant and not from the document itself."[66]

"I understand that, Sir," Karasik, his voice rising in anger, told the examiner. "This seems to me to raise one question and that is the degree of seriousness with which your Board, Sir, regards information received. Here we have an instance where the information . . . is not only inaccurate but highly untrue and at complete variance with the facts. . . . I think [it] lays grave doubts on the reliability of such information. . . . [It] will show you to what extent you can rely upon unsworn, uninterrogated information."[67]

Karasik added a footnote to this story which was even more damaging to Hartsfield. State Department records indicated that Gauss's dispatch had been part of the record in the Service case which had been before the board. "That puzzles me," Karasik said. "Why [was] Mr. Hartsfield . . . relying on the word of an informant when your records contain this document. . . [?]" Neither Bingham nor Hartsfield cared to answer Karasik's questions. "If there are no further questions," Bingham said quickly, "we will consider the hearing closed."[68]

Four days later Vincent flew back to Tangier, pleased with the way his hearing had ended and certain that his troubles must finally be over. There was no doubt in his mind—or Surrey's—that he would now be completely exonerated. Did he not testify fully and honestly? Was not the board's own examiner shown to be biased and negligent? What more proof did honest men require?

Unfortunately, Vincent again underestimated his enemies, for whom truth and justice meant little. They were moved by fear, malice, and ambition, and these played the decisive role in the final adjudication of the Vincent case. It was, Harry Blair later said, "one of the worst miscarriages of justice" he had ever observed.[69]

The Loyalty Review Board began its final debate in late October, when John Harlan Amen and Burton French met to discuss the case. It was immediately apparent that the two were at odds: Amen believed Vincent guilty of procommunism, while French thought him innocent of every charge. They could not have been further apart.

In an attempt to convert French, Amen summarized his views in a letter on the thirty-first. He admitted to being primarily influenced by the McCarran committee's conclusion that Vincent was responsible for policies "favorable to the Chinese Communists." Indeed, Amen thought so highly of the senator that he argued that it was not possible to clear Vincent without at the same time criticizing the committee—and Amen did not think any criticism was justified. It was not the last time that the senator cast his large shadow over the review board proceedings.

Amen listed seven other points which he thought sufficient to convict Vincent: Included were "Mr. Vincent's Communistic activities and opposition to . . . Chiang Kai-shek"; his "uniform and strict adherence to the Communist line without deviation"; and his association with "notorious Communist sympathizers" like Alger Hiss and Owen Lattimore. Amen also thought that Dooman, Hurley, Budenz, and Miles had been credible witnesses whose testimony he found "no good reason to reject." "The general pattern of Communistic activity seems to me to emerge clearly and unequivocally," he concluded. ". . .(I)t is inconceivable to me how a decision of eligibility could be substantiated."[70]

When Harry Blair read Amen's letter he was "astounded," and sent him an eighteen-page analysis which attacked each of Amen's seven points. Blair could not understand how Vincent could be accused of following the Communist line. "Vincent participated in the effort to [form a coalition government in China]," Blair wrote,

> which, from the hindsight wisdom of 1952 when we have become aware of the Kremlin's tactics, may be called a Communist "line." So did many others, including the President of the United States, who sent both Hurley and Marshall to China to accomplish it. None of us believes the President, Hurley, or Marshall are disloyal. Second, it is claimed that the "line" was to criticize Chiang Kai-shek, weaken his strength with his people, and eventually destroy him. The record is overflowing with statements of other Foreign Service officers, newspaper, magazine, and radio correspondents, American and other businessmen in China, Army officers (including General Wedemey-

255   More Damn Trouble

er . . .) all showing beyond dispute that . . . Chiang's Kuomintang *was* wholly corrupt, inefficient and obviously headed for disaster. For Vincent to have shut his eyes to these facts and refuse to report them . . . would have been a most reprehensible dereliction of duty.

Nor could Blair accept the veracity of the "prejudiced" Dooman, the often confused Hurley, and the "unreliable" Budenz. "I can discover no pattern of Communistic activity on the part of Vincent. . . ," Blair concluded. "[T]o me an impressive feature of the record is the unanimous faith and confidence in Vincent's loyalty by those who knew him best and were most intimate with him in his daily life": fellow diplomats, newspaper correspondents, and War and Navy Department officials. "They never saw the least evidence by deed or word of any Communist sympathy." Such evidence was sufficient to convince Blair that Vincent was completely loyal to his country.[71]

Blair's lengthy analysis demonstrated that he had studied not just the raw data in Vincent's file (a considerable effort in itself) but had also examined other congressional testimony and documents which he thought relevant to Vincent's case. Amen's letter, on the other hand, revealed that he had not read much beyond the examiner's reports before reaching a decision; in places his words were identical with those found in a supplementary report Hartsfield wrote earlier that month.[72] Once again, Amen showed that he was derelict in his duty.

Amen's letter may not have pleased Blair but it did impress Bingham. During the past few months he had failed in his own effort to find information to corroborate the worst charges against Vincent. He wrote to Patrick Hurley and Louis Budenz in July and September, asking for their help, but the ex-Communist did not reply and Hurley, in a typically incoherent twenty-three-page letter, said he had no evidence "to convict John Carter Vincent of disloyalty."[73] So Amen's letter, with its orderly presentation of a case against Vincent, must have appealed greatly to the chairman; indeed, after receiving a copy he rewrote it to read as if it were the final opinion of the *entire* panel. Not only did Bingham adopt all of Amen's seven points, he added another. The eighth point concerned the testimony of Louis Budenz, the McCarran committee's star witness: "Mr. Louis F. Budenz states that in 1943 and 1944, he knew from official Communist Party reports that Mr. Vincent was a secret or non-card carrying member of the Communist Party. Mr. Budenz, as a Communist Party official, certainly was in a position to know of Communist Party activities and affiliations during that time." The insertion of this clause into the final report would mean that the review board accepted Budenz's claim that Vincent was a Communist.

When Bingham submitted this new eight-point draft to the panel on December 11, a rebellion erupted. Blair, French, and Mrs. Doyle refused to sign it.[74] A heated discussion then ensued in which all participated. "To my surprise and intense delight," Blair later observed, "I found French and I had the same view we started with": That there was nothing in the record to justify a finding of reasonable doubt. "Amen still thought there was . . . but did not mention the Zaibatsu [question]." Bingham was "also against Vincent," while Marion Wade Doyle, who might cast the deciding vote, seemed to be undecided. But it soon became clear that she would side with Amen and Bingham, because she thought that Vincent's contribution to John Service's defense fund showed a "sympathy for Communism." Bingham and Amen were unimpressed by that argument but, out of deference to Mrs. Doyle, it was included in the panel's first report. Someone mentioned Budenz's testimony and Harry Blair flew into a rage: "I wouldn't believe him on a pile of Bibles as high as the Washington monument," he cried, then stalked out of the room.[75]

Bingham now had the majority he needed to recommend Vincent's dismissal and asked Amen to draft a new opinion. In this version, the board stated that it neither accepted nor rejected Budenz's charges or the McCarran committee's verdict—it did not say how they were interpreted. This change was apparently made as a concession to Blair and French. Amen also reduced the eight points to four, and, following Mrs. Doyle's suggestion, added a paragraph criticizing Vincent for contributing to Service's defense fund.[76]

Although this version of the board's report was slightly less condemnatory than Bingham's original eight-point draft, Blair and French still would not sign it and said again that they would file a separate opinion and send a copy to Vincent's attorneys. But Bingham had all the votes he needed: Mrs. Doyle's, Amen's, and his own. Thus, by a vote of three to two, the review board determined there was a reasonable doubt of Vincent's loyalty and recommended his dismissal from government service.

Bingham continued to handle the Vincent case in an unorthodox manner, even after a majority of the board reached a decision. Usually, the chairman sent the secretary of state the board's opinion along with a separate covering letter. (In the Service case, Bingham sent Acheson a five-page opinion and a two-page letter.)[77] But this time Bingham sent *no* opinion to Acheson, only a letter which summarized and in places *revised* the majority's findings. New words were added, while others were removed. "Without expressly accepting or rejecting the testimony of Louis Budenz . . . or the findings of the Senate [Judiciary] Committee," the letter *now* stated that the panel had "taken these factors into account." (Amen's draft was even more vague on how the panel interpreted this evidence.) Amen's charge that Vincent had been "overzealous" in promoting pro-Communist policies was erased, as was Mrs. Doyle's paragraph regarding Vincent's contribution to the Service fund. And Vincent was no longer accused of being (in Amen's words) "careless of his prerogatives of office."[78] The board's records do not indicate why Bingham decided to make these changes—perhaps he hoped that softening the language might persuade French and Blair to forgo their decision to file a separate opinion. If this was Bingham's motive he did not succeed; even though the case was now officially closed (as far as the board was concerned), Blair and French went ahead and wrote a nineteen-page dissenting opinion which they sent to their colleagues as well as to Dean Acheson and Walter Surrey.[79] Bingham's peculiar letter also had an unexpected effect on John Harlan Amen; he seems to have been displeased with the changes made in the majority opinion because he later gave Senator McCarran his own "individual conclusions" in the Vincent case.[80]

Bingham never explained to his fellow board members why he decided to send Acheson a letter instead of the final report. Blair suspected that "there were some things in the decision of which he did not approve, perhaps because [they were] not clearly condemnatory and he wanted to garble the majority opinion [and] by not sending . . . any opinion, there was unlikely to be inquiry as to different opinions, for the letter reads as if the opinion was that of the [entire] Board." Bingham's letter gave no hint that two members had refused to follow the majority.[81]

Bingham's entire performance in the Vincent case was extraordinary: He was unusually enthusiastic about reversing the State Department's decision when the case was first referred to the Board; he expanded the size of the panel and appointed himself chairman; he revised the majority opinion after the three approved it; and he did not send the secretary of state a full report. What motivated him? The evidence suggests that Bingham felt it politically necessary to recommend Vincent's dismissal. His predecessor was savagely attacked by the McCarthyites who were now watching and judging him. The McCarran committee had rendered its own critical verdict. A similar opinion from his board would enhance Bingham's popularity in the Congress. Self-protection was his chief motive, both Adrian Fisher and Harry Blair later argued, protection for himself and for his son Woodbridge, who was suspect simply because he was a professor of Chinese history at the University of California. Fisher thought that Bingham was afraid that McCarran might declare Woodbridge a "security risk." Blair, who observed Bingham closely during his tenure as chairman, believed that it was fear of McCarran which explained Bingham's behavior: "McCarran was Chairman of the powerful Judiciary Committee in the Senate," Blair said. "He was courted and kowtowed to by Republicans, in the Senate and generally. . . . Mr. Bingham was a politician and a Republican, and . . . was interested in keeping McCarran happy and [here was] a chance to back up the findings of the McCarran Committee, by a decision of a non-political and non-partisan board."[82]

Perhaps, too, the fire of ambition, still flickered in the seventy-five-year-old Bingham. In the 1920s, his political career seemed bright with promise: That decade saw him elected Connecticut's lieutenant-governor, governor, and United States senator. Then in 1929, he stumbled badly: He appointed a member of Connecticut's Association of Manufacturers to his staff and, as the *New York Times* put it, "introduced him into the secret sessions of a subcommittee engaged in drafting . . . tariff revision measures." The Senate Judiciary Committee accused Bingham of improper conduct and called him to testify. Bingham appeared and after a stormy session, claimed that the committee had used "police court methods" and had "twisted and tortured his testimony to ruin his reputation." Despite his defense, the Senate voted overwhelmingly on November 5, 1929 to condemn Bingham for activities contrary to "good morals and Senatorial ethics"; three years later, he was defeated for reelection. Eighteen years would pass before Bingham again served his government. Did Bingham hope that success as chairman of the Loyalty Review Board might wipe away the stain of Senate censure and give him another opportunity to resume his career? The record does not say, but it is reasonable to surmise that this might be so. Certainly, Bingham's earlier experience with the Judiciary Committee must have made him reluctant to challenge that body and again earn its disfavor. Whatever the final reason—fear, self-protection, ambition—Hiram Bingham consciously and maliciously set out to destroy the career of John Carter Vincent.[83]

Late on the night of December 15, 1952, Vincent received a telegram from the State Department informing him of the Bingham board's decision:

> For Vincent:
> The Department has received the following letter from the Loyalty Review Board of the Civil Service Commission:
> The Honorable The Secretary of State:
> In reference case of John Carter Vincent, Chief of Mission, Tangier, Morocco.
> Sir:
> Under the provisions of Regulation 14 of the Rules and Regulations of the Loyalty Review Board, a panel of the Board has considered the

259   More Damn Trouble

case of the above-named employee. The members of the panel reviewed the entire record in the case and heard the testimony of Mr. Vincent in person and argument of counsel on his behalf.

Without expressly accepting or rejecting the testimony of Louis Budenz that Mr. Vincent was a Communist and "under Communist discipline" or the findings of the Senate Committee on the Judiciary (A) that "over a period of years John Carter Vincent was the principal fulcrum of IPR pressures and influence in the State Department" and (B) that "Owen Lattimore and John Carter Vincent were influential in bringing about a change in United States policy in 1945 favorable to the Chinese Communists," the panel has taken these factors into account.

Furthermore, the panel calls attention to the fact that Mr. Vincent was not an immature or subordinate representative of the State Department but was an experienced and responsible official who had been stationed in China from April 1924 to February 1936 and from March 1941 to August 1943, and who thereafter occupied high positions in the Department of State having to do with the formulation of our Chinese policies.

The panel notes Mr. Vincent's studied criticism of the Chiang Kai-shek Government throughout a period when it was the declared and established policy of the Government of the U.S. to support Chiang Kai-shek's Government.

The panel notes also Mr. Vincent's indifference to any evidence that the Chinese Communists were affiliated with or controlled by the USSR.

Mr. Vincent's failure to properly discharge his responsibilities as Chairman of the Far Eastern Subcommittee of State, War and Navy to supervise the accuracy or security of State Department documents emanating from that Subcommittee, was also taken into account.

Finally, the panel calls attention to Mr. Vincent's close association with numerous persons who he had reason to believe were either Communists or Communist sympathizers.

To say that Mr. Vincent's whole course of conduct in connection with Chinese affairs does not raise a reasonable doubt as to his loyalty, would, we are forced to think, be an unwarranted interpretation of the evidence. While we are not required to find Mr. Vincent guilty of disloyalty and we do not do so, his conduct in office, as clearly indicated by the record, forces us reluctantly to conclude that there is reasonable doubt as to his loyalty to the Government of the U.S.

Therefore it is the recommendation of the Loyalty Review Board that the services of Mr. John Carter Vincent be terminated.

Very truly yours,
Hiram Bingham
Chairman, Loyalty Review Board

"In light of this action taken by the Loyalty Review Board," the secretary of state informed Vincent, "you are suspended effective immediately and you will be advised by the Department as to the final action to be taken in the case as soon as possible."[84]

Some years later, after discovering a copy of this message in her husband's papers, Betty Vincent reread it and wrote: "The stunning effect of this telegram received in Tangier, is still too poignant and devastating to recall. But from this moment on, JCV was finished—career-wise, job-wise, but not, happily, inner-spiritually wise." Seventeen-year-old Jack Vincent, who had inherited his father's dry wit, remarked when he was informed: "It looks like they hit us every Christmas!"[85]

Vincent's spiritual strength was evident the following morning, when he called his staff together to break the news. Because of the review board decision, he had been suspended from duty; this meant that the first secretary of legation was now in temporary command. He was not allowed to see classified cables or reports, even ones he himself had been drafting the day before. Vincent sensed immediately how saddened his colleagues were to hear this announcement. "Don't let's act like we are at the funeral," he laughed. "There is plenty of fight left in me and faith."[86]

This time, Vincent was feeling more anger than calm. "I am amazed at Bingham's letter," he wrote his attorneys on December 22. "How could that panel, if it gave any weight to my own record and testimony, support the four vague charges. . . ? And if the Panel, without accepting or rejecting the Budenz testimony, takes it 'into account,' does it also take 'into account' my own sworn statement? . . . I am doubtful . . . as to the honesty and intelligence of the Panel." For the first time since his troubles began five years before, Vincent seemed eager to fight back: "I should like to appear again before the Panel . . . I should like to bring before it every officer who has worked with, for, or over me during the period 1941-47, irrespective of their attitude toward me. Bring them in, under oath, and let them talk: . . . Mr. Grew, Dooman and Hornbeck, John Service and Davies. . . . As star witnesses bring in Byrnes, Marshall and Acheson. . . . Betty is full of ideas for testimonials from prominent persons . . . Mrs. Roosevelt, Oscar Chapman (she has a long list); and maybe Senators such as George, Maybank, Morse, Mike Mansfield, Fulbright. . . ." Perhaps a new board should be selected, he suggested, composed of "outstanding people" and retired Foreign Service officers familiar with the history of Chinese-American relations. "No matter what," he concluded, "I want some official undoing . . . of the damage done by the Review Board and, in the process, an exposure of its incompetence."[87]

If Bingham hoped his letter to Acheson would end Vincent's career immediately he was mistaken. The telegram aroused Vincent and his allies to make one last attempt to rescue his career.

10

Still Christians, Still Diplomats, Still Loyal Americans

On December 16, 1952, the State Department released the text of the Bingham decision, and the Vincent case again became the focus of national debate.

"The press here is dividing violently on whether the Board was right or wrong," observed James Reston in the *New York Times*. Pro-McCarthy newspapers, like the New York *Journal-American* and the *Philadelphia Inquirer*, called the news "hot and good" and were "elated" that the Review Board had "finally caught up with Vincent." Bingham's letter, Fulton Lewis, Jr. told a radio audience, was a "vindication of Senator Joe McCarthy."[1] Vincent's supporters worried about the effect the board's decision would have on the Foreign Service and its conduct of American diplomacy. Broadcaster Elmer Davis said "the obvious lesson" diplomats must draw from the Vincent case was that "no man who values his future can afford to do anything or think anything that may look like a mistake seven years later." "The Bingham Board has hoisted a warning to every member of the Foreign Service," declared the *Washington Post*. "He is given to understand that any enterprise on his part to find out, assay, and assess is taboo. He is informed, in short, that honest reporting is *verboten*."[2]

Foreign Service officers voiced the same concerns. The Board of Directors of the American Foreign Service Association joined the Editorial

Board of the *Foreign Service Journal* in publishing a special article in their magazine entitled "The Meaning of the Ruling in the Vincent Case for the National Interest." It said, in part:

> The Loyalty Review Board's [decision] . . . is causing bewilderment and misgiving in our ranks. It is disturbing not only because it recommends dismissal for a veteran officer who had already been cleared by the Department's Loyalty-Security Board, but because it implies doctrines which would prevent the Service from doing its full duty. . . . To us. . . , the letter means that any Foreign Service Officer reporting confidentially to his superiors may cast doubt on his own loyalty if his reports contain criticism of a friendly government. It also seems to mean that he will have to be ultra-cautious in admitting the strength of the opposition. . . . [I]f ever the reporters in the field or career civil servants at home must function in a climate of fear or in conformity to dogmas, the American people may never know in time whether a policy has failed. . . . If the supreme Loyalty Board accepts a principle capable of such vicious extension, then the most loyal supporters cannot report loyally. . . . [Officers] who read this letter may well feel themselves cast adrift without a compass.

The Foreign Service Association called on President Truman "to take a fresh look at the Vincent Case and at the whole loyalty procedure."[3]

A fresh look" was exactly what Vincent's attorney and friends were now working to achieve. Walter Surrey preferred the appointment of a special presidential commission and he had already discussed the idea with Vincent's friend Jim McHugh, the morning after the Bingham letter was made public. To head the new group Surrey suggested either former federal judge, Learned Hand, or Ambassador Joseph Grew. McHugh objected to Grew: "He just isn't big enough and is foreign service to boot." Hand was the better choice. Surrey finally agreed and said he would recommend the judge to Secretary Acheson and Adrian Fisher.[4]

When more than a week went by without any news, McHugh became "uneasy" and went to the State Department for a talk with Charles Bohlen, who was then serving as counselor. For over an hour Bohlen explained what was happening behind the scenes: "I was assured that Dean had gone to work on it in his office at the very moment I was talking to [Bohlen]. At least they now recognize that it is no longer a question of 'How did we ever let things come to this pass?' but rather, 'How do we get out of here in a manner which will stick?'"[5]

No doubt the first question bothered Acheson as much as the second.

Although he had often defended his department against charges of procommunism, he had also thrown sacrificial victims to the McCarthyites. His decision to send Vincent to Tangier in 1951 was one outstanding example. Now, a year later, Vincent was in deeper trouble. There seemed to be nothing that he could do to help Vincent—until he received Blair's and French's dissent. He had no idea that the board had been so divided, and he was immediately suspicious. He had always despised Bingham, and now, at last, he had an opportunity to act against him and at the same time save the career of a good friend and distinguished public servant. Acheson now assumed full responsibility for the Vincent case.

First, he asked President Truman to order each review board member to write an individual opinion and then turn these and other relevant documents over to the White House.[6] Bingham, Amen, and Mrs. Doyle hurriedly drafted reports which the chairman sent to presidential assistant Donald Dawson. (Mrs. Doyle admitted to being influenced by the FBI interviews with Wedemeyer and Judd, which, after "prayerful deliberation," had led her to reach a finding of reasonable doubt; Amen's and Bingham's brief opinions, almost identical in thought and language, simply restated the points listed in their majority report.) "Much of this material contains the names of people whom we regard as Communists," Bingham told Dawson. ". . . I trust that you will not let this material go beyond the White House." Charles Murphy, the president's counsel, examined the records, then passed them on to Acheson and Fisher.[7]

The secretary and his legal advisor found the majority report (which they were seeing for the first time) "utterly ridiculous." "I knew John Carter and the charges well enough to know the imputation of disloyalty was unfounded," Acheson later wrote in his memoirs, "and that the charges were in reality based upon policies that he had recommended and the valuations of situations he had made and that largely I accepted." Moreover, the report itself was thoroughly muddled. "I note a statement," Acheson told the president, "that the panel has not accepted or rejected the testimony of Mr. Budenz or the findings of the [McCarran] Committee . . . [but] has taken them into account. I am unable to interpret what this means." Because of the narrowness of the board's decision and its peculiar meaning, Acheson followed Surrey's suggestion and, with Truman's approval, appointed a new group "to review the record."[8]

Before making his decision public, Acheson conferred with John Foster Dulles, whom Eisenhower had chosen to be secretary of state. Acheson told Dulles that he thought the review board "had passed judgment not on Mr. Vincent's loyalty but on the soundness of the policy recommendations he had made. If disagreements on policy were to be equated with disloyalty, the Foreign Service would be destroyed." He described the plan he was considering, and asked the future secretary how he would respond to its findings. Dulles said that while he could not agree in advance to accept the board's decision he would consider its findings "helpful" and offered to "talk with any members who might wish to talk with him." (John McCloy, who had been invited to join the board, did call on Dulles and received the impression that their report "would have great weight with the new Secretary.")[9]

On January 3, President Truman announced the appointment of the five-man panel which would examine the record and determine whether Vincent should be reinstated or dismissed. Its chairman was Learned B. Hand, former chief judge of the United States Second Circuit Court of Appeals. Joining Hand was an equally distinguished group of public servants: John J. McCloy, former assistant secretary of war and high commissioner for Germany, now chairman of the board of the Chase Manhattan Bank (McCloy was also a close personal friend of General Eisenhower and was rumored to have been his first choice to be secretary of state); James Grafton Rodgers, a Republican like McCloy, who had served as assistant secretary of state under Henry Stimson; G. Howland Shaw, a career Foreign Service officer, who had also served as an assistant secretary of state under Cordell Hull; and, finally, Edwin C. Wilson, former ambassador to Panama and Turkey. Marquis Childs spoke for most of the press when he wrote that "the new commission is made up of men of knowledge, experience and unquestioned integrity."[10]

The news that Bingham's decision had been temporarily set aside infuriated Vincent's critics in the Congress. Republican Congressman Kit Clardy demanded that the Hand Commission be abolished before it produced an opinion which might embarrass the future Eisenhower administration. McCarran called its creation "illegal" and urged the establishment of an independent Loyalty Review Board which, he said, could not be "interfered with by the President or anyone else."[11]

Vincent's friends were naturally elated by Acheson's decision, word of which Vincent was the last to hear. "What has happened to the Department? Paralyzed?" he frantically wrote Surrey on January 6. "Not one word about what goes on. A crazy telegram asking me to keep them advised as to my whereabouts in case they want to telephone. Where in hell do they think my 'whereabouts' might be. And [nothing] about Dean's statement except from you. We still don't have the text. After all, I am an interested party!" He learned more about developments from Charles Owsley and Jim McHugh, who wrote a few days later. "The more I think about it," Owsley said, "the clearer it becomes that all our thanks should go to the three members of the Bingham Board (and whoever was responsible for drafting the letter) for being so unbelievably stupid. As it is, the case simply cries out for review and the procedure now developed seems to be getting a sympathetic response (except from McCarran and Co.). If the letter had simply been worded differently I think it would have *made* all the difference even though the conclusions would remain as wrong as ever. We are all as happy as can be." "It has come off better than we dared hope," wrote McHugh.

> Walter outlined it to me the morning after the bombshell exploded. . . . [G]etting John McCloy really did the trick. Phil Graham [publisher of the *Washington Post*] told me . . . that McCloy had taken the job only after insisting that Dulles agree to abide by and cooperate with the findings of the Board. . . . [Bohlen] had hinted pretty strongly when I saw him that Dulles and Eisenhower had agreed to the Board, which he said, would make it practically impossible for them to ignore or reject its findings. He also made the very logical point that the only way out of the mess would be to come up with a review after Dean and Truman left office; otherwise not only you but the whole Foreign Service would be sitting ducks. . . . I feel certain that the new Board is going to come through with something really classic . . . and I think you will thereby bequeath something to your children which they will have good reason to be proud of and cherish all of their lives.

And McHugh added: "You don't owe your friends a thing, either. What anyone has done to help bring this indescribable business out of the depths into which it had sunk will be ample reward, for we came very close to stepping off into the Moscow pit. This was 'It,' and Thank God, a few people saw it for just that."[12]

Vincent found these messages reassuring and was pleased to learn that his case was now being examined by a panel of knowledgeable and impartial judges. Personally, he hoped that Acheson would be the man "to undo the dirty work," but he recognized that the final decision would probably belong to Dulles who was to be Eisenhower's Secretary of State. "Officially it might be better to leave the task to Dulles," he wrote Surrey, "if, as we assume, there is to be reinstatement (we can but hope and have faith in man)." He told Surrey that he was ready to come home if the Hand board required further testimony, regardless of any "catcalls" he might elicit.[13]

His attorney advised him *not* to come home. "I do not want to have you around the country where one committee after another could subpoena you," Surrey told him. "Frankly I know of no [such] plans . . . [but] the

McCarran letter, plus a broadcast last night by Fulton Lewis, in which he . . . attacked [John] McCloy on the grounds that in 1945 and 1946 McCloy had testified that he did not refuse commissions to Communists, gives me a feeling that one of the Committees may get the urge to embarrass the Judge Hand Board. . . . I want to play it safe." Vincent accepted this advice, remained in Tangier, and waited.[14]

While he was "sitting the situation out patiently—Betty less patiently," the Hand board began its work. The chairman had reviewed most of the record by the first week in January but it took time to communicate with his colleagues and send them copies of Vincent's file. When it became clear that they would not reach a final decision by January 20, Hand informed Dean Acheson. "We have done a substantial share of the preliminary work and hope to make a report in due course," Hand said, "if Secretary Dulles wishes us to continue." In one of his last acts as secretary of state, Acheson thanked the judge and his associates for the work they had already done and their "willingness to continue to serve. I would not have asked you to take up this heavy burden," Acheson emphasized, "had I not believed that for you to do so was the best way to preserve the integrity of the Foreign Service and of the Department of State."[15]

Hand also wrote Dulles, asking whether he wished the board to proceed, but was so confident of Dulles's intentions that, without waiting for an answer, he called the panel together several times after Eisenhower's inauguration. By January 29, according to John McCloy, "we came to the informal conclusion that we could find nothing which indicated disloyalty on the part of Mr. Vincent. . . . [W]e were prepared to make our report." Two days later, on January 31, Hand telephoned McCloy with what must have been surprising news: Secretary Dulles had just informed him that "he was taking the matter out of the hands of the . . . Board." The secretary would make a decision without their advice, Hand told McCloy: The Vincent case "was no longer before us."[16]

Vincent's lawyers and friends were, of course, quite upset about Dulles's decision, as were two of the commission members. John McCloy believed that Dulles would at least consider their findings (had in fact been told so by the secretary) and was "disturbed" by Dulles's action.[17] G. Howland Shaw, who had worked with Vincent in the State Department, wrote Hand that "way down deep inside me I have to admit to a feeling of moral and intellectual discomfort and it is a very real feeling and a very strong one.

After my incomplete study of the record I do not believe that right has been done and that belief troubles me greatly." He asked to meet with the judge "to see if I cannot get a bit more perspective on the Vincent Case and feel a trifle happier about the whole wretched business."[18] Only Vincent remained remarkably untroubled by this serious development: "I have no concern about [Dulles]," he told family and friends. "I believe he will try to be fair . . . but he may be subjected to irresistible political pressures."[19]

Had Vincent known more about the background and personality of John Foster Dulles he would have found reason to be concerned. The man now judging his career was his complete opposite: Massive and bear-like in physique, ponderous and self-righteous—he was, in essence, "an austere nineteenth century moralist." Vincent, by contrast, was a quiet, elegant Jeffersonian—a believer in reason and the essential goodness of man. Vincent was warm, friendly, an extrovert. Dulles was cold, distant, and friendless. "He was a very awkward man in all social relations," recalled diplomat Joseph C. Green, who knew Dulles for forty years; "so self-centered in thought, . . . whose manners . . . seemed to reflect a complete lack of interest in the other person." Green could not forget one occasion when Dulles was visiting the family island in Lake Ontario: "He was sitting on the shore . . . cracking hazel nuts and eating them, when two boys in a small sailboat came up to land almost in front of him. They were driven by stress of weather . . . in great danger [and] landing to save their lives. Foster said to them, 'You're not permitted to land on this island.' They explained their predicament. He finally said, 'Well, all right, but just as soon as the wind abates get off.' That was all the welcome the two shipwrecked boys had." Even those who admired Dulles, and later worked for him, admitted that he was "remarkably impersonal in dealing with other people."[20]

He was, above all, a man with one obsession: becoming and remaining secretary of state. Both his grandfather (John W. Foster) and his uncle (Robert Lansing) had been secretaries of state, and Dulles considered the office his by hereditary right. But after finally winning the prize, could he survive in a Washington dominated by McCarthyites? The expectation, held by many, that Eisenhower's election would end McCarthy's hold over the Capitol soon proved false. The spotlight that once focused on Truman and Acheson now shifted to Eisenhower and Dulles. There was "heavy and severe and continuing pressure," said one man who worked closely with Dulles. "[Y]ou had this damn McCarthy . . . throwing the brickbats one after another. . . . We didn't know where the next thing would come [from]."[21] No one felt more in peril than Dulles. In 1946, as chairman of the board of the Carnegie Endowment for International Peace, he had recommended that Alger Hiss be appointed its president. Conservative Republicans had not forgotten this and that Dulles had served the odious Truman administration as a "consultant"—he had, at the president's request, negotiated the Japanese-American Peace treaty in 1951.[22] Now, as secretary of state, his first objective was to reassure the McCarthyites that he was not another Acheson, even if this meant destroying State Department and Foreign Service morale.

He began by separating himself from the department, which had the reputation of being a haven for Communists and homosexuals. He left the operation of the department to other men, like Donald Lourie, former president of the Quaker Oats Company and a diplomatic novice. Lourie, in turn, appointed Scott McLeod, a former FBI agent and staff assistant to Styles Bridges, chief of Department Security. "Scotty had a very black and white approach to things," one associate later recalled. "He was a conspirator by nature . . . [and] deeply suspicious of many of the things in the State Department he did not understand." The effect of Dulles's aloofness was disastrous. "I think that the State Department felt let down by Mr. Dulles," John Service has said, "partly because he, himself, had no interest in administration. . . . [H]e rather washed his hands of it, almost in an ostentatious way and left it to the people who were regarded as the butchers—people like McLeod, who almost rubbed their hands with glee at the idea of [firing] a lot of people."[23]

Dulles also let Foreign Service officers know that they were all suspect. In his first address as secretary of state, he told them that he demanded not only competence and discipline but "positive loyalty" to their president's policies. At the same time, he promised the American people that he would rid the department of "Communists" and their "sympathizers." Both statements "disgusted some Foreign Service Officers," Charles Bohlen later noted, "infuriated others, and displeased even those who were looking forward to the new administration."[24]

The appointments and statements were part of Dulles's general strategy of maintaining good relations with the McCarthyites in Congress and the country. It was to Walter Judd (Vincent's old adversary) that Dulles turned to for advice on filling the office of assistant secretary of state for the Far East. Judd recommended two men: General Wedemeyer and Virginia banker Walter Robertson—who had served briefly in the Chungking embassy. Robertson got the job.[25] The secretary was also responding warmly to the letters he was receiving from Alfred Kohlberg.

Kohlberg wrote Dulles twice in January 1953. First he sent Dulles copies of the Bridges memorandum, and pointed out what he thought were certain "discrepancies" between Vincent's earlier statements and his testimony before the McCarran committee. Vincent's testimony, Kohlberg said, "exhibits qualities of ignorance, laziness, misunderstanding, lack of interest, and lack of study" which he thought explained Vincent's "errors" from 1943 to 1947. Such (alleged) incompetency did not necessarily indicate disloyalty, Kohlberg argued in an apparent change of heart, but it did suggest that Dulles would have to remove incompetents "all down the line" before he could "restore the former high reputation of the State Department." In emphasizing competency rather than loyalty, Kohlberg recommended to Dulles the very standard Dulles was later to use in evaluating Vincent's career.[26]

Then Kohlberg sent Dulles "disturbing" news about Judge Hand. It seems that the judge had permitted the New York Emergency Civil Liberties Committee to use an extract from a recent speech, in their program announcing a conference on McCarthyism. The sponsors and the forum leaders (Professor Stringfellow Barr, Frank Lloyd Wright, Albert Einstein, among others) "include," Kohlberg said, "a number of persons who have been identified as Communist Party members, . . . a further number (making up the majority) who have long records as fellow travelers, and a very few of doubtful standing, not one . . . publicly known as an Anti-Communist." The judge's speech (a defense of civil liberties) "indicates," Kohlberg said, "a lack of knowledge and a misunderstanding that should disqualify him as Chairman of a Committee to study and advise you on the case of John Carter Vincent."[27]

Although Dulles once called Kohlberg "fanatical" (Kohlberg had accused his law partner Arthur Dean of being a Communist[28]), he now thanked him profusely for sending the documents. "It will be useful to me," Dulles wrote "to have such information."[29]

Kohlberg's letter (and McCarran's statements) must have reminded Dulles of the potential danger he faced in allowing the Hand commission to reach a favorable decision which might be critical of the Bingham board. Not long after receiving Kohlberg's second letter, he dissolved the commission and a short time later ordered Vincent home for what Betty called a "command appearance and interview."

The last few days before Vincent's departure were troubled ones. As usual, Betty was full of ideas and suggestions on how to fight the McCarthyites. For months she had been typing single-spaced lists of things to do:

> Have JCV go over every *Congressional Record* insertion about him, go over item by item and give the truth and the absurdity of such charges. . . . Senator George should be called on by JCV . . . [to]

enter the refutation in the *Congressional Record*. . . . Get testimonials [from] business men in China—ask JC [about] the Chase or Natl. Bank men—Standard Oil etc. etc.—there are many all around and in New York who have respected and loved JC for years. . . . [G]et in a word about Hornbeck being a contributor to *Amerasia*—also it was he who brought Alger Hiss into the China Division. . . . [Mrs.] Hornbeck who is I am told by everyone an alcoholic prattles on at every Washington dinner party about J.C. being a "RED.". . . Write a letter to her . . . warning her if she does not shut up I will sue—I think we might be able to scare 'the pants' off of her—how I would like to, for she has a malicious tongue and uses it constantly against JC. . . . Wish we might be able to scare "the pants" off of her—how I would like to, for Budenz are the two guys to convict, the rest can be let go. . . . I used to know [George] Sokolsky . . . who is in Kohlberg's closest confidence—through him perhaps some data could be forthcoming. He LOVES to talk . . . especially to a "pretty girl."[30]

She was tired of hearing from her husband that there was "nothing to do." For years she had been telling him that he was "operating on about two cylinders"—that he possessed "mental and spiritual tools he was not using to the full." Her latest advice (which even she called "badly conceived") was not well received.[31]

After Vincent left, Betty alternated between moods of resignation and agitation. "By now you must be on your way to Washington," she wrote him on the evening of February 21. "I am anxious to hear of your safe arrival. As for the final outcome with Dulles I have reached the point where it does not seem very important. This whole experience, now that I have had a night and a day alone to ruminate, has taken on a fantastic dreamlike quality that seems to have little to do with ultimate reality—you and me and Sheila and Jack as human souls with our own way to make toward personal salvation. . . . I think the passions of hope, fear, anger, resentment, revenge, envy have been spent. It has taken me longer than you to arrive at this tranquil state. The Bible and Emerson's essays were sustaining food taken at your early age and don't let Mr. Dulles overlook the fact."

But such passions were not entirely spent: The next morning she had more suggestions on how her husband should conduct himself "before the little men now in high places." "Your deepest instinct is to avoid [a fight] and then to use all the strength you have . . . in squaring the omissions, commissions, wrongs or mistakes. . . . It is part of your glorifying the works of God and not exorcizing the devil philosophy." But "the political game has to be played. . . . Publicity, the right men on the Hill. . . . You should play it out to the last card. That's where those other four cylinders might begin to be put to use and then they'd be oiled up for the next real showdown. . . . The betrayals of you INSIDE of the Department is [*sic*] what Mr. Dulles will be most interested in; he can have a field day trying to clean up the rotten insides of the Dept. . . . I wish you could give him a report on how things were done, because I think his greatest desire is to get credit . . . for putting the Dept. back into decent circulation. . . . I think a list of Dooman's evils should be somehow collected. . . . In discrediting Dooman it should be pointed out that his lack of loyalty to his own government, to his own Department, to his own group is what is his heinous crime. This is what will appeal to Dulles, NOT whether he is a sonuvabitch or not, but that he can be a dangerously disloyal man in a pinch. . . . He is a sick and evil man, consumed by hatred—those are the things that should be pointed out. . . . I do not believe Dulles wants that type in his newly cleaned up stable of good, strong, enduring, healthy, loyal . . . horses." The simple act of writing and of striking back at her husband's enemies in prose if not in fact, revitalized her. "Here I am at it again," she wrote, "but this isn't advice, it's morning and I'm feeling very 'smart' healthy and alive."[32]

In this spirit and still energetic she decided to "beard a lion" in his own den: She wrote to Henry Luce, whose *Time* and *Life* magazines had for years attacked her husband. "I know you and my husband did not agree on [China policy]," she told the publisher,

> but I also know you both love China and your own country; because you were said to be pro-Chiang Kai-shek I never doubted for a moment that you were not pro-American according to your own convictions, as John Carter has certainly been according to his. . . . My husband has never spoken out during the last five years of vilification. . . . After twenty-seven years of training as a career officer one cannot and should not if you are properly disciplined mix in with politics or engage in personal controversies. It is ironic that . . . because of these qualities, John Carter is entirely vulnerable to the McCarrans and McCarthys. . . . [T]o the McCarran Committee honor lies only with the 'ex-Communists' because as Senator Ferguson rather touchingly puts it, 'the only ones we can believe are those who were in the know—the ex-party boys.' I find at this moment in our career that our greatest difficulty is that we are not ex-anything, still Christians, still diplomats, still loyal Americans with no confession or quarter asked for. I just don't want *Time* and *Life* to be too harsh in their judgments unless they have the 'evidence'—the 'truth' before them.

Her purpose in writing, she told Luce in the end, was "to enlist your talents, power and good will to make the end a happier one than sometimes my nightmares permit me to believe possible."[33]

As Betty was writing to Luce, her husband arrived in Washington. It was the third time in sixteen months that he had been summoned there: first by General Snow, then by Chairman Bingham, now by Secretary Dulles. His first night he had dinner with his attorneys. "They don't know much and what they do know is contradictory," Vincent wrote Betty just before going to sleep. "But they are so warm and partisan that it is difficult not to be misled. What they don't reckon with is the preponderant element which is indifferent, and the hostile element which weighs just as much in the minds of the 'judges' as the friendly element and its anticipated cries of injustice. This is not a counsel of despair," he added, "it is an estimate of the situation." Characteristically, he remained somewhat optimistic. "Reason and justice may prevail, but not necessarily. Anyway, [soon] I shall see Dulles."[34]

It was, Walter Surrey later wrote, "a long and trying week." On the morning of February 23, Surrey and Vincent drove to the New State Department Building for their first meeting with John Foster Dulles. They took the elevator to the secretary's quarters on the seventh floor, and after a few minutes wait, were ushered into his office. Dulles rose from his desk, a dour and melancholy expression on his face. Greetings were briskly exchanged and the guests invited to sit. He seemed nervous, Vincent thought: Dulles's hands fluttered around his body, patting down his sandy grey hair, and adjusting his thin-rimmed glasses, straightening his paisley tie. When he began to speak, the voice was solemn and flat, the words slightly slurred. Mr. Vincent would be cleared of the doubts regarding his loyalty, he announced, but he must retire from the Foreign Service because Dulles had concluded that Vincent was guilty of poor judgment. If Vincent refused, he would be fired immediately and lose his pension.

Such a decision was not unexpected, but Vincent was still stunned and somewhat surprised: The character of his service had never been at issue during his hearings, and he knew that his personnel record was exemplary. Shaking his head, he expressed sharp criticism of the decision, but did agree to retire. He would not sacrifice his family's financial security for the satisfaction of having Dulles fire him.

For the first time since the meeting began, Dulles smiled and began to relax. The exact details of Vincent's retirement and the reasons behind it, would be discussed at their next meeting, which the secretary scheduled for the following Saturday. On that day, Vincent was to submit his resignation; until then there must be no public statements regarding these developments. To insure secrecy, Dulles insisted that they meet at his home and instructed Vincent to enter through the back door.[35]

"On the basis of the first meeting John had with the Secretary," Surrey later wrote Betty, "it became very clear that [Dulles] was determined to do two things: (1) get John out of the service; (2) announce immediately that he was getting John out of the service." Surrey thought Dulles's first preference was to fire Vincent on grounds of disloyalty or poor security but could find no legal basis to do so. Failing in this, his next hope was to dismiss Vincent without giving a public explanation but "was disuaded [sic] from doing so because he probably realized that having cleared him on loyalty and security to then fire him without retirement rights would not have been good for the Secretary himself." And "had anything unforeseen broken during the week of negotiations," Surrey added, he thought it likely that Vincent would have been immediately fired. "In these circumstances there was no advantage in approaching Senators or anyone else and that might well have been a disadvantage. The Secretary is a very stubborn and determined man."[36]

The final meeting took place on February 28 at Dulles's home. Each side had kept their silence during the past five days so there were no reporters or other spectators waiting outside the residence. It was a cold winter's day and the street was deserted and hushed.

As requested, Surrey and Vincent entered the house through the back door—Surrey feeling angry and uncomfortable, Vincent numb and resigned. They were shown to their host who offered drinks and invited them both to sit down and relax. Surrey was "astonished" at Dulles's cavalier behavior and remarked that this was hardly a social occasion. His client, however, accepted the drink and took a seat. Vincent gave Dulles his brief letter of resignation and was handed the draft of the statement Dulles planned to release to the press. The secretary wanted Vincent retired within the month, but Vincent doubted that he could close out his affairs in so short a time. He suggested May 15, the day on which he had joined the Foreign Service twenty-nine years before. Dulles was "sympathetic" and stated that he really did not care at all when retirement actually took place, but for "public relations reasons" would "stick to the earlier date"—March 31, 1953. Vincent hoped that "there would be no [more] congressional investigations directed at [him] after retirement" and asked Dulles to use his "personal influence" to head them off. "There is still talk of a perjury action," Dulles said casually. ("Smells of Ferguson," thought Vincent.) But Dulles did not seem to take the prospect seriously and assured Vincent that if the question of an indictment arose Attorney General Herbert Brownell "could take care of it."

Then they discussed Dulles's statement, which he admitted, still needed "more polishing." Why not "polish out" the reference in the third paragraph to his poor judgment, Vincent asked. Dulles "laughed"; yes, he'd been having "troubles" with that paragraph. Vincent argued again that the "main preoccupation in 1941-45 was fighting the Japanese rather than the Communists." Originally, Dulles said, he had "that idea in the statement" but "also had something 'bad' so he cut them both out." Vincent wondered whether Dulles might wish to consult with some distinguished Foreign Service officers on "the content and character of his statement" but the secretary made no response. "I think you are going to have head winds in coupling clearance and retirement," he told Dulles. "I expect to have bad sailing anyway," Dulles replied.

One question above all, "puzzled" Dulles. How, he asked, could "so many people in the government have underestimated the threat of Communism . . . during and immediately after the war?" (Dulles might well have, but did not, include himself in this group; it was not until 1946 that he read Stalin's *Problems of Leninism* and began to write and speak out about the dangers of communism).[37] Dulles showed Vincent a dog-eared copy of *Problems of Leninism* and asked him if he was familiar with it. Vincent said no. "If you had read [it]," Dulles insisted, "you would not have advocated the policies you did in China."

Again Vincent tried to explain how the world looked to him in the 1940s. "I told Dulles . . . of my desire for cooperation in China to defeat the Japanese; of my subsequent concern that the Chinese Communists and the Russians would get together at the end of the war unless we did something about it; and of my belief in the autumn of 1945 that we could 'take in the Communists in more ways than one. . . . [T]he most important factor in the failure of the Marshall Mission was the time factor; that if the war against Japan could have ended with the war against Germany and if the Marshall Mission could have taken place . . . [before] the break with Russia, it might have succeeded. I referred to the recent book by [Milovan Djilas] the Yugoslav which indicates that as late as 1946 Stalin was unsure which horse to back [in China]." To Dulles, such views had little merit. He saw the Chinese situation in colors of black and white: Mao was a Communist and an atheist while Chiang was a democrat and a "Christian" who had "suffered for [his] faith."[38]

Finally, Dulles asked him: "Mr. Vincent, what are your views on . . . China [now]? [You know] the situation there better than just about anybody." (When Vincent later told Charles Owsley about Dulles's question Owsley was astonished: "First telling the man he was incompetent and then asking a question in such a way that it showed clear recognition that indeed Dulles knew that JCV was one of the most competent men in that field, was an act of the highest cynicism, and I must say, was not a bit untypical. I am afraid that had I been in JCV's place at that moment I would have said 'why you son-of-a-bitch!' and promptly left."[39]) Vincent was not capable of such a reaction, even if justified, and he dutifully gave Dulles the benefit of his views. The secretary of state listened attentively, unaware of the tragic irony: that Vincent's counsel would have always been available had Dulles not decided to force him out of the Foreign Service.[40]

A few days after Vincent returned to Tangier, Dulles presented to the public his decision in the Vincent case. After "carefully" studying the record "with a view to discharging [his] legal responsibility in a way which will both protect the interests of the United States and do personal justice," he had reached the following conclusions:

1. I do not believe the record shows that Mr. Vincent is a "security" risk. . . .

2. I do not find that "on all the evidence there is reasonable doubt as to the loyalty" of Mr. Vincent to the Government of the United States. . . .

3. I have, however, concluded that Mr. Vincent's reporting of the facts, evaluation of the facts, and policy advice during the period under review show a failure to meet the standard which is demanded of a Foreign Service Officer of his experience and responsibility at this critical time. I do not believe that he can usefully continue to serve the United States as a Foreign Service Officer. . . .[41]

Of Dulles's decision two biographers later wrote: "It was a lonely and awesome responsibility deciding whether a man's career should be ended and his reputation blasted. Dulles felt it keenly. Despite immense pressures upon his time, he read the voluminous file with the utmost care."[42] State Department records do not support this view, expressed first by Dulles and later repeated by other writers.[43] It was not until February 20 that the secretary first saw the Loyalty-Security Board records, which included Vincent's personal statement, the six volumes of testimony and dozens of FBI reports. Therefore, Dulles had no more than three days in which to study the most important documents before reaching a decision. (It took the three-man Loyalty-Security Board six weeks to study the record; the five-man Bingham board spent eight weeks examining the case.) It is unlikely then that Dulles read the voluminous file as carefully as he claimed. Nor is there any indication that he ever saw Vincent's personnel file, which contained career evaluations—all positive, many excellent, spanning twenty-eight years. Since Dulles had never served in an administrative capacity in the State Department or Foreign Service, it is difficult to determine how and on what basis he devised a "standard" to evaluate Vincent's work. Dean Acheson later commented: "Mr. Dulles 'concluded' that Vincent's professional judgment . . . fell below a standard which Mr. Dulles demanded but did not define. [His] six predecessors, under all of whom Mr. Vincent served in the China field, did not find his judgment defective or substandard. On the contrary, they relied upon him and promoted him."[44]

In devising a standard, it might have been instructive for Dulles to have compared his views on world politics in the 1930s with Vincent's. Throughout the prewar decade, Dulles had been an isolationist, indifferent to the growth of German and Japanese fascism.[45] While Vincent was criticizing the Japanese take-over of Manchuria in 1931, Dulles called it "a logical and inevitable tendency" which the United States should do nothing to block. Five years later, Vincent was warning the State Department that Japanese aggression would ultimately threaten American security; Dulles, at the same time, was saying that "only hysteria entertains the idea that Germany, Italy, or Japan contemplates war upon us."[46] It was Dulles—not Vincent—who was guilty of poor judgment in the years before World War II, and a consideration of his own case might have made him more compassionate in handling Vincent's. But such emotions were apparently absent in Dulles, as even his sister Eleanor and brother Allen have agreed: "They sensed in [Foster]," their biographer writes, "a chilling capacity to be completely dispassionate, to reduce even the most anguishing problem to a question of expediency."[47] Political expediency, nothing less, explains Dulles's decision in the Vincent case, and that decision neither "protected the interests of the United States" nor did "personal justice."

The secretary's decision satisfied no one completely, not the Mc-Carthyites, not the Foreign Service and, least of all, Vincent. Senator McCarran called the decision "a subterfuge on the part of the Secretary of State, and the fact that Mr. Dulles sees fit to follow in the footsteps of Mr. Acheson doesn't do much credit to him, nor does it change my view of the situation based on the facts as I know them." Senator McCarthy was just as outraged: "Under no circumstances should anyone like Vincent, having been rejected by the Loyalty Board, be entitled to any pension," he told the press.[48] Congressman Clardy followed up on McCarthy's recommendation by introducing a bill in the House designed to deny Vincent his pension. "Vincent worked closely with Hiss on many things," Clardy said. "He helped make the disastrous policy that lost China to the Communists. He was under such heavy fire from Congress in 1947 because of his pro-Communist viewpoint he was sent out of the country. . . . I find nothing to justify his retention on a pension equal to approximately 3/4 of the salary paid to members of Congress—and way above the average national income. . . . I am glad he is no longer on the active list but I deplore the way it has been done. The price is too high."[49]

"Reaction among foreign service personnal was mixed," reported Neal Stanford in the *Christian Science Monitor* on March 5. "While most applauded the decision for vindicating one of their colleagues of charges of disloyalty, they found it hard to swallow his dismissal for poor reporting—which had not been the issue in the months of hearings, investigations, and conflicting decisions that had occurred." The result of Dulles's decision, the *Washington Post* noted, "is that the Administration and perhaps all future Administrations present an impossible problem to their professional personnel in the foreign service. Diplomats from now on will know that, in reporting from abroad, they are expected to be clairvoyants." Surrey heard similar sentiments and reported them to Vincent: "The general reaction is that the Secretary was wrong and vicious insofar as references to your ability are concerned . . . I have received many phone calls from Foreign Service and departmental people who express their considerable relief that you are cleared on loyalty and security and their bitterness concerning the 'volunteered' remarks of the Secretary."[50]

Surrey tried to emphasize the more positive aspects of Dulles's decision in his dealings with the press and the Vincents. To reporters he said that "Mr. Dulles unequivocally reverses the finding of the Loyalty Review Board and determines categorically that there is no reasonable doubt concerning Minister Vincent's loyalty and in addition that he is not and never was a security risk. It is equally clear that the reasons given or suggested for accepting Minister Vincent's retirement have nothing to do with loyalty or security."[51] He tried to reassure Betty, with limited success, that her husband had been vindicated and that it was "the best possible decision under the circumstances. I am convinced," he wrote her the day after the decision was announced, "that even if the Review Board had found in John's favor unanimously or otherwise that the Secretary would have dismissed him and would have done so in the same manner he did yesterday, that is, by making some statement concerning John's competence so that [Dulles] in his own mind can believe he is getting somewhere on the Hill." Mrs. Vincent was incapable of such objectivity: Rereading Surrey's letter a few months after Dulles's death in 1959, she scrawled on it: "The ends and means of Mr. Dulles and may God *not* rest your soul."[52]

Her husband managed to maintain his usual equanimity but in fact he was deeply hurt by Dulles's comments about his judgment. "I disagree heartily of course with Mr. Dulles' criticism of my work . . . ", he later told reporters. "The written record . . . will not support his comment; nor will the evaluation of my services under seven Secretaries of State who preceeded Mr. Dulles." In 1956 he noted that "my premature retirement . . . was solely on partisan political grounds, the Dulles citing of 'standards' notwithstanding. Frankly, based on my knowledge of his . . . predecessors, Mr. Dulles does not measure up to my standards for a Secretary of State but I am not . . . in a position to fire him."

As he prepared to leave Tangier, the letters of sympathy and support began to pour in. "It has been almost two years since this vindictive action against you began," his sister, Margaret, wrote. "You were caught between politics and the viciousness of McCarthyism. I have hoped that Dulles would be bigger than either of them—but he wasn't. I love you very much and my pride in you is always—as you must know—at the bursting point." Charles Owsley said that "now that the execution notices have been issued may I finally say how goddam sorry I am about what has happened. Some day I'm going to do some research and find out if you aren't the first career diplomat in U.S. history ever to have gotten a deal like this."[53]

"It's all over now," Vincent wrote a friend shortly before sailing for America. But it would never be entirely over. The State Department's Office of Security and the FBI continued to observe and record the final developments.[54] Chairman Bingham also could not resist a parting shot: In notifying the FBI of the final disposition of Vincent's case he stated that Vincent "retired after [an] adverse decision on loyalty by [the] Loyalty Review Board." There was no reference to the fact that Dulles said he had no doubts regarding his loyalty and security, and that the secretary of state's view superseded that of any government agency. Apparently, Bingham wanted the record to show that Vincent had been forced to retire because of *his* decision. Bingham's memorandum to Hoover was still in the files of the Civil Service Commission twenty-four years after Vincent left the Foreign Service.[55]

And, as usual, Vincent found reporters and photographers waiting to question him as his ship docked in New York Harbor on April 29, 1953. He and Betty posed for pictures and then Vincent read what he hoped would be the last statement he would ever have to make to the press. He spoke, without bitterness, but sharply, of Dulles's decision, typically expressing more concern about its consequences for the nation than for himself: "The Secretary's comments seem to derive from the idea that the [Truman] Administration, advised by a group of non-political career officers including me, failed to prevent and therefore caused the downfall of the National Government of China. [T]he fact of the matter is that it was the sheer and protracted stupidity of the National Government that lost China. . . . Nothing short of an American military protectorate, in fact if not in name, could have saved China. It has been quite a problem to save Southern Korea. China is an infinitely greater and more complex problem."

As for the future, he recommended that the Eisenhower administration abandon the notion that the United States lost China. "It has been a phony idea all along, peddled by the China Lobby," he said. "Then and only then can the Administration, with the aid of career officers freed from a fear that loyalty to Chiang Kai-shek is a test of loyalty to the U.S.A., begin to evolve and pursue an objective and we hope effective policy regarding China. It won't please everybody (no China policy ever has or will) but it will have the virtue of being an American policy and not a China Lobby policy."

Did he recommend that the United States withdraw its aid to Chiang, one reporter asked. No, Vincent replied, "but I do object to placing reliance on that aid as a major means of overthrowing the Communists in China. What we should do is keep constantly alert to detect and where possible promote any weakening in the ties between Moscow and Peiping and in the ties between Peiping and the outlying Chinese provinces." He thought the possibility of Titoism in China remote, but it was "a better bet than trying to re-establish Chiang."

"What about your own future?" asked another reporter. He said that he planned to look for something to do of a nongovernmental nature. To friends he still expressed the faith, despite all that had happened, "that things will work out all right." "I don't know what I want to do or can do but I know that I cannot afford, either spiritually or financially to retire. ... I am still young enough to learn and do know something about the world and people."[56]

Epilogue: The Man Who Should Be Standing Here Today

Shortly after his return to the United States, Vincent and his wife spent an evening with David Lilienthal, a veteran New Dealer and former chairman of the Atomic Energy Commission. "Vincent seemed exceptionally restless," Lilienthal later wrote in his diary. "I suppose the man is tired, with the hard life of a visitor who comes to New York from another world, for he has been in an out-of-the-way post in Africa, after a long time in China." Betty Vincent spoke about the problem of readjusting to America after living so many years abroad: It was, she said, "like Rip Van Winkle waking up after a long sleep."[1]

Vincent's first months of retirement were indeed difficult: For the first time in twenty-nine years he was without a job or a home. He had joined the Foreign Service directly after graduating from college, and it had been his home, his life, for nearly three decades. Now there was a void. "Everybody says write, write, write!" he complained to Walter Surrey at this time. "Write what?" Mrs. Alfred A. Knopf was urging him to write a book "about the development of China policy, or the roughing he had had," but, as he told Lilienthal, he did not "feel any strong urge [to] crusade against his detractors," or set the record "straight." Someday, perhaps, "in a scholarly exposition, . . . but not on a controversial or sensational basis."[2]

"What I really want is some kind of business-commercial connection," he told a friend in April 1953. At first a position with an international insurance firm, C. V. Starr and Company, seemed a likely prospect, but it did not work out. He contacted other firms in Boston, New York, and Washington, and a friend ran an advertisement in the *Wall Street Journal* describing "an ex-Foreign Service Officer with competence, experience and abilities which could be adopted to banking or industrial efforts in the Far East." But none of these efforts produced "any interest of consequence."[3]

Without a job to occupy him, he spent his time on family affairs. That first summer back, the Vincents motored West to visit Margaret and Allen Smith in Seattle, and on their return East, they stopped in Seneca, Kansas, Vincent's birthplace. It was in a way a sentimental journey: Having spent almost half his life abroad, and now lacking a permanent home, he was trying to rediscover his country, and in a more personal sense, his roots.[4]

By September, the Vincents were in Cambridge, Massachusetts, where they decided to live while Jack attended Harvard, and Sheila the Longy School of Music. With most of their life savings, they bought a three-story, fifty-year-old house on Garden Terrace, overlooking the university tennis courts. It had a magnificent backyard and garden where they would spend spring and summer nights dining alone or with friends. Vincent renewed his acquaintanceship with John K. Fairbank, professor of Chinese history, whom he had first met during the war. When Fairbank had contracted hepatitis in disease-ridden Chungking, Vincent had taken him into the embassy and put him in the ambassador's bed until he recovered. Now, in 1953, Fairbank introduced the Vincents to the community of scholars surrounding Harvard. "They were an attractive, sociable couple," Fairbank later said. "John Carter was handsome, formal looking, but informal in manner. He had the knack for good conversation; he could enter a room and break the ice. Within two years they knew everybody; they became old residents very soon."[5]

Vincent was still finding it difficult establishing a new career. There were no more responses to his ad in the *Wall Street Journal* and no other business opportunities presented themselves. Others, more wise than America's corporate managers, finally found a use for his talents. In 1955, he joined the Speakers' Bureau of the Foreign Policy Association and gave lectures on American-East Asian relations throughout the country. ("Mr. Vincent is recommended both for the large audience and the seminar type of group," read one bureau advertisement. "His friendliness makes him excellent in the question period.") During his first year as a public speaker he earned nearly nine hundred dollars; in 1956, over eleven hundred dollars. Although it entailed a good deal of travel and work, without much financial compensation, he did it happily. "It's a matter of self-discipline and a quixotic sense of duty," he told his attorney. As a Foreign Policy Association lecturer he was given a chance to comment on contemporary affairs, which remained a major interest despite his retirement from government service.[6]

He was deeply troubled by Dulles's diplomacy and what was happening to his colleagues in the China Service. In December 1953, John Davies was suspended from duty and ordered to undergo another loyalty investigation (his ninth). A special Security Hearing Board (none of whose members knew anything about China or the Foreign Service) deliberated for three months, then recommended his dismissal because of "lack of judgment, discretion, and reliability." Dulles fired him a short time later. In an open letter to the editors of the *Foreign Service Journal* Vincent called Dulles's action "cruel," reminiscent of his own retirement for failing to live up to a standard of conduct Dulles never defined. "It is Mr. Dulles' prerogative to 'review' policy toward China some ten years ago and find it wanting," Vincent wrote, "but of greater pertinence in my case was the circumstance that he was admittedly under pressure to say something critical of me on the occasion of my retirement. He chose the device of an undefined standard. A similar and unconvincing device seems to have been used in the case of John Davies with more drastic ... results than in my own." The *Washington Post* published a story on Vincent's letter—noting that it was the first time he had broken "his silence." State Department security officers clipped the story from the paper and added it to Vincent's loyalty file.[7]

By 1954, the Foreign Service had lost four of its ablest members: Edmund Clubb, John Service, John Carter Vincent, and now John Davies. The other prominent members of the China Service were serving in posts scattered throughout the world; none was serving in Asia or making policy in the State Department. "I see [Dulles] is taking no Far Eastern expert to [the] Geneva Conference," Vincent noted at that time. "Maybe he hasn't got a Far Eastern expert." He was very nearly right.[8]

Vincent's own separation from government service did not completely shield him from the barbs of his critics. In January 1956, he gave a lecture at a residential seminar on world affairs in St. Louis; soon afterwards, the chairman of the conference received a letter from J. W. Nystrom of the United States Chamber of Commerce, complaining about Vincent's appearance on the grounds that the *National Review* had called him "pro-Communist." Replying on behalf of the seminar, Richard W. Chubb told Nystrom that he had a high regard for the former diplomat and "could testify under oath that there was nothing pro-Communist about his presentation or remarks." He reminded Nystrom that John Foster Dulles had stated "that there was no question" regarding Vincent's loyalty. "As far as I know," Chubb concluded, ". . . Mr. John Carter Vincent is not only respectable, but is entitled to unusual consideration on account of his long service in the State Department." Chubb sent Vincent a copy of his letter but Vincent was too busy with problems closer to home to be troubled by Nystrom's complaint.[9]

Once again he was embroiled in controversy. Joseph DeGuglielmo, a member of the Cambridge City Council, was objecting to Vincent's appointment to the Civic Unity Committee, a citizen's group formed to combat racial discrimination. The Councilman wondered why Vincent should be allowed to serve on a quasi-official municipal body when Secretary Dulles had found his diplomatic career substandard. He recommended that Vincent be dropped from the committee and with other members convinced the mayor to call for an investigation of the group's activities. Vincent's supporters again came to his defense. Journalist Louis Lyon, in a radio broadcast, called Vincent one of the committee's "finest, most useful members." Mrs. Eleanor Goodridge wrote to the *Cambridge Chronicle Sun* accusing the mayor of trying to prevent "anyone unjustly accused of disloyalty to go back to normal human relations. They prefer to persecute him that they may pose to the uninformed as heroes fighting the Communist menace. This spells tragedy to many fine people and besmirches our reputation for fair play." In the end, the Civic Unity Committee, unlike Dulles, refused to submit to political pressure and dismiss Vincent. He remained with the group for many years.[10]

Vincent remained remarkably unaffected by these attacks, but he was slow to realize that the questions raised by Nystrom and the others continued to affect his ability to earn a living and also had an impact on the careers of friends and family. That September, the Foreign Policy Association informed Walter Surrey that it had been "criticized" for recommending Vincent as a lecturer because, the association stated, "[certain] parties allege he has been judged either 'disloyal' to the U. S. Government or a 'security risk.'" Richard Rowson, administrative assistant to the association's president, asked Surrey for a "precise statement" defining his client's "status in the eyes of the U. S. Government." Karasik informed Rowson that the secretary of state was ultimately responsible for determining an officer's loyalty and security and that Dulles had cleared Vincent of the charges against him. Despite this reassurance, the Foreign Policy Association did not renew its contract with Vincent, a development that surprised him, until he received a copy of Rowson's letter. "I found it hard to believe that the level of my lecturing during the winter of [19]55-56 was so low that the FPA had decided to part company with me on that account;" he told Karasik. "That it was simply caution, CAUTION—seems somehow to put me in a better light and mood; not that I have been moody over the matter since our separation."[11]

He would have been more angry had he known that his problems were causing difficulties for Abbott Low Moffat, a friend and former State Department colleague. While applying for a new government position in 1954, Moffat received an interrogatory from the Civil Service Commission stating that it heard that he had been associated with John Carter Vincent and Owen Lattimore—men described as being "influential in bringing about a change in United States policy ... favorable to the Chinese Communists." This information, Moffat was told, "might if true create a doubt concerning your loyalty to the Government of the United States." Shocked and angered by the commission's letter, Moffat sent it his own interrogatory. The commission "must be aware," he said, "that John Carter Vincent has been cleared by two different Secretaries of State ... yet here [you] officially brand him as a 'Communist, Communist Party member or Communist sympathizer'.... That is McCarthy philosophy; it is not American doctrine." A few months later he received an apology from the Commission, and eventually won the position he was seeking. Although his friendship with Vincent did not result in his dismissal from government service, the episode was acutely distressing. "Until one receives such [an interrogatory] oneself," Moffat noted, "it is literally impossible to comprehend the emotional and physical shock that such a paper produces."[12]

Government security agencies also investigated John Carter Vincent, Jr. In 1960, while a student at Harvard Law School, he joined an army reserve unit, which required a security check. He was therefore not surprised when he was asked to appear for an interview at the Boston army base. Only after arriving did he discover that he was being singled out for special treatment. Two army counter-intelligence agents escorted Jack to a private room, switched on a tape recorder, and asked a series of puzzling questions: Did he favor giving "arms and aid to Chiang Kai-shek and the Kuomintang Regime?" Did he think the United States "should pull out of Formosa?" Did he "think the U.S. should remain there and help Chiang Kai-shek?" Did he "think the U.S. should recognize Red China?" Jack did not have "the faintest idea what this was all about" and asked the agents "what the relevance and purpose of these questions were." Euclid E. Boucher, Jack later recalled, "answered that I might as well know at this point that his office in Washington wished to have my views on various aspects of American Foreign Policy on record, and to see whether they were similar to those of my father." Jack was confused and resentful but answered each question politely, as did his father on so many similar occasions. At the conclusion of the meeting, the agents asked whether he had a final statement to make. Yes, Jack replied, but first he wished to have a copy of the interview to show to his attorney. Boucher agreed to give him a transcript.

He called on Vincent the next day, bringing with him only one copy of the interview which he asked Jack to read and sign, Jack refused and again demanded his own copy. Boucher "seemed to be somewhat annoyed at this," Jack noted, "saying that this interview was really of very little consequence, and that his office only wanted to have my views on record, and that no doubt nothing more would come of it." Jack disagreed strongly: "As far as I was concerned," he said, "the interview was of considerable consequence to me: Why did the Defense Department want my views ... anyway, and if they wanted them now, why not every year or month." Boucher could not give him a satisfactory answer and two weeks went by before he received a copy of the interview (excised was Boucher's admission that the army wished to compare Jack's views with those of his father). Before signing it, Jack attached a personal statement objecting to the Pentagon interrogation.

He did receive his clearance and was appointed to the 305th Civil Affairs Group. Ironically, he became that unit's chief security officer and spent a good deal of his time investigating other men accused of being security risks.[13]

Jack's parents were greatly upset by this incident and the one involving Abbott Moffat. Betty again urged her husband to write his memoirs or an account of his continuing troubles with the witch-hunters, but he was still reluctant. She, as always, was more eager to fight. Betty was encouraged by a 1956 Supreme Court decision which found that the Civil Service Loyalty Review Board had acted illegally when it reviewed cases previously closed by an employee's department. Those dismissed because of an adverse ruling by the board were entitled to compensation, the court declared, among which was to have their records cleansed of the board's findings. Walter Surrey wrote to Secretary Dulles and Civil Service Commissioner Philip Young asking them, in light of *John P. Peters* v. *Oveta Culp Hobby, et al.*, to expunge Bingham's verdict from Vincent's records. Young agreed and asked Dulles and Hoover to take similar action. Both eventually complied, but the FBI handled the matter in its own peculiar fashion. The bureau decided that henceforth no mention of the board's decision would be made "in future documentations," but that previous reports would be left unchanged. "Such documentations in referring to the findings of the Loyalty Review Board were accurate at the time utilized," one FBI memorandum noted, and since the Civil Service Commission did not specifically order changes in these records none would be made. In effect, the FBI was ignoring the commission's order that Vincent's record be *completely* cleansed.[14]

Betty intensified her effort to absolve and vindicate her husband in the years that followed. In May 1957, she conferred with Adam Yarmolinsky of the Fund for the Republic; he urged her to collect and then publish all the records in the Vincent case. A few months later she went to Washington to meet with Harry W. Blair. Still alert, active, and eager to cooperate, he described in vivid and shocking detail how Bingham behaved and gave her copies of his personal correspondence with the other members of the board. After their meeting Betty wrote him:

> I wish I had your legal training . . . to improve my technique in trying to get background on the Review Board Panel's work. But I know you will forgive my meanderings, because it is hard to think straight and not "emote" when I think of the ruining of a career, and the possible ruining of another career that my son might choose—viz. any government work, connection with a university, a foundation job, even a job with a conservative law firm might be questioned bearing the name of John Carter Vincent, Junior. In the case of my husband the verdict of the Review Board has made ALL possible work for him impossible. This I know from the last five years experience. Fortunately I was able to lend a hand and see that our children received the good education they did. Even serving on a volunteer civic committee here in Cambridge, the presence of my husband was challenged. . . . [F]riends and associates of his are penalized for association with him. . . . My daughter Sheila is engaged to marry a young man who has a Political Science Research Office here in Cambridge. He has in the past received contracts from the Navy and other government offices for research in foreign countries. I fear, and not without reason, that his marrying the daughter of John Carter Vincent may interfere with HIS career. . . . I, myself, giving a talk before a Professional Women's Club in Boston was checked on by the local FBI. . . .
>
> . . . I could never have imagined, brought up as I was by a stern New England Congregational, intensely American, Mother, that I could fear this government (it is NOT mine) as I do. But *I* do not matter, and even John Carter is of secondary importance—he has accepted HIS tragedy, but for my two children I will fight and go on fighting. What can I say to you—who have been the one great help and encouragement to me? . . . My husband put[s] reliance on ultimate justice—and that is what perhaps you are helping to bring about. A nobler cause I cannot—nor can you embark on.[15]

Betty's hopes were raised again when writers Martin Mayer and Charles Clift researched the story in 1958 and 1959. But both of these

287   Epilogue

projects were abandoned. Later she hoped that President John F. Kennedy might rescue the China hands from the diplomatic oblivion to which Dulles had consigned them. Rose Kennedy was a close friend of John Davies's mother-in-law and the new secretary of state, Dean Rusk, had served with Vincent in the Truman administration. (Indeed, Vincent had urged Dean Acheson in 1946 to bring Rusk into the department—an action he later regretted.) But it quickly became apparent that the change from Dulles to Rusk would mean nothing for Vincent and the others. Milton Katz, a professor at Harvard and a friend of both Vincent and Rusk, wrote the secretary in 1961 "urging some kind of job for [Vincent]." Katz never received a reply.[16]

Vincent observed Betty's activities with mixed emotions. He was proud of his career and did not feel any need to be rehabilitated, but it was also clear that McCarthy's charges and Dulles's judgment still hung over him like some dark and offending cloud, affecting his future employment and that of his friends and family. Perhaps an article or a book about his experiences might dispel the doubts—which he still thought irrational and without foundation. He spent his time working on a study of the end of the extraterritorial system in China under the auspices of Harvard's East Asian Center (Harvard University Press published his monograph in 1970). And he gave seminars on Chinese history and politics at Radcliffe and made an occasional speech in Boston or New York. He was still intensely interested in world affairs and wrote letters to the *New York Times* and other newspapers.[17]

In his speeches, lectures, and letters Vincent criticized American diplomacy in the 1950s and 1960s. He warned repeatedly that anticommunism was distorting the American perception of Asian realities. Dulles thought too much in terms of friends and enemies, pacts and alliances, economic aid in return for allegiance to the "Free World." He considered it sheer idiocy to call Asian neutralism "immoral," as Dulles did in countless speeches. "We do not have to approve of it," he told one audience in the mid-1950s, "but we must realize that, at least for a considerable period, we shall have to accept it as a fact to which we should adjust ourselves—and our diplomacy—because we can't wish, talk or shoot it away. ... I would suggest that we respect their right to be neutral and refrain from trying to talk them into alliance on our side." Mutual respect was more important than mutual pacts. "We should endeavor to win and hold the friendship of these nations ... by seeking a better understanding of their problems and of their national psychology; and by helping them to do things—solve problems—in the way they think best rather than in the way we think best. ... Let us consult and cooperate; not simply provide and preach."[18]

No other development in American diplomacy worried Vincent more than the growing United States involvement in Indochina. As early as 1946, he had warned Under Secretary of State Dean Acheson that the French effort to regain their former colony would probably result in a guerrilla war that it was not in the American interest to support. While Vincent fought for a policy that recognized the vitality of Southeast Asian nationalism, Truman's administration (and its successor) backed the French in what it considered a struggle between democracy and communism. Later he recalled a conversation with George F. Kennan, then director of the State Department's Policy Planning Staff. Vincent had argued that colonialism in Asia was doomed, while Kennan answered: "John Carter, your views on Asian policy are quite sound from the traditional U.S. standpoint, but the immediate problem is to maintain the morale of Europe and its will to resist the Communist challenge."[19]

In 1964, while the United States planned a major escalation of its effort in Vietnam, Vincent was calling for a "neutralized Asia." "Of course there would be risks in such an approach," he wrote to the *New York Times* on June 17. "But isn't our present approach even riskier without much promise of success?" He called for a meeting of the Geneva Conference to negotiate an end to the Vietnam war; the creation of a neutralization agreement with all concerned Asian governments, including China; and the establishment of diplomatic relations with Communist China along with that country's admittance to the United Nations. His program offered "no panacea," he admitted, "but it would be a rational approach to a pressing problem. . . . Let us hope that the [Johnson] Administration will give it heed at the latest . . . after the November elections."[20]

Vincent's recommendations were ignored as President Johnson sought a military victory in Vietnam. Vincent was so disgusted with American policy that he could not bring himself to support Hubert Humphrey for the presidency in 1968. Nor would he vote for Richard M. Nixon, a former member in good standing of the McCarthyite wing of the Republican Party. In November he voted for the Socialist candidate: "Thus behaves a former U.S. [Minister] in this year of horrors, 1968," noted Vincent's friend Ross Terrill. Nixon's continued escalation of the war infuriated Vincent. When the President announced the American invasion of Cambodia over nationwide television in April 1970, Vincent leaped to his feet in anger. His reaction was "incredible," recalled Ross Terrill who was there to observe it. Vincent walked around his den, cursing Nixon, acting, Terrill thought, like a man half his age.[21]

Nixon could amuse as well as infuriate. The announcement in July 1971, that the president would soon visit the People's Republic of China was received by Vincent with some degree of hilarity; the thought that

Nixon would embrace Chou En-lai and Mao Tse-tung must surely have McCarthy and McCarran spinning in their graves, Vincent told a friend. The improvement in Chinese-American relations (which Vincent had been recommending for fifteen years) also had one unexpected personal result. One day in August, when the Vincents were visiting Abbott Moffat, he was introduced to a friend of his host's who cried: "John Carter Vincent! You've just been invited to China by Chou En-lai." Vincent's first reaction was one of amazement; he had spoken with Chou only a few times in Chungking, thirty years before. Moffat's friend must have him confused with another John—Service or Davies. No, the man insisted, it was Vincent; the story was in that day's *New York Times*. He was right: A dispatch from James Reston, then in Peking, noted that during an interview with Premier Chou En-lai, Chou had spoken of Vincent (along with Service, John Fairbank, and Owen Lattimore). "Take good wishes to them," Chou told Reston. "If they want to visit China we will welcome them." Vincent was thrilled to receive Chou's invitation and sent him a reply. "Dear and Esteemed Friend," he wrote, "Your message sent to us through Mr. Reston brought us great pleasure. Our first inclination was to accept your invitation at once, but Mrs. Vincent and I are scheduled to visit Europe [this] autumn and spend the winter in Santa Barbara where I have work with some University of California students. Hence we would very much like to make the visit in the early autumn of next year if it is convenient then. . . . I look forward very much to seeing you and China again."[22]

This hope was never realized. Although he talked of making the trip, as the fall of 1972 approached, he did not feel physically well enough to make actual plans. In 1967 he had suffered a heart attack, and since then, spells of dizziness left him weak and unsteady. Three months after celebrating his seventy-second birthday, he fell suddenly ill and was hospitalized for lung congestion. During the next few days his condition worsened; on the night of December 2, Betty visited him, for what was to be the last time. "He was having great difficulty breathing," she later noted, "and looked so tired." In the early morning hours of December 3, he died. A few hours later, Betty wrote to a friend: "I am sad but the comfort is J. C. did not want to live with his difficult breathing and voice almost gone. You have the real memory of him . . . as I have too."[23]

Vincent's friends and acquaintances were deeply affected by his death. John and Caroline Service wired: "We are filled with memories of a great person and much love." David H. McKillop, president of the American Foreign Service Association, told Betty that "even those of us who were not privileged to know him, nevertheless, have felt a close affinity with him. Who better reflected those qualities of courage, conviction, integrity, and excellence of performance in all that he did than he? . . . He has been an inspiration and example of what a Foreign Service Officer should aspire to be. We can all be proud to have him in our ranks." Betty was especially moved by I. A. R. Richards, who called to say that he had "never known a man meet adversity with more gallantry."[24]

Many of the nation's great newspapers (some originally hostile) noted Vincent's passing and eulogized him as a distinguished public servant. "Mr. Vincent was almost a picture-book diplomat," Alden Whitman wrote in the *New York Times*. "Elegant, mustached, with penetrating blue eyes and bushy brows, he possessed the courtliness of . . . 'an old fashioned Southern gentleman'. . . . In China, Mr. Vincent was on friendly terms with virtually every political, economic and military personality." Whitman and other writers reviewed his years in Ch'angsha, Mukden, Dairen, Chungking, and Washington, and recalled that he had been an early foe of Japanese imperialism, a critic of the Nationalist government, and an opponent of direct intervention in the Chinese civil war. Evaluating Vincent's views, the *Los Angeles Times* argued that "history has shown, long before he died, that he and a handful of other foreign service officers, who persisted in reporting what they felt to be the truth, were not . . . in error."[25]

The letters and the editorials were a source of great comfort to Betty, as was the presence of Jack and Sheila. Ross Terrill visited her on December 10, "a bit apprehensive about how [he] might find her." Later he wrote in his diary that Betty was "self-possessed and even regal. . . . Halfway through our talk she suddenly said, 'What I miss about John Carter is the conversation.' She is a terrier in conversation, and so, in his way was he a great conversationalist. . . . Only at the end did she become emotional . . . but I think she will be OK."[26]

On January 11, 1973, Vincent's family and closest friends gathered together in a requiem service to remember the man as well as the diplomat. "His skill as a diplomat came first of all from his intuitive comprehension of people," John Fairbank said, "what they felt and wanted, what they were up to. . . . We were fortunate that John Carter, with his special background in the China field and fresh from wartime Chungking, was [Chief of FE] in the late 1940s when we chose *not* to intervene militarily against the Chinese revolution in what could have been a super-super Vietnam." Walter Surrey recalled Vincent's gentleness, civility, and "unbreakable moral fibre." Dr. George H. Carter spoke of Vincent the neighbor—of "friendly greetings across the garden wall, growing curiosity and warm feelings about the whereabouts, the pursuits, the pleasures and the health of all the family members." Speaking for his family, Jack Vincent said, "We remember my father best as a lover of life—both animate and inanimate—small people and large, animals, plants—and neglected things—and his kindness. I am guided by his integrity, which I trust I and my son have inherited and will never deny."[27]

Thus spoke family and friends. What will history say about John Carter Vincent?

Despite its tragic and premature termination (Vincent was only fifty-two when forced to retire) his career was full, exciting, and valuable. Vincent's personality and character—even-tempered, detached, objective—was admirably suited to diplomacy. When Americans became hysterical in Ch'ang-sha, Vincent remained cool and with methodical care evacuated them from that troubled city without a loss of life. Later, in the Chungking embassy, he helped to bring order out of bureaucratic chaos, and his optimism infected the entire staff (and some foreign diplomats) and boosted morale during the darkest days of World War II. In the late 1940s, he fought against the crusaders and warriors who sought to make China a battleground of the cold war. Few diplomats in modern times have served in such dangerous places and have acquitted themselves as admirably.

Those qualities of poise and tact work as well for the nation as they do for the man. Over a hundred years before Vincent's birth, George Washington told his countrymen that "permanent, inveterate antipathies against particular nations and passionate attachments for others should be excluded" from the nation's foreign policy. "The nation which indulges toward another an habitual hatred or an habitual fondness is in some degree a slave." There was no place in diplomacy, Washington argued, for the strong emotions, passions, and hates which distorted judgment. This too was Vincent's creed. He tried to cut through the strands of propaganda that bound America to Chiang Kai-shek during the war and threatened, afterwards, to propel the United States into war against the Communists.

Ironically, Vincent's strengths as a diplomat made him vulnerable to attack from the partisans, the zealots, the extremists who suffered from an excess of emotion—from a passionate attachment to Chiang, and inveterate antipathy toward Russia. There was no place for John Carter Vincent among the ideologues who made the United States a slave of rabid anticommunism in the 1950s.

The life of John Carter Vincent also has something to tell us about the strengths, weaknesses, and relevance of modern American liberal values. As a representative liberal of his generation, Vincent was acutely aware of social and economic injustice, and his outlook gave him insight into the conditions and causes that contributed to the fall of the Nationalist government and the victory of the Chinese Communists. At the same time, however, his philosophy inhibited him from fully understanding that the United States could not create a liberal China—the foundation on which to build such a state was just too weak. Of course, Vincent was not alone in his beliefs: Many Chinese held similar views. Unfortunately, economic and social problems could be resolved only through revolution. Liberalism was more helpful in the diagnosis of Chinese ills than in their eradication. In the end, even Vincent, who had believed for so long that democratic reform was possible, realized that violent revolution was inevitable. Edward Rice, a colleague in the China Service, later remembered how "uncomfortable" Vincent was, working "in a period during which liberals were finding less and less middle ground on which to stand. ... Before he went to his ... post in Geneva [in 1947] I heard him remark: 'Well, now China is somebody else's problem. My bones are not the only ones already whitening upon its sands and I wonder how many of my successors will have to suffer the same fate.'" Vincent and the Americans were not the only ones to suffer: The failure to establish a liberal China meant not just the death of their dreams, but those of a generation of Chinese as well.[28]

Vincent's liberalism was more successful as a personal philosophy: It kept him open to new ideas and flexible when confronted by new challenges. It also sustained him during the most difficult moments of his life. In the 1950s, without realizing, or consciously seeking it, Vincent became, for many, a symbol of the American liberal temperament at its best: objective, generous, honest. Men with such qualities were hard to find in McCarthyite America.

Toward the end of his life, Vincent's career was beginning to receive the praise that it deserved. Scholars spoke highly of his dispatches from China. Daniel Ellsberg personally presented Vincent with an inscribed copy of *The Pentagon Papers* and lauded him for his foresight in predicting and opposing the Vietnam War. Historian James C. Thomson, Jr. and journalist David Halberstam argued that the purge of Vincent and the other China hands left the American government bereft of Asian experts who might have prevented or moderated America's involvement in Vietnam.[29] Indeed, without the political duplicity that attended the fall of China, it is not impossible to imagine Vincent as an important ambassador or under secretary of state in the Washington of John F. Kennedy or Lyndon B. Johnson. In the 1940s he helped to limit American involvement in the Chinese civil war; given his knowledge and experience, he surely would have fought just as tenaciously against a similar involvement in the Vietnamese civil war. Had he been given such an opportunity in the 1960s, American and Vietnamese life might not have been so tragically blighted. Perhaps too his quiet persistence and continuing belief in realism in foreign affairs might have helped to reconcile the United States to the existence of a Communist China long before formal diplomatic relations between the two countries finally began in January 1979. But due to the efforts of Alfred Kohlberg, Joseph McCarthy, and Hiram Bingham, along with the inadvertent cooperation of Harry Truman and Dean Acheson, policy-making in the State Department and the White House was dominated by other men, men who knew little about Asia. The result was disaster in Vietnam, and enmity and estrangement with China.

One month after Vincent's death, the men who had long believed that the United States and the People's Republic of China might be able to peacefully coexist in spite of cultural barriers and political differences were honored at a luncheon given by the American Foreign Service Association. On January 30, 1973, in the State Department's Benjamin Franklin Room, several hundred people gathered to celebrate the life and work of the China hands, and also perhaps to wonder about the "ifs" of history. Absent were Secretary of State William P. Rogers and Presidential Assistant Henry A. Kissinger; they were too busy to lunch with John Service, Edmund Clubb, and the others, despite the fact that the Nixon administration had adopted the policy the China hands had recommended nearly thirty years before. Service was selected to speak to his colleagues. He rose, and before beginning his address, acknowledged the presence in the audience of Mrs. John Carter Vincent. "We all knew John Carter as a staunch friend," Service said, "and as a capable, courageous, and loyal chief. He was the man who should be standing here today."[30]

Bibliography

Manuscript Collections

Joseph Alsop Papers. Mss. Div., Lib. of Congress, Wash. D.C.

William Benton Papers. State Hist. Soc., Madison, Wisc.

Styles Bridges Papers. New England College, Hanniker, N. H.

Ch'ang-sha Consular Post Volumes. Nat. Archives, Wash., D.C. Cited as Ch'ang-sha Vols.

U.S. Civil Service Commission Records. Wash., D.C. Cited as Civil Service Records.

Lauchlin B. Currie Papers. Private possession.

Department of State Files. Nat. Archives, Wash., D.C.

Department of State Papers. Dept. of State, Wash., D.C.

John Foster Dulles Papers. Princeton U., Princeton, N.J.

Federal Bureau of Investigation Records. Wash., D.C. Cited as FBI Records.

Herbert Feis Papers. Mss. Div., Lib. of Congress, Wash., D.C.

Joseph C. Green Papers. Princeton U., Princeton, N.J.

Learned B. Hand Papers. Harvard U., Cambridge, Mass.

295

Stanley K. Hornbeck Papers. Hoover Inst. on War, Revolution, and Peace, Stanford U., Stanford, Calif.

Cordell Hull Papers. Mss. Div., Lib. of Congress, Wash., D.C.

Patrick J. Hurley Papers. U. of Oklahoma, Norman, Okla.

Nelson T. Johnson Papers. Mss. Div., Lib. of Congress, Wash., D.C.

Ruth Kauke Papers. Private possession.

David D. Lloyd Papers, Harry S. Truman Lib., Independence, Missouri.

Joseph R. McCarthy vs. *the Post-Standard Co. of N.Y.*, Court Records, County of Onendago, N.Y., located in County Clerk's Office, Syracuse, N.Y.

Henry Morgenthau, Jr. Papers. Franklin D. Roosevelt Lib., Hyde Park, N.Y.

Office of Security Records. Dept. of State, Wash., D.C.

Willys R. Peck Papers. Hoover Inst. on War, Revolution and Peace, Stanford U., Stanford, Calif.

Franklin D. Roosevelt Papers. Franklin D. Roosevelt Lib., Hyde Park, N.Y.

Laurence Salisbury Papers. Private possession.

U.S. Congress, Senate Foreign Relations Committee, 1947 Records. Record Group No. 46, Nat. Archives, Wash., D.C.

Stephen J. Spingarn Papers. Harry S. Truman Lib., Independence, Missouri.

Joseph W. Stilwell Papers. Hoover Inst. on War, Revolution, and Peace, Stanford, U., Stanford, Calif.

Walter Sterling Surrey Papers. Private Possession, Wash., D.C.

Harry S. Truman Papers. Harry S. Truman Lib., Independence, Missouri.

Tsinan Consular Post Volume #800. Nat. Archives, Wash., D.C. Cited as TCPV #800.

Arthur K. Vandenberg Papers. U. of Michigan, Ann Arbor, Mich.

John Carter Vincent Papers. Possession of John C. Vincent, Jr., but will eventually be deposited at Harvard U., Cambridge, Mass. Cited as JCV mss.

John Carter Vincent Personal File, Dept. of State, Wash., D.C. Cited as JCV Personnel File.

Henry A. Wallace Papers. U. of Iowa, Iowa City, Iowa.

Government Documents

Dept. of State. *Department of State Bulletin*, vol. 28, Jan. 19, 1953.

———. *Biographic Register*. 74 vols. Annual. Wash., D.C. Govt. Printing Office, 1870-1951.

_____. *Foreign Relations of the United States, Diplomatic Papers: 1926.* vol. 1. Wash., D.C.: Govt. Printing Office, 1942. Cited as *FR 1926*, 1.

_____. *Foreign Relations of the United States, Diplomatic Papers: 1927.* vol. 2. Wash., D.C.: Govt. Printing Office, 1942. Cited as *FR 1927*, 2.

_____. *Foreign Relations of the United States, Diplomatic Papers: 1938.* vol. 4. Wash., D.C.: Govt. Printing Office, 1954. *Cited as FR 1938*, 4.

_____. *Foreign Relations of the United States, Diplomatic Papers: 1941.* vol. 5. Wash., D.C.: Govt. Printing Office, 1956. Cited as *FR 1941*, 5.

_____. *Foreign Relations of the United States, Diplomatic Papers: 1942, China.* Wash., D.C.: Govt. Printing Office, 1956. Cited as *FR 1942*, China.

_____. *Foreign Relations of the United States, Diplomatic Papers: 1943, China.* Wash., D.C.: Govt. Printing Office, 1957. Cited as *FR 1943*, China.

_____. *Foreign Relations of the United States, Diplomatic Papers: 1944.* vol. 6. Wash., D.C.: Govt. Printing Office, 1967. Cited as *FR 1944*, 6.

_____. *Foreign Relations of the United States, Diplomatic Papers: 1945.* vol. 7 Wash., D.C.: Govt. Printing Office, 1969. Cited as *FR 1945*, 7.

_____. *Foreign Relations of the United States: 1946.* vol. 9. Wash., D.C.: Govt. Printing Office, 1972. Cited as *FR 1946*, 9.

_____. *Foreign Relations of the United States: 1946.* vol. 10. Wash., D.C.: Govt. Printing Office 1972. Cited as *FR 1946*, 10.

_____. *Foreign Relations of the United States: 1947.* vol. 7. Wash., D.C.: Govt. Printing Office, 1972. Cited as *FR 1947*, 7.

_____. *United States Relations with China: With Special Reference to the Period 1944-1949.* Cited as *China White Paper*. Stanford: Stanford U. Pr., 1967.

U. S. Congress. House. 80th Cong. 2nd sess. Committee on Appropriations. *Department of State Appropriations Bill for 1949, Hearings.* 1 pt. Wash., D.C., 1949.

U.S. Congress, Senate. Committee on Armed Services and the Committee on Foreign Relations. *Military Situation in the Far East, Hearings.* 82nd Cong., 1st sess. 5 pts. Wash., D.C., 1951. Cited as *Military Situation*.

_____. Committee on Foreign Relations. *The Evolution of U. S. Policy Toward Mainland China.* 92nd Cong., 1st sess. 1 pt. Wash., D.C., 1971.

_____. Committee on the Judiciary, Subcommittee to Investigate the Administration of the Internal Security Act and Other Internal Security Laws. *The Amerasia Papers: A Clue to the Catastrophe of China.* 91st Cong., 1st sess. 2 vols. Wash., D.C., 1970.

_____. Committee on the Judiciary, Subcommittee to Investigate the Administration of the Internal Security Act and Other Internal Security Laws. *Institute of Pacific Relations, Hearings.* 82nd Cong., 1st and 2nd sess. 15 pts. Wash., D.C., 1951-1952.

_____. Committee on the Judiciary, Subcommittee to Investigate the Administration of the Internal Security Act and Other Internal Security Laws. *Morgenthau Diary: China.* 89th Cong., 1st sess. 2 vols. Wash., D.C., 1965.

_____. Subcommittee of the Committee on Foreign Relations. *State Department Employee Loyalty Investigation, Hearings.* 81st Cong., 2nd sess. 3 pts. Wash., D.C., 1950.

Books, Articles, and Dissertations

Acheson, Dean G. *Present at the Creation: My Years in the State Department.* N.Y.: Norton, 1969.

Adler, Selig. *The Uncertain Giant.* N.Y.: Macmillan, 1965.

Allman, Norwood F. *Shanghai Lawyer.* N.Y.: McGraw, 1943.

Alperovitz, Gar. *Cold War Essays.* Garden City, N.Y.: Anch. Doubleday, 1970.

_____. *American Foreign Service Journal.* vol. 2, No. 4, Apr. 1925.

Alsop, Joseph. "The Strange Case of Louis Budenz," *Atlantic Monthly*, Apr. 1952.

Anderson, Clinton P. and Milton Viorst. *Outsider in the Senate.* N.Y.: World Pub. Co., 1968.

Anderson, Jack, and Ronald W. May. *McCarthy: The Man, the Senator, the 'Ism.'* Boston: Beacon Pr., 1952.

Barnard, Ellsworth. *Wendell Willkie: Fighter for Freedom.* Marquette: Northern Mich., 1966.

Barnes, William, and John H. Morgan. *The Foreign Service of the United States: Origins, Development and Function.* Wash., D.C.: Hist. Office, Bureau of Public Affairs, Dept. of State, 1961.

Barnet, Richard J. *Intervention and Revolution.* N.Y.: World Pub. Co., 1966.

Barrett, David D. *The Dixie Mission.* Berkeley: U. of California Pr., 1970.

Bendiner, Robert. *The Riddle of the State Department.* N.Y.: Farrar & Rinehart, 1942.

Blum, John M., ed. *The Price of Vision: The Diary of Henry A. Wallace,* 1942-1946. Boston: Houghton Mifflin, 1973.

Bohlen, Charles E. *Witness to History, 1929-1969.* N.Y.: Norton, 1973.

Bontecou, Eleanor. *The Federal Employee Loyalty Program.* Ithaca: Cornell U. Pr., 1953.

Borg, Dorothy. *American Policy and the Chinese Revolution, 1925-1928.* N.Y.: Amer. Inst. of Pacific Relations, 1947.

_____. *The United States and the Far Eastern Crisis of 1933-1938.* Cambridge: Harvard U. Pr., 1964.

_____., and Shumpei Okamoto, eds. *Pearl Harbor as History.* N.Y.: Columbia U. Pr., 1973.

Braeman, John, Robert H. Bremner, and David Brody, eds. *Twentieth-Century American Foreign Policy*. Columbus: Ohio St. U. Pr., 1971.

Brown, Ralph, S., Jr. *Loyalty and Security: Employment Tests in the U.S.* New Haven: Yale U. Pr., 1952.

Buhite, Russell D. *Nelson T. Johnson and American Policy Toward China, 1925-1941*. East Lansing: Michigan St. U. Pr., 1968.

————. *Patrick J. Hurley and American Foreign Policy*. Ithaca: Cornell U. Pr., 1973.

Burns, James M. *Roosevelt: The Soldier of Freedom*. N.Y.: Harcourt, Brace, Jovanovich, 1970.

Butow, Robert J. C. *Tojo and the Coming of the War*. Stanford: Stanford U. Pr., 1961.

Byrnes, James F. *Speaking Frankly*. N.Y.: Harper, 1947.

Campbell, John Franklin. *The Foreign Affairs Fudge Factory*. N.Y.: Basic, 1971.

Chun-tu Hsueh. *Huan Hsing and the Chinese Revolution*. Stanford: Stanford U. Pr., 1961.

Clubb, O. Edmund. *Twentieth Century China*. N.Y.: Columbia U. Pr., 1964.

————. *The Witness and I*. N.Y.: Columbia U. Pr., 1975.

Cochran, Bert. *Harry S. Truman and the Crisis Presidency*. N.Y.: Funk & Wagnalls, 1973.

Cohen, Warren I. *America's Response to China*. N.Y.: Wiley, 1971.

Congressional Quarterly Service. *Congressional Quarterly*, 1953, pt 2. Wash., D.C. 1954.

————. *Congress and the Nation: 1945-1964*. Wash., D.C., 1965.

Cook, Fred J. *The Nightmare Decade: The Life and Times of Senator Joe McCarthy*. N.Y.: Random, 1971.

Crow, Carl. *Handbook for China*. Shanghai: Crow, 1925.

Crowley, James B. *Japan's Quest for Autonomy: National Security and Foreign Policy*. Princeton: Princeton U. Pr., 1968.

Davies, John Paton, Jr. *Dragon by the Tail*. N.Y.: Norton, 1972.

de Toledano, Ralph. *Spies, Dupes and Diplomats*. New Rochelle: Arlington Hse., 1967.

Dennett, Tyler. *Americans in Eastern Asia*. N.Y.: Macmillan, 1922.

Dillon, Mary E. *Wendell Willkie*. Phil.: Lippincott, 1952.

Douglass, Bruce, and Ross Terrill, eds. *China and Ourselves*. Boston: Beacon Pr., 1970.

299   Bibliography

Dulles, Foster Rhea. *American Policy Towards Communist China, 1949-1969*. New York: Crowell, 1972.

Fairbank, John K. *The United States and China*. 3rd ed. Cambridge: Harvard U. Pr., 1971.

Feis, Herbert. *The China Tangle*. Princeton: Princeton U. Pr., 1953.

Ferrell, Robert H. *American Diplomacy*. N.Y.: Norton, 1969.

———. *American Diplomacy in the Great Depression*. New Haven: Yale U. Pr., 1957.

———. *Frank B. Kellogg 1925-1929 - Henry L. Stimson 1929-1933*. American Secretaries of State and Their Diplomacy, ed. by Robert Ferrell and Samuel Flagg Bemis, vol. 2. N.Y.: Cooper Square, 1963.

Fleming, Peter. *The Siege at Peking*. London: Hart-Davis, 1959.

Frank, Benis M. and Henry I. Shaw, Jr. *Victory and Occupation: History of U.S. Marine Corps Operation in World War II*. 5 vols. Hist. Branch, U.S. Marine Corps, Wash. D.C.: Govt. Printing Office, 1968.

Freeland, Richard M. *The Truman Doctrine and the Origins of McCarthyism*. N.Y.: Knopf, 1971.

Freidel, Frank. *Franklin D. Roosevelt: The Apprenticeship*. Boston: Little, 1952.

———. *Franklin D. Roosevelt: Launching the New Deal*. Boston: Little, 1973.

Fried, Richard M. *Men Against McCarthy*. N.Y.: Columbia U. Pr., 1976.

Graebner, Norman A. *The New Isolationism*. N.Y.: Ronald, 1958.

———, ed. *The Uncertain Tradition: American Secretaries of State in the Twentieth Century*. N.Y.: McGraw, 1961.

———., ed. *Ideas and Diplomacy*. N.Y.: Oxford U. Pr., 1964.

Griffith, Robert. *The Politics of Fear: Joseph R. McCarthy and the Senate*. Lexington: U. Pr. of Kentucky, 1970.

Halberstam, David. *The Best and the Brightest*. N.Y.: Random, 1972.

Harper, Alan D. *The Politics of Loyalty*. Westport, Conn.: Greenwood, 1969.

Hartman, Susan M. *Truman and the 80th Congress*. Columbia: U. of Missouri Pr., 1971.

Heinrichs, Waldo H., Jr. *American Ambassador: Joseph C. Grew and the Development of the United States Diplomatic Tradition*. Boston: Little, 1966.

———. "Bureaucracy and Professionalism in the Development of American Career Diplomacy," in John Braeman, Robert H. Bremner, and David Brody, eds., *Twentieth-Century American Foreign Policy*. Columbus: Ohio St. U. Pr., 1971.

Hofstadter, Richard. *The Age of Reform.* N.Y.: Knopf, 1958.

————. *The Paranoid Style in American Politics and Other Essays.* N.Y.: Knopf, 1965.

Holcombe, Chester. *The Real Chinese Question.* N.Y.: Dodd, 1900.

Hoopes, Townsend. *The Devil and John Foster Dulles.* Boston: Little, 1973.

Hosoya, Chihiro. "Miscalculations in Deterrent Policy: Japanese-American Relations, 1938-1941." *Journal of Peace Resolution,* May 1968.

Hume, Edward H. *Doctor's East and Doctor's West.* N.Y.: Norton, 1946.

Hume, L.C. *Drama at the Doctor's Gate.* New Haven: Yale-in-China Assoc., 1960.

Ilchman, Warren Frederick. *Professional Diplomacy in the United States, 1779-1939.* Chicago: U. of Chicago Pr., 1961.

Iriye, Akira. *The Cold War in Asia.* Englewood Cliffs, N.J.: Prentice-Hall, 1974.

Israel, Jerry. *Progressivism and the Open Door.* Pittsburgh: U. of Pittsburgh Pr., 1971.

Kahn, E.J., Jr. *The China Hands: America's Foreign Service Officers and What Befell Them.* N.Y.: Viking, 1975.

Keeley, Joseph. *The China Lobby Man: The Story of Alfred Kohlberg.* New Rochelle: Arlington Hse, 1969.

Koen, Ross Y. *The China Lobby in American Politics.* N.Y.: Octagon, 1974.

————. "Two Postscripts to the McCarran Hearings." *Bulletin of Concerned Asian Scholars,* vol. 4, May 1969.

Kohlberg, Alfred. "The State Department's Left Hand." *Plain Talk,* July 1947.

————. "The Great Debate." *The Freeman,* Jan. 8, 1951.

————. "Why Was Vandenberg Misled?" *The Freeman,* May 21, 1951.

Kolko, Joyce and Gabriel. *The Limits of Power.* N.Y.: Harper & Row, 1972.

LaFeber, Walter, ed. *America in the Cold War.* N.Y.: Wiley, 1969.

Langer, William L., and S. Everett Gleason. *The Challenge to Isolation: The World Crisis and American Foreign Policy.* N.Y.: Harper & Row, 1952.

Lattimore, Owen. *Ordeal by Slander.* Boston: Little, 1950.

Link, Arthur. *Wilson.* 5 vols. Princeton: Princeton U. Pr., 1947-1965.

————. *Woodrow Wilson and the Progressive Era.* N.Y.: Harper & Row, 1954.

Lippman, Walter. *Living Age.* vol. 333, July 1, 1927.

301   Bibliography

————., ed. *The United States in World Affairs, 1932*. N.Y.: Harper & Bros., 1935.

May, Gary. "The China Service of John Carter Vincent, 1924-1953." Ph.D. dissertation, U.C.L.A., 1974.

McCarthy, Joseph R. *The Fight for America*. Hamilton: Montana, 1952.

Mei, Y.P. "Thus We Live in Chungking." *Asia*, July 1941.

Melby, John F. *The Mandate of Heaven*. N.Y.: Anch. Doubleday, 1972.

Merli, Frank J., and Theodore A. Wilson, eds. *Makers of American Diplomacy: From Roosevelt to Kissinger*. N.Y.: Scribner, 1974.

Millis, Walter, and E. S. Duffield, eds. *The Forrestal Diaries*. N.Y.: Viking, 1951.

Morris, Margaret F., and Sandra L. Myers, eds. *Essays on American Foreign Policy*. Austin: U. of Texas Pr., 1974.

Mosley, Leonard. *Dulles: A Biography of Eleanor, Allen, and John Foster Dulles and Their Family Network*. N.Y.: Dial, 1978.

New York Times. 1951-1953.

Ogata, Sadako N. *Defiance in Manchuria: The Making of Japanese Foreign Policy, 1931-1932*. Berkeley: U. of California Pr., 1964.

Packer, Herbert L. *Ex-Communist Witnesses: Four Studies in Fact Finding*. Stanford: Stanford U. Pr., 1962.

Parmet, Herbert L. *Eisenhower and the American Crusades*. N.Y.: Macmillan, 1972.

Paterson, Thomas G. "American Businessmen and Consular Service Reform 1890s to 1906." *Business History Review*, 40, Spring 1968.

Payne, Robert. *Forever China*. N.Y.: Dodd, 1945.

————. *The Story of General Marshall*. N.Y.: Prentice-Hall, 1951.

Peck, Graham. *Two Kinds of Time*. 2nd ed., rev. Boston: Houghton Mifflin, 1967.

Ramsdell, Daniel B. "The Nakamura Incident and the Japanese Foreign Office." *The Journal of Asian Studies*. vol. 25, Nov. 1965.

Rappaport, Armin. *Henry L. Stimson and Japan, 1931-1933*. Chicago: U. of Chicago Pr., 1963.

Romanus, Charles F., and Riley Sunderland. *Stilwell's Mission to China*. Wash., D.C.: Office of the Chief of Military Hist., Dept. of the Army, 1953.

———. *Stilwell's Command Problems.* Wash., D.C.: Office of the Chief of Military Hist., Dept. of the Army, 1956.

———. *Time Runs Out in CBI.* Wash., D.C.; Office of the Chief of Military Hist., Dept. of State, 1959.

Roosevelt, Elliott. *As He Saw It.* N.Y.: Duell, Sloan & Pearce, 1946.

Rose, Lisle A. *After Yalta: America and the Origins of the Cold War.* N.Y.: Scribner, 1973.

Rosenman, Samuel I. *Working with Roosevelt.* N.Y.: Harper & Row, 1952.

Rovere, Richard H. *Senator Joe McCarthy.* N.Y.: Harcourt, Brace, Jovanovich, 1959.

Schapsmeir, Edward L., and Frederick H. *Prophet in Politics: Henry A. Wallace and the War Years.* Ames: Iowa St. U. Pr., 1970.

Schram, Stuart. *Mao Tse-tung.* N.Y.: Simon & Schuster, 1967.

Schroeder, Paul W. *The Axis Alliance and Japanese-American Relations, 1941.* Ithaca: Cornell U. Pr., 1958.

Service, John S. *The Amerasia Papers: Some Problems in the History of U. S.-Chinese Relations.* Berkeley: U. of Calif. Pr., 1971.

Sherwood, Robert E. *Roosevelt and Hopkins.* 1st ed. N. Y.: Harper & Row, 1948.

Shewmaker, Kenneth E. *Americans and Chinese Communists, 1927-1945: A Persuading Encounter.* Ithaca: Cornell U. Pr., 1971.

Simone, Vera, ed. *China in Revolution.* Greenwich, Conn.: Fawcett Publications, 1968.

Smith, Robert. "Alone in China: Patrick J. Hurley's Attempt to Unify China, 1944-45." Ph.D. dissertation, U. of Oklahoma, 1966.

Snow, Edgar. *Journey to the Beginning.* N. Y.: Random, 1958.

———. *Red Star Over China.* N. Y.: Grove, 1961.

Spence, Jonathan. *To Change China.* Boston: Little, 1969.

Stanton, Edwin. *Brief Authority.* N.Y.: Harper & Row, 1956.

Stimson, Henry L., and McGeorge Bundy. *On Active Service in Peace and War.* 1st ed. New York: Harper, 1948.

Stewart, Maxwell. "Exit Pat Hurley." *Nation,* Dec. 8, 1945.

Stuart, Graham H. *American Diplomatic and Consular Practice.* N. Y.: Appleton-Century-Crofts, 1952.

303   Bibliography

Stuart, John Leighton. *Fifty Years in China*. N. Y.: Random, 1954.

Tang Tsou. *America's Failure in China: 1941-1950*. Chicago: U. of Chicago Pr., 1963.

Te-kong Tong. *United States Diplomacy in China, 1844-1860*. Seattle: U. of Wash. Pr., 1964.

Theoharis, Athan G. *Seeds of Repression*. Chicago: Quadrangle, 1971.

_____. *The Yalta Myths*. Columbia: U. of Missouri Pr., 1970.

Thorne, Christopher. *The Limits of Foreign Policy: The West, the League, and the Far Eastern Crisis, 1931-1933*. N.Y.: Putnam, 1973.

Time. 1945-46, 1951-53.

Toynbee, Arnold J. *Survey of International Affairs: 1926*. London: Oxford U. Pr., 1927.

_____. *Survey of International Affairs: 1927*. London: Oxford U. Pr., 1928.

Truman, Margaret. *Harry S. Truman*. N.Y.: Morrow, 1972.

Truman, Harry S. *Year of Decisions*. 1st ed. Garden City, N.Y.: Doubleday, 1955.

_____. *Years of Trial and Hope*. Garden City, N.Y.: Doubleday, 1955.

Tuchman, Barbara W. "If Mao Had Come to Washington: An Essay in Alternatives." *Foreign Affairs*, Oct. 1972.

_____. *Stilwell and the American Experience in China, 1911-1945*. N.Y.: Macmillan, 1970.

Ulam, Adam. *The Rivals: America and Russia Since World War II*. N.Y.: Viking, 1971.

Ungar, Sanford J. *FBI*. Boston: Little, 1976.

U.S. News and World Report. 1951-1953.

Vandenberg, Arthur H., Jr., ed. *The Private Papers of Senator Arthur Vandenberg*. Boston: Houghton Mifflin, 1952.

Varg, Paul A. *The Closing of the Door: Sino-American Relations, 1936-1946*. East Lansing: Michigan St. U. Pr., 1973.

Wallace, Henry A. "My Mission to China." *The New Leader*, Nov. 19, 1951.

_____. *Soviet-Asia Mission*. N.Y.: Reynal & Hitchcock, 1946.

Washington Post. 1950-1953.

Wedemeyer, Albert C. *Wedemeyer Reports!* N.Y.: Holt, 1958.

Weinstein, Allen. *Perjury: The Hiss-Chambers Case*. N.Y.: Knopf, 1978.

Welles, Sumner. *Seven Decisions That Shaped History.* N.Y.: Harper & Row, 1948.

Wertenbaker, Charles. "The Strange World of Alfred Kohlberg." *The Reporter.* Apr. 19, 1952.

Westerfield, H.B. *Foreign Policy and Party Politics: Pearl Harbor to Korea.* New Haven: Yale U. Pr., 1955.

White, Theodore H. *In Search of History: A Personal Adventure.* N.Y.: Harper & Row, 1978.

————., and Annalee Jacoby. *Thunder Out of China.* 1st ed., N.Y.: W. Sloane Associates, 1946.

Williams, Frederick W. *The Life and Letters of S. Wells Williams.* N.Y.: Putnam, 1889.

Willkie, Wendell L. *One World.* N.Y.: Simon & Schuster, 1943.

Wilson, David. "Leathernecks in North China, 1945." *Bulletin of Concerned Asian Scholars,* Summer 1972.

Young, Marilyn B. *The Rhetoric of Empire.* Cambridge: Harvard U. Pr., 1970.

Interviews

Buss, Claude A., Apr. 1972, San Jose, Calif.

Drumright, Everett F., Apr. 1973, San Diego, Calif.

Fairbank, John K., May 1973, Cambridge, Mass.

Fisher, Adrian S., May 1973, Wash., D.C.

Karasik, Monroe, July 1971 and May 1973, Wash., D.C.

Kauke, Ruth R., May 1973, Los Angeles, Calif.

Moffat, Abbott, May 1973, Princeton, N.J.

Service, John S., Apr. 1972, Berkeley, Calif.

Surrey, Walter S., May 1973, Wash., D.C.

Terrill, Ross, May 1973, Cambridge, Mass.

Thomson, James C., Jr., May 1973, Cambridge, Mass.

Vincent, Elizabeth T., Feb., July 1971; Feb., Mar. 1972; May, Sept. 1973, Santa Barbara, Calif., and Cambridge, Mass.

Vincent, John Carter, Feb., July 1971; Feb., Mar. 1972, Santa Barbara, Calif., and Cambridge, Mass.

Notes

Full bibliographic information for books cited is given in the preceding Bibliography.

Chapter 1

1. Sec. of state to JCV, Dec. 15, 1952, *John Carter Vincent Papers* (hereafter cited as JCV mss).

2. Silas Benjamin Simmons to JCV, Feb. 3, 1952, JCV mss.

3. Lula F. Vincent to JCV, Aug. 18, 1948, p. 1, JCV mss.

4. Interview with JCV, July 1971. For information on the Vincent family's history see John Martin Vincent Papers, Henry Huntington Library, San Marino, Calif.

5. John Martin Vincent Papers, Huntington Lib., San Marino, Calif.

6. Interview with JCV, July 1971.

7. Interview with JCV, July 1971.

8. Interview with JCV, July 1971.

9. Sheila Vincent Cox to author Oct. 5, 1976; interview with JCV, July 1971.

10. JCV to author, Aug. 24, 1971.

11. "Statement of John Carter Vincent before State Department Loyalty Security Board, Dec. 17, 1951," p. 1, JCV mss; Lula Vincent to JCV, Aug. 18, 1948, JCV mss; interview with JCV, July 1971.

12. Interview with JCV, July 1971; "Transcript of Grades," John Carter Vincent, Sidney Lanier High School, Macon Georgia.

13. Interview with JCV, July 1971.

14. Interview with JCV, July 1971; Wilson is quoted in Merli and Wilson, p. 66.

15. Interview with JCV, July 1971.

16. Interview with JCV, July 1971; for the offer of the clerkship see handwritten notations on "Application for Appointment," Nov. 11, 1922, John Carter Vincent Personnel File (hereafter cited as JCV Personnel File).

17. "Influences Shaping American Policy Toward China": Draft of an address before residential seminar, La Fayette College, 1955, pp. 4-5, JCV mss; Interview with JCV, July 1971.

18. Quoted in L. C. Hume, p. 69.

19. Spence, p. 162.

20. Quoted in ibid., p. 162.

21. "Influences Shaping American Policy Toward China," p. 5, JCV mss.

22. JCV to Margaret Vincent Smith, May 16, 1928, p. 1; JCV mss; Edward H. Hume, pp. 27-28.

23. Interview with JCV, Mar. 1972.

24. For a complete list of the religious organizations operating in Hunan Province during this period, see JCV to Americans in Hunan Province, Jan. 12, 1927, Ch'ang-sha Consular Post Volumes (hereafter cited as Ch'ang-sha Vols.).

25. JCV to Margaret Vincent, Mar. 17, 1925, p. 1, JCV mss; Interview with JCV, July 1971.

26. JCV to Margaret Vincent, Feb. 23, 1925, pp. 1-2, JCV mss; JCV to Margaret Vincent, Jan. 4, 1925, JCV mss.

27. "Reporting of Ratings," Wilbur J. Carr to JCV, Apr. 27, 1925, JCV Personnel File.

28. For specific information on Vincent's performance on the examination see May, p. 29.

29. Wilbur J. Carr to JCV, Apr. 27, 1925; JCV to Margaret Vincent, June 1925, JCV mss.

30. JCV to Margaret Vincent, Apr. 29, 1925, p.1, JCV mss.

31. A good introduction to China's agonies after 1911 is Tuchman, *Stilwell,* pp. 36-37, 68-69.

32. For an excellent discussion of Russian efforts to control the Chinese revolution, see Spence, pp. 184-204.

33. Tuchman, *Stilwell,* pp. 92-93.

34. Ibid., pp. 93-95.

35. Kauke, undated letter, 1926; Kauke to Mr. and Mrs. J. Kauke, Sept. 18,

307   Notes

1926, Kauke Papers. I am grateful to Mrs. Kauke for allowing me to examine and quote from her letters written while visiting Ch'ang-sha in 1926.

36. Kauke to "Folks," Aug. 17, 1926, Kauke Papers.

37. Ibid.

38. Interview with Ruth Kauke, May 1973, Los Angeles, Calif.

39. JCV to J.V.A. MacMurray, Jan. 13, 1927, p. 3, Ch'ang-sha Vols.

40. Ibid., p. 2.

41. Ibid., p. 3.

42. Interview with JCV, Feb. 1972.

43. Allen Smith to author, May 22, 1972, pp. 2-4; interview with JCV, Feb. 1972.

44. Chapin to JCV, Dec. 26, 1926; enc. with letter to JCV, Jan. 8, 1927, p. 2, Chiang-sha Vols.

45. Ibid.

46. JCV to Derr, Jan. 5, 1927, p. 2, Ch'ang-sha Vols. JCV to Lewis, Jan. 21, 1927, p. 3, Ch'ang-sha Vols.

47. For information on the crisis at Hankow see J.V.A. MacMurray to the sec. of state, Nov. 29, 1926, *Foreign Relations of the Unites States, Diplomatic Papers: 1926* vol. 1, p. 655 (multivolume works in this series are hereafter cited as *FR* followed by the year and volume number or geographical designation); MacMurray to sec. of state, Dec. 4, 1926, p. 657, *FR 1926,* 1. For Vincent's view and the effect of the crisis on developments in Ch'ang-sha see JCV to MacMurray, Jan. 13, 1927, p. 1; JCV to U.S. consul general, Jan. 11, 1927, p. 1; JCV to Americans in Hunan province, Jan 12, 1927; JCV to MacMurray, Jan. 25, 1927, p. 1; JCV to MacMurray, Feb. 15, 1927, p. 1; all in Ch'ang-sha Vols.

48. For missionary reaction to the withdrawal order see C.N. Dubbs to JCV, Jan 27, 1927, p. 1. Frank A. Keller to JCV, Jan. 14, 1927; Dominic Faugenbacher to JCV, Jan. 27, 1927; all in Ch'ang-sha Vols. See also JCV to Margaret Vincent, Jan. 31, 1927, p. 2, JCV mss.

49. JCV to Lockhart, Feb. 1, 1927, p. 1, Ch'ang-sha Vols.

50. JCV to MacMurray, Feb. 10, 1927, p. 1, Ch'ang-sha Vols.; for discussion of specific problems see JCV to MacMurray, Feb. 15, 1927, *FR 1927,* 2; I.F. Czarnetzki to JCV, Feb. 17, 1927, Ch'ang-sha Vols.; JCV to Tung Wei Chi, Feb. 17, 1927, Ch'ang-sha Vols.

51. JCV to Vanderburgh, Feb. 15, 1927, Ch'ang-sha Vols.; for Vincent's criticism of American missionaries see JCV to Elizabeth Spencer, Dec. 8, 1930, p. 2, JCV mss.

52. JCV to Reverend Agathe Purtill, Mar. 22, 1927, Ch'ang-sha Vols.

53. JCV to MacMurray, Jan. 13, 1927, p. 3; JCV to MacMurray, Feb. 15, 1927, p. 2, Ch'ang-sha Vols.

54. JCV to MacMurray, Jan. 13, 1927, Ch'ang-sha Vols.

55. For a discussion of American China policy during this period, see Borg, *American Policy and the Chinese Revolution,* pp. 47-83, 242-431; Cohen, pp. 100-25; Ferrell, *Kellogg and Stimson,* pp. 64-81; Buhite, *Johnson,* pp. 19-52.

56. JCV to Margaret Smith, Mar. 22, 1928, p. 2, JCV mss.

57. JCV to Margaret Smith, Feb. 13, 1927, JCV mss., ibid.

58. For a brief discussion of the "Nanking Incident" see May, pp. 61-64.

59. MacMurray to sec. of state, Mar. 25, 1927, *FR 1927,* 2, 265.

60. JCV to Margaret Smith, June 14, 1927, p. 1, JCV mss.

61. JCV to J.V.A. MacMurray, May 19, 1927, p. 1, Ch'ang-sha Vols.

62. JCV to Margaret Smith, June 14, 1927, pp. 1-2, JCV mss.

63. Pan's report is quoted in JCV to J.V.A. MacMurray, May 21, 1927, pp. 1-2, Ch'ang-sha Vols.

64. JCV to MacMurray, May 21, 1927, p. 2, Ch'ang-sha Vols.

65. JCV to Margaret Smith, June 14, 1927, p. 4, JCV mss.

66. JCV to Margaret Smith, May 14, 1928, p. 6; May 22, 1928, pp. 5-7; Aug. 29, 1928, p. 4; all in JCV mss. For more information on developments in Hunan province in 1927-28 see May, pp. 72-75.

67. For a discussion of differing American views on Chiang's regime see Cohen, pp. 121-22; Vincent's views can be found in JCV to Margaret Smith, May 22, 1928, pp. 2-3 and June 14, 1927, p. 4, both in JCV mss.

68. Harvey to Johnson, May 28, 1927; "Annual Efficiency Report," Aug. 1, 1927; MacMurray to Wilbur J. Carr, July 8, 1927 all in JCV Personnel File. Yale-in-China later honored Vincent with a special dinner and watch: interview with JCV, July 1971.

69. JCV to Margaret Smith, May 14, 1928, p. 6, JCV mss.

70. Tuchman, *Stilwell,* p. 65.

71. For a history of the student-interpreter program in China see May, pp. 90-114.

72. Stanton, p. 8.

73. Tuchman, *Stilwell,* p. 66; interview with JCV, July 1971; JCV to author, Aug. 16, 1971, p. 1.

74. Samuel Sokobin to author, June 12, 1972, pp. 34-35.

75. The quotes are from memo on student-interpreter life by D.B. Lasseter, Jan. 10, 1921, enc. with C.C. Eberhardt to sec. of state, Apr. 2, 1921, 122.56/57, pp. 1-3, Dept. of State Files.

76. JCV to Margaret Smith, Aug. 8, 1929, p. 1, JCV mss; Elizabeth Spencer to Mrs. J.H. Slagle, Sept. 15, 1930, p. 2, JCV mss; interview with JCV, July 1971.

77. JCV to Margaret Smith, Nov. 11, 1929, pp. 1-2, JCV mss.

78. Elizabeth Spencer to Mrs. J. Slagle, Oct. 3, 1929, p. 2; Elizabeth Spencer to Hugh, Oct. 15, 1929, p. 1, both in JCV mss.

79. Elizabeth Spencer to Hugh?, Oct. 15, 1929, JCV mss.

80. JCV to Margaret Smith, June 10, 1929, JCV mss.

81. JCV to Margaret Smith, Nov. 11, 1929, pp. 1-2, JCV mss.

82. JCV to Smith, Nov. 11, 1929, pp. 1-2, JCV mss.

83. JCV to Smith, Nov. 11, 1929, pp. 1-2, JCV mss; interview with JCV, July 1971; JCV to author, Aug. 16, 1971.

84. Interview with JCV, July 1971.

85. Spencer to Mrs. J. Slagle, Nov. 3, 1929, p. 1, JCV mss.

86. Spencer to Mrs. J. Slagle, Nov. 25, 1929, pp. 5-6; Spencer to Hugh, Oct. 7, 1929, pp. 1-2, both in JCV mss.

87. The quotations are drawn from a series of evening outings in Peking. See Elizabeth Spencer to Mrs. J. Slagle, Nov. 3, 1929, p.1; Spencer to Hugh, Oct. 15, 1929, p. 3; Spencer, "Going To The Theatre in Peking," pp. 1-2, all in JCV mss.

88. Spencer to Mrs. J. Slagle, Nov. 15, 1930, p. 1; see also Spencer to Hugh, Apr. 4, 1930, p. 2; Spencer, diary, Apr. 8, 1930 entry, pp. 25-26, all in JCV mss.

89. See Spencer, "Sun Yat-sen Day"; also diary entries for Mar. 28, 29, 30, 1930, pp. 15-18; JCV to Spencer June 23, June 25, July 1, July 7, July 15, Sept. 28, 1930, all in JCV mss.

90. Spencer to Reynolds, Mar. 8, 1930, pp. 2-3, JCV mss.

91. Spencer to Mrs. J. Slagle, Sept. 15, 1930, p. 3.

92. Interview with JCV, July 1971.

93. Spencer to Mrs. J. Slagle, Oct. 30, 1930, p. 4, 5, pp. 6-9.

94. For information on political developments in Tsinan and Shantung provinces see C.D. Meinhardt to Nelson T. Johnson, Oct. 7, 1930; Johnson, Oct. 31, 1930; Johnson, Dec. 4, 1930, Johnson, Jan. 2, 1931, Feb, 3, 1931, Mar. 5, 1931, all in Tsinan Consular Post Volume #800 (hereafter cited as TCPV #800).

95. JCV to Spencer, n.d., 1930, JCV mss.

96. JCV to Spencer, Jan. 20, 1931, pp. 2-3; see also JCV to Spencer, Dec. 8, 1930, p. 3, both in JCV mss.

97. JCV to Spencer, Dec. 8, 1930, pp. 1-2, JCV mss. For more on Vincent's views on missionaries see JCV to Spencer Dec. 15, 1930, pp. 1-4, JCV mss.

98. JCV to Nelson T. Johnson, Dec. 4, 1930, p. 4, TCPV #800.

99. JCV to Spencer, 1931, p. 3, JCV mss.

100. JCV to Geroge D. Wilder, Dec. 20, 1930, p. 2, TCPV #800. See also JCV to Nelson T. Johnson, Feb. 3, 1931, pp. 5-6 ibid.; JCV to Spencer, n.d., 1931, pp. 1-5, JCV mss.

101. JCV to Spencer, Feb. 1, 1931, p. 3, JCV mss.

102. Elizabeth Vincent to Mrs. J. Slagle, Spr. 12, 1931, pp. 1-3, JCV mss.

103. Elizabeth Vincent to Mrs. J. and John Slagle, Mar. 8, 1931, p. 1, JCV mss.

104. JCV to Margaret Smith, July 1, 1931, pp. 4-5; Elizabeth Vincent to Mrs. J. Slagle, July 14, 1931, p. 3, both in JCV mss. Interview with JCV, July 1971. For information on Manchuria as the flashpoint of Sino-Japanese relations (with special attention to the Wanpaoshan and Nakamura incidents) see JCV to sec. of state, June 15, 1931, pp. 3-6, 893.00 PR Mukden/49; JCV to sec. of state, Aug. 11, 1931, pp. 8-9, 893.00 PR Mukden/51; JCV to sec. of state, Sept. 12, 1931, pp. 2-3, 893.00 PR Mukden/63, all in Dept. of State Files. See also Ogata, pp. 53-59; Crowley, p. 82-121.

105. On the outbreak of the Mukden Incident, see Ferrell, *American Diplomacy in the Great Depression* pp. 123-30; Butow, pp. 34-35; Ogata, pp. 59-64. For the consulate-general's initial report see Andrew G. Lynch to sec. of state, Sept. 20, 1931, 793.94/2216, p. 1, Dept. of State Files.

106. JCV to author, Aug. 17, 1971, pp. 2-5; interview with JCV, July 1971.

107. Memo by JCV, Sept. 26, 1931, pp. 1-4, enc. with M.S. Myers to sec. of state, Sept. 26, 1931, 793.94/2217, Dept. of State Files.

108. Memo by JCV, pp. 5-7, Dept. of State Files.

109. M.S. Myers to sec. of state, Oct. 6, 1931, pp. 2-3, 793.94/2358, Dept. of State Files; Elizabeth Vincent to Mrs. J. Slagle, Oct. 10, 1931, pp. 2-3, JCV mss; JCV to sec. of state, Dec. 6, 1931, p. 1, 793.94/3395, Dept. of State Files; memo, Oct. 15, 1931, pp. 1-2, enc. M.S. Myers to sec. of state, Jan. 7, 1932, 793.94/7496 Dept. of State Files.

110. Elizabeth Vincent to family, Oct. 13, 1931, pp. 2-3, JCV mss. For more on Vincent's reporting on developments in Mukden, see May, pp. 159-63.

111. JCV to Maxwell H. Hamilton, Nov. 9, 1933, pp. 1-7, 800 File; see also JCV to Joseph Grew, Dec. 29, 1933, pp. 3-18, 800 File, both in Dept. of State Files.

112. JCV to Margaret Smith, Aug. 8, 1934, pp. 2-6, JCV mss; see also JCV to Margaret Smith, Aug. 29, 1933, pp. 2-6, ibid; JCV to Joseph Grew, Oct. 27, 1933, pp. 1-2, 800 File, Dept. of State Files; for more information on Vincent's observations of Dairen see May, pp. 163-70.

113. Elizabeth Vincent to family, Sept. 21, 1938, p. 3, JCV mss.

114. Roosevelt's "Quarantine Speech" can be found in Graebner, ed., *Ideas and Diplomacy* pp. 587-90; for an excellent analysis of the speech see Borg, *United States and the Far Eastern Crisis* pp. 369-98.

115. JCV to Hornbeck, July 23, 1938, p. 7; see also JCV to Sumner Welles, Jan. 23, 1949, pp. 6-7, both in JCV mss.

116. JCV to Sumner Welles, pp. 5-6, JCV mss.

117. JCV to Sumner Welles, p. 8; Vincent to Hornbeck, July 23, 1938, pp. 8-9; for additional statements of Vincent's views, see JCV to Hamilton, Oct. 11, 1938; JCV to Hornbeck, Feb. 1, 1939, Mar. 23, 1939, Apr. 7, 1939, Apr. 23, 1939, all in JCV mss.

118. JCV to Sumner Welles, Jan. 20, 1939, p. 5, JCV mss. For views of the "Japanese hands" see, for example, Raymond C. Mackay to Hamilton, Apr. 26, 1939 and Joseph Ballantine to Hamilton, Apr. 24, 1939, enc. JCV to Hornbeck, Apr. 19, 1939, Far Eastern Div. Records, Dept of State Files. For Hamilton's views see memo by the chief of FE, Oct. 10, 1938, *FR 1938*, 4, 62-65; interview with JCV, July 1971. The quote can be found in Chihiro Hosoya, "Miscalculation in Deterrent Policy: Japanese-American Relations, 1938-1941," *Journal of Peace Research* (May 1968), p. 102.

119. Quoted in Heinrichs, *American Ambassador*, p. 272.

120. Elizabeth Vincent to Mrs. J. Slagle, Nov. 16, 1938, p. 2; see also Elizabeth Vincent to Mrs. J. Slagle, July 21, Oct. 22, 1938, both in JCV mss.

121. Elizabeth Vincent to Mrs. J. Slagle, Feb. 3, 1939, p. 1, JCV mss.

122. Elizabeth Vincent to ?, Sept. 3, 1939, p. 3, JCV mss.

123. JCV to Jim ?, Feb. 1, 1940, pp. 1-2, JCV mss. JCV to John Slagle, Mar. 1, 1940, p. 4, JCV mss. JCV to James K. Penfield, Mar. 4, 1940, p. 3, JCV mss.

124. JCV to John Slagle, Mar. 1, 1940; JCV to Margaret Smith, Mar. 14, 1940, p. 3; "Geneva Diary" entires for Sept. 9, 1939, Jan. 7, 1940; JCV to Isidor Lubin, Aug. 24, 1940, pp. 2-3, all in JCV mss.

125. See Dept of State, efficiency reports for Sept. 1932, Oct. 1932, Aug. 1935, Oct. 1935, Aug. 1936, Aug. 1939, Mar. 1, 1951, all in JCV Personnel File.

Chapter 2

1. Sec. of state to Amer. consul general, Shanghai, Feb. 7, 1941, John Carter Vincent File, Hornbeck Papers; interview with JCV, July 1971.

2. JCV to Elizabeth Vincent, letter diary: Feb. 14, 1941-Feb. 20, 1941, JCV mss.

3. JCV to Elizabeth Vincent, letter diary, Feb. 20 entry, JCV mss.

4. The quotations are from a number of letters written on shipboard and in the months that followed: JCV to Elizabeth Vincent, diary entry Feb. 20, 1941; JCV to Elizabeth Vincent, n.d., spring 1941; Apr. 11, 1941; July 12, 1941; July 26, 1941, pp. 2-3, all in JCV mss.

5. For Johnson's view of his successor and important comments on a variety of problems in Sino-American relations (including the KMT-CCP conflict), see Johnson to Hornbeck, Jan. 9, 1941, pp. 1-2; Jan. 16, 1941, pp. 1-2; Feb. 11, 1941, pp. 1-3; Feb. 14, 1941, pp. 1-3; Feb. 25, 1941, pp. 1-2; Mar. 4, 1941, p. 1; Mar. 13, 1941, pp. 1-2; Mar. 20, 1941, pp. 1-2; Apr. 11, 1941, pp. 1-3; Apr. 16, 1941, pp. 1-2; Apr. 25, 1941, pp. 1-2. See also chargé d'affaires to sec. of state, May 16, 1941. For one view of Johnson by a long time associate, see W. R. Peck to Hornbeck, Feb. 2, 1941. All of the above are in the Johnson File #258, Box 262, Hornbeck Papers. For a historian's view of Johnson, see Buhite, *Johnson*.

6. Sec. of state to Amer. consul general, Shanghai, June 3, 1941; Gauss to sec. of state, June 12, 1941, both in JCV File, Hornbeck Papers.

7. JCV to Margaret Smith, n.d., 1941, p. 1, JCV mss. Payne, *Forever China*, p. 13.

8. Mei, p. 349.

9. JCV to Margaret Smith, n.d., 1941, JCV mss.; Mei, p. 350; Payne, *Forever China*, p. 12; Tuchman, *Stilwell*, p. 334; JCV to Elizabeth Vincent, July 17, 1941, p. 1, JCV mss.; memo by FE, May 8, 1942, p. 3, Gauss File, #175, Hornbeck Papers.

10. Mei, p. 439; Atcheson to Hornbeck, Aug. 15, 1943, p. 3, Atcheson file Box #21, Hornbeck Papers.

11. Mei, p. 350; Tuchman, *Stilwell*, pp. 334-35; JCV to Elizabeth Vincent, July 12, 1941, p. 1, JCV mss.

12. JCV to Margaret Smith, n.d., 1941, p. 2; JCV to Elizabeth Vincent, Aug. 7, 1941, p. 1, and Sept. 9, 1941, p. 1; all in JCV mss. See also Gauss to Hull, Sept. 5, 1941, p. 1, Gauss File, Hornbeck Papers.

13. JCV to Margaret Smith, n.d., 1941, p. 2, JCV mss.

14. Peck, p. 63; Payne, pp. 24-25.

15. Gauss to Hornbeck, Nov. 10, 1941, p. 4, Gauss File #175, Hornbeck Papers; JCV to Elizabeth Vincent, July 26, 1941. For more on the problems of obtaining an automobile for the American embassy in Chungking, see Hornbeck to Breckinridge Long, Oct. 28, 1941, Gauss File, Hornbeck Papers.

16. JCV to Margaret Smith, n.d., 1941, p. 2; JCV to Elizabeth Vincent, Aug. 7, 1941, p. 1, both in JCV mss.

17. JCV to Elizabeth Vincent, July 26, 1941, p. 1, JCV mss.

18. For a brief discussion of Magruder's mission, see Tuchman, *Stilwell*, p. 221.

19. For Vincent's view of the activities of one such advisor, Owen Lattimore, see JCV to Elizabeth Vincent, July 17, 1941, p. 1; July 25, 1941, p. 1; Aug. 7, 1941, p. 1, all in JCV mss. For Lattimore's selection as advisor to Chiang, see Currie to Roosevelt, Apr. 29, 1941; Isaiah Bowman to Currie, May 2, 1941; H. E. Yarnell to Currie, May 2, 1941; Roosevelt to Hull, May 19, 1941; Hull to Roosevelt, May 21, 1941, all in PSF China File, Roosevelt Papers.

20. JCV to Currie, Aug. 7, 1941, JCV mss. See also Davies, p. 2; JCV to author, Apr. 28, 1972, p. 1; memo by Hornbeck, May 8, 1942, p. 2, Gauss File #175, Hornbeck Papers.

21. Davies, p. 163.

22. Interview with JCV, Mar. 1972

23. Gauss to Hornbeck, Nov. 10, 1941, p. 4, Gauss File, Hornbeck Papers.

24. Johnson to Hornbeck, Nov. 10, 1941, p. 4, Hornbeck Papers.

25. JCV to Elizabeth Vincent, July 26, 1941, p. 2,; JCV to Currie, Aug. 7, 1941, p. 2, both in JCV mss.

26. JCV to Currie, p. 1.

27. Ibid., p. 2.

28. Ibid.

313   Notes

29. JCV to Elizabeth Vincent, Aug. 7, 1941, p. 2, JCV mss.

30. JCV to Currie, Aug. 4, 1941, p. 1, JCV mss.

31. See JCV to Elizabeth Vincent, July 26, 1941, p. 1, JCV mss.

32. JCV to Currie, Aug. 4, 1941, p. 2. See also Gauss to sec. of state, Aug. 20, 1941; John Carter Vincent, *FR 1941*, 5: 533-36.

33. JCV to Currie, Aug. 4, 1941, p. 4, JCV mss.

34. Quoted in Tuchman, *Stilwell*, pp. 233; Roosevelt to Currie, May 15, 1941, PSF China File, Roosevelt Papers.

35. Quoted in Tuchman, *Stilwell*, p. 234.

36. As Gauss's first secretary and later counselor, it was Vincent's job to prepare telegrams and dispatches for the ambassador. After discussing the subject, Vincent would write the dispatch which Gauss would sign to be forwarded to the State Department.

37. Gauss to sec. of State, Dec. 14, 1941, telegram, pp. 1-2, quoted in statement before State Dept. Loyalty-Security Board, JCV mss.

38. Memo of conversation by 1st sec. of embassy, Dec. 30, 1941, *FR 1942*, China: 429-32. For Gauss's report to the secretary of state on his discussions with Chiang, see Gauss to sec. of state, Dec. 30, 1941, *China White Paper*, pp. 471-72. See also Feis, p. 19.

39. JCV to Elizabeth Vincent, Jan. 30, 1942, p. 1, and Jan. 4, 1942, p. 1, both in JCV mss.

40. See JCV to Vincent, Jr., Jan. 2, 1942; JCV to Sheila Vincent, Jan. 3, 1942, both in JCV mss.

41. JCV to Elizabeth Vincent, Jan. 4, 1942, pp. 1-2, JCV mss.

42. JCV to Elizabeth Vincent, Jan. 10, 1942, p. 4, JCV mss.

43. Ibid., p. 5. See also amb. in China to sec. of state, Jan. 7, 1942, *FR 1942*, China: 192-93.

44. JCV to Elizabeth Vincent, Jan. 10, 1942, p. 6, JCV mss.

45. Ibid., p. 7.

46. Ibid., p. 8; JCV to Elizabeth Vincent, Jan. 13, 1942, p. 2, JCV mss.

47. Gauss to Hull, Jan. 8, 1941, *China White Paper*, p. 476; Feis, p. 19. See also Gauss to Hull, Jan. 17, 1942, *FR 1942*, China: 5; Gauss to Hull, Mar. 6, 1942, *FR 1942*, China: 25-26; Gauss to Hull, Mar. 7, 1942, *FR 1942*, China: 27-28.

48. For the view from Washington see Hornbeck to Hull, Jan. 23, 1942, pp. 1-2, Memo, Dispatch, Correspondence File: Nov. 1941-Feb. 1942, Box 464, Hornbeck Papers. See also Hornbeck memo ("For the Secretary's Conversation with the President"), Jan. 23, 1942; "Proposed Loan to China," Jan. 28, 1942; memo, Jan. 29, 1942, all in Hornbeck papers; see also Hornbeck to Hull, Jan. 10, 1942, *FR 1942*, China: 433-34; *Feis*, p. 20; Hornbeck and Welles, Feb. 16, 1942, *FR 1942*, China: 20-22. For Henry Stimson's view, see Stimson and Bundy, p. 531. For Roosevelt's view see Roosevelt to Marshall, Mar. 8, 1943, p. 1, Naval Aide's Files: China FDR Map Room, Box 165, Roosevelt Papers.

49. JCV to Elizabeth Vincent, July 12, 1941, p.1, JCV mss.

50. Treasury representative Manuel Fox and Claire Booth Luce, wife of the publisher of *Time*, were critical of Gauss and urged his replacement to officers of the State Department in 1942. See memo by Atcheson, May 8, 1942, pp. 3-5, Hornbeck Papers. See also Currie to JCV, Oct. 1, 1942, p. 1, Currie Papers. I am indebted to Dr. Currie for making this letter available to me from his private papers. See also Raymond Clapper, "Error in Judgment," *Washington Daily News*, Sept. 5, 1942, JCV mss.

51. Anonymous to Roosevelt, Oct. 15, 1941, PSF China Folder, Roosevelt Papers. Roosevelt passed these observations along to Hull on Nov. 21, 1941. See Roosevelt to Hull, Nov. 21, 1941, PSF China File, 1-41, Roosevelt Papers. Gauss remained in Chungking as ambassador until Nov. 1944.

52. Quoted in Davies, p. 233.

53. Davies to Hornbeck, Apr. 27, 1942, Davies File, Box 138, Hornbeck Papers.

54. JCV to Elizabeth Vincent, n.d. (probably Apr. 1942), p. 1, JCV mss.

55. JCV to Sheila Vincent, Jan. 3, 1942, pp. 1-2, JCV mss.

56. My discussion of an average day in the life of First Secretary Vincent is drawn from several sources: notations in Vincent's letter-diary for 1942, including entries for Feb. 21, an undated reference of the spring, May 8, Aug. 12, and Aug. 19; as well as interviews with JCV in 1971 and 1972, and an interview with Service, Apr. 1972.

57. JCV to Elizabeth Vincent, Jan. 31, 1942, p. 1, JCV mss.

58. JCV to Elizabeth Vincent, winter 1942, p. 1, JCV mss.

59. JCV to Elizabeth Vincent, Jan. 31, 1942, pp. 1-3, JCV mss.

60. JCV to Elizabeth Vincent, Feb. 21, 1942, p. 3, JCV mss.

61. Elizabeth Vincent to Mrs. J. Slagle, Apr. 11, 1939, p. 3; JCV to Sheila Vincent, Jan. 3, 1942, p. 2; JCV to Elizabeth Vincent, Feb. 12, 1942, p. 1, Feb. 21, 1942, p. 3, and Mar. 31, 1942, p. 2; all in JCV mss.

62. Elizabeth Vincent to JCV, July 2, 1941, p. 1, JCV mss.

63. Elizabeth Vincent to JCV, n.d. (probably Nov. 1941), pp. 1-3, and Mar. 12, 1942, pp. 2-3, both in JCV mss.; memo by John G. Erhardt, Oct. 18, 1941, JCV Personnel File; memo by G. Howland Shaw, Jan. 29, 1942, JCV Personnel File.

64. Feis, pp. 24-34.

65. Quoted in Feis, p. 41. See also, memo by advisor of political relations, May 7, 1942, *FR 1942*, China: 40-41, and memos of May 20, 1942, *FR 1942*, China: 49-51.

66. See memo by chief of FE, *FR 1942*, China: 51-54; also memo of June 17, 1942, *FR 1942*, China: 71-82.

67. Diary entry, May 1942. See also entry for May 11, 1942, both in JCV mss.

68. Diary entry, May 18, 1942, JCV mss.

69. Diary entry, May 13, 1942, JCV mss.

70. Memo of conversation by counselor of embassy in China, May 6, 1942, *FR 1942*, China: 197-98.

71. Diary entry, May 27, 1942, JCV mss. See also, Gauss to Hull, May 28, 1942, *FR 1942*, China: 59.

72. JCV to Elizabeth Vincent, July 12, 1942, p. 2, JCV mss.

73. JCV to Elizabeth Vincent, May 28, 1942, p. 2; see also diary entries for May 29 and June 24, 1942, all in JCV mss.

74. Tuchman, *Stilwell*, p. 303; Feis, pp. 42-44.

75. Tuchman, *Stilwell*, pp. 312-13; Feis, p. 44.

76. JCV to author, Aug. 14, 1971. See also Gauss to Hull, Jan. 17, 1942, *FR 1942*, China: 4-5; Gauss to Hull, Jan. 22, 1942, ibid., p. 8; memo of conversation, Jan. 24, 1942, ibid., pp. 9-10; Gauss to Hull, Feb. 21, 1942, ibid., pp. 24-25; Gauss to Hull, Mar. 7, 1942, ibid., pp. 27-28; Vincent is the author of all of the above. See also memo by counselor of embassy in China, June 28, 1942, ibid., pp. 106, 107; Gauss to Hull, July 9, 1942, ibid., pp. 104-5; memo of conversation by amb., July 11, 1942, ibid., pp. 109-114.

77. JCV to Elizabeth Vincent, July 9, 1942, p. 1, JCV mss.

78. JCV to Elizabeth Vincent, July 7, 1942, p. 1; JCV to Elizabeth Vincent, July 7, 1942 p. 1, JCV mss.

79. Diary entry, July 12, 1942; JCV to Elizabeth Vincent, n.d., p. 1, both in JCV mss.

80. Annalee Jacoby to author, Apr. 28, 1976, pp. 1-2.

81. JCV to Elizabeth Vincent, Sept. 1942, p. 1, JCV mss.

82. The phrase is excerpted from a memo by Maxwell Hamilton quoted in Tuchman, *Stilwell*, p. 322.

83. Memo by counselor of embassy to China to amb., July 22, 1942, *FR 1942*, China: 213-14.

84. Ibid., pp. 213-14.

85. Ibid., p. 226. For a detailed discussion of Vincent's memo, see May, pp. 244-54.

86. See Tuchman, *Stilwell*, pp. 323-24.

87. Quoted in ibid., p. 324.

88. See Roosevelt to Chiang, Aug. 21, 1942, *FR 1942*, China: 140.

89. JCV to Elizabeth Vincent, Sept. 1, 1942, p. 3, JCV mss.

90. JCV to Elizabeth Vincent, Oct. 5, 1942, p. 2, JCV mss.

91. Ibid., p. 3.

92. Ibid.

93. Ibid. See also Davies, pp. 254-55.

94. JCV to Sheila and Vincent, Jr., Oct. 15, 1942, p. 1, JCV mss.

95. JCV to Elizabeth Vincent, Oct. 5, 1942, p. 4, JCV mss.

96. Willkie, p. 141. See also Tuchman, *Stilwell*, pp. 334-35.

97. JCV to Elizabeth Vincent, Oct. 5, 1942, p. 4, JCV mss.

98. Willkie, pp. 145, 135, 118.

99. Tuchman, *Stilwell*, p. 333.

100. JCV to Elizabeth Vincent, Sept. 3, 1942, p. 2, JCV mss.

101. JCV to Elizabeth Vincent, Sept. 6, 1942, p. 1, JCV mss.

102. JCV to Elizabeth Vincent, Nov. 15, 1942, p. 2, JCV mss.

103. JCV to Elizabeth Vincent, n.d. (autumn), 1942, JCV mss.

104. JCV to Elizabeth Vincent, Nov. 24, 1942, p. 1, JCV mss.

105. JCV to Elizabeth Vincent, Dec. 30, 1942, pp. 1-2, JCV mss.

106. Elizabeth Vincent to JCV, Jan. 1943, p. 1, JCV mss.

107. For information on the famine in Honan and its consequences, see Tuchman, *Stilwell*, p. 261 and 234; Gauss to sec. of state, Feb. 15, 1943, *FR 1943*, China: 208-9; JCV to sec. of state, Mar. 30, 1943, *FR 1943*, China: 221; JCV to sec. of state, Apr. 23, 1943, *FR 1943*, China: 224-25. See also White and Jacoby, pp. 166-78, and White, pp. 144-56.

108. JCV to sec. of state, May 8, 1943, *FR 1943*, China: 233. See also Drumright to JCV, May 5, 1943, *FR 1943*, China: 233-36.

109. Memo by 3rd sec. of embassy in China, Jan. 23, 1943, *FR 1943*, China: 195-96.

110. Gauss to sec. of state, Dec. 16, 1942, *FR 1942*, China: 265. Vincent is the author of this dispatch.

111. JCV to sec. of state, May 6, 1943, *FR 1943*, China: 232.

112. Interview with JCV, July 1971.

113. Dept. of State, annual efficiency report, Aug. 1, 1942, JCV Personnel File.

Chapter 3

1. Elizabeth Vincent to JCV, July 2, 1941, pp. 1-3, JCV mss: interview with JCV, July 1971.

2. JCV to Elizabeth Vincent, July 1942, JCV mss.

3. JCV to Elizabeth Vincent, n.d., summer 1942, p. 1, JCV mss.

4. Interview with JCV, Feb. 1942.

5. JCV to Elizabeth Vincent, July 1941, JCV mss.

6. Interview with JCV, Feb. 1942.

7. Laurence Salisbury to author, Apr. 15, 1972, p. 1. Mr. Salisbury was an assistant chief of FE from 1941 to 1944.

8. Service, *Amerasia*, pp. 97-99; Service to author, Dec. 12, 1972, p. 1.

9. Adams to author, Mar. 16, 1972, p. 2. Mr. Adams was a member of FE from 1941 to 1943.

10. Ibid.

11. Edwin Stanton to Conrad Snow, Dec. 22, 1951, JCV mss.

12. Hornbeck to Hull, Jan. 15, 1942, Memo, Dispatch, Correspondence File, Nov. 1941-Feb. 1942, Box 464, Hornbeck Papers.

13. Laurence Salisbury to author, Apr. 15, 1972.

14. Ibid.

15. Ibid.

16. JCV to Shaw, Jan. 17, 1944, JCV Personnel File.

17. My account of the events leading to the removal of Hornbeck is based on a diary kept by Salisbury and on conversations with Vincent and other former officials of FE.

18. Salisbury diary, Salisbury papers.

19. Ibid.

20. Salisbury to author, Apr. 15, 1972.

21. See Hornbeck testimony in "Transcript of Proceedings," State Dept. Loyalty-Security Board, in the matter of John Carter Vincent, Dec. 17, 1951, pp. A4-A6, JCV mss.

22. For Hornbeck's view of the effect of his removal on American Far Eastern policy, see Hornbeck's testimony in "Transcript of Proceedings," State Dept. Loyalty-Security Board, pp. A20-A23, JCV mss. See also Hornbeck to Rusk, June 7, 1950, Rusk File, Box 368, Hornbeck Papers, and Hornbeck to Eugene Dooman with enc. Mar. 26, 1964, Dooman File, Box 150, Hornbeck papers.

23. Interview with JCV, Feb. 1972.

24. Gauss to sec. of state, Feb. 3, 1944, *FR 1944*, 6:322.

25. For embassy reports on the "Young General's Plot," see Gauss to sec. of state, Jan. 6, 1944, *FR 1944*, China: 302-03; Gauss to sec. of state, Feb. 3, 1944, ibid., pp. 319-26; Gauss to sec. of state, Feb. 15, 1944, ibid., pp. 334-36.

26. For embassy reports on Chinese geographical disintegration, see Gauss to sec. of state, Nov. 18, 1943, *FR 1943*, China: 380-82; Gauss to sec. of state, Nov. 27, 1943, ibid., p. 385; Gauss to sec. of state, Dec. 22, 1943, ibid., pp. 390-91; Gauss to sec. of state, Jan. 15, 1944, *FR 1944*, 6:305-7; Gauss to sec. of state, Feb. 1, 1944, *FR 1944*, 6:318.

27. Madame Sun's remarks can be found in Gauss to sec. of state, Feb. 16, 1944, *FR 1944*, 6:341-42; Gauss to sec. of state, Feb. 23, 1944, ibid., pp. 351-52. Sun Fo's

comments can be found *FR 1944*, 6:385-87. See also Gauss to sec. of state, Apr. 3, 1944, ibid., pp. 392-93; Gauss to sec. of state, May 4, ibid., p. 410.

28. Gauss to sec. of state, June 8, 1944, *FR 1944*, 6:449.

29. For details on ICHIGO, see Romanus and Sunderland, *Stilwell's Command Problems*, pp. 316-20.

30. Gauss to sec. of state, June 15, 1944, *FR 1944*, 6:101.

31. JCV to Elizabeth Vincent, n.d., 1942, p. 1, JCV mss.

32. JCV to Elizabeth Spencer, n.d., 1930, JCV mss.

33. Interview with JCV, Mar. 1972.

34. Memo from under sec. of state to dir. of FE, May 24, 1944, *FR 1944*, 6:230; Wallace, "My Mission to China," p. 2. See also draft of "Mission to China," File 300, 299N, Wallace Papers; memo of conversation by the deputy dir. of FE, Mar. 19, *FR 1944*, 6:217.

35. Memo by under sec. of state, May 24, 1944, *FR 1944*, 6:230.

36. Wallace to Kohlberg, Oct. 4, 1950, p. 2, File #251, 069M, Wallace Papers; Wallace to McCarran, Aug. 5, 1952, p. 2, File #350, 173M, Wallace Papers.

37. Feis, p. 145. See also Tang, p. 162.

38. For Chinese press reaction to the announcement of Wallace's impending visit, see *Ta Kung Pao*, Apr. 13, 1944, *National Herald*, May 28, 1944; *Hsin Chung Kuo Erh Pao (New China Daily News)*, May 23, 1944; *Ta Kung Pao*, May 22, 1944; *China Times*, May 22, 1944; *Sin Hua Erh Pao*, May 22, 1944; *Sao Tang Pao*, Apr. 15, 1944; all in Files #30557M through #30557P, Wallace Papers.

39. Schapsmeir and Schapsmeir, pp. 86-87. See also Rosenman, pp. 483-45.

40. U.S. Senate, Committee on the Judiciary, Subcommittee to Investigate the Administration of the Internal Security Act and Other Internal Security Laws, *Morgenthau Diary: China*, vol. 2, p. 1103 (hereafter cited as *Morgenthau Diary*, 1 or 2).

41. Interview with JCV, July 1971.

42. Interview with JCV, July 1971.

43. Memo of conversation by deputy dir. of FE, Mar. 14, 1944, *FR 1944*, China: 218.

44. Wallace to Hull, Mar. 24, 1944, File #30429M, Wallace Papers. See also, *FR 1944*, 6:219. For Hull's reply, see Hull to Wallace, Mar. 29, 1944, File #30417M, Wallace Papers; see also *FR 1944*, 6:219-20.

45. Wallace to Hull, Apr. 25, 1944, File #30621N, Wallace Papers. See also *FR 1944*, 6:226; Wallace to Hull, Apr. 29, 1944, File #30627M, Wallace Papers; *FR 1944*, 6:226, n. 28.

46. Interview with JCV, July 1971.

47. *IPR Hearings*, pp. 1804-5.

48. Memo on Chiang by John Davies, Jr., Dec. 31, 1943, p. 1, File #30127R,

Wallace papers. An expurgated version of this memo can be found in *FR 1943*, China: 398-99.

49. Report on his trip from Peiping to Chungking by G.M. Hall, Mar. 4, 1943, Wallace Papers.

50. John Davies, Jr., "The American Stakes in Chinese Unity," p. 3, File #30127P, Wallace Papers; see also *FR 1943*, China: 258-66.

51. Interview with JCV, Feb. 1972.

52. Davies, "The American Stakes in Chinese Unity," pp. 6-7, File #30127P, Wallace Papers.

53. Interview with JCV, Mar. 1971; memo by deputy dir. of FE to under sec. of state, Feb. 15,1944, *FR 1944*, 6:330-31; memo of conversation by chief of Chinese Affairs Div., May 8, 1944, ibid., p. 413.

54. JCV to sec. of state, May 6, 1943, *FR 1943*, China: 231. See also memo by John Davies, Jr. to Currie, Aug. 6, 1942, p. 2, Davies File #138, Hornbeck Papers.

55. Memo by 2nd sec. of embassy in China, Jan 15, 1944, *FR 1944*, 6:307-8. For Stettinius' reaction to Davies's memo on the observer mission, see Stettinius to Ballantine, Feb. 17, 1944, ibid., p. 331, n. 51a. For Gauss's view, see Gauss to sec. of state, Feb. 16, 1944, ibid., pp. 345-46.

56. Sec. of state to sec. of war, Apr. 4, 1944, *FR 1944*, 6:393-94; memo by sec. of state to Roosevelt, Apr. 4, 1944, ibid., p. 394; sec. of war to sec. of state, Apr. 8, 1944, ibid., p. 395.

57. Roosevelt's attempts to win Chiang's permission for the observer mission can be found in the following communications: Roosevelt to Chiang, Feb. 9, 1944, *FR 1944*, 6:329; Chiang to Roosevelt, Feb. 22, 1944, ibid., pp. 348-49; Roosevelt to Chiang, Mar. 1, 1944, ibid., p. 367. See also, Davies, pp. 303-4; Romanus and Sunderland, *Stilwell's Command Problems*, p. 303; Feis, pp. 157-59.

58. Interview with JCV, Mar. 1972.

59. Interview with JCV, Mar. 1972.

60. Wallace, *Soviet-Asia Mission*, p. 25.

61. *Time*, July 3, 1944, p. 19.

62. Interview with JCV, Mar. 1972.

63. Madame Chiang to Wallace, Apr. 15, 1944, Trip File, Wallace Papers; interview with JCV, July 1971.

64. Wallace diary, June 20, 1944 entry, Wallace Papers; see also Blum, p. 350. Descriptions in the original Wallace diary are somewhat more explicit than those in Blum.

65. Wallace diary, June 20, 1944 entry, Wallace Papers.

66. For a full report of the Wallace-Chiang conversations see John Carter Vincent, "Summary Notes of Conversations between Vice President Henry A. Wallace and President Chiang Kai-shek, June 21-24, 1944," in *China White Paper*, pp. 549-59 (hereafter cited "Summary Notes"); see also May, pp. 311-29.

67. Vincent, "Summary Notes," *China White Paper*, p. 551; see p. 552 for references to Stilwell.

68. Ibid., p. 554.

69. Interview with JCV, Mar. 1972.

70. Wallace diary, June 24, 1944 entry, Wallace Papers; see also Blum, p. 352.

71. Blum, p. 555. See also May, p. 322.

72. Interview with John S. Service, Apr. 1972. For Service's view of the role of the observer mission see memo for the vice-pres., File 31363P, Wallace Papers (the memo is unsigned but Service acknowledges that he is the author—Service to author, Dec. 12, 1972). On the telegram from Roosevelt, see Wallace diary, June 24, 1944 entry, Wallace Papers; see also Blum, p. 352.

73. Vincent, "Summary Notes," *China White Paper*, p. 557; memo by 2nd sec. of embassy in China, June 23, 1944, *FR 1944*, 6: 461, 462.

74. Quoted in Blum, p. 352.

75. Ibid.

76. Vincent, "Summary Notes," *China White Paper*, pp. 558-59; see also, *IPR Hearings*, p. 1362.

77. Vincent, "Summary Notes," *China White Paper*, p. 599.

78. Ibid.

79. *IPR Hearings*, pp. 1368-69.

80. Wallace diary, June 23, 1944 entry, Wallace Papers.

81. Ibid., June 26, 1944 entry.

82. Alsop, "Budenz," p. 4; see also "The Strange Case of Louis Budenz—First Draft," Atlantic File, Box 35, Joseph Alsop Papers; *IPR Hearings*, p. 1363.

83. Alsop, "Budenz."

84. *IPR Hearings*, pp. 1346-47.

85. Ibid., p. 1445.

86. Ibid.

87. Ibid.

88. Alsop, "Budenz," p. 6.

89. *IPR Hearings*, pp. 1365, 1447-48.

90. Ibid., p. 1448.

91. Ibid., pp. 1365, 1448.

92. Wallace to pres. in "The Officer in Charge at New Delhi to the Secretary of State," June 28, 1944, *FR 1944*, 6:235.

93. Ibid., pp. 236-37.

94. "Summary Report of Vice President Wallace's Visit to China," July 10, 1944, enc. Wallace to Truman, Sept. 19, 1951, in Truman to Vice-Pres. Alban Barkley, Sept. 22, 1941, p. 4, Lloyd Papers. For an expurgated version of this report, see *FR 1944*, 6:240-44. For more on Wallace's "new coalition," see *IPR Hearings*, pp. 1367-68, and Wallace to McCarran, p. 3, Wallace Papers.

95. "Summary Report," enc. Wallace to Truman, Sept. 19, 1951, Lloyd Papers, p. 4.

96. Ibid.

97. Schapsmeir and Schapsmeir, p. 97. For statistics on miles traveled during the Wallace mission, see Wallace, *Soviet-Asia Mission*, "Itinerary."

98. Cochran, pp. 1-21. See also Margaret Truman, pp. 168-91.

99. Interview with JCV, July 1971.

100. JCV to Hull, Aug. 28, 1944, p. 2, PSF China File, 1942-1945, Roosevelt Papers. Emphasis in original; for more on Vincent's view of Chinese politics, see memo for Roosevelt, Aug. 15, 1944, *FR 1944*, 6:141-43; memo for pres., Aug. 28, 1944, *FR 1944*, 6:524-25; sec. of state to amb. in China, Sept. 9, 1944, *FR 1944*, 6:567-69; memo by chief of Chinese Affairs Div., Sept. 19, 1944, *FR 1944*, 6:581; memo by sec. of state to Roosevelt, Sept. 25, 1944, *FR 1944*, 6:594 (Vincent is the author of this memo); memo for pres., Oct. 25, 1944, *FR 1944*, 6:181-82. For Service's report, see Service, *Amerasia*, pp. 200-207.

101. Quoted in Roosevelt, p. 205. Roosevelt's animosity toward career diplomats can be found in William L. Langer and S. Everett Gleason, *The Challenge to Isolation: The World Crisis and American Foreign Policy* (N.Y.: Harper & Row, 1952), p. 8; Welles, p. 216; Sherwood, pp. 756-57; Rosenman, pp. 9, 165, 207. For an example of one liberal journalist's view of the State Department, see Bendiner.

102. My selection of eighteen prominent members of the foreign service in China was determined by the list of drafting officers whose reports were thought important enough by the State Department Historical Office to be included in the *Foreign Relations* volumes on China. The State Department's *Biographic Register*, 1943, provided the statistics on place of birth and educational background.

103. Of the eighteen selected for examination, only two were born in the East; four in the South, four in the Midwest, and three in the Far West. Five were born outside the United States. None attended an Eastern university as an undergraduate.

104. Freidel, *Apprenticeship*, p. 334.

105. Ibid., p. 34.

106. Tuchman, *Stilwell*, p. 220.

107. Quoted in ibid., p. 320.

108. Quoted in Campbell, p. 45.

109. Roosevelt to Chiang, Aug. 19, 1944, p. 2, Roosevelt Papers.

110. Interview with JCV, July 1971.

111. Buhite, *Hurley*, p. 148.

112. Cochran, p. 297.

113. Interview with JCV, July 1971.

Chapter 4

1. Roosevelt, pp. 193, 204.

2. Tuchman, *Stilwell*, p. 612. See also memo by under sec. of state, Aug. 3, 1944, *FR 1944*, 6: 247; Buhite, *Hurley*, pp. 148-49.

3. Buhite, *Hurley*, p. 149. See also memo by under sec. of state, Aug. 9, 1944, *FR 1944*, 6: 247-48.

4. Smith, p. 49. See also Hurley to Truman, May 20, 1945, *FR 1945*, 7: 110. Roosevelt to Hurley, Aug. 17, 1944, Roosevelt Papers.

5. Buhite, *Hurley*, p. 152; White and Jacoby, p. 219; Tuchman, *Stilwell*, p. 616; Hurley to Roosevelt and Marshall, Sept. 7, 1944, *FR 1944*, 6: 154. See also, Smith, p. 56.

6. Roosevelt to Marshall, Mar. 8, 1943, p. 1. For Roosevelt's view of Stilwell, see Roosevelt to Marshall, Oct. 3, 1942, PSF China File, Roosevelt Papers. Hurley to Roosevelt, Oct. 10, 1944, *FR 1944*, 6: 170. For details on Stilwell's removal from China-Burma-India, see Tuchman, *Stilwell*, pp. 617-50.

7. Interview with Gauss, *China Tangle* File, Box 10, Feis Papers.

8. Smith, p. 75.

9. For a discussion of Hurley's negotiations, see amb. in China, Jan. 31, 1945, *FR 1945*, 7: 193.

10. Barrett, pp. 56-57.

11. Ibid., p. 57.

12. Memo of conversation, Nov. 8, 1944, *FR 1944*, 6: 680; Barrett, pp. 62-63. See also "Revised Draft by the Chinese Communist Party Representative," *FR 1944*, 6: 687-88.

13. Buhite, *Hurley*, p. 171; amb. in China, Jan. 31, 1945, *FR 1945*, 7: 195; "General Hurley's message to Secretary Morgenthau," enc. #1, Harry White to Morgenthau, Dec. 8, 1944, vol. 801, p. 263, Morgenthau Papers.

14. Roosevelt to Hurley, Nov. 17, 1944, *FR 1944*, 6: 700.

15. Hurley to Roosevelt, Dec. 14, 1944, Map Room, Box 20, Folders 4-5, Roosevelt Papers.

16. For the Nationalist proposals, see 2nd counterdraft by Chinese gov. representative, n.d., *FR 1944*, 6: 703-4, and 3rd counterdraft, n.d., *FR 1944*, 6: 706-7. These documents were given to Hurley by T.V. Soong on Nov. 17 and 20, respectively.

17. Barrett, p. 70; Barrett to Wedemeyer, Dec. 19, 1944, *Fr 1944*, 6: 728-31; Chou En-lai to appointed amb. Dec. 16, 1944, *FR 1944*, 6: 739.

18. Adler to White, Feb. 12, 1945, vol. 829-II, pp. 331, 333, Morgenthau Papers.

19. Harold Isaacs, "The Situation in China Since Stilwell's Recall," Dec. 22, 1944, p. 3, enc. in Currie to Roosevelt, Jan. 17, 1945, PSF China File, Roosevelt Papers.

20. Jacoby to author, Apr. 28, 1976, p. 3.

21. Appointed amb. in China to sec. of state, Dec. 24, 1944, *FR 1944*, 6: 745-48.

22. Memo by chief of the Chinese Affairs Div., Dec. 26, 1944, *FR 1944*, 6: 750.

23. Ibid., pp. 750-51.

24. Ibid., p. 750. See also memo by chief of Chinese Affairs Div., Jan. 2, 1945, *FR 1945*, 7: 153.

25. Memo by sec. of state to Roosevelt, Jan 4, 1945, *FR 1945*, 7: 154. Vincent is the author of this memo.

26. For a detailed discussion of Service's reportage, see May, pp. 382-92.

27. John S. Service, "First Informal Impressions of the North Shensi Communist Base," July 28, 1944, *FR 1944*, 6: 517-20.

28. U.S. Congress, Senate, Committee on Foreign Relations, *The Evolution of U.S. Policy Toward Mainland China*, 92nd Cong., 1st sess., 1 pt, 1971, p. 11 (hereafter cited as *Evolution of U.S. Policy*).

29. Memo of conversation with Mao, Aug. 25, 1944, *FR 1944*, 6: 607, 608; report of 2nd sec. of embassy in China, Sept. 18, 1944, ibid., pp. 576-77; *Evolution of U.S. Policy*, p. 11.

30. John S. Service, "Desirability of American Military Aid to the Chinese Communist Armies," Aug. 29, 1944, *FR 1944*, 6: 618-19.

31. John S. Service, "The Need of an American Policy Toward the Problems Created by the Rise of the Chinese Communist Party," Sept. 3, 1944, *FR 1944*, 6: 616-17.

32. Memo of conversation by 2nd sec. of embassy in China, July 27, 1944, *FR 1944*, 6: 52 2.

33. Interview with John Service, Apr. 17, 1972.

34. For Gauss's views, see amb. in China to sec of state, Aug. 29, 1944, *FR 1944*, 6: 526. See also Gauss to sec. of state, Sept. 1, 1944, ibid., p. 534; Gauss to sec. of state, Sept. 28, 1944, ibid., p. 601.

35. Gauss had first suggested the creation of a military council in July (see Gauss to sec. of state, July 4, 1944, *FR 1944*, 6: 116-17 and also July 12, 1944, ibid., p. 215). The concept appealed to Vincent and others in FE and a telegram was drafted instructing Gauss to discuss the subject with Chiang (see sec. of state to Gauss, July 8, 1944, ibid., p. 120 and Sept. 9, 1944, ibid., pp. 567-68). But Chiang "did not appear more than politely responsive to the suggestion" (Gauss to Hull, Sept. 4, 1944, ibid., pp. 567-68 and Sept. 16, 1944, ibid., pp. 573-74). For Service's view of this proposal, see Service, *Amerasia*, pp. 67-73.

36. Amb. in China to sec. of state, Sept. 28, 1944, *FR 1944*, 6: 601-2.

37. For a candid statement of this view, see Service, "The Need for Greater Realism in Our Relations with Chiang Kai-shek," Oct. 10, 1944, *FR 1944*, 6: 707-10. See also, Service, *Amerasia,* pp. 712-14.

38. Davies, pp. 344-64.

39. Interview with JCV, Mar. 1972.

40. JCV to Elizabeth Vincent, Feb. 18, 1942, p. 1, JCV mss.

41. JCV to Elizabeth Vincent, Oct. 5, 1942, p. 2, JCV mss.

42. Interview with JCV, Mar. 1972.

43. "Address Before the Foreign Policy Association," Dec. 13, 1944, p. 10, JCV mss.

44. JCV to Elizabeth Vincent, n.d., Feb. 1941, p. 1, JCV mss.

45. Nelson T. Johnson testimony, "Transcript of Proceedings" in Vincent case, Loyalty-Security Board; pp. 79-85, JCV mss.

46. White, p. 73.

47. Memo by JCV on Anglo-American-Soviet policy to China, Jan. 11, 1945, p. 2, 893.00/1-1145, Dept. of State Files; memo on American policy toward China, Mar. 2, 1945 (written in collaboration with Everett Drumright and Edwin Stanton), *FR 1945,* 7:251; memo by the chief of the Chinese Affairs Div., Jan. 29, 1945, *FR 1945,* 7:38.

48. Roosevelt to Leahy, Dec. 8, 1944, classified State Department messages to and from, Map Room, Box 20, Folders 4, 5, Roosevelt Papers.

49. Hurley to Roosevelt, Feb. 8, 1945, *Foreign Relations of United States: The Conferences at Malta and Yalta* (Wash., D.C. 1955), p. 960.

50. Roosevelt to Leahy, Dec. 8, 1944, Map Room, Box 20, Folders 4, 5, Roosevelt Papers.

51. For a discussion of Hurley's activities at this time, see Buhite, *Hurley,* pp. 184-87.

52. Adler to White, Feb. 12, 1945, vol. 829-II, p. 331, 333, Morgenthau Papers.

53. Chargé in China to sec. of state, Feb. 24, 1944, *FR 1945,* 6:238-39.

54. Chargé in China to sec. of state, Feb. 26, 1945, *FR 1945,* 6:239-40.

55. Buhite, *Hurley,* p. 191; Davies, pp. 385-88; Wedemeyer, pp. 318-19.

56. Service to sec. of state, Dec. 8, 1945, *FR 1945,* 7:737.

57. White and Jacoby, p. 247. See also Smith, p. 123.

58. Buhite, *Hurley,* pp. 189-90.

59. Acting political advisor in Japan to sec. of state, Dec. 8, 1945, *FR 1945,* 7:733.

60. Adler to White, Feb. 12, 1945, vol. 829-II, p. 331, Morgenthau Papers.

61. Memo by chief of Chinese Affairs Div., Mar. 1, 1945, *FR 1945*, 7:248.

62. Ibid.

63. For an earlier and different statement of this view, see memo by chief of Chinese Affairs Div., Jan. 29, 1945, *FR 1945*, 7:38, and "American Policy with Respect to China," ibid., p. 252.

64. *Evolution of U.S. Policy*, p. 18.

65. Adler to White, Fed. 25, 1945, *Morgenthau Diary*, 2:1422.

66. Memo by John Service and Raymond Ludden to commanding general, U.S. Forces, China theater, Feb. 14, 1945, *FR 1945* 7:216-18. For a discussion of this memo, see Service, *Amerasia*, pp. 186-87.

67. Service, *Amerasia*, p. 188; U.S. Senate, Subcommittee of the Committee on Foreign Relations, *State Department Loyalty Investigation, Hearings*, 82st Cong., 2nd sess., 3 pts., p. 1974 (hereafter cited as *State Dept. Loyalty Investigation*).

68. *Evolution of U.S. Policy*, pp. 1-7.

69. Chargé in China to sec. of state, Feb. 28, 1945, *FR 1945*, 7:246.

70. *State Dept. Loyalty Investigation*, p. 1974; Service, *Amerasia*, pp. 188, 112, and 113, n. 30.

71. Adler to White, Feb. 25, 1945, *Morgenthau Diary*, 2:1422.

72. *Evolution of U.S. Policy*, p. 18.

73. Memo by chief of Chinese Affairs Div., Mar. 1, 1945, *FR 1945*, 7:248-49; interview with JCV, July 1971.

74. Memo by acting sec. of state to Roosevelt, Mar. 2, 1945, *FR 1945*, 7:254. Vincent is the author of this memo.

75. Ibid. See also memo in PSF China File 1942-1945, Roosevelt Papers. The aide's notation is written in pencil on p. 1 of the memo.

76. Smith, p. 159.

77. Memo by dir. of FE, Mar. 6, 1945, *FR 1945*, 7:263. For Atcheson's view of Hurley's accusations, see Atcheson to sec. of state, Dec. 8, 1945, ibid., pp. 732-33.

78. Memo by dir. of FE, Mar. 6, 1945, *FR 1945*, 7:263.

79. Smith, p. 165.

80. For the effect of the Yalta Agreement on Sino-American relations, see Buhite, *Hurley*, p. 187; Service, *Amerasia*, pp. 114-16; *Evolution of U.S. Policy*, pp. 33-34; Tuchman, "If Mao Had Come to Washington," p. 55.

81. Hurley's later explanation was that Roosevelt sent him to Europe to revise the Yalta Agreement (see Hurley testimony, U.S. Senate, Committee on Armed Services and the Committee on Foreign Relations, *Military Situation in the Far East*, 82nd Cong., 1st sess., 5 pts, pp. 2883-93 (hereafter cited as *Military Situation*). Hurley's testimony does not coincide with his position as reflected in more reliable contemporaneous documents. See, for example, amb. in China to sec. of state, Apr. 14, 1945, *FR 1945*, 7:330; Feis, p. 280, n. 7.

82. Service, *Amerasia,* p. 91.

83. Tuchman, "If Mao Had Come to Washington," p. 57, n. 3.

84. Interview with JCV, July 1971.

85. The two were Walter Robertson (later assistant secretary of state for the Far East under President Eisenhower) and Ellis O. Briggs, who was to have a distinguished career in the Foreign Service.

86. Service, *Amerasia,* pp. 90-93.

87. Tuchman, "If Mao Had Come to Washington," p. 58.

88. Roosevelt, pp. 143, 53.

89. Tuchman, *Stilwell,* p. 513-14; Roosevelt, pp. 153-54, 163, 164; Snow, *Journey to the Beginning,* p. 347.

90. Romanus and Sunderland, *Time Runs Out,* p. 338, n. 14.

91. Gauss interview, *China Tangle* File, Box 10, Feis Papers.

92. Ulam, pp. 88-90.

Chapter 5

1. Smith to JCV, Sept. 24, 1945, pp. 7-8, JCV mss.

2. Quoted in Byrnes, p. 321.

3. JCV to Elizabeth Vincent, Feb. 20, 1941.

4. Herbert Feis interview with Acheson, Truman Lib. See also Feis, p. 351.

5. Directive by Truman to the supreme commander for the Allied powers in Japan, Aug. 15, 1945, *FR 1945,* 7:530-31.

6. Truman, *Year of Decisions,* pp. 447-48.

7. Ibid., p. 447.

8. Wilson, pp. 33-34.

9. Joint Chiefs of Staff to commanding gen., United Forces, China theater, Sept. 18, 1945, *FR 1945,* 7:565.

10. Wilson, p. 34.

11. Chargé in China to sec. of state, Oct. 2, 1945, *FR 1945,* 7:573.

12. Memo by dir. of FE to under sec. of state, Sept. 20, 1945, *FR 1945,* 7:566-67.

13. Memo by dir. of FE to under sec. of state, Sept. 27, 1945, *FR 1945,* 7:570-71.

14. Memo by under sec. of state to dir. of FE, Sept. 28, 1945 *FR 1945,* 7:571.

15. Report by Joint Chiefs of Staff, Oct. 22, 1945, *FR 1945,* 7:593-94; memo by

dir. of FE, Nov. 12, 1945, ibid., p. 615; report by Joint Chiefs of Staff, Oct. 22, 1945, ibid., p. 598.

16. Memo by dir. of FE to sec. of state, Sept. 28, 1945, *FR 1945*, 7:616-17.

17. Ibid., p. 617.

18. Wilson, p. 35.

19. Wedemeyer, p. 359. See also Frank and Shaw, p. 573.

20. Commanding gen., U.S. Forces, China theater, to chief of staff, U.S. Army, Nov. 20, 1945, *FR 1945*, 7:653. For an interesting portrait of Wedemeyer, see Spence, pp. 265-78.

21. Millis and Duffield, p. 106.

22. Minutes of meeting of secs. of state, war, and navy, Nov. 6, 1945, *FR 1945*, 7:606-7.

23. Millis and Duffield, p. 106.

24. Minutes of meeting of secs. of state, war, and navy, Nov. 20, 1945, *FR 1945*, 7:646.

25. Millis and Duffield, p. 112.

26. Quoted in Martin Weil, *A Pretty Good Club: The Founding Fathers of the Foreign Service* (N. Y.: Norton, 1978), pp. 222-23.

27. Interview with JCV, July 1971.

28. For Vincent's view of Truman, see Blum, p. 525.

29. Memo by chief of Chinese Affairs Div. to sec. of state, Feb. 8, 1945, *FR 1945*, 7:855.

30. Frank and Shaw, p. 572.

31. JCV to Acheson, Nov. 15, 1945, pp. 1-2, 893.00/11-1545, Dept. of State Files.

32. JCV to Byrnes, Nov. 6, 1950, p. 1, JCV mss.

33. See, for example, U.S., Congress, *Congressional Record* (hereafter cited as CR), 79th Cong., 2nd sess., Vol. 91, pt. 8, pp. 11007, 11156. For the views of individual congressmen, see Congressman Hugh DeLacy to Acheson, Oct. 3, 1945, 740.00 119 DW/10-345, Dept. of State Files. For Congressman Michael Mansfield's view, see JCV to Acheson, Oct. 16, 1945, 740.0019 PW/10-1645, Dept. of State Files.

34. Acheson, p. 194. See also "Marshall Directive," p. 1, JCV mss.

35. Interview with JCV, July 1971.

36. JCV to Stettinius, Oct. 6, 1944, 003.1193/10-644, Dept. of State Files.

37. JCV, "Our Far Eastern Policies in Relation to Our Overall National Objectives," Oct. 12, 1946, pp. 6-9, JCV mss.

38. Memo by dir. of FE on U.S. military position in China, Nov. 19, 1945, *FR*

1945, 7:642-43; JCV to Acheson and Byrnes, Nov. 25, 1945, FW 893.00/11-2445, Dept. of State Files. For a similar view expressed by David E. Barbey, see chargé in China to sec. of state, Nov. 24, 1945, *FR 1945*, 7:668-69.

39. Acheson, p. 195. See also minutes of meeting of secs. of state, war, and navy, Nov. 27, 1945, *FR 1945*, 7:668-69.

40. Feis, p. 414, n. 4.

41. Acheson, pp. 195-96.

42. Millis and Duffield, pp. 98-99. See also Buhite, *Hurley*, pp. 211-41.

43. Amb. in China to sec. of state, Sept. 11, 1945, *FR 1945*, 7:557.

44. Hurley to Truman, Nov. 26, 1945, p. 2, Official File, Truman Papers. See also, amb. in China to Truman, Nov. 26, 1945, *FR 1945*, 7:722-26 and *China White Paper*, vol. 2, pp. 581-84.

45. Millis and Duffield, p. 113. For contemporary reactions to Hurley's resignation, see *Time*, Dec. 10, 1945, p. 18; *Newsweek*, Dec. 10, 1945, p. 34; Maxwell Stewart, "Exit Pat Hurley," *Nation*, Dec. 8, 1945. For an historian's analysis, see Buhite, *Hurley*, pp. 270-72. Truman's remark is found in Blum, p. 519.

46. Blum, pp. 520-21.

47. Anderson and Viorst, p. 79.

48. Truman, *Years of Trial*, pp. 66-67. See also the oral history interview with Edwin Locke, Jr., p. 35, Truman Lib.

49. Memo by dir. of FE, Nov. 28, 1945, *FR 1945*, 7:745-47.

50. Memo by Marshall to William Leahy, Nov. 30, 1945, *FR 1945*, 7: 474-78; Acheson, p. 198.

51. "U.S. Policy Toward China," enc. in Marshall to William Leahy, Nov. 30, 1945, *FR 1945*, 7: 749-51; Vincent's insertion can be found in an undated State Department memo on China policy, *FR 1945*, 7: 756, first paragraph. See also, Feis, p. 414, n. 4, and memo by sec. of state for War Dept., *FR 1945*, 7: 760-61.

52. Memo by Marshall to sec. of state, Dec. 10, 1945, *FR 1945*, 7: 766; Memo by Hull to Marshall, Dec. 8, 1945, *FR 1945*, 7: 758-59.

53 Memo of conversation by Hull, Dec. 10, 1945, *FR 1945*, 7: 762. See also memo of conversation by Marshall, Dec. 11, 1945, *FR 1945*, 7: 767.

54. Memo of conversation by Marshall, Dec. 11, 1945, *FR 1945*, 7: 767.

55. Memo by dir. of FE to sec. of state, Dec. 9, 1945, *FR 1945*, 7:760.

56. Memo of conversation by Marshall, Dec. 11, 1945, *FR 1945*, 7: 768. See also memo of conversation by Marshall, Dec. 14, 1945, *FR 1945*, 7: 770.

57. Marshall to William Leahy, Nov. 30, 1945, *FR 1945*, 7: 748.

58. Truman to Wallace, Dec., 18, 1945, p. 2, Official File, Truman Papers.

59. Acheson, pp. 199-200.

60. Memo by dir. of FE to sec. of state, Dec. 9, 1945, *FR 1945*, 7: 759.

61. *Time,* Dec. 26, 1945, p. 26.

62. For a discussion of Marshall's first months in China, see Melby, pp. 62-133; Varg. pp. 238-52. Marshall's activities can be followed on an almost daily basis in *FR 1946,9.*

63. Payne, *Marshall,* p. 270.

64. For these incidents, see *China White Paper,* pp. 143-44; Melby, pp. 110, 115, 116, 117.

65. Melby, p. 123.

66. Minutes of meeting between Marshall and Chou En-lai, Apr. 23, 1946, *FR 1946,* 9: 791.

67. Acheson, p. 205.

68. Kolko and Kolko, p. 267.

69. Marshall to Truman, May 22, 1946, *FR 1946,* 9: 882.

70. Tang, p. 420. See also, Melby, pp. 154-55.

71. Press release issued by Chiang Kai-shek, June 6, 1946, *FR 1946,* 9: 982. See also Marshall to Truman, June 6, 1946, ibid., p. 983.

72. Melby, p. 164; Acheson, p. 275.

73. For criticism of Marshall's activities by the Chinese, see minutes of meeting between Marshall and Chou En-lai, June 3, 1946, *FR 1946,* 9: 951-65. See also counselor of embassy in China to sec. of state, June 3, 1946, ibid., pp. 973-74; Marshall to Marshall Carter, June 10, 1946, ibid., pp. 1020-21; counselor of embassy in China to sec. of state, June 22, 1946, ibid., p. 1151; Marshall to Truman, June 26, 1946, ibid., pp. 1201-2.

74. For Stuart's activities, see Marshall to Walter Robertson, June 11, 1946, *FR 1946,* 9: 1023.

75. Minutes of meeting between Marshall and Yu Tai-wei, Apr. 22, 1936, *FR 1946,* 9: 788-89; Cohen, p. 189.

76. Memo by 2nd sec. of embassy in China, June 13, 1946, *FR 1946,* 9: 1046; Marshall to Truman, June 17, 1946, ibid., pp. 1100-1101; Tang, p. 425.

77. Marshall to acting sec. of state, July 2, 1946, *FR 1946,* 9: 1278.

78. Theodore H. White, "In Search of China Policy," *The New Republic,* Dec. 15, 1946, p. 26.

79. Acting sec. of state to Marshall, July 4, 1946, *FR 1946,* 9: 1295-96.

80. Ibid., pp. 1296-97.

81. Ibid., p. 1297.

82. Dir. of FE to under sec. of state, Aug. 21, 1946, *FR 1946,* 10: 58-59.

83. Memo by dir. of FE to acting sec. of state, Sept. 18, *FR 1946,* 10: 205-6.

84. JCV to Elizabeth Vincent, Feb. 14, 1943, p. 1, JCV mss.

85. Memo by conversation by acting sec. of state, Sept. 7, 1945, *FR 1945*, 7: 551.

86. Memo by dir. of FE to under sec. of state, Apr. 8, 1946, *FR 1946*, 10: 826.

87. Memo by sec. of state to State Dept. member of State-War-Navy Coordinating Committee, Jan. 5, 1946, *FR 1946*, 10: 810-11.

88. Wedemeyer to chief of staff, Jan. 21, 1946, *FR 1946*, 10: 811-16.

89. Memo by Joint Chiefs of Staff to State-War-Navy Coordinating Committee, Feb. 13, 1946, *FR 1946*, 10: 819.

90. Memo by dir. of FE to sec. of state, Feb. 19, 1946, *FR 1946*, 10: 821-22.

91. Directive to secs. of state, war, and navy, n.d. *FR 1946*, 10: 823, n. 28.

92. For Vincent's reaction to Wedemeyer's attempt to attach a Shangai station command to the Military Assistance Advisory Group, see memo by dir. of FE to sec. of state, Mar. 13, 1946, *FR 1946*, 10: 854-55; memo to dir. of FE, Mar. 8, 1946, ibid., p. 854.

93. Confidential source.

94. Interview with John J. McCloy, Dec. 8, 1952, *China Tangle* File, Box 10, Feis Papers.

95. Memo of conversation by dir. of FE, Aug. 13, 1946, *FR 1946*, 10: 24.

96. Memo of conversation by dir. of FE, Sept. 9, 1946, *FR 1946*, 10: 164.

97. Tang, p. 427. See also statement by Marshall and Dr. Stuart, Aug. 10, 1946, *FR 1946*, 10:1.

98. Tang, p. 425. See also, *China White Paper*, p. 356.

99. *IPR Hearings*, pp. 2253-54.

100. Chiang's statement is quoted in Tang, p. 430. For Chiang's letter to Truman, see Chiang to Truman, Aug. 28, 1946, *FR 1946*, 10: 92. For Vincent's reaction to Chiang's message to Truman, see memo by dir. of FE to under sec. of state, Aug. 28, 1946, *FR 1946*, 10: 92-93; see also, Acheson and JCV to Marshall, Aug. 30, 1946, *FR 1946*, 10: 147, n. 38.

101. Marshall to Truman, Sept. 23, 1946, *FR 1946*, 10: 217-19.

102. Memo by dir. of FE to acting sec. of state, Sept. 26, 1946, *FR 1946*, 10: 227-28.

103. Marshall to under sec. of state, Oct. 2, 1946, *FR 1946*, 10: 273. For Vincent's reaction to Marshall's cable, see memo by dir. of FE to under sec. of state, Oct. 3, 1946, *FR 1946*, 10: 276-77.

104. Marshall to Marshall Carter, Oct. 6, 1046, *FR 1946*, 10: 298-99; Tang, p. 434; Acheson, p. 280.

105. Tang, p. 434.

106. Quoted ibid., p. 435.

107. Minutes of meeting between Marshall and Dr. Stuart, Dec. 5, 1946, *FR 1946*, 10: 591. See also, Marshall to Truman, Dec. 20, 1946, *FR 1946*, 10: 663.

108. Minutes of meeting between Marshall and C. P. Lee, Dec. 26, 1946, *FR 1946*, 10: 659.

109. For the Communist view of the National Assembly, see amb. in China to sec. of state, Jan. 1, 1947, *FR 1946*, 10: 672-79.

110. Minutes of meeting between Marshall and Chou Tsien-chung, Dec. 21, 1946, *FR 1946*, 10: 649.

111. Marshall to Truman, Dec. 28, 1946, *FR 1945*, 10: 662-63. See also minutes of meeting between Marshall and T.V. Soong, Jan. 7, 1947, ibid., p. 690.

112. Marshall to Truman, Dec. 28, 1946, p. 665.

113. Memo by dir. of FE to under sec. of state, Dec. 31, 1946, *FR 1946*, 10: 671-72. See also, Byrnes, p. 229.

114. Marshall Carter to Marshall, Jan. 3, 1947, *FR 1946*, 10: 680.

115. Melby, p. 218.

Chapter 6

1. Tang, pp. 443-44.

2. For details on the termination of the executive headquarters and withdrawal of American marines, see memo by dir. of FE to sec. of state, Mar. 8, 1946, *FR 1946*, 10:854; memo by dir. of FE to the sec. of state, Nov. 5, 1946, ibid., pp. 879-82; memo by dir. of FE to the sec. of state, Jan. 24, 1947, ibid., pp. 706-8; Colonel Marshall S. Carter to Colonel George V. Underwood, Jan. 27, 1947, ibid., pp. 709-10; amb. in China to sec. of state, Jan. 29, 1947, ibid., p. 710. See also Melby, p. 228.

3. Memo by dir. of FE to Sec. of state, Feb. 7, 1947, *FR 1947*, 7:790-91.

4. Ibid., pp. 792-93; for a similar view, see memo by Philip Sprouse, n.d., ibid., pp. 786-89.

5. For Marshall's view, see the minutes of meeting of the secs. of state, war, and navy, Feb. 12, 1947, *FR 1947*, 7:796-97.

6. See memo by dir. of FE to sec. of state, Feb. 7, 1947, *FR 1947*, 7:793-94.

7. Minutes of meeting, Feb. 12, 1947, *FR 1947*, 7:796.

8. Sec. of war to sec. of state, Feb. 26, 1947, *FR 1947*, 7:799-802; Patterson's view of the Chinese Communist movement can be found in *FR 1947*, 7:800, 801.

9. Sec. of state to sec. of war, Mar. 4, 1947, *FR 1947*, 7:805-8.

10. For Vincent's reaction to the decision to have the Joint Chiefs prepare a study, see memo by dir. of FE to sec. of state, Mar. 27, 1947, *FR 1947*, 7:1094; for Vincent's use of the Joint Chiefs study as a means to block Pentagon initiatives, see memo by dir. of FE to sec. of state, May 2, 1947, ibid., p. 826.

11. For information on Chinese economic developments, see, for example, amb. in China to sec. of state, Mar. 4, 1947, *FR 1947*, 7:53-54; Report of assist. military attaché, May 7, 1947, enc. in amb. in China to sec. of state, May 16, 1947, ibid., pp. 126-27; Melby, p. 232; Tang, p. 451; *China White Paper*, pp. 369-70.

12. For information on Chinese military developments, see amb. in China to sec. of state, Mar. 12, 1947, enc. in amb. in China to sec. of state, May 8, 1947, ibid., pp. 114-17; amb. in China to sec. of state, May 15, 1947, ibid., pp. 119-20; *China White Paper*, p. 316; Tang, p. 451.

13. For information on Chinese political developments, see amb. in China to sec. of state, May 20, 1947, *FR 1947*, 7:131-33; amb in China to sec. of state, May 21, 1947, ibid., pp. 137-38; amb. in China to sec. of state, May 27, 1947, ibid., pp. 147-48; amb. in China to sec. of state, May 30, 1947, ibid., pp. 154-55; *China White Paper*, pp. 238-42; Tang, p. 451.

14. Amb. in China to sec. of state, Apr. 22, 1947, *FR 1947*, 7:1104. See also amb. in China to sec. of state, Apr. 25, 1947, ibid., p. 115.

15. For China's formal request, see Chinese amb. to sec. of state, May 13, 1947, *FR 1947*, 7:1119-20.

16. On this point, see Vincent's comment in memo of conversation by sec. of state, May 8, 1947, *FR 1947*, 7:1115.

17. For the views of Senator Vandenberg, see Vandenberg, pp. 519-23; Tang, p. 448; for Bridges's views, see Tang, p. 448; for the Republican Party's position on the China issue in 1947, see Freeland, pp. 198-99.

18. The quotation from Truman's speech is from Barnet, pp. 119-20; for the text of Truman's address, see Lafeber, pp. 49-55.

19. On this point, see Freeland, p. 100.

20. Interview with JCV, July 1971; Marshall, Byrnes, and Baruch are quoted in Freeland, pp. 100-101.

21. Tang, pp. 449, 452; on the Nationalist campaign to win American aid, see Millis and Duffield, p. 285.

22. Study on the military aspects of U.S. policy toward China, enc. by Joint Chiefs of Staff to State-War-Navy Coordinating Committee, June 9, 1947, *FR 1947*, 7:840, 846.

23. Ibid., pp. 842-43.

24. Ibid., pp. 842, 843-44. For details on specific programs recommended by the military, see chief of the Army Advisory Group to amb. in China, June 28, 1947 and chief of the Naval Advisory Group Survey Board to amb. in China, June 19, 1947, enc. in amb. in China to sec. of state, July 7, 1947, ibid., pp. 874-76.

25. Memo by dir. of FE to sec. of state, June 20, 1947, *FR 1947*, 7:849.

26. Ibid. For Vincent's view of Russian policy toward China, see dir. of FE to sec. of state, July 18, 1947, *FR 1947*, 7:1169.

27. For Vincent's concern, see acting sec. of state to amb. in the Soviet Union, Apr. 2, 1947, *FR 1947*, 7:814, n. 66.

28. For Vincent's views on limited military assistance to the Nationalist government, see acting sec. of state to amb. in the Soviet Union, Apr. 7, 1947, *FR 1947*, 7:817-18; memo by dir. of FE, May 26, 1947, ibid., pp. 833-34; minutes of meeting of the secs. of state, war, and navy, June 26, 1947, ibid., p. 851; memo by dir. of FE, June 27, 1947, ibid., pp. 852-64.

29. Memo by dir. of FE, June 27, 1947, *FR 1947*, 7:854.

30. Memo by dir. of FE to sec. of State, May 16, 1947, *FR 1947*, 7:1121. See also memo by dir. of FE to sec. of state, May 23, 1947, ibid., pp. 1124-25.

31. Memo by dir. of FE to assist. sec. of state for Economic Affairs, Mar. 18, 1947, *FR 1947*, 7:1092; memo by the dir. of FE to sec. of state, Mar. 27, 1947, ibid., pp. 1093-94; memo by chief of the Div. of Investment and Economic Development to dir. of the Office of Departmental Administration, Apr. 23, 1947, ibid., pp. 1105-7.

32. Memo by dir. of FE to sec. of state, Mar. 14, 1947, *FR 1947*, 7:1088-89; memo by dir. of FE to under sec. of state for Economic Affairs, Mar. 17, 1947, ibid., p. 1091; memo by dir. of FE to sec. of state, Mar. 27, 1947, ibid., pp. 1093-94; memo by dir. of FE, May 26, 1947, ibid., p. 1125; proposed memo by dir. of the Office of Financial and Development Policy and dir. of FE to sec. of state, June 4, 1947, enc. in memo by dir. of the Office of Financial and Development Policy to under sec. of state, June 4, 1947, ibid., pp. 1130-32.

33. Memo of conversation by sec. of state, May 8, 1947, *FR 1947*, 7:1115.

34. Interview with JCV, July 1971.

35. Memo of conversation by sec. of state, May 8, 1947, *FR 1947*, 7:1114-15; see also memo by sec. of state to dir. of FE, Mar. 4, 1947, ibid., p. 1085; memo by dir. of FE to under sec. of state for Economic Affairs, Mar. 17, 1947, ibid., p. 1091; memo of conversation by dir. of the Office of Financial and Development Policy, June 11, 1947, ibid., pp. 1132-34.

36. For information on the origins and activities of the Wedemeyer mission, see *FR 1947*, 7:635-784; for Wedemeyer's own account, see Wedemeyer, pp. 381-404; see also Tang, pp. 454-62.

37. For Marshall's views on aid to China in 1948, see *China White Paper*, pp. 380-84; Tang, pp. 470-77.

38. Iriye, p. 154.

39. *CR*, 80th Cong., 1st sess., p. 534.

40. Bridges to Vandenberg, Mar. 27, 1947, Vandenberg Papers.

41. The best scholarly study of the China Lobby remains Koen.

42. Keeley, pp. 24-25.

43. Subcommittee of the Committee on Foreign Relations, "Tydings Committee Report," July 20, 1950, p. 146, *State Dept. Employee Loyalty Investigation, Hearings*.

44. Quoted in Wertenbaker, pp. 20-21.

45. For a list of the Board of Directors of the American China Policy Association, see "Statement on China White Paper," Aug. 29, 1949, Official File, Truman Papers.

46. Hannah Arendt, "'Ex-Communists' Remain Totalitarian at Heart," *Washington Post,* May 3, 1953.

47. Kohlberg, "Great Debate," p. 264. Kohlberg first presented his program publicly during a session of the Senate Committee on Appropriations on June 8, 1948. See "Statement of Alfred Kohlberg" in U.S. Cong., 2nd sess., Committee on Appropriations, *Economic Cooperation Administration* (Washington, D.C., 1948) in Bridges Papers.

48. Kohlberg, "Great Debate." The papers of Alfred Kohlberg are deposited at the Hoover Institution on War, Revolution and Peace, Stanford, California, but are closed to researchers until 1999. Those interested in Kohlberg's views can turn to his voluminous published articles, letters, and speeches. See, for example, *Plain Talk,* Jan. 1947-Mar. 1949, and:

Letters:

Kohlberg to Herbert Brownell, Jr., June 28, 1944, *CR,* 81st Cong., 2nd sess., p. A7433.
Kohlberg to Robert S. Allen, Aug. 1, 1949, *CR,* 81st Cong., 1st sess., pp. A5066-7.
Kohlberg to Wallace, Oct. 23, 1950, Wallace Papers.
Kohlberg to Wallace, Nov. 29, 1950, Wallace Papers.

Speeches:

"McCarthyism and Korea," Senate, *CR* 82nd Cong., 1st session. (Apr. 13, 1951), pp. A2070-71.
"Speech," Senate, *CR,* 82nd Cong., 1st sess. (Aug. 10, 1951), pp. A5046-51.
For brilliant essays on the new conservatism exemplified by Kohlberg and others on the radical right, see Hofstadter, *Paranoid Style,* pp. 41-151.

49. Koen, pp. 56-57.

50. Dulles, pp. 73-74; Tang, p. 466; Westerfield, pp. 241-68.

51. Theoharis, *Yalta,* p. 6; see also Theoharis, *Seeds,* pp. 14-15.

52. Kohlberg to Hurley, Mar. 14, 1947, Box 105, Hurley Papers. I am indebted to Professor Russell D. Buhite for assistance in obtaining important documents from the Hurley collection.

53. Vandenberg to Bridges, Mar. 25, 1947, Vandenberg Papers.

54. Memo pp. 1-4, enc. Bridges to Vandenberg, Apr. 7, 1947, Bridges Papers. For Kohlberg's earlier view of Vincent, see "Questions for Mr. John Carter Vincent," n.d., Box 105, Hurley Papers.

55. JCV to Acheson, Apr. 9, 1947, p. 1, JCV mss.

56. Ibid.

57. Ibid.

58. Ibid., p. 5

59. Acheson to George, Apr. 18, 1947, p. 1, JCV mss.; for Acheson's analysis of the charges, see "Analysis of Allegations against Mr. John Carter Vincent," pp. 1-2, enc. with Acheson to George, JCV mss.

60. Kohlberg, "State Department's Left Hand," pp. 12-17.

61. Kohlberg, "Kremlin Agent in the State Department," enc. Kohlberg to Hurley, Apr. 10, 1947, Box 105, Hurley Papers.

62. "Press Release," *Plain Talk,* May 12, 1947, enc. with Vandenberg to George, May 9, Senate Committee on Foreign Relations, 1947 Records.

63. Both can be found in Senate Committee on Foreign Relations, 1947 Records.

64. Busbey represented the district where Mrs. Vincent's brothers lived. Interview with Elizabeth Vincent, 1972; see also *CR,* 80th Cong., 1st sess., pp. 2580-81. Busbey also sent a copy of Kohlberg's article to the State Department: see memo, June 1947, and W. W. Chapman, Jr., to Hamilton Robinson, June 9, 1947, both in Office of Security Records.

65. Interview with JCV, 1971.

66. Interview with JCV, 1971.

67. Undated memo, Senate Committee on Foreign Relations, 1947 Records.

68. Kohlberg, "State Department's Left Hand," p. 12.

69. Interview with JCV, 1972.

70. Vincent's nomination to be minister to Switzerland was sent to the Senate on July 21, 1947, and was confirmed on July 23, 1947. See memo to pres., July 21, 1947, Official File, Truman Papers. See also *CR,* 80th Cong., 1st sess., p. 9844.

71. "Executive Session," July 22, 1947, p. 2, Senate Committee on Foreign Relations, 1947 Records.

72. Vandenberg to A. Scott Petersen, June 4, 1947, Vandenberg Papers.

73. Kohlberg to Vandenberg, Nov. 25, 1947, quoted in Kohlberg, "Why Was Vandenberg Mislead?" p. 520.

74. Acheson, p. 400.

75. For Republican criticism of Truman's policies and the president's response, see Griffith, pp. 327-28; Freeland, pp. 115-34; Theoharis, *Seeds,* pp. 101-2; Hartmann, *passim,* Tang, p. 453; Acheson, p. 400.

76. Vandenberg to Kohlberg, n.d., quoted in Kohlberg, "Why Was Vandenberg Misled?"; see also Tang, p. 453, and Freeland, p. 202.

77. Quoted in Griffith, p. 38.

78. Ibid., p. 328.

79. Ibid., p. 40.

80. House Committee on Appropriations, *Department of State Appropriations Bill for 1949,* pp. 182-83.

81. The identification of Kohlberg as Clare's "confidential informant" is based on the following evidence:

a. The informant told Clare that "information relating to this incident is in possession of Senator Styles Bridges." Only a few men knew of the existence of the Bridges's memorandum which Kohlberg had authored, Kohlberg chief among them.

b. A reference to the incident appears in the first draft of Kohlberg's essay "The State Department's Left Hand," written in April 1947, four months before Clare's report. The story does not appear in the final version of the article. See "Kremlin Agent in the State Department," p. 8, enc. Kohlberg to Hurley, Apr. 10, 1947, Hurley Papers. In this letter, Kohlberg notes explicitly that he had received this information from Hurley.

c. The subject of Clare's investigation was the Institute of Pacific Relations; Kohlberg was one of its first members to charge the group with procommunism. Being such a prominent critic of the organization, it seems likely that Kohlberg would be interviewed during a general inquest into the Institute's activities.

d. Finally, Kohlberg's offices were lcoated in New York, where Clare's own office was located. The other men involved in blocking Vincent's confirmation in 1947—Hurley, Judd, La Moore, and Bridges—lived outside Clare's investigatory jurisdiction.

82. For information on the *Amerasia* affair see Koen, pp. 61-66.

83. For the original story, see Clare to R. D. Clark, Aug. 25, 1947; Clark to T. F. Fitch, Aug. 25, 1947; telegram, State Dept., Wash., to State Dept., N.Y., Jan. 15, 1948; "Interview with General William J. Donovan concerning John Carter Vincent," Clare to Special Agent in Charge, N.Y. Div., Jan. 16, 1948, pp. 1-2; also telegram, State Dept., N.Y., to State Dept., Wash., Jan. 16, 1948. For the State Department's view, see "Statement Regarding John Carter Vincent," n.d, John E. Peurifoy to sec., Sept. 9, 1948, pp. 1-2. All of the above documents are in the Office of Security Records. Robinson is quoted in House Committee on Appropriations, *Department of State Appropriations Bill*, pp. 190-91.

84. House Committee on Appropriations, *Department of State Appropriations Bill*, pp. 190-91.

85. Griffith, p. 44.

86. Ibid., p. 46; see also, Irwin Ross, *The Loneliest Campaign* (N.Y.: New Amer. Lib., 1968), pp. 54-57.

87. Two general surveys of American life between 1945-1950 are Eric F. Goldman, *The Crucial Decade and After* (N.Y.: Knopf, 1960), and Joseph C. Goulden, *The Best Years* (N.Y.: Atheneum, 1976).

88. For McCarthy's speeches, see Griffith, pp. 28-30, 48-49; Cook, pp. 147-49.

89. Cook, p. 164. See also *CR*, 81st Cong., 2nd sess., Feb. 20, 1950, p. 2045.

90. *CR*, 81st Cong., 2nd sess., Feb. 20, 1950, p. 1959.

91. Ibid., p. 1960.

92. Rovere, p. 132.

93. *CR*, 81st Cong., 2nd sess., p. 1960.

94. *N.Y. Times*, Feb. 26, 1950, p. 6; Cook, p. 178.

95. Quoted in special agent in charge (hereafter SAC), Wash. Field, to dir., FBI, June 19, 1950, FBI Records.

96. Dir., FBI, to assist. to attorney gen., Apr. 21, 1950, p. 3, FBI Records;

see also, dir., FBI, to Peyton Ford, assist. to the attorney general, May 2, 1950, ibid.

97. Hoover to legal attaché, Oct. 31, 1947, FBI Records. For a discussion of the role played by "legats" (FBI agents serving as U.S. embassies abroad), see Ungar, pp. 223-45.

98. Ladd to dir., May 22, 1948, pp. 1-2, FBI Records. Hoover's handwritten comment is clearly visible on the bottom of page 1.

99. Dir., FBI, to attorney general, May 17, 1948, pp. 1-2, FBI Records.

100. Ladd to dir., May 26, 1948, FBI Records.

101. For Hoover's comment, see ibid.

102. Peurifoy to Peyton Ford, June 5, 1948, Office of Security Records.

103. Quoted in Ladd to dir., July 13, 1948, p. 1, FBI Records.

104. Ibid.; see also office memo., Aug. 24, 1948, FBI Records.

105. For the notation, see request for report on loyalty data, Apr. 5, 1949, FBI Records; for the origins of the decision to append the notation, approved by Hoover, see office memo., Apr. 8, 1949, p. 2, FBI Records.

106. Office memo., May 13, 1949, pp. 1-2, FBI Records. See also memo, June 28, 1949, FBI Records, noting the receipt of a letter charging that Vincent had a "pro-Soviet attitude toward China." This letter was added to Vincent's FBI file.

107. Office memo, Mar. 21, 1950, FBI Records. See also "John Carter Vincent: Allegations by Senator McCarthy—Case No. 2," n.d., but probably Feb. 24, 1950, FBI Records.

108. Dir., FBI, to assist. to attorney general, Apr. 21, 1950, pp. 1-2, FBI Records. Hoover also sent Ford a copy of Kohlberg's article "The State Department's Left Hand." When eleven days passed without a reply from the attorney general's office, Hoover sent a second letter. See dir., FBI, to Peyton Ford, May 2, 1950, FBI Records.

109. Memo to dir., May 5, 1950, p. 1: see also memo, May 12, 1950, p. 2, both in FBI Records.

110. Dir., to SAC, Wash. Field, May 10, 1950, pp. 1-10, FBI Records.

111. Hoover to S. D. Boykin, May 5, 1950. See also James E. Webb to Amer. embassy, London, May 19, 1950, p. 1, and D. L. Nicholson to Ellis O. Briggs, June 12, 1950, all in Office of Security Records.

112. Ungar, pp. 225-26.

113. S. D. Boykin to Hoover, May 19, 1950, pp. 1-2, Office of Security Records.

114. See for example: "Statement by Mr. Edward E. Rice," May 29, 1950, pp. 1-3, enc., Spencer S. Beman to D. L. Nicholson, May 29, 1950; "Request for Opinion on Loyalty of Mr. John Carter Vincent," June 21, 1950, enc., Ellis O. Briggs to D. L. Nicholson, June 21, 1950; W. B. Hussey to S. D. Boykin, June 28, 1950; "Statement Made by Loy W. Henderson, American Foreign Service Officer, Regarding John Carter Vincent, American Foreign Service Officer, at the Request of the Federal Bureau of Investigation in Connection

with an Investigation of Mr. Vincent Based upon Information to the Effect That He Possesses Pro-Communist Sympathies," enc., S. D. Boykin to Hoover, July 13, 1950; "Interrogatory," pp. 1-2, June 28, 1950, enc. with William R. Langdon to D. L. Nicholson, June 28, 1950; telegram June 8, 1950 (Stanton to Amer. Embassy, Bangkok), and Walter S. Pedigo to Regional Security Headquarters, Manila, July 21, 1950, enc. with Walter S. Pedigo to D. L. Nicholson, July 21, 1950; "Interview had by F. S. O. Harold D. Finley with F. S. S. Dorothy St. Clair regarding Mr. and Mrs. John Carter Vincent, July 25, 1950," enc. S. D. Boykin to Hoover, Aug. 23, 1950; "Paris Inquiry of Apr. 27, 1951, re Mr. John Carter Vincent," May 16, 1951, Alexander Schnee to the ambass., enc. Ellis O. Briggs to D. L. Nicholson, May 18, 1951; all in Office of Security Records.

115. Dir., FBI, to SAC, Wash. Field, May 19, 1950; see also telegram, dir. to FBI, Wash. Field, May 16, 1950, both in FBI Records.

116. Hoover to legal attache, Paris, May 5, 1950; for the decision to interview Vincent, see memo, May 12, 1950; for a record of the interview, see legal attaché, to dir., June 6, 1950, pp. 1-5; all in FBI Records.

117. FBI report, Kansas City, Missouri, May 23, 1950, pp. 1-4; see also SAC, Kansas City, Missouri, to Dir., FBI, May 19, 1950, both in FBI Records.

118. FBI report, Atlanta, Georgia, May 27, 1950, pp. 1-5, FBI Records.

119. FBI report, Charlotte, N.C., May 26, 1950, pp. 1-3, FBI Records.

120. See telegram, Nicholson to Hussey, May 13, 1950; also "Resumé of John Carter Vincent Case as of Sept. 10, 1951"; and Spencer S. Beman to Nicholson, May 29, 1950; all in Office of Security Records.

121. Telegram, James E. Webb to Lewis Douglas, May 19, 1950, pp. 1-2, Office of Security Records.

122. Telegram, Lewis Douglas to sec. of state, June 5, 1950; for the full interviews, see Hussey to Nicholson, June 13, 1950, pp. 1-10, both in Office of Security Records.

123. Dir., FBI, to SAC, Wash. Field, July 19, 1950, FBI Records.

124. JCV to Peurifoy, Mar. 7, 1950, pp. 1-2, JCV mss.

125. Ibid., p. 2.

126. Ibid.

127. Ibid., pp. 2-3.

128. Ibid., pp. 3-4.

129. JCV to sec. of state, May 12, 1950, Office of Security Records.

130. James E. Webb to JCV, May 13, 1950, Office of Security Records.

131. James E. Webb to Amer. embassy, London, May 13, 1950, Office of Security Records. This telegram and the one above are both time stamped 1 p.m.

132. From time to time, McCarthy would mention "Case Number 2" but usually outside the Committee Hearing Room. See the *N. Y. Times,* May 8, 1950; May 11, 1950; *Washington Post,* May 12, 1950.

133. *Baltimore Sun,* May 14, 1950.

134. Kohlberg made his files available to McCarthy shortly before his first address at Wheeling, W.V., in Feb. 1950, and the following month he conferred with the senator's staff and personally gave McCarthy the "story of the China sell-out step by step and in chronological order." See Keeley, pp. 2-3; also, Irene C. Kuhn, "He Lobbies Against Communism," in *CR,* 82nd Cong., 2nd sess., July 5, 1952, p. A4702.

135. Like Vincent, Owen Lattimore had long been a target of Alfred Kohlberg's attacks. See, for example, "Kremlin Agent in the State Department," p. 2, enc. Kohlberg to Hurley, Apr. 10, 1947, Box 105, Hurley Papers; "Owen Lattimore: Experts' Expert," *China Monthly,* 6 (Oct. 1945), pp. 10-13, 26; "Reply to a Reply," *China Monthly,* 6, Mar. 1946, p. 104. For Lattimore's view, see Lattimore, *passim.*

136. *N.Y. Times,* May 14, 1950.

137. Griffith, p. 100.

138. Subcommittee of the Committee on Foreign Relations "Tydings Report," July 20, 1950, p. 146, State Dept. Employee Loyalty Investigation Hearings.

139. Ibid., p. 95.

140. Quoted in Griffith, p. 101; *N.Y. Times,* May 8, 1950.

141. Griffith, p. 134.

142. McCarthy to Davis, n.d., quoted in James H. Rowe, Jr., to Bailey Aldrich, June 19, 1953. I am grateful to Mr. Joseph Alsop and Mr. Rowe for making this letter available to me. The letter, dated Sept. 11, 1950, can be found in "Statement of Donald A. Surine," Feb. 18, 1953, *Joseph R. McCarthy* vs *the Post-Standard Co. of N.Y.*

143. Carlisle Humelsine to Senator William Benton, Oct. 16, 1951, pp. 3-4, Box 5, Benton Papers.

144. "Report of Investigation," p. 2, enc. David K. E. Bruce to D. L. Nicholson, Jan. 18, 1951, Office of Security Records.

145. Ibid.; Newsweek, Mar. 25, 1951, p. 28.

146. "Report," p. 2. enc. Bruce to Nicholson, Jan. 18, 1951, Office of Security Records.

147. McCarthy to Davis, Aug. 15, 1950, Exhibit 11, *McCarthy* vs. *Post-Standard Co.*

148. Davis to McCarthy, Aug. 7, 1950; McCarthy to Davis, Aug. 11, 1950, both in *McCarthy* vs. *Post-Standard Co.*

149. "Statement of Charles Davis," pp. 137-38, *McCarthy* vs. *Post-Standard Co.;* Carlisle Humelsine to Senator William Benton, pp. 2-3. For Davis's statement to American officials in Paris and a photostat of the receipt, see "Statement by Charles Davis, Oct. 5, 1950," pp. 1-4, enc. Bruce to Nicholson, Jan. 18, 1951, Office of Security Records. Davis also admits sending a copy of the telegram to McCarthy in "Charles Davis to Senator, 9/50," Office of Security Records. For general discussions the Davis Case, see Griffith, p. 135, and Anderson and May, pp. 199-201.

150. Davis's plans are sketched out in a letter to McCarthy quoted in "Statement of Charles Davis," pp. 146-47.

151. Memo of conversation, Nov. 17, 1950, p. 1, enc. Bruce to Nicholson, Jan. 18, 1951, Office of Security Records.

152. Ibid., p. 2. See also Donald A. Surine to Charles Davis, Nov. 28, 1950, Exhibit 14, *McCarthy* vs. *Post-Standard Co.* McCarthy's view of Davis can be found in "Statement of Joseph R. McCarthy," p. 128, 156, *McCarthy* vs. *Post-Standard Co.* The Story of Davis's arrest and trial is told in the *N. Y. Times,* Feb. 13, Feb. 14, July 27, Oct. 10, Oct. 14, Oct. 16, Oct. 17, 1951. For Vincent's view of the Davis affair, see "Charles Davis Case," Surrey Papers.

153. *N. Y. Times,* Oct. 16, 1951.

154. "Statement of Joseph R. McCarthy," p. 152, *McCarthy* vs. *Post-Standard Co.*

155. Memo for pres., Jan. 11, 1951, Official File, Truman Papers. For the public announcement of Vincent's transfer, see *N. Y. Times,* Mar. 4, 1951, *Washington Post,* Mar. 3, 1951, *Washington Evening Star,* Mar. 3, 1951, *N. Y. Herald Tribune,* Mar. 3, 1951.

156. JCV to Durbrow, Jan. 19, 1951, JCV mss.

157. JCV to Mrs. Lula Vincent, Mar. 4, 1951; JCV to Durbrow, both in JCV mss.

158. *N. Y. Herald Tribune,* Mar. 3, 1951.

159. JCV to Lula Vincent, Mar. 4, 1951, JCV mss.

160. Personnel Action Sheet, Dept. of State, Aug. 7, 1951, JCV mss.

161. For McCarthy's and Kohlberg's statements see *N. Y. Herald Tribune,* Mar. 3, 1951; Kohlberg, "McCarthyism and Korea," a speech reprinted in *CR,* 83rd Cong., 1st sess., Apr. 13, 1951, p. A2070.

162. *Time,* Mar. 12, 1951, pp. 20-21.

163. "Scrambled Diplomats," *Washington Post,* Mar. 7, 1951; Charles L. Stout to editor, *Washington Post,* Mar. 7, 1951.

164. McHugh to JCV, Mar. 7, 1951, pp. 1-3, JCV mss. See also McHugh to JCV, Feb. 16, 1951, JCV mss.

165. JCV to Lula Vincent, Mar. 4, 1951, JCV mss.

166. JCV to C. M. Ravndal, Oct. 8, 1948, pp. 1-2, JCV mss.

167. JCV to Florian Niedeier, Apr, 3, 1951, JCV mss.

168. Quoted in Griffith, p. 132.

169. See in Cabell Phillips, *The Truman Administration: The History of a Triumphant Succession* (N.Y.: Macmillan, 1965), p. 345.

170. Quoted in Griffith, p. 145.

171. *CR,* 83rd Cong., 1st sess., Aug. 9, 1951, p. 9918.

172. "Special Release," Aug. 10, 1951, JCV mss; see also N.Y. *Herald Tribune* (Paris ed.), Aug. 11, 1951, pp. 1, 6. For an editorial comment on McCarthy's charges, see *Washington Post,* Aug. 15, 1951.

173. Clipping, Aug. 12, 1951, JCV mss.

174. Interviews with John Service; John Fairbank; Adrian Fisher; Monroe Karasik; Walter Surrey.

175. For Vincent's attitude toward Republican attacks, see JCV to Ken Browne, June 29, 1951, JCV to Surrey, July 17, 1952, JCV to Benjamin Katz, Feb. 13. 1953, all in JCV mss.

176. JCV to Benjamin Katz, Feb. 13, 1953, all in JCV mss.

177. Elizabeth Vincent to Sheila and John Carter Vincent, Jr., Aug. 1951, JCV mss.

Chapter 7

1. U.S. Cong., Senate, 82nd Cong., 1st sess., Committee on the Judiciary, *Institute of Pacific Relations,* pt. 2, p. 625, 626, 632 (hereafter cited as *IPR,* pt., etc.).

2. Ibid., pp. 625-26.

3. Ibid., p. 626.

4. Alsop, "Budenz," p. 30.

5. JCV to Elizabeth Vincent, n.d., 1951; telegram and statement, Aug. 24, 1951, both in JCV mss.

6. Alsop, "Budenz," p. 29; Packer, pp. 120-24; Griffith, pp. 80-81.

7. Alsop, "Budenz," p. 30.

8. *IPR,* pt. 2, p. 514.

9. Alsop, "Budenz," p. 29.

10. Ibid.

11. Packer, p. 124.

12. Keeley, p. 270.

13. Schapsmeir, pp. 213-14; see also Wallace to William F. Knowland, Oct. 11, 1952, Wallace Papers.

14. Quoted from *CR,* 82nd Cong., 1st sess., Sept. 24, 1951, pp. 11936-40; see also *Herald Tribune,* Sept. 25, 1951.

15. Alsop, "Matter of Fact," in *CR,* 8nd Cong., 1st sess., Sept. 24, 1951, p. 11939.

16. Ibid., pp. 11939-40.

17. William V. Shannon, "The Strange Case of Louis Budenz," *New Republic,* Oct. 22, 1951, p. 9; for Lehman's comments on Alsop's series and Brewster's response, see *CR,* 82nd Cong., 1st sess., Sept. 14, 1951, pp. 11344-45; McCarran is quoted in *Washington Post,* Sept. 24, 1951.

18. Truman to vice-president, Sept. 22, 1951, Lloyd Papers.

19. Wallace to Truman, Sept. 19, 1951, pp. 1-2, Truman Papers.

20. Ibid., p. 2.

21. "The Vincent Episode," *N.Y. Herald Tribune*, Sept. 25, 1951.

22. *New Republic*, Oct. 1, 1951, p. 6.

23. *CR*, 82nd Cong., 1st sess., Sept. 24, 1951, pp. 11936-40; see also *N.Y. Herald Tribune*, Sept. 25, 1951.

24. JCV to Elizabeth Vincent, Aug. 21, 1951, p. 1, JCV mss. See also JCV to Elizabeth Vincent, n.d., and JCV to Elizabeth Vincent, Aug. 30, 1951, p. 3, both in JCV mss.

25. Quoted in *N.Y. Post*, Oct. 10, 1951, pp. 2, 23.

26. JCV to McCarran, Sept. 7, 1951, JCV mss.

27. JCV to Elizabeth Vincent, Sept. 15, 1951, pp. 1-2; JCV to Frank Vincent, Sept. 28, 1951; JCV to Frank Vincent, Ascension Day, p. 3; Vincent to Frank Vincent, July 30, 1951, pp. 3-4, all in JCV mss.

28. JCV to Elizabeth Vincent, Sept. 15, 1951, pp. 1-2; JCV to Elizabeth Vincent, Sept. 17, 1951, p. 4; JCV to Elizabeth Vincent, n.d.; JCV to Frank Vincent, Nov. 21, 1951, p. 1, all in JCV mss.

29. Quoted in. Rose, pp. 181-82.

30. For general accounts of the impact of McCarthyism on American life, see Parmet, pp. 227-28; Robert Vaughn, *Only Victims* (N.Y.: Putnam, 1973); Stefan Kanfer, *A Journal of the Plague Years* (N.Y.: Viking, 1973); Lillian Hellman, *Scoundrel Time* (Boston: Little, 1976); Jessica Mitford, *A Fine Old Conflict* (N.Y.: Knopf, 1977).

31. For information on Davies, Clubb, and Service, see Kahn; Richard Fried, pp. 169-70.

32. *IPR*, pt. 4, pp. 1082-86; Alsop, "Budenz," pp. 32, 33.

33. Alsop, "The Strange Case, 1st Draft," p. 7, Alsop Papers.

34. For the text of Alsop's letter to McCarran, see *Washington Post*, Oct. 7, 1951.

35. Shannon, p. 9.

36. Schapsmeir, p. 213.

37. Shannon, p. 10.

38. For excerpts from Wallace's statement, see *N.Y. Post*, Oct. 10, 1951.

39. Atwood, p. 10. For more criticism of McCarran, see Arthur Krock, "In the Nation," *N.Y. Times*, Oct. 11, 1951.

40. *IPR*, pt. 5, p. 1368.

41. Ibid. pp. 1342-43.

42. *N.Y. Post*, Oct. 20, 1951, Wallace Papers.

43. *IPR*, pt. 5, pp. 1474-75.

44. Ibid., p. 1404.

45. Ibid.

46. Ibid., p. 1472.

47. Ibid., pp. 1472-73.

48. *N.Y. Herald Tribune*, Oct. 16, 1951; Charles Owsley to author, Mar. 30, 1972.

49. *N.Y. Herald Tribune*, Oct. 16, 1951.

50. JCV to Frank Vincent, Nov. 21, 1951, p. 1, JCV mss.

51. JCV to McCarran, Nov. 9, 1951, "JCV: Letters to and from McCarran File," Surrey Papers.

52. See "Department of State for the Press," Nov. 16, 1951, Spingarn Papers.

53. *N.Y. Times*, Nov. 19, 1951; *N.Y. Daily Compass*, Nov. 19, 1951; *Philadelphia Inquirer*, Nov. 19, 1951.

54. McCarran to JCV, Nov. 16, 1951, "JCV: Letters to and from McCarran File," Surrey Papers.

55. *N.Y. Daily Compass*, Nov. 19, 1951.

56. *Washington Post*, Nov. 22, 1951.

57. For information on the operations of the State Department Loyalty-Security Board, see "Statement of Brigadier Gen. Conrad E. Snow, Ret., Before a Subcommittee of the Senate Foreign Relations Committee," Apr. 5, 1950, pp. 1-5, Truman Papers. See also Snow to sec. of state, Jan. 8, 1953, p. 2, Appendix B., enc. interview with Snow, Truman Lib.

58. For information on Humelsine, Snow, Snipes, and Moyer, see Snow to sec. of state, Jan. 8, 1953, p. 2; also Clubb, pp. 146-47.

59. Snow to JCV, Nov. 19, 1951, pp. 2-3, 4, JCV mss.

60. Hoover to SAC, N.Y., May 26, 1950, FBI Records. For information on Joseph Kamp, see Seymour Martin Lipset and Earl Raab, *The Politics of Unreason: Right-wing Extremism in America, 1790-1970* (N.Y.: Harper & Row, 1970), p. 244; also Anderson and May, p. 242.

61. FBI report, N.Y., July 13, 1950, pp. 1, 32, FBI Records.

62. FBI, Report, Wash., D.C., July 28, 1950, pp. 1-61, FBI Records; see also Civil Service Commission, Loyalty Review Board, "Post-Audit Report," Apr. 14, 1952, p. 39, Civil Service Records (hereafter cited as "Post-Audit").

63. FBI report, Wash., D.C., July 28, 1950, p. 1, FBI Records.

64. For information on the selection of the members to serve on Vincent's panel, see "John Carter Vincent," Nov. 20, 1951, Office of Security Records. For information on Kimball and Nufer, see the State Department's *Biographic Register*, 1951.

65. The FBI interview with Judd is quoted verbatim in Marion Wade Doyle,

"The Case of John Carter Vincent," Dec. 24, 1952, pp. 3-4, Loyalty Review Board, Civil Service Records. See also letter to the dir., Aug. 15, 1950, p. 6, FBI Records.

66. Quoted in Doyle, "The Case of John Carter Vincent," pp. 2-3. See also Loyalty Review Board, "Post-Audit," p. 7, Civil Service Records.

67. For a brief sketch of the activities of Admiral Miles in Chungking, see Davies, pp. 287-89. Wedemeyer is quoted in *Diaries*, pp. 288-89. For information on Chiang's secret police, see Fulton Lewis, Jr., "Washington Report," Feb. 15, 16, 19, 1951, *N.Y. Journal American*, enc. SAC, N.Y., to dir., FBI, Feb. 26, 1951, FBI Records.

68. Quoted in Loyalty Review Board, "Post-Audit," p. 6, Civil Service Records.

69. Kohlberg, "State Department's Left Hand." Congressman Busbey sent a copy of the Kohlberg piece to the secretary of state on June 5, 1947. See Dept. of State memo, n.d. and draft of letter to Fred E. Busbey attached, Office of Security Records. See also W. W. Chapman to T. F. Fitch, June 9, 1947, Office of Security Records. A copy can also be found in Senate Foreign Relations Committee, 1947 Records.

70. For a description of the Vincent-Kohlberg conversation, see p. 61-62; see also, "Results of Investigation," pp. 2-4, enc. SAC, N.Y., to dir., FBI, Oct. 24, 1951, FBI Records.

71. Kornfeder tells his life story briefly in *IPR*, pt. 3, pp. 865-66.

72. Kornfeder is quoted in Loyalty Review Board, "Post-Audit," p. 36, Civil Service Records.

73. Kornfeder to Snow, Dec. 8, 1951, Office of Security Records.

74. See letter to dir., FBI, Dec. 30, 1952, FBI Records.

75. Budenz's interview with the FBI is quoted in Blair to Amen, Nov. 12, 1952, pp. 9-10, JCV mss.

76. I.F. Stone, "How Budenz Was Coaxed to Smear Vincent," *N.Y. Daily Compass*, Feb. 8, 1952, in FBI Records.

77. Memo for the file, Dec. 26, 1951, State Dept. Loyalty-Security Board, Office of Security Records.

78. Acheson, pp. 17, 439.

79. Interview with Fisher.

80. Interview with Fisher.

81. Interview with Fisher.

Chapter 8

1. JCV to Surrey, Aug. 4, 1952, JCV mss; Interview with JCV, July 1971.

2. Interviews with Surrey and Karasik, July 1971, May 1973. For Vincent's telegram, see Surrey Papers. For responses, see "Statement by Clarence Edward Gauss," Dec.

18, 1951; Clayton to JCV, Dec. 18, 1951; Benton to JCV, Dec. 22, 1951; Hilldring to JCV, Dec. 18, 1951, all in Office of Security Records.

3. On Dec. 6 and 17 the board questioned two of Vincent's critics: Eugene H. Dooman and Stanley K. Hornbeck. Vincent and Surrey were permitted to observe the proceedings. See Dept. of State Loyalty-Security Board., "Transcript of Proceedings," in the matter of John Carter Vincent, Dec. 6, 17, 1951, JCV mss (hereafter cited as "Transcript," with appropriate dates).

4. Clubb, p. 147.

5. Loyalty-Security Board, "Transcript," Dec. 17, 1951, pp. B3-B5, JCV mss; Clubb, p. 147.

6. Loyalty-Security Board, "Transcript," Dec. 17, 1951, pp. B8-B18, JCV mss.

7. Ibid., pp. B20-C55.

8. Loyalty-Security Board, "Transcript," Dec. 18, 1952, p. A1, JCV mss.

9. Ibid., p. A2, A4.

10. Ibid., p. A11.

11. Ibid., pp. A18-19; see also pp. A21-24.

12. See ibid., pp. D15-21 (for Vincent's view of Hiss); pp. C26-29 (of Lattimore); pp. D-21-23 (of Currie).

13. Ibid., pp. A38-39, 40.

14. Ibid., pp. A-58-60, B1.

15. Ibid., pp. B22-24.

16. Ibid., pp. A52-53.

17. Ibid., pp. D23-28.

18. For the witnesses' view of Vincent's politics, see Loyalty-Security Board, "Transcript," Dec. 20, 1951, pp. 61, 79-82, 83, 104, 118, and "Transcript," Dec. 21, 1951, pp. 13-14, JCV mss.

19. Loyalty-Security Board, "Transcript," Dec. 20, 1951, pp. 120-21 (Bess); pp. 9-10 (Magruder), p. 29 (Hamilton), ibid., Dec. 21, 1951, p. 7 (Mayer), JCV mss.

20. Loyalty-Security Board, "Transcript," Dec. 20, 1951, p. 123 (Bess), p. 68 (Seitz), pp. 51-52 (Mayer), JCV mss.

21. Ibid., pp. 118-20.

22. For a complete list of the documents demanded by McCarran, see McCarran to Acheson, Jan. 2, 1952, Surrey Papers; see also *IPR,* pt. 6, pp. 1915-16.

23. McCarran to JCV, Nov. 30, 1951, Office of Security Records; JCV to McCarran, Dec. 3, 1951, Surrey Papers; McCarran to JCV, Jan. 2, 1952, Surrey Papers; see enc., "John Carter Vincent: Documents Requested," in Surrey Papers; JCV to McCarran, Jan. 14, 1952, Surrey Papers.
The State Department referred McCarran's request to President Truman who

refused to give McCarran the documents on the grounds that public release of internal State Department records and executive loyalty files would demoralize the Foreign Service and "undermine the integrity of the Loyalty System." See Truman to Acheson, Jan. 24, 1952, Surrey Papers. Also "Background of President" letter of Jan. 24 to sec., Office of Security. A copy of Truman's letter to Acheson is attached.

24. See "Issues Which May Be Raised in Hearing of John Carter Vincent before McCarran Committee," pp. 1-4, "JCV's Associations with Individuals," both in Surrey Papers.

25. House Committee on Un-American Activities, "The Role of the Communist Press in the Communist Conspiracy," 82nd Cong., 2nd sess., 1952, pp. 2151-52, p. 2165, pp. 2168-69. Vincent also discussed the Granich case during his appearance before the McCarran Committee: See *IPR*, pt. 6, pp. 1973-77.

26. All in the Office of Security Records; *Chicago Daily Tribune*, Jan. 11, 1952; *Washington Times Herald*, Jan. 10, 1952; *N.Y. Times*, Jan. 10, 1952.

27. Quoted in Kahn, p. 237.

28. Joseph and Stewart Alsop, "Matter of Fact," *N.Y. Herald Tribune*, Feb. 4, 1952; *Washington Post*, Feb. 3, 1952; Lowell Mellett, "Senators Give Victim a Lesson," *Washington Star*, Feb. 6, 1952; *Louisville Courier-Journal*, Feb. 4, 1952.

29. *Louisville Courier-Journal*, Feb. 4, 1952.

30. Kohlberg claimed that Vincent's actions followed the Communist line as expressed in two documents: *The Program of the Communist International and Its Workers,* and "The Revolutionary Movement in the Colonies and Semi-Colonies" (Bridges memo., p. 1, Bridges Papers). The committee asked Vincent about both documents. See *IPR*, pt. 6, p. 1690. Kohlberg argued that Vincent had criticized General MacArthur in Sept. 1946 (Bridges memo., 2). See *IPR*, pt. 6, p. 1686 for the committee's questions. Kohlberg raised questions about Vincent's role in the Marshall mission (Bridges memo, p. 2). See *IPR*, pt. 7, pp. 2250-53. Kohlberg attacked Vincent's speech before the National Trade Council (Bridges memo and "State Department's Left Hand," p. 13). See *IPR*, pt. 7, pp. 2256-65. Kohlberg charged that Vincent sent Communists to American consular posts in China and Japan (Bridges memo). See *IPR*, pt. 6, pp. 1901-2.

In his speech to the Senate in Aug. 1951, McCarthy charged that Vincent urged that Kim Koo-Sek, a Communist, be made president of South Korea (*CR*, 83rd Cong., 1st sess., Aug. 9, 1951, p. 9918). The McCarran committee also took up this charge. See *IPR*, pt. 6, p. 1880.

In Jan. 1951, the Army Intelligence received a report from Kuomintang officials entitled: "Information on the Activities of U.S. and Foreign Nationals Assisting the Chinese Communist Party in An Attempt to Overthrow the Chinese Nationalist Government." The report included two pages on Vincent (Dept. of the Army Papers). The committee incorporated some of this material in their questioning of Vincent. See *IPR*, pt. 6, pp. 1787-92, pp. 2000-2002.

31. Sourwine is quoted in the *Baltimore Sun*, Feb. 4, 1952; see also *N.Y. Times*, Feb. 3, 1952.

32. "Statement of John Carter Vincent, Diplomatic Agent and Consul at

Tangier, before Senate Subcommittee on Internal Security, January 30, 1952," p. 1-2, JCV mss. Copy also in Spingarn Papers.

Following the reading of this statement, Vincent also read into the record his letter, JCV to Under Sec. John Peurifoy, Mar. 7, 1950, JCV mss.

33. *IPR*, pt. 6, p. 1689.

34. Willard Shelton, "Powerful Pat McCarran," *The Progressive*, May 1, 1952, p. 24.

35. *IPR*, pt. 6, p. 1780.

36. Ibid., p. 1894.

37. Ibid., p. 1819.

38. *IPR*, pt. 7, pp. 2021-22.

39. Ibid., p. 2112.

40. Interview with Elizabeth Vincent, July 1971.

41. These quotations are taken from a series of exchanges between Vincent and the committee during the six-and-a-half days of hearings. They can be found in *IPR*, pt. 7, p. 2010; *IPR*, pt. 6, pp. 1960-61; *IPR*, pt. 7, p. 2217.

42. *IPR*, pt. 7, pp. 2175-76; see also *Washington Post*, Feb. 2, 1952, *N.Y. Times*, Feb. 2, 1952.

43. *IPR*, pt. 7, p. 2183.

44. Ibid., p. 2281; Vincent is quoted in Kahn, p. 237.

45. *Washington Star*, Feb. 3, 1952; *N.Y. Herald Tribune*, Feb. 3, 1952; *N.Y. Times*, Feb. 3, 1952; *Baltimore Sun*, Feb. 4, 1952.

46. The board is quoted in Civil Service Commission, Loyalty Review Board, "Post-Audit Case," p. 41, Civil Service Records. See also John W. Sipes to D. L. Nicholson, Dec. 27, 1951, Office of Security Records.

47. "Statement of Loyalty-Security Board," Feb. 6, 1952, Office of Security Records. See also "Decision of Loyalty-Security Board—Vincent, John C.," Feb. 6, 1952, Office of Security Records.

48. Humelsine to Vincent, Feb. 18, 1952, JCV mss; see also copy in Office of Security Records, and "Department of State—For the Press," Feb. 19, 1952, Spingarn Papers.

49. McCarran is quoted in *N.Y. Times*, Feb. 20, 1952.

50. "Statement by Vincent made in New York before returning to Tangier, Feb. 20, 1952," Spingarn Papers.

51. JCV to Elizabeth Vincent, Feb. 20, 1952, JCV mss.

52. JCV to Elizabeth Vincent, Feb. 29, 1952, pp. 1-2, JCV mss. For Benton's letter, see Benton to JCV, Feb. 20, 1952; and JCV to Benton, Apr. 7, 1952, both in JCV mss.

53. See, for example, E.A. Damour, F.S. Hardeman, Jr., Teddy Hart, and

Rufus Evans to JCV, Jan. 1952, JCV mss; Jack and Fran Creighton to JCV, Feb. 7, 1952, JCV mss.

54. Simmons to JCV, Feb. 3, 1952, JCV mss. For more critical mail, see Edith D. Moses to JCV, Feb. 3, 1952, and Harold L. Meyer to JCV, Jan. 31, 1952, both in JCV mss.

55. See Griffith, pp. 157-64.

56. JCV to Surrey and Karasik, Mar. 2, 1952, JCV mss.

57. JCV to Frank and Leleah Vincent, Mar. 11, 1952, pp. 1-3, JCV mss.

58. JCV to Woodbridge Bingham, Mar. 17, 1952, JCV mss.

59. Untitled parody, n.d., pp. 1-4; see also JCV to Surrey and Karasik, Mar. 2, 1952, JCV mss.

60. JCV to Surrey, Mar. 21, 1952; JCV to Frank and Leleah Vincent, Mar. 11, 1952; see also JCV to Surrey, June 12, 1952, all in JCV mss.

61. Surrey to JCV, Apr. 2, 1952, JCV mss.

62. Nicholson to Clark, Apr. 1, 1952; Clark to Nicholson, Apr. 2, 1952; see also N.Y. Field Office to Investigations Branch, State Dept., Apr. 15, 1952, pp. 1-3, all in Office of Security Records.

63. SAC, Wash. Field Office, to dir., FBI, Feb. 15, 1952; memo, Mar. 28, 1952; see also memo, Apr. 9, 1952, all in FBI Records.

64. Hoover to Chief, Investigative Div., Apr. 15, 1952, Civil Service Records; see also dir., FBI, to assist. attorney general, July 2, 1952, FBI Records.

65. James E. Hatcher to D.L. Nicholson, Feb. 29, Mar. 27, Apr. 8, Apr. 22, May 2, 1952. all in Civil Service Records.

66. Loyalty-Security Board statement, Mar. 14, 1952, Office of Security Records; Chronology of Vincent Case, n.d.; memo, May 25, 1952; see also "Decision of Loyalty-Security Board—Vincent John Carter," Mar. 17 and May 27, 1952; D.L. Nicholson to William H. McMillan, May 28, 1952; memo, May 28, 1952; Loyalty-Security Board statement, Aug. 5, 1952; "Decision of Loyalty-Security Board—Vincent John Carter," Aug. 7, 1952; memo, Aug. 15, 1952; John W. Ford to Raymond K. Greenfield, Aug. 18, 1952; all in Office of Security Records.

67. For facts on the subcommittee's investigation of the IPR., see CR, 83rd Cong., 1st sess., Jan. 3, 1953, pp. 683-84.

68. Quoted in CR, 83rd Cong., 2nd sess., p. 9113.

69. For a study of the IPR, see John N. Thomas, *The Institute of Pacific Relations: Asia Scholars and American Politics* (Seattle: U. of Washington Pr., 1974).

70. "McCarran's Revenge," *Washington Post*, July 4, 1952.

71. U.S. Congress, Senate, 82nd Cong., 2nd sess., Committee on Judiciary, Report No. 2050 Pursuant to Senate Res. 366, *Institute of Pacific Relations* (McCarran committee report), pp. 224, 225.

72. Ibid., p. 226.

73. Surrey to JCV, July 2, 1952, JCV mss.

74. Surrey to JCV, July 3, 1952, pp. 1-8, JCV mss.

75. JCV to Surrey, July 17, 1952, JCV mss.

76. Humelsine to JCV, July 9, 1952, JCV mss; for Bingham's letter to the State Department, see Bingham to Snow, July 7, 1952, Civil Service Records. See also memo for the file, July 8, 1952, Office of Security Records.

77. JCV to Humelsine, July 17, 1952, Office of Security Records.

78. Surrey to Vincent, July 24, 1952, JCV mss.

79. JCV to Surrey, July 17, 1952, JCV mss.

80. Surrey to JCV, July 24, 25, 1952, JCV mss. See also Karasik to JCV, Aug. 14, 1952, JCV mss.

81. The quotations can be found in JCV to Surrey, Aug. 4, 1952, pp. 2-3; JCV to Surrey, Aug. 7, 1952, p. 2, and JCV to Karasik, Aug. 25, 1952, JCV mss.

82. JCV to Karasik, Aug. 25, 1952, p. 1; JCV to W. K. Scott, Aug. 29, 1952, Office of Security Records.

Chapter 9

1. Karasik to JCV, Aug. 14, 1952, JCV mss.

2. Creighton to JCV, n.d., 1951, JCV mss.

3. For a discussion of the board's role, see "Statement by Seth Richardson, Chairman, Loyalty Review Board, Civil Service Commission," Truman Papers; pp. 45-46; Brown, pp. 45-46, Bontecou, pp. 278-79.

4. For Republican criticism of Truman's loyalty program, see, for example, McCarthy to Acheson, July 23, 1951, Humelsine to McCarthy, July 25, 1951, both in *CR,* 82nd Cong., 1st sess., pp. 9705-6.

5. *N.Y. Times,* June 7, 1956.

6. *CR,* 82nd Cong., 1st sess., p. 9706; *CR,* 82nd Cong., 2nd sess., pp. 105-6.

7. *CR,* 82nd Cong., 1st sess., pp. 3354-57; Lowell Mellett, "Rule by Reasonable Doubt," *Washington Evening Star,* Dec. 20, 1951, clipping in Green Papers; for the evolution of federal loyalty standards, see Congressional Quarterly *Congress and the Nation,* pp. 1684-85; for criticism of the "reasonable doubt" standard, see Bontecou, pp. 68-72; also Alan Barth, "The High Cost of Security," *The Reporter,* July 24, 1951, pp. 13-16.

8. For Bingham's views, see the transcript of a meeting of the Loyalty Review Board reprinted in de Toledano, pp. 237-49. The quotations are in ibid., p. 240 and McCarthy, p. 29.

9. See Appendix, *CR,* 82nd Cong., 1st sess., vol. 97, pt. 15, pp. A5744-46.

10. *CR,* 82nd Cong., 1st sess., p. 9706.

11. For the Loyalty Review Board decision on John S. Service, see "Opinion of

the Loyalty Review Board," Dec. 12, 1951, pp. 12-17, enc. in "Department of State for the Press," Dec. 13, 1951, Spingarn Papers.

12. See Busbey's remarks in *CR,* 82nd Cong., 1st sess., p. 9706, p. A5744; *CR,* 82nd Cong., 2nd sess., pp. 105-6.

13. D. L. Nicholson to Raymond E. Greenfield, Feb. 27, 1952, Civil Service Records.

14. Bingham explained the board's procedure in "Catching the Disloyal," *U.S. News and World Report,* Nov. 23, 1951, pp. 25, 26-27, and in his American Bar Association speech in Sept. 1951; see note 9 above.

15. Loyalty Review Board, "Post-Audit," Apr. 14, 1952, pp. 39-42, Civil Service Records.

16. Bingham is quoted in Apprendix, *CR,* 82nd Cong., 1st sess., p. A5745.

17. Charles Clift notes, JCV mss.

18. Loyalty Review Board, "Post-Audit," pp. 18-19, Civil Service Records.

19. Ibid., p. 15, pp. 39-40. Hartsfield also stated, incorrectly, that fifteen men testified on Vincent's behalf. In fact, there only were eight. See page 3 for this error.

20. Hartsfield to Burton L. French, Nov. 3, 1952, Civil Service Records. Said Welch in *May God Forgive Us,* a book which Hartsfield recommended to French: It is "a certainty" that there are "more Communists and Communist sympathizers in our Government today than ever before." Quoted in Daniel Bell, ed., *The Radical Right.* (Garden City, N.Y. Doubleday, : 1963), p. 243.

21. For a brief biographical sketch of Burton L. French, see *Who Was Who in America,* vol. 3, 1951-1960 (Chicago: Marquis, 1960); for Harry W. Blair's background, see ibid., 4:29. Information on John Harlan Amen was found in his obituary in the *N.Y. Times,* Mar. 11, 1960. For their appointment to the Vincent panel, see Bingham to French, Apr. 7, 1952; French to Bingham, Apr. 9, 1952; Bingham to Amen, May 12, 1952, all in Civil Service Records.

22. French to Bingham, June 13, 1952; French to Hartsfield, June 13, June 21, 1952, both in Civil Service Records.

23. Bingham to French, May 29, 1952; Bingham to Amen, June 2, 1952; Amen to Bingham, June 4, 1952; French to Bingham, June 13, 1952, French to Hartsfield, June 13, 1952, all in Civil Service Records.

24. French to Hartsfield, June 21, 1952, Civil Service Records. For Blair's description of his meeting with French see Charles Clift notes, JCV mss.

25. Blair to Elizabeth Vincent, Apr. 4, 1958, p. 1. See also Clift notes, JCV mss.

26. Hoover to James Hatcher, July 2, 1952, FBI Records; James Hatcher to D. L. Nicholson, July 11, 1952, Office of Security Records; "Secret Security Information," Aug. 1, 1952, Office of Security Records," French to D. L. Nicholson, July 25, 1952, Civil Service Records.

27. Meade to W. K. Scott, July 24, 1952, Office of Security Records.

28. "Statement—Loyalty-Security Board," Aug. 5, 1952; "Confidential Security Information," Aug. 5, 1952; decision of Loyalty Security Board—Aug. 7, 1952; office memo, Aug. 15, 1952; all in Office of Security Records.

29. John Ford to Raymond Greenfield, Aug. 18, 1952, Office of Security Records; a copy of the letter is also in the Civil Service Records; see also memo of decision: Loyalty Review Board, Aug. 20, 1952, Civil Service Records; memo on the Vincent case, Aug. 19, 1952, Office of Security Records; French to Conrad Snow, Aug. 22, 1952, Office of Security Records.

30. Charles Clift notes, JCV mss.

31. "Regulations for the Operations of the Loyalty Review Board," p. 1, in Civil Service Commission statement by Seth Richardson, chairman, Loyalty Review Board, Dec. 17, 1947, Truman Papers.

32. Bingham is quoted in Appendix, *CR,* 82nd Cong., 1st sess., p. A5745; see also Bingham, "Catching the Disloyal," *U.S. News and World Report,* Nov. 23, 1951, p. 23.

33. Woodbridge Bingham to author, June 16, 1972, p. 1.

34. For Meade's drawing, see Dept. of State memo, Oct. 1, 1952, Office of Security Records.

35. On the selection of the date to begin the hearing, see W. K. Scott to JCV, July 29, 1952; memo for the record, July 30, 1952; JCV to W. K. Scott, Aug. 7, 1952; W. K. Scott to JCV, Aug. 25, 1952, all in Office of Security Records.

36. Loyalty Review Board, "Regulation 14 Hearing in the Case of Mr. John Carter Vincent," Oct. 7-8, 1952, p. 2021, Civil Service Records; see also ibid., pp. 15-16, 22, 24-25, 41-43 (hereafter cited as Review Board Hearing).

37. Ibid., p. 105.

38. For a brief discussion of the conflicting views on Japan, see Kolko and Kolko, pp. 319-20. Vincent discusses his own views in Review Board Hearing, pp. 96-105; the quotes are from interview with JCV, July 1971, and Martin Weil, *A Pretty Good Club: The Founding Fathers of the U.S. Foreign Service* (N.Y.: Norton, 1978), p. 215.

39. I. F. Stone, "The Pearl Harbor Diplomats," *Nation,* July 1945, pp. 26-27.

40. Loyalty-Security Board, "Transcript," Dec. 6, 1951, p. 52, JCV mss.

41. Interview with JCV, July 1971.

42. Loyalty-Security Board, "Transcript," Dec. 6, 1951, p. 50, JCV mss.

43. Ibid., pp. 55-56.

44. Ibid., pp. 55-56. See also Dooman to Hornbeck, Mar. 13, 1964, Box 150, Hornbeck Papers.

45. See *Newsweek,* issues for Dec. 1, 1947, pp. 36-38, and Dec. 20, 1948.

46. For Hoover's order that Kearn be interviewed, see dir., FBI, to SAC, N.Y., May 29, 1950, FBI Records; Kearn's expurgated interview can be found in FBI report, N.Y., July 13, 1950, pp. 8-9, FBI Records, and "Supplemental Analysis in the Case of John Carter

Vincent," by Weldon B. Hartsfield, Oct. 3, 1952, p. 10, Civil Service Records. The summaries of Kearn's articles can be found in FBI report, N.Y., July 13, 1950, pp. 6-7, FBI Records.

47. Dooman's interview with the FBI is summarized in Loyalty Review Board, "Post-Audit," pp. 8-10, Civil Service Records; for his testimony before the McCarran Committee, see *IPR*, Pt. 3 pp. 703-743; for his testimony before the State Dept. Loyalty-Security Board., see Loyalty-Security Board, "Transcript," Dec. 6, 1951, pp. 1-70, JCV mss.

48. Review Board Hearing, Oct. 7-8, pp. 82-84, Civil Service Records.

49. See, for example, Loyalty-Security Board, "Transcript," Dec. 6, 1951, pp. 12-13, JCV mss.

50. See, for example, Vincent's testimony before the McCarran committee: *IPR*, pt. 6, pp. 1862-65 and Review Board Hearing, p. 84. Vincent's testimony is borne out by a comparison of the "U.S. Initial Post-Defeat Policy Relating to Japan," which was approved by all the top officials on Aug. 31 and the final version entitled "U.S. Initial Post-Surrender Policy for Japan," which President Truman adopted on Sept. 6, 1945. On this controversy, see memo by sec. of state to Truman, n.d., *FR 1945*, 7:619. The final version can be found in *Department of State Bulletin*, Sept. 23, 1945, pp. 423-27.

51. Review Board Hearing, Oct. 7-8, 1952, p. 84, Civil Service Records.

52. For a discussion of the development of FEC-230, see Kolko and Kolko, pp. 320-22, 514-16.

53. Review Board Hearing, Oct. 7-8, 1952, p.90, 100 Civil Service Records.

54. Loyalty-Security Board, "Transcript," Dec. 6, 1951, p. 52, JCV mss.

55. Ibid.

56. Ibid., pp. 5, 44-46.

57. Ibid., pp. 45-46.

58. Ibid., p. 46.

59. Ibid., pp. 28, 64.

60. JCV to Elizabeth Vincent, n.d., 1951, JCV mss.

61. Review Board Hearing, Oct. 7-8, 1952, p. 85, Civil Service Records.

62. Dooman to Hornbeck, Review Board Hearing, Oct. 7-8, 1952, p. 85, Civil Service Records.

63. Blair to Elizabeth Vincent, Apr. 4, 1958, pp. 2, 3, JCV mss.

64. Review Board Hearing, pp. 23, 24, 46, Civil Service Records. The charge can be found in Loyalty Review Board, "Post-Audit," pp. 7-8, Civil Service Records.

65. Review Board Hearing, Oct. 7-8, 1952, pp. 219-20, Civil Service Records. For the dispatch itself and the comment by A.S. Chase of the China Division, see amb. in China to sec. of state, Sept. 8, 1944, *FR 1944,* China: 559-62, and memo by A.S. Chase, Sept. 26, 1944, *FR 1944,* China: 595-96.

66. Review Board Hearing, Oct. 7-8, 1952, p. 220, Civil Service Records.

67. Ibid., pp. 221-22.

68. Ibid., pp. 222-23, 224. Hartsfield was guilty of more errors than he knew. The charge in question originated in an FBI exhibit—an article which appeared in Kohlberg's *Plain Talk* in 1946. This article, summarized in Hartsfield's report, was part of the public record. The examiner was therefore mistaken as to his source and the nature of its confidentiality. The article was disowned by its author in 1950; Emmanuel Larsen told the Tydings committee that it had been rewritten by Kohlberg and the editors of *Plain Talk*. For a discussion of the controversy surrounding this article, see Griffith, pp. 97-98.

69. Quoted in Elizabeth Vincent to Blair, Dec. 22, 1957, JCV mss. See also Clift notes, p. 9, JCV mss.

70. Amen to French, Oct. 31, 1952, pp. 1-3, JCV mss.

71. Blair to Amen, Nov. 12, 1952, pp. 1-18, JCV mss.

72. See Amen's letter, point 2, p. 2, Amen to French, Oct. 31, 1952, JCV mss, and Hartsfield's "Supplemental Analysis in the Case of John Carter Vincent," pp. 7, 8, Civil Service Records.

73. Bingham to Hurley, July 8, 1952, Box 101—Post-World War II Folder-Post-World War II-Far East-China, Hurley Papers; Hurley to Bingham, n.d., 1952, Hurley Papers; Budenz, Sept. 17, 1952, Civil Service Records.

74. See "Loyalty Review Board-Bingham Suggested Draft," n.d., pp. 1-2, JCV mss. Also Elizabeth Vincent to Blair, Jan. 12, 1958, p. 3, JCV mss.

75. My description of the panel's debate is drawn from Blair to Elizabeth Vincent, Apr. 4, 1953, p. 3, and the Clift Notes, pp. 6-7, JCV mss.

76. "Loyalty Review Board," Dec. 11, 1952, pp. 1-2, Civil Service Records.

77. See "Letter from the Chairman of the Loyalty Review Board to the Secretary of State," Dec. 13, 1951, pp. 1-2, and "Opinion of the Loyalty Review Board," Dec. 13, 1951, pp. 12-17, in "Department of State for the Press," Dec. 13, 1951, Spingarn Papers.

78. See Bingham to sec. of state, Dec. 12, 1952, Civil Service Records.

79. See State Dept. "Dissenting Opinion Re John Carter Vincent," Dec. 19, 1952, JCV mss; copies can also be found in Office of Security and Civil Service Records.

80. Elizabeth Vincent to Blair, Jan. 12, 1958, p. 5, JCV mss; see also Blair to Elizabeth Vincent, Apr. 4, 1958, p. 3, JCV mss.

81. Blair to Elizabeth Vincent, Apr. 4, 1958, p. 2, JCV mss.

82. Ibid.; interview with Adrian Fisher.

83. For information on Bingham's problems with the Senate see, *N. Y. Times,* Nov. 4, 5, 1929.

84. Telegram, sec. of state to JCV, Dec. 15, 1952, JCV mss.

85. Mrs. Vincent's comments appear on p. 2 of the telegram. For Jack Vincent's comments see JCV to Surrey, Jan. 6, 1953, p. 4, JCV mss.

86. For Vincent's reaction to the news see JCV to Arthur Rosett, Dec. 23, 1952; John Dorman to Elizabeth Vincent, Feb. 12, 1953, both in JCV mss.

87. JCV to Surrey, Dec. 22, 1952, JCV mss.

Chapter 10

1. *N.Y. Times,* Dec. 18, 1952; the other comments are quoted in the State Dept.'s "Daily Opinion Summary—Vincent Case," Dec. 17, 1952, and Jan. 5, 1953, Office of Security Records.

2. Elmer Davis is quoted in "Daily Opinion Summary," Dec. 17, 1952, Office of Security Records; *Washington Post,* editorial , Dec. 17, 1952.

3. *Foreign Service Journal,* Jan. 1953, pp. 17, 60; *Washington Post,* editorial, Dec. 17, 1952.

4. McHugh to JCV, Dec. 30, 1952; see also McHugh to JCV, Jan. 6, 1953, both in JCV mss.

5. McHugh to JCV, Jan. 6, 1953; see also Charles Owsley to JCV, Dec. 22, 1952, both in JCV mss.

6. *N.Y. Times,* Dec. 31, 1952; Bingham to Dawson, Dec. 29, 1952, Civil Service Records.

7. For the individual opinions, see Marion Wade Doyle, "The Case of John Carter Vincent," Dec. 24, 1952, pp. 1-2, Civil Service Records; Hiram Bingham, "Opinion in Regard to the Loyalty Case of John Carter Vincent," Dec. 22, 1952, pp. 1-3, Office of Security Records; John Harlan Amen, "Opinion Regarding the Loyalty Case of John Carter Vincent," n.d., Civil Service Records; see also Bingham to Dawson, Dec. 30, 1952, Civil Service Records.

8. Acheson, p. 711; memo for the pres., Jan. 3, 1953, pp. 1-2, Office of Security Records; interview with Adrian Fisher. See also memo for the pres., Jan. 8, 1952, Office of Security Records.

9. Acheson, p. 712; Acheson to Elizabeth Vincent, Mar. 17, 1967, JCV mss; Marquis Childs, "The Vincent Case," Dec. 24, 1952, JCV mss; interview with Adrian Fisher. Fisher later said that Acheson believed he had won Dulles's support for the creation of the board.

10. For the announcement of the Hand board, see memo for the pres. and memo to sec. of state, Jan. 3, 1953, Office of Security Records; *Department of State Bulletin,* Jan. 19, 1953, pp. 122-123; *N.Y. Times,* Jan. 4, 1953, pp. 1, 3; *Washington Post,* Jan. 4, 1953, p. 1; Childs, "The Vincent Case." For McCloy's relationship with Eisenhower, see Hoopes, p. 130.

11. For Clardy's comment, see "Weekly Report," *Congressional Quarterly, 1953,* pt. 2, p. 145; McCarran's remarks can be found in *CR,* 83rd Cong., 1st sess. (Jan. 9, 1953), pp. 286-88. See also, Surrey to JCV, Jan. 13, 1953, JCV mss.

12. JCV to Surrey, Jan. 6, 1953, pp. 2-3; Charles Owsley to JCV, Jan. 7, 1953; James McHugh to JCV, Jan. 11, 1953, pp. 1-2, all in JCV mss. See also, Surrey to JCV, Jan. 6, 1953, p. 2, JCV mss.

13. JCV to Surrey, Jan. 6, 1953, pp. 2-4, JCV mss.

14. Surrey to JCV, Jan. 13, 1953, p. 1; Charles Owsley to JCV, Jan. 24, 1953, both in JCV mss.

15. Hand to Acheson, Jan. 17, 1953; Acheson to Hand, Jan. 20, 1953, both in Hand Papers. A copy of Acheson's letter to Hand can also be found in the Office of Security Records.

16. See Hand to Dulles, Jan. 20, 1953, Hand Papers. For Hand's belief that Dulles would allow them to continue their work, see Hand to James Grafton Rodgers, Esq., Jan. 6 and Jan. 12, 1953, Hand Papers; Hand to Edwin H. Wilson, Esq., Jan. 12, 1953, Hand Papers; Hand to G. Howland Shaw, Esq., Jan. 12, 1953, Hand Papers; John McCloy to author, Aug. 21, 1972. For Dulles's decision see, Dulles to Hand, Jan. 29, 1953, in "Department of State for the Press," Jan. 31, 1953, Office of Security Records.

17. Surrey to JCV, Feb. 5, 1953, p. 1, JCV mss. See also Arthur Krock, "In the Nation," *N.Y. Times*, Jan. 6, 1953.

18. Shaw to Hand Jan. 31, 1953, Hand Papers.

19. Vincent's view of Dulles can be found in JCV to Henry Grady, Jan. 23, 1953; JCV to Surrey, Jan. 26, 1953; JCV to unidentified correspondent, Feb. 14, 1953; all in JCV mss.

20. Joseph C. Green interview, p. 18, 20-21, Dulles Oral Hist. Coll. Dulles Papers; Dulles's "admirer" was Herman Phleger, his legal advisor; see Herman Phleger interview, p. 10, Dulles Oral Hist. Coll., Dulles Papers.

21. John Hanes interview, p. 78, Dulles Oral Hist. Coll., Dulles Papers.

22. For Dulles's relationship with Hiss, see Weinstein, pp. 366-72; for Dulles's work on behalf of the Truman administration, see Hoopes, pp. 85-113.

23. See Hanes interview, p. 82, Dulles Oral Hist. Coll., for the statement about McLeod; John S. Service interview, p. 19, Dulles Oral Hist. Coll. For Dulles's relationship with the State Department, see Hoopes, pp. 151-60.

24. For Dulles's speech, see Hoopes, pp. 4-9; Bohlen, p. 312.

25. Interview with Judd, Dulles Oral Hist. Coll., Dulles Papers.

26. Kohlberg to Dulles, Jan. 5, 1953, Dulles Papers.

27. For the excerpt from Hand's speech, see Kohlberg to Dulles, Jan. 14, 1953, Dulles Papers.

28. Dulles to Walter Judd, Feb. 2, 1948, quoted in interview with Judd, Dulles Papers.

29. Dulles to Kohlberg, Jan. 14, Jan. 24, 1953, Dulles Papers.

30. See "Suggestions for JCV," pp. 1-2, and memo for Mr. Surrey, p. 3, JCV mss.

31. Elizabeth Vincent to JCV, Feb. 21, 1953, pp. 1-2, JCV mss.

32. Ibid., pp. 2-4.

33. Elizabeth Vincent to Luce, Feb. 22, 1953, pp. 1-2, JCV mss.

34. JCV to Elizabeth Vincent, Feb. 22, 1953, JCV mss.

35. Surrey to Elizabeth Vincent, Mar. 6, 1953, JCV mss. Interview with Elizabeth and John Carter Vincent, Mar. 1972.

36. Surrey to Elizabeth Vincent, Mar. 6, 1953, JCV mss.

37. For Dulles's views on communism, see Hoopes, pp. 63-67.

38. Hoopes, p. 78.

39. Owsley to author, Mar. 30, 1972, p. 6.

40. For information on the Feb. 28 meeting, see JCV to Surrey, n.d., "Unfinished Business," pp. 5-6, JCV mss.

41. Memo by sec. of state in the matter of JCV, Mar. 4, 1953, in "Dept. of State for the Press," Office of Security Records. See also, *N.Y. Times,* Mar. 5, 1953.

42. Diane and David Heller, *John Foster Dulles: Soldier for Peace* (N.Y.: Holt, Rinehart & Winston, 1960) p. 169.

43. Joseph and Stewart Alsop, "The Clearing of Vincent," *N.Y. Herald Tribune,* Mar. 8, 1953; *Washington Post,* Mar. 5, 1953; see also Louis L. Gerson, *John Foster Dulles,* (N.Y.: Cooper Square, 1967), p. 112.

44. Acheson, p. 713.

45. Hoopes, pp. 46-49.

46. Quoted in Peter Lyon, *Eisenhower: Portrait of the Hero* (Boston: Little, 1974), p. 437; Dulles's quote on Manchuria can be found in I.F. Stone, *The Haunted Fifties* (N.Y.: Random, 1963), p. 13.

47. Mosley, p. 93.

48. Both senators are quoted in the *Baltimore Sun,* Mar. 5, 1953.

49. Clardy is quoted in *CR,* 83rd. Cong., 1st. sess., pp. A2646 and *CR,* 83rd Cong., 1st. sess., p. 1631.

50. *Christian Science Monitor,* Mar. 5, 1953; *Washington Post,* Mar. 5, 1953; Surrey to JCV, Mar. 16, 1953; JCV mss.

51. "Statement by Walter Surrey," enc. with Surrey to JCV, Mar. 5, 1953, JCV mss.

52. See Surrey to JCV, Mar. 5, 1953, p. 2, JCV mss, for Mrs. Vincent's comments.

53. Margaret Smith to JCV, Mar. 5, 1953; Owsley to JCV, Mar. 5, 1953, both in JCV mss.

54. See letters to dir., Dec. 16, 1952, Jan. 7, 1953, and Jan. 19, 1953, FBI Records. Vincent's file contained a copy of Dulles's decision and an editorial on his case which appeared in the *Foreign Service Journal* in Apr. 1953.

55. Bingham to Hoover, July 3, 1953, Civil Service Records.

56. Remarks made to the press by JCV, Apr. 29, 1953; JCV to Benjamin Katz, Mar. 26, 1953, both in JCV mss.

Epilogue

1. David E. Lilienthal, *The Journals of David E. Lilienthal: The Venturesome Years 1950-1955* (NY: Harper & Row, 1966) p. 400-401.

2. Ibid.; Harold Strauss to JCV, Mar. 11, 1953, JVC mss; JCV to Harold Strauss, Mar. 26 1953, JCV mss; JCV to Surrey, Dec. 1, 1953, Surrey Papers.

3. JCV to C. V. Starr, Esq. Apr. 9, 1953; JCV to Frank Vincent, Apr. 26, 1953; JCV to Leleah Vincent, Oct. 2, 1953, p. 1, all in JCV mss.

4. JCV to Leleah Vincent, Oct. 2, 1953, pp. 2-4, JCV mss.

5. "An Appreciation by John K. Fairbank," John Carter Vincent Memorial Service, p. 3, JCV mss.

6. JCV to Surrey, Dec. 1, 1954; JCV to Surrey, July 10, 1954, both in JCV mss. Interview with JCV, 1972. The Foreign Policy Association advertisement is quoted in Kahn, p. 256.

7. On Davies's dismissal see Kahn, pp. 257-63; JCV to editors of *Foreign Service Journal,* Dec. 10, 1954, enc. JCV to Surrey and Karasik, Dec. 10, 1954, JCV mss; *Washington Post,* Jan. 8, 1955, copy in Office of Security Records.

8. JCV to Surrey, July 10, 1954, JCV mss. On the scattering of the China hands see Ross Terrill, "When American Lost China: The Case of John Carter Vincent," *The Atlantic Monthly,* Nov. 1969, p. 78.

9. Chubb to Nystrom, Mar. 26, 1956, pp. 2-3, JCV mss.

10. "Broadcast by Louis M. Lyon," Apr. 5, 1956, copy in JCV mss; Goodridge to editor, *Cambridge Chronicle-Sun,* Apr. 12, 1956, copy in JCV mss; JCV to ed., *Cambridge Chronicle-Sun,* Apr. 12, 1956, copy in JCV mss; interview with JCV, 1972.

11. Rowson to Surrey, Sept. 23, 1957; JCV mss; Karasik to Rowson, Sept. 27, 1957, JCV mss; JCV to Karasik, Oct. 1, 1957, Surrey Papers.

12. "Interrogatory," May 20, 1954, original in possession of Mr. Abbott Moffat, Princeton, N.J.; Moffat to Pierce Gerety, July 28, 1954, pp. 1-3, also in Mr. Moffat's possession.

13. Jack Vincent's story can be found in "Statement of John Carter Vincent, Jr.," July 28, Aug. 7, Aug. 20, 1960. Original in Mr. Vincent's possession, Boston, Mass.

14. JCV to Leleah Vincent, Feb. 14, 1953, p. 1, JCV mss; office memo, Oct. 19, 1955, FBI Records; see "Security of Government Employees," June 10, 1955, FBI Records; Surrey to Young, Sept. 9, 1955, JCV mss; Surrey to Dulles, Sept. 9, 1955, copy in JCV mss; Young to Surrey, Oct. 12, 1955, JCV mss; Young to Dulles, Oct. 12, 1955, copy in JCV mss.

15. Elizabeth Vincent to Blair, Dec. 17, 1957, JCV mss. See also Elizabeth Vincent to Surrey, May 28, 1957, Surrey Papers; interview with Elizabeth Vincent, 1972.

16. For information on Mrs. Vincent's activities see Elizabeth Vincent to Surrey, Apr. 23, 1957, Apr. 10, 1958, Apr. 30, 1958, May 28, 1957, all in Surrey Papers. See also Charles Clift to Surrey, Apr. 10, 1959, Surrey Papers. For the Katz story see Ross Terrill's

diary, Aug. 13, 1970 entry, in Mr. Terrill's possession. I am greatly indebted to Mr. Terrill for making portions of his diary available to me.

17. Interview with Ross Terrill, May 1973.

18. "Notebook," pp. 27-28, JCV mss; see also letters to the editors, *N. Y. Times,* Mar. 9, 1955, and Oct. 27, 1959.

19. Kennan is quoted in Halberstam, p. 105; see also letter to editor, *Boston Globe,* Sept. 15, 1969; for Vincent's 1946 memo to Acheson see Mike Gravel, ed., *The Pentagon Papers* (N.Y.: Beacon Pr. 1971), vol. 1, p. 29.

20. Letter to the editors, *N. Y. Times,* June 17, 1964, JCV mss.

21. Diary of Ross Terrill, Nov. 14, 1968 entry; interview with Ross Terrill.

22. For James Reston's interview with Chou En-lai see *Report From Red China* (NY: N.Y. Times, 1971) p. 76, interview with Abbott Moffat.

23. Interview with JCV, 1972; diary of Ross Terrill, Aug. 16, 1972 entry; Elizabeth Vincent to author, Dec. 4, 1972.

24. John and Caroline Service to Elizabeth Vincent, Dec. 6, 1972; JCV mss; McKillop to Elizabeth Vincent, Dec. 22, 1972, JCV mss; Richards is quoted in the diary of Ross Terrill, Dec. 10, 1972 entry.

25. *N. Y. Times,* Dec. 5, 1972, p. 48; *L.A. Times,* Dec. 7, 1972.

26. Diary of Ross Terrill, Dec. 10, 1972 entry.

27. Remarks on Vincent can be found in "John Carter Vincent Memorial Service," pp. 3-4, (Fairbank); pp. 12-13, (Carter); pp. 1-2 (John C. Vincent, Jr.) JCV mss.

28. Vincent is quoted in "Statement by Mr. Edward E. Rice, May 29, 1950," enc. Spencer S. Beeman to D.L. Nicholson, May 29, 1950, Office of Security Records.

29. Interview with Elizabeth Vincent, 1973; on the Foreign Service Association luncheon see Kahn, pp. 297-307, also *N. Y. Times,* Feb. 4, 1973.

30. For Thomson's views see James C. Thomson, Jr. "How Could Vietnam Happen: An Autopsy," *The Atlantic Monthly,* Apr., 1968, pp. 48-49; Halberstam, pp. 462-78.

Index

360

Palmer, A. Mitchell, 222
Pan, J. S., 37, 38
Patterson, Robert, 135, 136, 141, 147, 154
Pearl Harbor, 68
Pehle, John, 97
Peking, China, 30, 31, 38, 40-48, 132, 153, 155
Perkins, Mahlon F., 46
Peurifoy, John E., 175, 178-180, 238
Political Consultative Conference (PCC), 142-143
Political Science Clique, 71, 83
Potsdam Conference, 131, 135

Quo Tai-chi, 96

Reston, James, 262, 290
Reynolds, Florence, 46
Rice, Edward, 293
Richards, I. A. R., 291
Ringwalt, Arthur, 127
Robertson, Walter, 269
Robinson, Hamilton, 168, 169, 170
Rodgers, James Grafton, 265
Rogers, William P., 294
Roosevelt, Franklin, 55, 56, 57, 65, 72, 73, 80, 83-84, 86, 92, 96, 99, 103, 104, 106-107, 108, 109-111, 112, 113, 114, 116, 122, 126, 127, 128-129, 131
Rosenberg, Ethel and Julius, 171
Rosinger, Lawrence K., 206
Rowell, Chester, 53
Rowson, Richard, 284
Rusk, Dean, 288

SACO (Chinese Intelligence), 208
Salisbury, Lawrence, 92, 93
Schapsmeir, Edward and Frederick, 199

Seitz, Hugo F., 221
Service, John S., 16, 91, 103, 108, 117-119, 120, 121, 123, 124, 127, 128, 169, 197, 212, 241, 242, 249, 253, 254, 257, 269, 283, 290, 291, 294
Shanghai, China, 30, 38, 59, 61, 63, 132, 155
Shannon, Nancy, 203
Shannon, William V., 193
Shansi, China, 98
Shantung province, China, 49-50, 98, 155
Shaw, G. Howland, 92, 265, 267
Shimato, Lieutenant Colonel, 52-53
Sinkiang, China, 38
Sipes, John W., 204, 215, 218-219, 252
Smith, Allen E., 32-33, 36, 130, 282
Smith, Lawrence, 162
Smith, Willis, 201, 226, 231
Smyth, Robert, 77
Snow, Conrad E., 203-204, 205, 208, 210, 211, 215, 216, 222, 230, 252
Sobel, Morton, 171
Sokolsky, George, 271
Soong family, 83
Soong, T. V., 96, 100, 114
Sourwine, J. G., 200-201, 225, 227, 229
South Manchuria Railway Company, 51, 52
Spencer, Elizabeth. *See* Vincent, Elizabeth Spencer
Spiker, Clarence J., 40
Stalin, Joseph, 122, 126, 135
Stampfli, Emil, 183
Stanford, Neal, 278
Stanly, Dr., 50
Stanton, Edwin, 92, 93
Stassen, Harold E., 171
State-War-Navy Coordinating Committee (SWINCC), 146; Post-Initial Surrender Policy to Japan, 250
Stefan, Karl, 168, 169, 170
Stettinius, Edward, 92, 94, 112

Born in Los Angeles, Gary May studied at U.C.L.A., where he received his Ph.D. in 1974. His doctoral dissertation, "The China Service of John Carter Vincent," won the 1975 Allan Nevins Prize from the Society of American Historians. He has taught at U.C.L.A., Colgate University, and is now an associate professor at the University of Delaware, where he specializes in modern American diplomatic and political history. He lives in Newark, Delaware, with his wife and children.